DEADLY MEDICINE

They are the pillars of society. Beyond reproach, above suspicion. But hidden behind their crisp white uniforms and fancy diplomas lurk insane murderers who used their positions of trust to take the lives they were supposed to save.

Now, from the authentic files of TRUE DETECTIVE MAGAZINE, read the frightening true crime accounts of these medical monsters — doctors, nurses, pharmacists and technicians — who kill.

You'll never trust your doctor again.

FROM THE FILES OF <u>TRUE DETECTIVE</u> MAGAZINE

MEDICAL MURDERERS

Edited by ROSE G. MANDELSBERG

PINNACLE BOOKS
WINDSOR PUBLISHING CORP.

The editor wishes to thank the following individuals whose help was instrumental in making this book possible: Sara Heredia-Pearl, Inspector Alva Busch, Crime Scene Technician of the Illinois State Police; Lieutenant William Fletcher, Commander of the Violent Crime Squad, Cincinnati Police Department; Prosecutor John Kaye and Captain William Lucia of the Monmouth County Prosecutor's Office; and Julie Malear.

For more true crime reading, pick up *True Detective, Official Detective, Master Detective, Front Page Detective* and *Inside Detective* magazines on sale at newsstands every month.

PINNACLE BOOKS

are published by

Windsor Publishing Corp.
475 Park Avenue South
New York, NY 10016

First Pinnacle Books printing: February, 1992

Printed in the United States of America

TABLE OF CONTENTS

"GREEDY DOCTOR'S Rx FOR MURDER!"

by Channing Corbin

At about 6:45 a.m. on Sunday, June 17, 1984, on a perfectly beautiful spring morning, an exercise rider took three-year-old Swale out for a brief gallop around the race track at Belmont Park, N.Y. Swale, conservatively valued at 40 million dollars, enjoyed his run and was playful. Minutes later, while being hosed down, Swale, Kentucky Derby winner classified as the champion race horse in his class, let out an eerie moan, collapsed on the ground and died. The immediate diagnosis was that the horse had died of a heart attack. A three-hour autopsy refuted the diagnosis and failed to ascertain the actual cause of death.

Said one of two veterinarians flown in from the University of Pennsylvania to conduct the postmortem on the colt, "We may never find the answer, just the same as with humans." This equine parable contains numerous fascinating parallels to a death which occurred early on the morning of July 15, 1983 in the small town of Douglas, Wyoming and which claimed the life of Kay Marie Schmunk, age 44. For a long time, subsequent to Mrs. Schmunk's mysterious and untimely demise, it was feared that her case was destined to become one of those ascribed to by the veterinarian while discussing the inex-

7

plicable death of Swale, which occurred only 11 months later.

Douglas, Wyoming is the county seat of Converse County and the designated site for the Wyoming Police Officers Training Academy. Located a short distance south of Casper on Interstate 25 with an approximate population of 6,009 citizens, the small, conservative town is a somewhat unlikely setting for a bizarre murder mystery. Moreover, Kay Marie Schmunk, active in church affairs and president of the local chapter of the National Right to Life Organization, was an extremely atypical candidate for a murder victim.

Throughout the 1960s, Kay and her first husband had resided in the Detroit suburb of Mount Clemens with their three children. Their family physician was Dr. R.F. Schmunk who was also happily married.

The two marriages were torn asunder when the doctor-patient relationship between Kay and the benign, somewhat jocular Dr. Bob Schmunk evolved into a tempestuous, romantic affair which became so intense that it had eventually destroyed both of their marriages. Kay's divorce was especially bitter and lasted for 18 months. It ended with the court awarding custody of the three young children to their natural father. Within the year, Kay initiated legal action seeking to overturn the custody ruling. She and Robert Frank Schmunk openly pursued their relationship subsequent to their divorces.

Kay eventually won her court battle to gain custody of her children and after her marriage to Dr. Schmunk in 1972, her children came to live with the couple. As a general practitioner in a closeknit suburb, Dr. Schmunk frequently found himself the target of scandalous, even downright malicious gossip which seemed to have its origin in his affair with Kay and the subsequent devastation of both of their marriages.

Then, while on a trip to a gun show in Findlay, Ohio

8

in 1971, they'd taken along 10-year-old Larry Sam Wilson, Kay's son. The threesome was traveling in Dr. Schmunk's camper when a tragic accident occurred. A butane gas bottle exploded destroying the camper and killing the boy.

He and his wife discussed relocating to a place where they could be assured of peace and a brand new start in life. Together, they pored over maps and studied their options. Both favored the west with a preference for Wyoming. They selected the town of Douglas after establishing that Converse County would welcome the settlement of a good family doctor in their locale.

During the latter part of 1979, Dr. Bob, as he was fondly called by his patients and friends, had settled his family on 8.5 acres of land located outside of Douglas, and had applied for a Wyoming medical license which was granted in January, 1980. He maintained his office at his place of residence and he and his wife became quite active in local church affairs. Kay described herself as a born-again Christian who'd previously been associated with the Catholic and Jehovah Witness denominations but was now a devout Baptist as was her husband.

The Schmunks were accorded a warm welcome by residents of the hospitable community and they acquired a varied circle of friends. Even today, no one can say, with any degree of accuracy, exactly when and how Kay died.

Was her death perhaps self induced—suicide or even an accident? Some were even inclined to strongly suspect that Kay had died of natural causes when she was pronounced dead at the Converse County Memorial Hospital on July 15, 1983. A physician had heroically worked over the victim in the hospital's emergency room where she'd arrived via an ambulance after police and medics had responded to an emergency call from the Schmunk residence a short while earlier. The victim's grief-stricken husband had accompanied his wife to the hospital. He and the attending physician were acquainted, and although he was positive Mrs. Schmunk was already dead, he persisted in his attempts at resuscitation awaiting a cue from Dr. Schmunk saying all that could be done had already been accomplished.

At this stage, all anyone knew for certain was what the distraught doctor had told them. He said he had awakened at about 6:30 a.m. to find his wife's still and cold body lying in bed beside him. He mentioned reddish fluids around her mouth and nose and had noticed that her face was ashen and mottled. He had checked for a pulse or a heartbeat but found no vital signs. Schmunk became almost frantic and shouted for his stepson John to telephone the police and request an ambulance. Douglas Police Officers Robert Wegner and Robert Miller and an ambulance were at the residence within minutes.

The police officers found Dr. Schmunk administering CPR (cardiopulmonary-resuscitation) to his wife on the bed in the master bedroom. Medics hastily prepared the stricken woman for the code-three run to the hospital, a trip which took three minutes. The attending physician immediately attempted to revive the victim. Schmunk, on the verge of hysteria, stood nearby wrapped in a sheet. At one point, he mumbled something about having injected his wife with a quarter of a grain of morphine during the night after she complained of an acute headache. One quarter of a grain is by no means a massive dosage of morphine, a commonly used pain-killer and a derivative of opium. As a precautionary measure, however, the physician prepared to administer a narcotic antagonist by injection and was dismayed when he was unable to locate a vein.

This factor indicated either the victim had suffered a long-term illness or she might be an addict. The physician spent 40 minutes in his efforts to revive Kay who he felt may have been clinically dead on arrival (DOA). He'd managed to administer the drug antagonist by injection without results. Several times, Dr. Schmunk had

10

asked him to discontinue his efforts if he felt they were fruitless. Dr. Schmunk was grief stricken, although he appeared to be in control of his emotions. As a man of medicine, he was quite familiar with death.

A nurse pulled a sheet over the decedent's face. An autopsy was ordered. Ordinarily, a postmortem examination is not required in cases where a patient expires in a hospital or while under a doctor's treatment. Usually, the death can be attributed to the condition for which the patient was being treated.

However, in the case of Kay Marie Schmunk, in the physician's opinion, there was no apparent cause of death. At the mention of an autopsy, Dr. Schmunk, shocked by the sudden, inexplicable death of his wife, was aghast and he protested.

"Do you have to know everything? Does everything have to be in black and white? Please God, have mercy," the bereaved physician moaned.

While the physician was entirely sympathetic to his colleague's sentiments, he felt obligated to act against Dr. Schmunk's feelings. He gently advised the decedent's husband that he was duty bound to follow prescribed procedures. Dr. Schmunk subsequently made mention of the fact that he'd also given his wife methadone and me- peridrine (Demerol) during the night after she com- plained of an excruciating headache. Being a doctor himself and cognizant of the proper procedures involved, Dr. Schmunk appeared reconciled that his wife's body would be autopsied.

At 7:45 a.m. that fateful Friday morning, the Con- verse County coroner was somewhat surprised when he received a telephone call from Dr. Schmunk apprising him of the sudden death of his wife Kay. Dr. Schmunk had implied that, in accordance with his and his wife's religious beliefs, he desired to make arrangements for the immediate cremation of her remains. The coroner replied that this would require the execution of certain forms of

11

authorization. While filling out these documents, Dr. Schmunk apprised the coroner that the cause of death was, "cardio-pulmonary failure."

On Saturday, June 16, 1983, the day after Kay Schmunk had expired so abruptly and mysteriously in the bedroom of her home, her remains were transported to Casper, Wyoming in adjacent Natrona County and released to Dr. Ronald Waeckerlin, a forensic pathologist who agreed to autopsy the decedent's body.

Dr. Waeckerlin commenced his scheduled postmortem examination on that date. Having learned of the dead woman's history of severe headaches accompanied by pain so strong that it could barely be alleviated, he fully expected to discover that Kay had succumbed to a brain tumor or aneurysm. Dr. Waeckerlin was also aware that the victim's bladder was found to be bereft of urine or "bone dry" during prior examinations conducted at the Converse County hospital. This factor was distinctively unique in that morphine, Demerol and methadone are urine retentive drugs and there should have been at least 10 residual cubic centimeters left inside the bladder. For some reason, it had been voided.

A visitor from Converse County, Wyoming was present in the morgue examination room with official permission throughout the course of the autopsy. His name was James Davey, a criminal investigator assigned to the Converse County Sheriff's Office in Douglas. Astoundingly enough, during those fleeting 24 hours which had elapsed between the time Mrs. Schmunk's heart ceased to beat and the time her body, draped with a green sheet, was wheeled into the morgue facilities in Casper, hints of veiled, often fleeting suspicions had infiltrated the offices of Mr. Frank Peasley, Converse County Attorney, and his deputy, Mike Hubbard. The innuendo was that there was much more to Mrs. Schmunk's death than met the eye.

Nevertheless, Peasley found it difficult to ignore the rash of unfounded rumors. As matters stood, he knew

12

that he would have only one genuine opportunity to either refute all hint of suspicion or to validate them, and the only way to do that was through a postmortem. A cremation, however, was in the offing, a process which would destroy the evidence.

One relative of the deceased was somewhat surprised upon hearing about Dr. Schmunk's plans to have his wife's body reduced to an urn of ashes in view of the fact that she'd abhorred fire after it had claimed the life of her young son.

Still in somewhat of a daze and aware that he was stymied in making any further plans for funeral services pending the release of his wife's remains by the Converse County coroner, Dr. Schmunk maintained his role as a recently bereaved widower. He received considerable comfort from friends and fellow church associates.

On July 19th, four days after his wife's death, Dr. Bob visited the office of a Douglas dentist who was an acquaintance. Schmunk had confided in the dentist, talking of the profound love he'd harbored for his departed wife, exclaiming, "She's better off now. She'd thank us for what we've done." The doctor had bought a rifle from the dentist earlier in the year saying it was "for his girlfriend."

Investigators learned Dr. Schmunk was really into guns and possessed a collection of firearms valued at $40,000. He and his wife also enjoyed ivory and had accrued a collection appraised at $10,000. Probers also found out that Kay Schmunk had recently had all of her teeth pulled in an effort to eradicate the cause of her agonizing headaches. Nothing had given her any relief except the injections of potent pain-killers administered by her caring husband which eased her agony long enough to allow her to get a bit of sleep.

John V. Wilson Jr., Kay's eldest son by her first marriage, now 17, appeared despondent after his mother's death. Candidly speaking, he said he and his 53-year-old

13

stepfather had not been on the best of terms. He knew that he'd been named in his mother's will but was uncertain of his exact inheritance. Kay had executed her will in February, 1981 naming her husband as both executor and principal heir to her estate comprised of $200,000 worth of real estate, four cars, four trailers worth over $25,000 and personal savings of $2,500.

Her daughter was not named in the will. She'd left nothing but one rifle to her son, requesting that Dr. Schmunk be appointed as the youth's guardian until he reached the age of 19. Mrs. Schmunk's life was insured for $12,000 when she expired. When the will was filed for probate on August 29, 1983 by Dr. Schmunk, it was evident that his wife had, in a manner of speaking, been holding the purse strings when she died and that she'd literally disinherited both of her children.

At the conclusion of the autopsy performed in Casper by Dr. Waeckerlin, one salient factor evolved. The postmortem examination had failed to identify the cause of Kay Marie's death. The procedures had been so precise that three needle puncture sites were located on the body. Only one of the three tiny punctures could have been self-administered by the victim. The total number of needle marks was consistent with Dr. Schmunk's ultimate statement that during the night of July 14-15, 1983 and at his wife's specific request, he'd given her 15 milligrams of morphine at about 12:15 a.m., 100 milligrams of Demerol about two hours afterward and a third injection of 10 milligrams of methadone several hours later.

Although the combination of pain-killing drugs was incompatible, the net amount given the decedent by injection was, if accurate, far from being massive or lethal. All of Mrs. Schmunk's family and numerous close friends knew about her severe headaches and the torturous pain the poor woman suffered during her frequent bouts with her malady. Her husband had taken her to see several specialists none of whom were able to offer any

14

relief. Dr. Waeckerlin had no other professional alternative except to follow through in his endeavors. By no means is an autopsy the last recourse in such cases.

He set about to collect numerous body fluid, tissue, and vital organ specimens for transmittal to forensic laboratories in both Wyoming and Utah. He examined the stomach contents of the body closely and had failed to detect any indications that any drugs had been ingested orally.

Some specimens were dispatched to Michael Peat, a toxicologist at the University of Utah. Others were transmitted to Dr. Rosemary Kincaid with the Wyoming Chemical Testing Program located in Cheyenne. Both technicians performed a battery of tests to ascertain the true cause of Mrs. Schmunk's death. Her body was, in time, released to her husband who proceeded with his plans to have it cremated. During the interim, certain suspicions were converted to facts

Converse County Sheriff's Detective Davey was joined by Lou Dekmar, an ace investigator assigned to the county prosecutor's staff. Both sleuths were fairly certain as early as 48 hours subsequent to Mrs. Schmunk's death that foul play was involved. Bluntly speaking, their convictions at this phase were predicated mainly upon the strong suspicions held by the residents in Douglas.

Davey and Dekmar learned of Dr. Schmunk's odd behavior in the emergency room of the Converse County Memorial Hospital while a doctor spent 40 minutes working over Mrs. Schmunk's lifeless body. They were further intrigued when they established that the bereaved man had contacted the county coroner soon after his wife was formally pronounced dead, to announce emphatically that he wished to have her remains cremated immediately. What was the hurry? detectives wondered. Most of the dead woman's family resided in Michigan. Dr. Schmunk's plans wouldn't even have given them time to arrive for the services.

15

Detectives decided to probe further. They interviewed numerous witnesses and relatives of the victim. The latter class of interviews were conducted with Kay Marie's son and the youth's stepfather. Dr. Schmunk was adamant that his previous quotes about the amounts of drugs he had administered to his wife on the night she died were correct.

His stepson told police that while the doctor and his wife were always compatible in public, they often argued in the privacy of their home.

The investigators located a close friend of the victim who said she had spent the day of July 14th with Kay who had been suffering from one of her splitting headaches. She'd earlier seen Mrs. Schmunk take several pills which caused her to become severely depressed. Later on that day, she chatted with the victim by telephone and was told that she was still in agony from the headache. This witness told police that she suspected Kay might be on some kind of drug because of her frequent bouts of depression and irrationality. She stressed, however, that she always felt the couple loved each other.

From the outset of the complex investigation, sleuths learned from a variety of sources that Dr. Schmunk had a very unsavory past. All they had to do, these informants explained, was to conduct an in-depth probe into the doctor's past before he and his family relocated to Wyoming from Michigan in 1979. In due time, County Attorney Frank Peasely became so intrigued that he dispatched several detectives to Michigan to delve into Dr. Schmunk's background. It was to be a trip well worth the expense. The state of Michigan had withdrawn Dr. Schmunk's license to practice medicine.

Dr. Schmunk's troubles commenced when he was tried on a morals charge in 1976. The scandal in the Detroit suburb was eventually brought to the attention of the medical board of examiners and Schmunk's license was revoked. Michigan's revocation of Schmunk's license evidently had no bearing on his being granted a license expeditiously by the Wyoming Board of Medical Examiners.

Police also found considerable evidence that Kay Marie was more than somewhat dissatisfied with her marriage and with Wyoming during the last months of her life. It was learned that she intended to leave her husband and return to Michigan.

Much of the information gleaned during the probe established a viable motive for murder. Almost everything Dr. Schmunk and his wife had owned was in her name. Her departure, separation and perhaps a divorce could present serious consequences for Dr. Schmunk, detectives surmised. It would assuredly create another scandal and might well result in the doctor's ruination. The plot continued to thicken as forensic scientists in Utah, Wyoming and now Arizona persisted in their intensive efforts to establish beyond all doubt the real cause of Kay's sudden death. Considerable progress was being made in this aspect of the bizarre case. Testings conducted in Cheyenne were showing five times the amount of drugs Dr. Schmunk had admitted giving his wife just prior to her death. As the toxicologist in Salt Lake City would later state, "The level of Demerol in Kay Schmunk's blood was the highest he'd ever perceived in any living person."

Dr. Schmunk was now the prime suspect in the investigation, but no one was jubilant. Everyone close to the probe knew that they had a long way to go before they could even begin to file any charges. They were still talking to Dr. Schmunk and often these interviews were videotaped. This was essential to build a solid case although the prime suspect made no admissions.

Finally, in early September, 1983, all of the clinical reports of examination related to the death of Kay Schmunk were in. It was blatantly obvious that the victim had succumbed as the direct result of a drug overdose and there was evidence she might have been a long-term addict. Probers knew only one person could have introduced the massive dosages of pain-killing drugs into the victim's veins.

Toxicologists' reports proved that five times the amount of narcotics had been given the victim over the amount declared by Dr. Schmunk. The drug dosage was so massive that it eliminated all margin of professed error. According to sound reasoning, it would have been impossible for a doctor to have accidentally made such a profound mistake.

With all the evidence in, Prosecutor Peasely wanted to pursue one other avenue of the probe prior to taking the case before a Converse County grand jury. He planned to review and inspect the records on file with the Wyoming State Board of Medical Examiners. He was told that such records were sealed and confidential and not available for scrutiny, even by county prosecutors preparing to file a murder charge against a physician practicing within the state who'd had his license suspended for cause in another. Peasely took the matter up with the State Supreme Court.

Investigators established through a review of narcotic drug records on file from January 1, 1983 and mid-July that Schmunk had given a total of 26 shots of morphine with 23 of those injections going into Kay Marie's veins. During this same period of time, he'd administered 44 shots of methadone of which 41 were given to his wife, meaning that she'd received 90% of all narcotics dispensed by Dr. Schmunk during those six months preceding her death.

Peasely had good reason to believe that complaints relative to drug abuse had found their way into Dr. Schmunk's files in Cheyenne. Nevertheless, he failed in his attempt to attain access to Schmunk's records when the Supreme Court ruled against him. As one editorial published in a Cheyenne newspaper described it, the ruling amounted to the law closing ranks to protect a physician from prosecution. The decision of the judges involved was predicated primarily on Wyoming state statutes, which allowed them very little latitude in such cases. It stymied the Schmunk probe.

Undaunted, the Converse prosecutor proceeded with his endeavors to bring the matter before the grand jury with a request that a warrant be drawn up for the arrest of Dr. Robert F. Schmunk on a charge of first-degree murder. Despite the fact that he'd been subjected to frequent interviews by police, Dr. Schmunk was unaware that he was the prime suspect in the murder case. That is, until Monday, September 12, 1983 when a story was published in a newspaper describing the case in considerable detail, but without identifying the doctor by name.

Ironically, the leak which precipitated the article could have purportedly originated only at the state echelon. The newspaper was widely read in Douglas where any resident who read it could draw correct correlations. The story had the distinction of being the first article published about the 60-day investigation into the death of Kay Schmunk, and it placed investigators in a quandary. Fearful that the news might prompt the suspect into taking flight, Peasely arranged to have him placed under tight surveillance. He needed 72 hours to finalize his presentation to the grand jury. It was to be three days of high drama and tension.

Investigators Lou Dekmar and Jim Davey had, by now, interviewed dozens of witnesses, including doctors, nurses and close relatives of the victim.

Late on the afternoon of Wednesday, September 14, 1983 the Converse County grand jury, after a secret session, charged Dr. Schmunk with one count of first-degree murder. The accused, at his specific request, had testified during the closed-door hearings. A statement issued by the county attorney's office implied that the death penalty might be sought in the event the physician was convicted. Dr. Schmunk also requested that he be allowed to surrender himself to the authorities, thus avoiding the disgrace associated with being arrested.

He was promptly taken into custody and booked into the Converse County Jail in Douglas. Prior to his incarceration, he issued his own personal statement for publication in the Douglas weekly newspaper. He was arraigned on September 19th, four days after his arrest, in Eighth District court in Douglas. Accompanied by two lawyers from Milwaukee, Wisconsin, Schmunk did not enter a plea. Judge Taylor set bail at $50,000 on a first-degree murder charge declining a defense motion to reduce it to $25,000. A number of the accused's church associates were present during the hearing.

Dr. Schmunk managed to make bail by putting his gun and ivory collections up as property bond. On October 17, 1983 he returned to the Converse County District Court before Judge Taylor and entered a plea of not guilty exclaiming, "I plead not guilty, your honor." A trial date of February 6, 1984 was set. Schmunk had been ordered to appear for hearings before the state medical board, an action which he resisted through his defense counsel.

Schmunk's legal counsel requested, and was granted, a change of venue, moving the trial to Sheridan, Wyo. His trial did not commence until May 3, 1984 after a jury of nine men and five women were selected. Prosecutor Frank Peasely, during his opening statements, declared dramatically that the defendant had effectively reduced his wife to a genuine drug addict and that their marriage was fraught with a "dark counter-current" during which she underwent a slow descent into the private hell of drug dependence. He touched upon the ethical aspects involved in a case where a doctor treated his own wife. He pointed out the deviousness involved as well as the fact that the portly doctor endeavored to match wits with the forensic science community.

Throughout the nine-day trial, the prosecution presented a massive array of physical and circumstantial evidence as well as eye-witness testimony.

The two Douglas police officers who had responded to the emergency call on the morning of July 15, 1983 stated that they didn't feel the doctor was administering CPR correctly and that Schmunk had told them he'd only given his wife one injection but was unable to recall what it was. Most damaging was testimony that showed seven minutes after Kay Marie was pronounced dead, the defendant made a telephone call to arrange for her cremation.

The fact that he resisted a postmortem procedure was also deemed damaging. Numerous family members of the victim testified for the prosecution as did a number of toxicologists, pathologists and members of the medical profession. Dr. Peat, an internationally renown toxicologist, told the jurors that the victim died of an acute drug OD, one more massive than he ever encountered.

The defense put Dr. Schmunk on the witness stand to testify in his own behalf. The crux of his testimony was in his statement, "I did not kill my wife." Dr. Schmunk was on the stand most of the day, Friday, May 11, 1984. He'd wept while describing his wife's death and his attempts to revive her.

During his closing arguments, the prosecutor told the jurors, "He (Schmunk) wasn't her doctor. He was her executioner." The prosecutor's most emphatic description of the defendant was that he was "a master of manipulation."

The jury received the case for deliberation at 1:30 p.m., May 12th and returned nine hours later with a verdict of guilty as charged. Even before the mandatory life sentence could be imposed, the accused defense counsel cited their intent to appeal the conviction.

Schmunk was given life in prison on Friday, May 18, 1984. Judge Taylor allowed him to remain free on bond pending the outcome of his appeal, which was subsequently denied by the district court.

"DID THE KINDLY DOCTOR BECOME A BLOODLUSTING BUTCHER?"

by Bud Ampolsk

The message went out at 7:05 p.m. on Friday, September 21, 1985. It was terse, brief, couched in the language of professionals who use special terms to avoid words such as "death," which trigger intense emotional reactions.

The message was received almost simultaneously by Deputy Prosecutor William R. Coleman and noted defense attorney Matthew K.L. Pyun. To them it meant that the trial which had been set to begin on October 9, 1984 would never take place.

The cryptic announcement was also received at Honolulu Police Headquarters. To Detective Gerald Lee, who had worked so painstakingly since December 28, 1978 on the baffling mystery, it meant that the murder was likely to remain an open case in his files for the foreseeable future.

The announcement from St. Francis Hospital was that Dr. Richard K.C. Chang, a cardiac arrest admission in the hospital's I.C.U., had expired.

Had the death of Dr. Chang occurred prior to June 15, 1983, it undoubtedly would have been recorded in the position of honor on obituary pages of Hawaii newspapers.

Because it had taken place on Sept. 21, 1984, it was

23

to be splashed across the state's front pages with all the accompanying notoriety that goes with being a principal in a sensational homicide investigation.

It was only natural that Dr. Chang's death would spark vivid memories of veteran police officers, prosecutors, defense attorneys, key witnesses, family members and associates of the three people whose destinies had been become so intimately intertwined almost six years before.

For investigating officers, it all had started at precisely 4:30 p.m. on Dec. 28, 1978. It was at that moment that they received the call from the posh 12th floor, two-bedroom condo apartment with its magnificent panoramic view of the Pacific Ocean.

"Something terrible has happened! Come quickly!" the distraught caller had pleaded.

Indeed, as they stood on the deep pile carpeting at the entrance to the apartment, the reporting officers became aware that the frantic caller had understated the situation.

There was blood everywhere. It drenched the carpet, spattered the walls and soaked the pajama-clad bodies of the two elderly people lying jammed just inside the doorway.

"I found them just that way," the neighbor reported. "I had brought up their mail for them. I tried to open the door. It seemed to be stuck. I pushed hard against it. Then I saw the bodies."

The neighbor, who possessed a key to the apartment, and building employees quickly identified the murdered couple as Ted and Alyce Char.

"Who'd have wanted to kill such lovely people?" one of the assembled group of lookers-on wondered aloud.

Kneeling beside the cadavers, the investigators were wrestling with their own question. It was, "Who could have hated this elderly couple with such demonic fury and needed to savage them this way?"

The Chars had been well-known throughout the islands. Ted, having started from very humble surroundings, had built a fabulously successful business career through a series of astute real estate deals. At age 78, he and his wife, Alyce, now in her mid-60's, counted some of the biggest names in finance, literature, culinary pursuits and the arts as close friends.

They'd raised their children and when the younger people had moved to the mainland, they'd sold their palatial estate and moved into the condo.

There, the Chars had continued to entertain lavishly. And the couple's varied activities had not been limited to merely socializing. Together, they had written such well received books as "The Gourmet's Encyclopedia of Chinese-Hawaiian Cooking."

They'd traveled frequently to places as far away as Hong Kong in order to participate in bridge and mah-jongg tournaments.

The couple had been completely devoted to each other. Their great joy had been in giving lavish dinners which they themselves prepared for their VIP guests and having those guests sign their register.

Ted's story closely rivaled that of Horatio Alger. Born the son of a handyman, he'd worked his way through college by peddling pots and pans door-to-door. He'd received a degree in accounting from the University of Illinois in 1928. In 1932, he had been the first accountant to be given certification by the territory of Hawaii.

His investments were conservative and not the kind to arouse enmity. He specialized in buying unimproved land and holding it until it attracted developers' interest. His holdings soon spread to California and his mainland ventures were to prove as lucrative as those in Hawaii.

Slightly built, Alyce had combined sound business

sense with a flair for the artistic. Quickly she became known as a perfect hostess, a concerned neighbor who busied herself in charity and community enterprises, and an astute businesswoman. She formed Royal Dragon Arts, a wholesale importing company specializing in far eastern artifacts.

There was seemingly nothing in the background of Ted or Alyce Char to answer the questions running through the minds of those who now moved through the gore-spattered Char apartment in search of some something which might make sense out of this senseless double murder.

To the detectives and representatives of the medical examiner's office, the advanced age of the two victims made the viciousness of their murders a prime example of overkill.

Ted Char lay sprawled closest to the doorway. Puncture wounds covered his torso. (Later, the medical examiner's report would indicate that he had been stabbed 44 times by a sharp, narrow-pointed instrument, probably a kitchen knife almost two inches wide and approximately eight inches long. His hand was twisted at a crazy angle. It was obvious the hand had been broken by his killer when Char had tried to defend himself.

Nearby, Alyce Char was sprawled on her back. She too had been stabbed repeatedly. In all, some nine knife thrusts had ripped into her body. There was little doubt that she'd died because she had attempted to come to the aid of her husband.

With practiced eyes, the police officers moved beyond the bodies. Perhaps if the signs of violence had spread throughout the apartment, they might have been an indication that robbery was the motive.

But the theory didn't hold. Beyond the vestibule, the beautifully furnished and well-kept condo apartment was as neat and clean as it had ever been. It became obvious that the Chars had met their killer at the door. Once he had murdered them, he'd left the apartment without probing the other rooms.

The Christmas decorations which hung from the apartment door gave a particularly bizarre touch to the death scene. Of special interest was the card which dangled from the decorative knocker. What had been a season's greeting of joy and good will had been turned gruesome by the superimposition of a bloody fingerprint.

Carefully, the forensic people bagged and tagged the card. They reasoned that their entire case might someday rest on this one tangible bit of evidence.

Now with Detective Gerald Lee of the Honolulu Police Department taking a key role, investigators began fanning through the building. They figured that from the clothing of the victims the lethal assault might have taken place in the early morning hours. Most likely, Ted and Alyce Char had been awakened from their sleep by their caller and had not even had a chance to don robes over their pajamas before admitting the perpetrator.

If the theory were to be taken a step further, it would seem likely that the caller had been known to the Chars, otherwise the usually prudent tenants of the apartment would not have allowed him into it.

The urgent need was to find somebody who might have seen the person either coming into the building, on its premises, or leaving it.

The checking by police officers hit the jackpot.

A neighbor who lived on the 11th floor, recalled that on the morning of the 28th, shortly before 6 a.m., he had decided to go to the building's lobby to pick up his morning newspaper.

The witness said that when the elevator had stopped at his floor, the door had opened to reveal a stockily built Oriental man, whom the tenant described as being between 50 and 60 years old.

The tenant had greeted the Oriental, but had received no reply. He remembered the other man as having kept his arms folded in front of his chest and as having acted preoccupied and somewhat confused.

Instead of riding down in the elevator with the tenant, the man had hurriedly left the car at the 11th floor. The tenant had then proceeded downstairs, picked up the newspaper and returned to his own apartment. He'd told his wife about the incident.

The information offered by the witness was valuable, but somewhat sketchy. Would the tenant agree to undergo a session with a hypnotist in hopes of coming up with further details?

Being a public spirited citizen, the tenant said he would. The police arranged the session for three days later. With a hypnotist associated with the Honolulu Police Department taking the witness step by step through his encounter of the fateful morning, the tenant was able to sharpen his recollection. He now reported that the Oriental had been wearing a dark suit, dark tie, brown belt, black shoes with laces and a watch on the left wrist with the face on the inside.

The Oriental had been round faced, smooth-shaven. There'd been a mark, perhaps a birthmark or a blemish, on the left side of his face, near his chin. The stranger had been portly, with a bulging stomach. He'd been perspiring profusely with beads of sweat running down his nose.

The description lent further weight to theories that the assailant had been known to his victims. It was now believed that they'd had no reason to fear him until he'd attacked.

Now Detective Lee and his associates began the arduous task of reconstructing the Chars' last days. It had been unusual for the gregarious couple to be so alone during the Christmas holidays. By tradition, the Yule season had always been one of open hospitality and celebration for them.

With the growing belief that there could have been some previous association between the murdered couple and their killer, Lee and his men searched out friends and relatives of the Chars.

The more they delved, the more apparent it became to the investigators that an ironic twist of fate had taken over to expose the elderly couple to their destroyer.

It never would have been that way, had not a chain of seemingly unrelated incidents gotten underway on a late night in October, some 4,000 miles away from Honolulu on a roadway in Connecticut.

It was on that night that a man driving a Mustang ran a stop sign and collided with a car in which the Chars were passengers. (They'd been visiting close relatives in the Constitution State.)

Alyce had suffered what at first had appeared to be a superficial head injury in the crash. But instead of shaking the effects quickly, the elderly woman began to suffer memory lapses, and coordination difficulties. Medical examinations produced the diagnosis that the accident had caused a more serious injury than had been thought.

Alyce was forced to undergo surgery for a blood clot on the brain. An anticipated Christmas holiday trip to Hong Kong had to be abandoned. The Chars canceled the tickets they held for a December 22nd flight to the British Crown Colony.

Despite the disappointment at the medically forced change of plans, the Chars had reason to be happy. Once the brain clot had been removed surgically, Alyce's recuperation had proved uneventful. She'd even made something of a game of fashioning attractive head turbans to hide the fact that her hair was still growing back in.

She'd been aware and concerned enough to exchange warm Christmas greetings with relatives and to affix the Yule card to her front door to give a festive motif to her apartment.

The Chars believed the year would end on an upbeat note and that 1979 would bring a return of all good things to them.

They were reinforced in this optimism by close relatives and friends who paid casual visits to them. The evening of December 27th was a particularly happy occasion for them. They dined at home with a close relative. By now Alyce was well enough along in her recovery to help Ted fix dinner and even sip a Scotch and soda. They discussed Alyce's operation and engaged in the loving family banter which made such meetings so enjoyable. Every so often, the conversation would get back to the thought that if it hadn't been for the automobile accident, the Chars would now be in Hong Kong.

The quiet evening ended happily at about 10 o'clock. It was the last time the couple were to be seen alive.

While the interviews with friends and relatives went on, the investigators waited impatiently for word from Washington on the bloody fingerprint on the Char Christmas card. The FBI ran the telltale clue through its batteries of computers, but came up with nothing. The print did not match anything in their files.

As the days ticked by and there were no further developments, it became apparent to Deputy Prosecutor Jan Futa and Detective Lee that they were up against a stone wall. Every promising lead seemed to come to nothing. The bits and scraps of information and evidence were gone over and over. New theories were de-

30

veloped and abandoned. The weeks turned into months and the months into years.

Somewhere, someone knew something which would untie the Gordian Knot. But who was that someone and how could Lee reach him?

The dedicated police officer went about his work, taking on new cases, carrying out other successful investigations. But constantly at the back of his mind was the knowledge that a vicious killer was still at large. Lee would not rest until that killer was brought to justice.

"I knew sooner or later something would surface," he says.

It wasn't until May of 1982 that Lee was to get his big break in the case. It was then that the Honolulu Police Department was to publicize the Char killings in its "Crime Stoppers" program. The publication was backed by an ad placed in Sunday newspapers by Char relatives, posting a $20,000 reward for information leading to the arrest and conviction of the couple's killer or killers.

There was no reason to believe that the promotion and offer would bring any more immediate results than all of the other efforts in the grisly discovery of the two bodies. But this time was to prove quite different.

The day the ad offering the award appeared, a man was to clip it carefully, fold it neatly and place it in his wallet. The following morning, the man was to contact the authorities, informing them he had important information to divulge about the double slaying.

Not willing to allow themselves to become too elated over the call for fear that it would only lead to the kind of disappointment they had suffered during the four and a half years of their investigation, the detectives set up a meeting with the man.

His story was short, graphic, complete. The man said

31

he had reported to his job as a parking lot attendant in the condo's garage at 5 a.m., as usual, on the morning of the Char murders.

He'd been at work for only a few minutes when a black Corvette, driven at high speed, had entered the lot. The car pulled into a parking stall.

The driver got out of the car and walked toward the elevator which gave access to the upper floors of the condo. Seeing and recognizing the attendant, the man greeted him by name.

According to the witness, he and the man had become acquainted some years before when the attendant had worked at another lot in the city. The attendant had also been aware that the man to whom he was now talking was a physician.

The man quoted the doctor as saying, "This is an emergency. I'm going to the 12th floor."

The witness went on to describe how he'd opened the door to the elevators for the doctor and how the doctor had then pressed a $20 bill into his hand as a tip.

Said the witness, "I waited for him to come down again. I wanted to thank him for the tip."

About a half hour later, without saying a word, the doctor returned to the lot and hurriedly got into his Corvette and drove up the ramp with such speed that his tires squealed in protest.

Could the witness provide the doctor's name?

Yes, he was Dr. Richard K.C. Chang.

The investigators could hardly believe their ears. Richard Chang was not only a physician, but had been one of the most respected medical men on the island. The 56-year-old gastroenterologist had been thought to be the personification of what a dedicated doctor should be.

Like Ted Char, Chang had worked his way up from the most humble surroundings. Where Char had supported himself in his youth by selling pots and pans, Chang had grown up driving a delivery truck and toting 100-pound sacks of rice. He'd gone to the mainland and received his diploma from Creighton University in Nebraska.

Back in the islands, he soon won renown for his diagnostic ability. Recalled one relative, "He could diagnose a case after a patient had seen everyone else in town. That's why patients loved him—because he made them well."

Others described him as a kind-hearted man whose service to his patients included advising them on personal as well as medical matters and interceding in behalf of their family members.

It had been nothing for the physician to dip into his own funds to pay the medical bills of some of those he treated. In one case, he had been reputed to have lent $50,000 to a person he didn't know because another man had vouched for the stranger.

As the ultimate praise, one acquaintance was to recall, "Why, he even made house calls." Other doctors paid tribute to Chang for his sense of compassion in the care of his patients. They called him an excellent physician in the truest sense of the word.

Yet, despite these glowing testimonials, there were other things about Chang which were designed to keep him from being ruled out as a prime suspect in the condo slayings.

The first was the similarity between his photograph and the police artist's drawing of the intruder on the elevator who'd been surprised by the 11th floor tenant.

An even stronger bit of evidence was the fact that when Honolulu authorities took a set of Chang's fingerprints from their own files (they'd been there as were those of other Honolulu medical personnel for purposes of identification) and sent them to FBI headquarters, word was flashed back from Washington that the print of Chang's index finger on his right hand matched the bloody print on the Christmas card which had been affixed to the Char's door.

Now the investigators put new emphasis on their efforts. They were aware of the need to delve deeply into the possibly darker side of Chang's personality.

Deputy Prosecutor William R. Coleman, who took the case after Futa had left the prosecutor's office, noted the need to build a strong case of circumstantial evidence which would transcend the bloody fingerprint and tie Chang more closely to the Char killings.

"People want to know why," he said. "It's a normal reaction. They want a motive."

His opinion coincided with Futa's. Futa comments: "It's hard for a jury to convict someone of murder. And in a case like this, when you have a pillar of society, the jury wants a motive. A motive gives them peace of mind."

Indeed, as they dug more deeply, the investigators began discovering a side of Dr. Chang that his adoring patients and admiring colleagues had either never seen or never mentioned.

While a former wife was saying, "I could never be able to accept the fact that he could possibly do anything like that (commit murder)," others painted a somewhat different picture of the physician. They reported that Chang had been busy speculating in real estate over the years. His dream of a realty empire was smashed when he had invested heavily in a proposed $20 million, 276-bed medical facility.

The project collapsed and Chang had filed a $7 million breach of contract suit. It took him three years to obtain an out-of-court settlement for $1.5 million. Although his backers got their money back, Chang's own attorneys had sued him for non-payment of their fees.

34

Chang's personal life had taken an unexpected twist in 1975 when he divorced his wife of 25 years to marry a woman some 15 years younger than he was. The split-up with his first wife was on amicable grounds. Their property was evenly divided and they remained friends as well as business partners.

But Chang's second marriage had proved much less tranquil. With the financial pressures upon him, Chang began to suffer from stress and high blood pressure. In 1980 he began to experience episodes of gastro-intestinal bleeding and chest pains. He flew to Houston, Texas for coronary bypass surgery, but the symptoms were not alleviated. He was told by concerned physicians that he would have to limit his own medical activities because of his continuing distress.

Now Chang sought relief by taking a number of potent prescription drugs such as Demerol and Percodan. Those close to him believed the powerful medication impaired his ability to think. He fell into periods of deep depression. He began having irrational outbursts and found it impossible to control his temper. He fell into periods of deep depression.

Those who had lived most closely to him reported they had suffered physical abuse at his hands. One relative sought the advice of a psychiatrist who warned him that Chang's threats were not to be taken lightly. They were of a most serious nature. When informed that Chang had taken to keeping a loaded gun concealed in the glove compartment of his automobile, the relative said the psychiatrist had advised that it be secretly removed.

On July 1, 1981, Chang's second marriage broke up. His closest relatives said they fled to the mainland in fear of their lives.

Having put all the available pieces together, Lee and Coleman now felt they were ready to move.

On June 15th, the Oahu grand jury brought down a true bill, charging Dr. Richard K.C. Chang with two counts of murder in the deaths of Ted and Alyce Char.

Detective Andrew Glushenko was dispatched to the physician's house, where he took the ailing and financially broke Chang into custody. Unable to make the $200,000 bail, he was remanded to jail to await trial.

Preparations went resolutely ahead for the courtroom showdown. Coleman and defense attorney Pyun prepared cases which would hinge on their ability to make a jury believe their case, without the irrefutable proof of the proverbial "smoking gun."

Coleman would base his case on these points:

Although they were not closely associated, Chang and the Chars had been known to each other. Chang had once been a guest in the Char house. Both had traveled in the same social circles. Both had been involved in real estate dealing.

The more frenzied of the attacks on the Chars had been carried out on Ted. Alyce, from the position of her body, had probably been slain when she came to the defense of her beleaguered husband. This indicated that Chang could possibly have had a real or fancied grievance against Char.

The fact that the Chars had opened their door to the killer at 6 a.m., indicated that the murderer was known to one or both of them.

A credible witness had put a man answering Chang's description on the elevator at about the time of the slayings. The witness, under hypnosis, had recalled that the man on the elevator had been in a highly agitated state.

The parking lot attendant had spoken to Chang and had seen him fleeing from the lot in a frenzied state.

A close relative of Chang's had found the man hurriedly washing blood from his clothing upon his return on the morning of the murder. Chang had told the relative that he had suffered an attack of bleeding diarrhea. However, the relative swore that there had only been blood on paper toweling in the bathroom. No blood had been visible on Chang's clothing.

The FBI report on the bloody Christmas card fingerprint was that it was the same as that of Chang.

In recent years, Chang's personality had deteriorated into one of violence and physical abuse which had terrorized his closest relatives.

For his part, defense counsel Pyun was set to stress the reasonable doubt issue in the case. He would have attacked the prosecution on these points:

The FBI fingerprint analysis had not been conclusive. Pyun would have produced two expert witnesses who would have testified that the blood prints lacked sufficient points of likeness—ridges, arches, loops and whorls—to conclusively prove they were Chang's. He would say, "We've never had a case where the experts are so convinced that identification cannot be made."

The key prosecution witness had an axe to grind in putting Chang at the scene of the parking lot. Arguing that the witness had waited four and a half years following the murder to come forward with his testimony, the defense attorney would contend that the man had been motivated by his desire to claim the $20,000 reward offered by members of the Char family for information leading to the conviction of the killer. Pyun would point out that the witness himself possessed a criminal record for having passed bad checks and would not be above concocting a false story for self gain.

In a legal maneuver, Pyun would attempt to exclude testimony by Chang's former wife concerning her conversations with him in their bathroom when Chang had been alleged to have been washing out blood stains. He would cite the prohibition of a spouse testifying against her mate.

He would downplay evidence that Chang suffered a knife wound in the palm of his hand on the morning of the murder. The prosecution's theory about the wound was that it had occurred when Chang's knife had bounced in his hand after striking one of Char's ribs. Pyun's contention would be that Chang had performed intricate surgery on a patient on the day following the double murder. Had he suffered a hand wound, he would not have had the manual dexterity to carry out the procedure so soon afterwards.

Pyun would produce a witness who would testify that on the day of the murders she had seen three men approaching her in the condo's garage. The men had divested themselves of coveralls they were wearing. After the men had left, the woman had recovered the coveralls of one. However, when she had taken them home and attempted to wash them, she had found stains which looked like they were bloodstains and had thrown the garments out.

He would contend that the witness who'd delivered the Chars' mail and discovered their bodies had heard the dead bolt snap when she'd used her key. That indicated that whoever had entered the apartment to kill the Chars had locked the door from the outside.

Whose premise the jury which was never impaneled would have believed will never be known. Death had intervened.

Suffice it to say that Dr. Chang went to his grave with over 300 friends and relatives paying their last respects to him. A minister confined his eulogy of the physician's contributions to his profession and his patients.

He commented, "For Dr. Chang, it's a crowning day rather than a day of defeat. You see his mortal body at peace."

As the words were spoken, investigators, relatives of both the slaughtered Chars and the fallen Chang, and just about everybody in the sophisticated city of Honolulu had his own ideas of what had gone on in the 12th floor luxury condo apartment the morning of December 28, 1978.

What is your theory?

"MURDERED THE
WRONG VICTIM"
by W.T. Brannon

The trial of William R. Hill, 27, for murders in 1974
and 1975 opened in the Criminal Court of Circuit
Court Judge John J. Moran in Chicago on the morning
of July 25, 1977 when the selection of a jury began.
Under Illinois law, a defendant may decide whether to
have a bench trial, with the judge deciding his fate, or
a trial by jury, whose members would determine his
destiny.

Like most other defendants, Hill had decided to put
his lot in the hands of the jury.

While the jurors were being selected, First Assistant
State's Attorney Barry Gross discussed the case. Although Hill was on trial for the murders of two men,
three men besides Hill had been involved.

Allen Ziperstein, 61, a pharmacist and co-owner with
Robert Fields, 47, in five drug stores—which had been
given the fancier name Medical Centers. His office was
in the Haymarket Drug Store, on West Madison Street
in the heart of the skidrow section, inhabited by winos
who slept in cheap flophouses and in doorways when
the weather was not too cold.

The four other medical centers were located in sections where people were poor and mostly on welfare.
Fields was not a pharmacist but formerly had operated

a pawn shop on West Madison Street across the street from the drug store. A close friend of Fields was Dr. Max Murphy Kaye, a dentist whose office was about half a block from the drug store.

When they heard the drug store was for sale, Fields and Dr. Kaye discussed the possibility of buying it. But Fields had another acquaintance, Allen Ziperstein, a pharmacist who was younger than Dr. Kaye. Without telling Dr. Kaye, they bought the store as co-owners. When Dr. Kaye heard of this he was furious.

To get capital for buying the store, Fields had sold his pawn shop. He had made many friends when he was a pawn broker and persuaded them to bring their prescriptions to him. Most did.

Dr. Kaye came to the drug store and in the back there ensued one of a long series of shouting matches between him and Fields. Dr. Kaye said he should have a share of the profits and Fields promised to cut him in.

Later Fields gave Dr. Kaye a few dollars and this infuriated the dentist, whose business had dropped off. Medicaid had paid for dental work, dentures and prescriptions written by Dr. Kaye. He had lost some of this business when the law was changed, but he still wrote prescriptions which were filled at the Haymarket Drug Store. The volume of these was so large that he was being investigated along with Ziperstein and Fields. It was believed that many of the prescriptions were not filled although Medicaid paid for them.

On August 23, 1974, a black man entered the drug store on West Madison Street and asked the clerk if he could see Mr. Festenstein.

He told the man there was no one there by that name and that he probably wanted to see Mr. Ziperstein. The man nodded.

Allen Ziperstein was at his desk in a back room and came out when the clerk told him of the caller. It was then 9:18 a.m. Ziperstein came out and said to the man: "What can I do for you?"

Without a word the black male whipped out a .32 caliber chrome-plated automatic and pumped seven shots pointblank into the body of the druggist. Then he turned and strode out the door. He soon was lost among the people on the crowded street.

The clerk called Central Police Headquarters and within minutes, Commander Joseph DiLeonardi was at the scene. Police Officers Toolis and Coe who had been cruising nearby at the time of the shooting quickly roped off the front of the store to keep out curiosity seekers.

Commander DiLeonardi soon was joined by Lieutenant Walter Bosco, head of Area One homicide. He was followed by the squad of James Dvorak, Michael Caccitolo and John Glenn. At the time Glenn was on furlough, but returned a few days later.

The clerk and other witnesses described the gunman as a black male, 25 to 33 years old. He was about six feet tall, weighed about 170 pounds and was well dressed in a neat suit, white shirt and tie.

Witnesses were questioned and Investigator Caccitolo finally found one who recalled seeing the fleeing gunman board a northbound bus. Commander DiLeonardi was notified and he immediately put investigators to work contacting patrol cars and district stations between Madison Street and the city limits at Howard Avenue, a distance of about 10 miles.

Investigators Caccitolo and Dvorak concentrated on the block on which the drug store was located. Caccitolo found a merchant who told of hearing the loud arguments from the drug store. However, this was several days after the murder and the merchant said the arguments had been heard since the murder. This meant they had not been between Ziperstein and Fields.

Meanwhile, Investigator Dvorak tried to find a motive. But everyone who knew Ziperstein said he was a very friendly, mild-mannered man and it was improbable that he was arguing with his partner. About this time, Caccitolo learned that the shouting matches had continued after the druggist's death. This tended to clear Fields, who already had furnished an alibi.

Investigator Glenn returned and added muscle to the probe. The three men had other duties but every spare moment was devoted to the case. But it still was unsolved on January 18, 1975. On that day, a well dressed black male watched Fields get out of his car and start for the drug store. Fields was shotgunned in the back and the gunman paused only momentarily to brandish the weapon at spectators. Then he hurried to the corner and boarded a northbound bus.

Investigators Dvorak, Caccitolo and Glenn were at the scene in minutes. Dr. Tae Lyons An, a medical examiner, also was there as well as identification men and crime lab technicians. A routine investigation was made but it yielded no clues.

The homicide men were more determined than ever. Records of the welfare department showed that Dr. Kaye was 72 instead of the 65 he claimed to be. These records also showed that Festenstein had been the name of the second victim until he had it legally changed to Fields. However, according to merchants on the block where the drug store was located, Dr. Kaye refused to recognize the changed name. That was the name given to the drug clerk, who didn't know that Fields once had been named Festenstein.

But who had hired him to murder Festenstein? Was it Dr. Kaye?

Some witnesses said a young black male was behind the gunman and fled after the shooting. The investigators stopped a young black man three days after the shooting. He was identified by the witnesses as the man who had been standing behind the killer. He had fled when the shots were fired but in a different direction. He identified himself as Edgar Wiley, 20.

Wiley denied that he had been a witness and said he had arrived after hearing of the shooting. He was released after he had given his address. The investigators continued concentrating on the block.

They found a man who said he was not a witness but he had heard from a fellow merchant that the gunman was a security guard and that he was a close friend of Wiley. The detectives went to the other merchant, who said he had heard the story from a girl who was a secretary-receptionist for a small medical center on the west side. The investigators went to see her.

She told them one security guard, William R. Hill, 27, saw her reading a newspaper account of the murder of Ziperstein and said, "I killed that guy."

When she asked him why, he replied that a man had made a contract with him to do the job and he was to receive $25,000 from a Dr. Kaye, a dentist with offices near the drug store. She told him she was busy and didn't have time for fairy stories.

The girl called Hill a loudmouth and a braggart, that he claimed to have been a Sicilian Commando when he was overseas. Still posing as a member of the Mafia, he had learned a few Italian phrases.

The girl said Hill talked repeatedly about the murder and two days after it occurred, he came in looking very dejected. When she asked him what was wrong, he said he had shot the wrong man and Dr. Kaye was very angry. He said Festenstein was the man known as Fields.

After the dentist had simmered down, he gave Hill another chance, although he had reduced the contract fee to $10,000. Hill said he got $5,000 from Dr. Kaye and $2,500 from an employee of the dentist. He said he was to get the balance after the hit.

Hill gave her a running account of his progress. It had been decided to wait a few months until the heat was off. Then Fields was shot on January 18, 1975. Hill told the girl about it and said she intended to inform the police after the Ziperstein murder, but waited too long and Fields was killed. After that she didn't know what to do. After Wiley was questioned he didn't show up for work.

The investigators went to the address Hill had given the security agency, but it was phony. Then they went to the address Wiley had given and found him at home. He was informed of his rights and was taken to Central police headquarters. A lineup was arranged and several skidrow witnesses viewed it. Wiley was picked out as the man.

One who was acquainted with both men said that Wiley worshipped Hill. The informer said he thought the plan was to make Wiley the fall guy. Wiley said Hill wouldn't do anything like that. "Okay," said the investigator, "suppose you tell us where Hill can be found. You're going to be charged with being an accessory, at the least, and probably with murder."

Wiley gave Hill's address and he was picked up. Assistant State's Attorney Joseph Urso had just arrived when the officers brought Hill in.

Hill tried some plea bargaining. "I'll dictate a typewritten confession to a court reporter if Assistant State's Attorney Joe Urso, with you all as witnesses, will give me a written statement that I will be guaranteed a sentence of fourteen years to fourteen years and a day."

The witnesses included Prosecutor Urso, Investigators Dvorak, Caccitolo and Glen, Commander DiLeonardi and Lieutenant Bosco.

Hill's proposal was refused at once. One of the investigators said he already had given a verbal confession. Hill was charged with murder and Wiley as an accessory. Both were held until they later were indicted by a Cook County grand jury, Hill for murder, Wiley as an accessory. They were held without bond in the Cook County jail.

When the case came to trial, Wiley agreed to testify against Hill and the accessory charge was dropped.

In his opening address, Prosecutor Scott Peterson said of Hill: "He fancied himself as a Mafia hit man. He always ate at good restaurants, ordering such things as lasagna. He even learned to speak Italian. He is a man who has schooled himself in the very fine art of killing human beings."

Despite interruptions from Hill's attorney, William O'Malley, Peterson told the jury that the murders resulted from a feud between Fields and Dr. Max Murphy Kaye. Peterson said the prosecution would provide witnesses to testify that Kaye hired Hill to kill Fields after the two had quarreled bitterly over a plan to swindle the welfare department.

He said Dr. Kaye sent business to Fields, some of it legal, some of it illegal. The prosecutor said Dr. Kaye's apparent motive was money. He said welfare investigators had learned that Dr. Kaye had fleeced the state on welfare medical bills, writing hundreds of prescriptions for medicine that was not needed.

Prosecutor Peterson said that Ziperstein was shot to death by Hill because of a mixup in names. Peterson said that Hill was paid a total of $6,800 after Fields had been shot down outside the drug store on January 18, 1975.

William O'Malley, the attorney who had been appointed by the court to represent Hill, asked the jury of six women and six men to pay particular attention to the testimony of Edgar Wiley. "See if you don't think the wrong man is sitting in front of you." O'Malley said that Hill was a man who "worked two and three jobs, none of them high-paying."

One of the jobs was in a metal working shop, where Hill had the means to repair and remodel guns, two of which the prosecutors charged, were used in the slayings.

Pointing at the defendant, Prosecutor Peterson said: "All of the evidence and all of the witnesses will point their fingers in just one direction, William Roderick Hill." In Hill's apartment, Peterson said, the police found a "beautifully illustrated pamphlet telling how to kill. He had a motto, Kill Without Joy, and that's exactly what he did."

When the trial got under way, the clerk in the drug store at the time of both murders testified that about a week before the slaying of Ziperstein, Dr. Kaye came into the drug store and asked for Bob, the name he normally called Robert Fields. Fields was in a back room and Dr. Kaye went in there.

The clerk said he could hear Fields and Dr. Kaye shouting at each other but that he didn't know what the quarrel was about. He said he was eating lunch in a restaurant on Halsted the next day when Dr. Kaye strode in. He whipped out a gun and waved it in the air toward the clerk and said: "You tell Bob to stay away from me." Then he left.

The receptionist Hill confided in said she also was a medical technician and had worked two weeks in the Haymarket Drug Store in 1974. However, this was prior to the murder of Ziperstein. She said she met Hill first when both were employed by a Medical Center on West Chicago Avenue in November, 1974.

One day, she testified, "he asked me if he fit the description of the man who killed Allen Ziperstein and I said, 'I guess so.' He said: 'Well, I should because I killed him.'"

During two hours of testimony, the witness told of Hill's efforts to woo her. He took her to Kung Fu movies and Italian restaurants. She said he frequently took her to Italian restaurants, where Hill sometimes talked in what sounded to her like Italian.

One day, she testified, Hill came to work wearing a brown-checked jacket and told her: "This is the jacket I was wearing when I killed Allen Ziperstein."

"Did he tell you how he did that?" Prosecutor Peterson asked.

"He said he walked into the Haymarket Drug Store and he asked for Allen Ziperstein. He told me he shot him six times in the chest and once in the leg so he would fall."

This conflicted with what the investigators had learned. According to what they had been told, Hill asked for Festenstein, Fields' former name, probably known only to Dr. Kaye among the principals in the case. There was no apparent reason for Hill to ask for Ziperstein.

Assistant State's Attorneys Peterson and George Lynch introduced in evidence the jacket Hill supposedly had worn when he killed Ziperstein as well as a manual on how to commit murder, found by police in Hill's apartment.

Assistant State's Attorney Joseph Urso testified that on the night Hill was arrested, January 22, 1975, he made a verbal confession of the murder of Fields at Area One police headquarters.

"He said," Urso testified, "that like a good Sicilian soldier, he was following orders. He said he killed Mr. Fields and that he did it without any emotion—it had to be done."

48

Urso testified that Hill told him he had arranged to kill Fields for $10,000. He said the deal was made through one of Kaye's employees. He said that when he arrived at Area One headquarters, police were playing a tape recording of a statement made by Edgar Wiley.

The tape was played for Hill, Urso testified, and "Hill's eyes began to water. It was the first time he had showed emotion. He said to me: 'You have me, on Fields but not on Ziperstein.'" Urso said Hill had refused an attorney at first and even gave written permission to have his apartment searched. But later he asked for a lawyer.

Prosecutor Urso testified that the defendant offered to plead guilty to both murders if Urso would give him a written guarantee that he would receive the minimum sentence, which is 14 years.

"That's no deal," Urso said he told Hill.

The witness said that after he had listened to Wiley's confession and talking to the police, Wiley asked Urso if he was Italian. He said Hill used such phrases as "parla Siciliana" — speak Sicilian — and "Capiche Siciliana" — do you understand Sicilian? — frequently.

Urso said Hill told him he posed as a gas meter reader to get into Fields' home and make diagrams of the interior. Urso also said that Hill had a good knowledge of Fields' car, clothing and home.

Under cross-examination, Hill's attorney, William O'Malley, asked why the police tape-recorded Wiley's statement but didn't tape one by Hill.

Urso replied that Hill wouldn't make a statement to be tape recorded.

Another important witness was a woman, who said she had worked as a receptionist and dental technician for Dr. Max Murphy Kaye. He had assigned her to act as go-between for William R. Hill and Dr. Kaye, who had been carrying on a feud with Fields.

The witness told the judge and jury that she had passed information and money between Dr. Kaye and Hill.

Questioned by Assistant State's Attorney Lynch, the 24-year-old woman testified that she had heard Dr. Kaye say: "Bob is no good. I'd kill that bum if I thought I could get away with it. I'd pay five thousand dollars if I could find somebody to put a hit on Bob."

She added she had heard Dr. Kaye say this after a quarrel between Dr. Kaye and Fields.

She testified she told Hill of Dr. Kaye's comments and Hill told her: "I'll do it." The witness told him, she said, "I'll bet you would."

She said she then gave Hill an envelope from Dr. Kaye. It was addressed to Hill and it contained a detailed description of Fields' car and his neighborhood. It also contained a photograph of Fields.

The technician testified that she talked to Hill about a week later and he said, "he couldn't do it" because the police were harassing him.

However, she testified, on the day Ziperstein was gunned down Dr. Kaye answered the telephone and she heard Dr. Kaye's end of the conversation: "What? He hit the wrong man? Somebody walked in and shot Al's guts out!"

Later that night, the witness testified, Hill called her and said: "We did the job and I want my money."

She testified that when Dr. Kaye was asked about it, he replied that Hill should be paid only half of the sum agreed upon because he had killed the wrong person.

The witness said that she then delivered a white, unsealed envelope to Hill. She said it contained $20, $50 and $100 bills. She said that Hill was working as a security guard at the Medical Center on West Chicago Avenue, where he first had become acquainted with the receptionist who had testified earlier.

Prosecuting attorneys said that Hill received a total of $6,800 from Dr. Kaye.

There were other witnesses but the main witnesses already had testified to an extent to establish Hill's guilt. The state rested.

However, in his own defense Hill said he was innocent, and that his former roommate, Edgar Wiley, was the real killer.

The prosecution asked for the death penalty under Illinois' new capital punishment law. This case qualified under two of the provisions of the law—a contract murder or multiple killings.

In asking for the death penalty, Assistant State's Attorney Lynch said it was Hill and no one else who chose his "profession."

"This man chose to become an assassin, a hired killer," the prosecutor said. "He received money for what he did and in return for the money, he killed two.

Assistant State's Attorney Scott Person also asked for the death penalty. "We would like you to tell William R. Hill that you have killed enough people," Peterson said. "You have boasted enough of your hellish deeds of killing people."

"Tell the William R. Hills out there on the streets of Chicago that this type of crime doesn't pay—it's not what it's cracked up to be."

Defense Attorney O'Malley was critical of the fact that the jury was not told that it was to hear a capital case. He also criticized the failure to ask prospective jurors if they objected to the death penalty while the panel was being selected.

After the jury was given legal instructions by Judge

Moran, they retired to deliberate Monday afternoon. The deliberation lasted only a short time; the verdict was guilty of conspiracy and the contract murders of Ziperstein and Fields.

Under Illinois law, after the verdict is in, the defendant has two options. He can choose to be sentenced by the judge or put his fate in the hands of the jury. Hill decided to let the jury make the decision.

The jurors could sentence to imprisonment or give the death penalty. They deliberated three and a half hours and then returned their verdict — death in the electric chair.

The law requires an automatic appeal to the Illinois Supreme Court. There are many avenues of appeal and O'Malley vowed that he would take the case to the Illinois Supreme Court. The prosecuting attorneys said there were so many avenues of appeal in the state and federal courts — all the way to the United States Supreme Court — that the case could go on for years.

Defense Attorney O'Malley asked Judge Moran to overturn the verdict on the grounds that Hill's age, 27, had not been established before the trial began.

The judge rejected the request, saying that Hill's age clearly had been established.

Although the two murders were committed before the state's new capital punishment law went into effect, the former death penalty law still was on the books. Judge Moran said the Untied States Supreme Court had ruled that under a capital punishment law in effect when the crime was committed, the new law can be invoked, even though the high court had thrown out the former law.

The former capital punishment law was found unconstitutional by the Supreme Court because it permitted no discretion to impose a lesser sentence in some cases.

Almost immediately after the ruling by the high

court, the Illinois legislature went to work on a new death penalty law, one that would be upheld by the Supreme Court. The new law was passed and quickly signed in June, 1977, by Governor Thompson.

William R. Hill was the first person to be convicted under the new law. It remains to be seen whether he is the first to be executed. The last person to be executed in Illinois was James E. Dukes, who was convicted of shooting to death a plainclothes police officer in 1956. He finally went to the chair on August 24, 1962.

Hill was interviewed by newsmen in the office of Acting Warden Robert E. Glotz, on August 16th, the day after his conviction and sentence. They saw a sketch of a man sitting in an electric chair that was hanging in his cell.

Hill said he drew the sketch and hung it up the night before, shortly after he had been sentenced to die in the electric chair. "I look at it every hour," the convict said. "It makes me think of how people are mistreating me for their own gain."

Insisting that he was not guilty of the two hit murders, he accused the prosecutors of trying to "build political gain," and said his conviction was one way they hoped to do it.

The only persons known to voice regret were Hill and his attorney, O'Malley, who appeared to believe firmly in Hill's innocence.

According to two jurors who discussed the case, there never was any doubt about Hill's guilt. Marc Anthony, 31, said there was one main thought in everybody's mind: It was "that this man was cold-blooded and had no feelings.

"All of us felt capital punishment was needed in Illinois. We felt we were speaking for most people in the state. We're tired of people killing others and then getting back on the street after a thirty or forty-year prison term. The fact Hill might have killed again, had we sentenced him to prison, bothered us."

The jury had no sympathy for a murderer who "would put seven slugs into another man." He said the jurors didn't look kindly on a man who would "make a mistake and kill the wrong man—and still come back to kill another," Anthony said.

Anthony said he didn't feel squeamish about the verdict. "I have no second thoughts about sending Hill to the electric chair," he said. "He deserves the penalty he is getting."

The juror said there were two considerations that added to his aversion to the murders. Hill's execution would deter others from committing murder.

Another was Hill's military record. He was court-martialed three times—once for possession of marijuana, another time for the theft of a TV set and a third time for battery. He was dishonorably discharged.

The dishonorable discharge was approved by a Marine Corps chaplain. The chaplain had said Hill could not be "redeemed," that Hill had negative feelings about military service and recommended his dishonorable discharge.

Anthony said that on the first ballot for sentencing, the vote was 10 for the death penalty and two for imprisonment. The next ballot was 11 to one. The decision was unanimous on the third ballot.

However, Anthony said those who voted for imprisonment were not opposed to capital punishment.

"They told us later," Anthony said, "that they wanted us to get deep into the case in our discussions so there would be no doubt in our minds that we were doing the right thing."

Doctor Max Murphy Kaye didn't live to go to trial. Seven months after the indictment he died of a heart attack.

As this was written, William R. Hill was held in the Cook County jail while the appeals process ground on.

EDITOR'S NOTE:
Edgar Wiley is not the real name of the person so named in the foregoing story. A fictitious name has been used because there is no reason for public interest in the identity of this person.

"HOW MANY CORPSES FOR THE EVIL DOCTOR OF DEATH?"

by Richard Walton

Dressed head to foot in camouflage combat gear, the hunter moved with the stealth of a predator through the silent night, ears attuned to the slightest noise. His mission, however, was not to terminate life. In fact, he was about to save one.

The naturalist was seeking nocturnal badgers and toads known to frequent the dense bushes and parkland of Keston Lakes in Bromley, England, and, as he crept slowly forward, he was listening in particular for the rasping croak of the toads.

It was an intensely cold night with a temperature way below zero. Perhaps it was to be expected on that night of Saturday and Sunday, January 4-5, 1986, in that part of Southern England from midnight on.

Avoiding a frosted area of grass that would crunch underfoot, he tiptoed toward some holly bushes fringing a car park but suddenly stopped, the hairs prickling alarmingly on the nape of his neck.

There was something alien there, in back of the stygian gloom — a shape of indistinct form, yet vaguely human and hissing at him.

He crept closer, peering through the mist swirling off the water of the lakes. There was a head there but the mouth was too wide and low, gaping open like that of some gigantic toad.

And then he jerked back with an involuntary gasp of horror as he identified his monstrous apparition.

It was a mortally wounded woman, fighting for breath with her throat gashed open from ear to ear.

A few minutes later, the naturalist was pounding on the door of the nearby home of wealthy city businessman Harold Drake and his wife, Agnes, who were hosting a New Year's dinner party for several guests. Theirs was the only house around the park which he could find at 1:00 a.m. with lights still burning.

Mrs. Drake answered the door, a little alarmed to see a combat-clad stranger pleading with her to call the police as he almost fell into the hall.

"Help me!" he gasped. "There's a girl in the park back there and someone has tried to cut her head off!"

The Drakes and their guests rallied immediately to the emergency, one alerting the police on the telephone and the others in tuxedos and dinner gowns running back with the man to the lakes half a mile away.

Mrs. Drake threw a blanket over the icy-cold injured woman, who was wheezing for breath through a slashed windpipe. And she rubbed warmth into the victim's chilled hands and talked gently to her, assuring her that help would be arriving very soon.

It was, but four other things beyond an ambulance crew saved the woman's life—the miraculous arrival of the man on his toad safari, the Drakes' prompt response to his plea, a surgeon who performed an emergency operation in the local hospital soon afterwards, and, most of all, the intense cold of that night.

Hypothermia had set in, reducing the amount of blood she was losing from that ghastly wound. Otherwise, she would have bled to death before the man arrived, estimated death being only a scant 30 minutes away had he not done so.

Her identity was soon established. She was the 43-year-old Indian-born wife of a respected local man, John Baksh, also Indian. Both were in general practice as doctors in the district of Eltham nearby.

They lived in a luxury $400,000 house three miles from where she was found. The police had already heard from John Baksh late the previous night.

At 9:30 p.m. he had telephoned them. He and his wife—it was a second marriage for both of them—had been due to celebrate their second anniversary that night.

She had left the house at 5:00 p.m. to do some last-minute shopping in nearby Bromley but had not returned home. He had found her gray Ford Orion abandoned in the town center near the magistrates' court and feared that she had been the victim of abductors.

As she lay unconscious in a hospital later that following morning recovering from the life-saving operation, police appealed through the press for any witnesses to the snatch to contact them.

Meanwhile, certain coincidental stories circulated which, while not positively identifying anyone, pointed a finger in certain investigative directions.

Reports appeared in January that Scotland Yard detectives were to watch the exhumation of a 36-year-old British woman's body from a grave in southern Spain. She happened to be the wife of a London-based family doctor and had died while on holiday three years earlier, apparently the victim of a heart attack.

Around the same time, Murder Squad detectives were also reported to be probing the mystery deaths of three family doctors who worked at the same surgery in South London, all thought to have suffered heart attacks. But new evidence suggested that they could have been drugged to bring on or simulate this condition.

Two of these doctors were bachelors who died in the 1970's and had been cremated, a fact that made queries into their deaths more difficult.

Detectives had quizzed a man in custody about all three deaths, one report said, and Scotland Yard was also looking into something else very interesting. . . .

All three were heavily insured. The same man collected large payouts in each case.

A Yard spokesman was quoted as saying: "It may be weeks or even months before we know whether we are dealing with a multiple murder investigation or a series of extraordinary coincidences."

In the meantime, Baksh's wife had regained consciousness in the hospital to face a somewhat bizarre confrontation, while courting couples who had been making out in their vehicles in the car park near where she was found that night were lining up at Farnborough Police Headquarters to tell detectives what, if anything, they knew.

Then on Friday, January 10th, Dr. John Baksh was suddenly charged with the attempted murder of his second wife. In February, magistrates at his local Bromley court sent him for trial to London's Central Criminal Courts.

By August, however, another charge was added—that of having murdered his 47-year-old first wife (Ruby) in Almeria, Spain, three years earlier.

Anyone having read those earlier coincidental press reports now saw a certain light.

It is the tendency in England today for press speculation in advance of a trial to run rife, but this time it was conspicuous by its absence. It was left mainly to the second wife to reveal an amazing story in her court evidence about the respected family doctor who had picked up over $100,000 from his first wife's life insurance, and stood to gain another $125,000 from the second wife's own demise. After, that is, Crown prosecutor Allan Green, a bespectacled, jovial-looking but extremely astute lawyer, had outlined a few basic facts.

John Baksh had practiced in the Eltham and Chislehurst districts of South London and his first wife for 21 years was also a doctor in the practice. Then, in 1979, a shy, petite woman doctor, who had been born in Lucknow, joined the firm, too.

The woman had arrived in England in 1968. She was married in 1969 and had two children—a boy and a girl. In 1980, her husband left her.

A Fellow of the Royal College of Surgeons of Edinburgh and a member of the Royal College of Gynecologists, she was an undoubted asset to the practice, but Baksh found her attractive in a more physical way.

One night he visited her Bromley apartment with a bottle of champagne, asking her: "Why are you alone? This is a permissive society!" This shy woman told him that he might think so, but she did not. After drinking the champagne, all she gave the amorous doctor was dinner.

By October, 1982, Baksh was pressing for an affair, but she flatly refused. She was prepared, however, to marry him—but only after he divorced his first wife (Ruby).

When December came, Baksh said that he felt in need of a little sunshine, so he took his wife and their own two children to spend a holiday in the family villa outside Almeria in southern Spain.

But early on New Year's Day of 1983, Baksh suddenly summoned an elderly Spanish doctor he had met at a party. He claimed that after a strenuous New Year's party, his wife had collapsed with a heart attack and was dead.

The elderly physician signed the death certificate to confirm that. She was buried in Spain, although Baksh complained bitterly about the high funeral expenses.

Baksh then returned with the children to England. He had telephoned the woman he wanted for a mistress to inform her of the tragedy. Feeling sorry for him, she agreed to look after him and his own children, too.

Two weeks after that first wife's death, they went through a mock Hindu marriage ceremony in her apartment bedroom as the sickly-sweet scent of incense permeated the air. In front of an idol to the god Krishna, she knelt in submission at Baksh's feet as he placed his dead wife's wedding ring on her finger.

They became lovers the following week, and after her own divorce came through, they were married officially on January 7, 1984.

Baksh's motive for murdering his first wife, Prosecutor Green maintained, had been chiefly financial, although he also wanted to pursue his conquest of the new business partner.

But, by the end of 1985, he was in deep financial trouble with a $12,000 revenue bill on unpaid taxes, a large bank overdraft and heavy school fees overdue.

It was time to trade in his second wife for cash, too.

She confirmed by her own testimony in court that she had been a silent accomplice after-the-fact in the murder of the first wife, although the authorities contemplated no action against her.

She had learned of the crime in a startling way.

In May of 1983, four months after the first wife's death in Spain, she was with Baksh in a hotel bedroom in Montparnasse, Paris. It was early morning and she was getting changed as he still lay in bed. He asked her to come closer and she did so.

Standing in the Central Criminal Court witness box wearing a high-neck dress to cover the wound across her throat, she described what then happened. She never once looked in her husband's direction in the dock nearby.

"John started to cry," she said. "I was surprised, stroked his head to comfort him and asked what the trouble was. He told me he had sacrificed his first wife for me."

She had asked him to explain what he meant, to clarify the statement, and he had done so. "I thought I had dropped from the sky down to the level of earth," she whispered quietly, "for I could not believe it."

Baksh told her that every night he took his wife a drink of hot milk, but on that particular New Year's Eve, he put some drug tablets in it to knock her out. Then he injected a massive dose of morphine into her thigh.

She had not suffered, he said. Then he cried again for a time, turned over and went back to sleep, starting to snore.

Mrs. Baksh told the jury: "I was sitting there on the bed beside him in a mixture of fury, disbelief and depression. I wanted to run out and shout to the world what he had told me.

"I felt shattered. My first marriage had been very unhappy, and now I found this man was a murderer, and I was sleeping next to him."

She woke Baksh up and told him that she was frightened. She hoped that all he had said was not true.

He took her in his arms, consoled her, cried some more and went back to sleep.

A few weeks later she asked him bluntly why he had done it and he told her: "If I had not done so, I would not have got you!"

At that stage, she felt in fear for her own life. Baksh was a highly respected doctor and she thought no one would believe her story if she repeated it.

A few nights later she told him that if he could do that to his first wife, he might one day do the same to her—grimly prophesying her own near-fate. But he cried yet again and accused her of being cruel to him, adding, "What I have done is the biggest sacrifice anyone can make for love."

And so, for two years, the new Mrs. Baksh kept that terrible secret—until questioned by detectives as she lay in a hospital after "demon doctor" John, finding loot finally more important than love, ran a foot-long carving knife across her throat.

But first, her bizarre encounter in the hospital with the deadly doctor after her miraculous recovery from almost certain death drew the jury's rapt attention.

Her first vision on regaining consciousness was her husband's smiling face bending over her in a caring bedside manner, a bouquet of flowers in one hand, a look of fond love on his features. But naked fear ranged wide in his eyes as he kissed her three times on the forehead.

And, to ensure that police and nurses around the bedside nearby did not understand him, he spoke to her in Hindi, begging her to save him by covering up his murder attempt.

He asked her in hoarse appeal to "remember" masked men approaching her while she'd been out shopping. But she shook her head, indicating "no," because she could not yet speak.

Then he asked how many men there were, but she had put up one finger and pointed it straight at him to indicate: "It was you!"

Baksh then began to plead abjectly with her to save his life and keep him out of jail.

"I wanted to push him away but my mind said no. He must not think I would not cooperate, and I was worried about the children."

So, she agreed to tell the police a false story. But when Baksh had gone she scrawled on a blackboard these words: "My husband is a killer. Tell the judge he killed his first wife."

When able to speak properly again, she told detectives the true story of what had happened, and repeated that early-morning bedroom confrontation in Paris.

Her final comment on the man who almost killed her was that she had loved him too much because he was everything she wanted in a man.

Kind and gentle, he had seemed to be a perfect husband and father. But there had been something more than just her word to confirm the murder of the first wife.

When the body was exhumed in Spain, the pathologist, Dr. Iain West, found traces of morphine still in it. Unknown to Baksh, the body had been wrapped in plastic sheeting before interment in the coffin, which helped preserve it longer than normal.

Yet Baksh was still trying to wriggle out from under in his early statements to the police, and in court.

The first wife, he said, had taken an overdose of drugs when she had discovered that he had been having an affair with their new lady partner from Lucknow. He had told his wife that he would break off the relationship, he claimed, but she had still remained sad and pensive.

When the Spanish doctor certified death from heart failure it was Baksh himself who accepted it.

As for the Paris bedroom pillow-talk with his second wife, he said that he had made up the story about the killing in Spain to impress his new love—to prove he would do anything for her.

He had not killed his first wife, he insisted, nor had he tried to kill the second, describing her slashed throat as an accident.

That fateful day, he said, should have been one of celebration, but it turned into sheer hell, laced with arguments, violence, drink and drugs.

He had planned during the day to take his wife to see a theater performance of *Dr. Jekyll and Mr. Hyde*. What Mrs. Baksh had not suspected, however, was that she, herself, would painfully learn that her husband was no mean performer when it came to a dual-personality role.

He told the jury that during the early evening she had attacked him with a knife. He snatched it from her hand and tried to calm her down. Then she complained of an intense pain in her chest and he gave her, with consent, a heavy morphine injection.

Shortly, after they drank some champagne, but she started to quarrel again, so he suggested that they drive out to see some friends and talk over their domestic problem. He maintained that he took the knife with him to show these friends how desperate the domestic situation had become.

At Keston Lakes, he stopped the car so they could stroll in the fresh air for a few moments to clear away the fuzziness of drink and the effect of some pills he himself had also taken.

At that point, he said, his wife suddenly asked him where the knife was, and foolishly, he returned to the car for it. He wanted to demonstrate to her how it felt to have a knife pointed at oneself, to be threatened with it, as she had threatened him earlier in the day.

But, as he held the knife to her throat, she grabbed for it, and the blade slashed across her own throat in a deep five-inch-long gash.

Later he assured his lawyer, Robin Simpson Q.C., that he had not deliberately done it, nor had he known she was dying when he left her there. He had thought that she would be able to walk back home unaided and alone.

Having left a glove at the spot when he drove off in

something of a panic, he returned shortly afterwards. She was still lying in the same position on the grass, breathing normally.

Even his own lawyer found this difficult to believe, for there was incredulity in his voice as he asked Baksh: "But why in heaven's name didn't you telephone for an ambulance or take her to a hospital?"

"I couldn't think properly," Baksh muttered with downcast eyes.

So, he returned home and reported her missing to the police with his phony theory of a possible kidnap by masked men, leaving her own car conveniently in the center of Bromley to be found later.

He said he didn't want a scandal about two respectable doctors drinking to excess, taking drugs and quarrelling. He didn't want anyone else to know their "dark secrets."

In fact, he had drugged the champagne which was drunk by his wife earlier, and when she was comatose he injected her with a near-fatal dose of morphine. Then he drove out to the parkland to commit his diabolical second wife-murder, leaving her in agony, fighting for each breath, for nearly four hours.

This was the man who had told Detective Superintendent Norman Stockford earlier that it was the animal in him which made him drug his second wife and slit her throat, yet that he was still deeply in love with her, wanting her back home for the sake of their four children—and to be the right hand in his medical practice.

"One doesn't realize the importance of a person until their absence," he explained.

On Thursday, December 18th, the jury of seven men and three women found him guilty on both charges. Baksh, son of a priest, clasped his hands together and bowed weeping in prayer as the recorder of London, Sir

James Miskin, passed a minimum 20-year sentence on him for the murder and 14 years concurrently for the attempt.

"You are a danger to those close to you," the Recorder said. "You killed your first wife skillfully to gratify your lust for the second, and in doing so deprived your two relatively young adopted children of a mother."

Dr. Baksh confirmed his own Jekyll-and-Hyde image when confessing to another officer, Detective Inspector Tom Hamilton: "We are all two people—and it was the bad one in me that did this. . . ."

Ironically, if Baksh, with his medical skill, had cut his second wife's jugular vein, she would have bled to death within seconds. But, according to police, he cut her throat less efficiently, so that she would bleed more slowly, giving him time to return home and set up his alibi.

Now he joins the ranks of Britain's infamous wife-murdering medicos, like Hawley Crippen and Buck Ruxton.

An advocate of euthanasia, Baksh had told police that there came a time when people outlived their usefulness. These sinister words prompted an inquiry into other deaths around him.

Although his 80-year-old mother had been in remarkably good health, shortly after a visit from her son five years ago, she had died in a southern England nursing home, apparently of a heart attack.

And then there were those two former bachelor partners, Dr. David Jones, who had collapsed and died on a golf course in Spain in April 1978, and Dr. John Groome, who had collapsed and died five months later. Both left Baksh flourishing practices in South London.

In fact, detectives later scrutinized all of Baksh's medical records on dead patients in cases in which he had issued "natural causes" certificates.

According to what his surviving wife exclusively told the *People* newspaper on December 21st last year, she believed that her Svengali husband might one day have harmed her children, too.

She continues in practice, although her speech is still impaired from the injury in which the knife had sheared through muscles, tendons, nerves and blood vessels in her neck.

And now serving his sentence is the man who cold-bloodedly left her to die on the coldest night of the year, never dreaming that a toad hunter, of all people, would foil his diabolical plan to trade in her life for cash.

EDITOR'S NOTE:
Harold and Agnes Drake are not the real names of the persons so named in the foregoing story. Fictitious names have been used because there is no reason for public interest in the identities of these persons.

"MURDERING ANGEL
OF MERCY!"
by Barbara Geehr

On a warm morning in mid-July 1988, Captain Cliff Miller of the Putnam County, Florida, Sheriff's Office received the first phone call about possible murders at a nursing home near the Putnam-Alachua County line. A news reporter from a Gainesville television station advised Miller that he'd just received information from a male anonymous caller about such a possibility and thought the sheriff's office would want to check it out.

"Exactly what did this anonymous caller say?" the captain asked.

"Just that someone was killing patients at the New Life Acres Nursing Home which, as you probably know, is located just east of the sprawling town of Melrose."

"And what did the caller base his information on?"

"He said he heard some man in a Whiskey River bar bragging about killing five patients at New Life Acres," answered the television news reporter.

The second call came about an hour later. A volunteer worker at a Gainesville crisis intervention center reported receiving a call on the hot line from a highly agitated person who identified himself as "Jeff."

The worker said, "Jeff stated he worked at New Life Acres Nursing Home, had already killed five residents there and had just been thwarted in his attempt to kill a sixth. He gave a blow-by-blow description of what happened."

"How did he describe it?"

"He said he placed a chair outside this particular patient's window and removed a screen to gain entry. Once inside, he said he closed the room door, walked over to the bed and was just about to kill the woman sleeping there when someone knocked on the door. Scared that he could be caught in the act, he went back out through the window, replaced the screen and escaped.

"He was really calling for help," explained the crisis intervention center volunteer. "He was afraid he would kill again. I tried to keep him talking. I got him to give me the names of the five people he said he'd already killed and of the sixth person he was about to kill when the knock came on the door."

Captain Miller took down the information and dispatched Deputy Terry Beautein and Detective Chris Hord to the New Life Acres Nursing Home. There, while Hord talked with the female nursing home director, Beautein examined the room of the patient where "Jeff" said he'd been thwarted before he could kill his sixth victim.

From the nursing home director, Detective Hord learned that the only staff member with a first name Jeff was Jeffrey Lynn Feltner, 26, a nurse's aide. "Jeff first came to us through a relative who has worked here for many years," the director said. "He is a good employee and he does a good job. We've never had any complaints about his performance. He always shows up; he always reports for duty on time."

"How about today?" Hord asked.

"He's on the late shift."

Detective Hord wanted to know how long Feltner had worked at the nursing home.

The director checked employment records. "Actually," she said, "this is Jeffrey's second stint with us. He originally worked here from July of eighty-six until March of

70

eighty-seven. He left for several months at that time but returned in November and has been with us ever since."

"You're talking about November of eighty-seven?"

"Right."

"Okay, can you look up the dates of the deaths of the five patients whose names were given to the crisis intervention center in Gainesville as having been murdered?"

A check of the patients' records showed that all five residents had died between February 7th and April 6th of 1988.

"Well within the period of Feltner's second period of employment," Hord commented.

"Yes. Look, there was nothing suspicious about any of the deaths. All were attributed to heart attacks or just plain old age. That's the kind of place this is. The residents here are elderly people. We keep them as comfortable as we can until they expire. Most of them get cremated."

"What about the five this Jeff claims to have killed?"

The nursing home director again checked through the records. "Two of them were cremated; the other three were buried," she said.

Since Jeffrey Feltner was not due to report for work until the late shift, Detective Hord obtained the nurse's aide's home address and went there. Feltner was questioned by Hord who taped an interview in which Feltner denied making telephone calls to either the Gainesville television station or to the crisis intervention center in that city.

The detective then took the tape to the television station.

The reporter identified the voice on the tape as that of the anonymous caller who'd reported overhearing a man in a Whiskey River bar brag about killing five residents at New Life Acres Nursing Home.

Hord obtained a warrant and arrested Jeffrey Feltner on charges of first-degree murder and robbery. Following the arrest, Feltner admitted making the phone calls but denied he'd killed anyone. "I made the phone calls as a way of trying to get someone to investigate the poor conditions in nursing homes and the poor treatment the elderly patients are getting," he said.

Meanwhile, Deputy Beautein, back at New Life Acres, had completed his examination of the room in which an attempted sixth murder had, according to the telephone call to the crisis intervention center, been thwarted. Beautein found no evidence to indicate that a would-be killer had entered or left the designated room through a window, as the caller had stated.

A chair had been taken from a nearby patio and placed outside the window, but no weight seemed to have been placed on it. Beautein could find no depressions in the soft sand on which the chair stood. Additionally, longstanding debris on the windowsill appeared not to have been disturbed; no latent prints had been left and nothing in the room looked as though it had been disturbed.

"There was absolutely nothing to indicate that Jeffrey Feltner nor anyone else had entered or left that room through a window," Captain Miller commented, upon learning the results of the examination. "If someone did, he would have had to fly in and fly out. The whole thing looks like a setup. Someone probably placed a chair outside the window of that particular room to make it look as though it had been broken into. I can't tell you why anyone would do that, but apparently someone did. Maybe it was to give credence to the story of being thwarted in a sixth murder attempt."

The longer the investigation continued, the more likely it seemed that the five patients Feltner was said to have originally claimed he'd killed at New Life Acres had instead died of natural causes and moreover, that Feltner, as he claimed, might indeed have fabricated the story to draw attention to the poor care elderly patients were re-

72

ceiving at nursing homes. Miller said the investigation did not indicate that the nurse's aide had killed anyone. "We investigated Feltner's admission and refuted them," he said. "Murder charges against him could not be substantiated. There is a possibility that Feltner made the admissions to bring attention upon himself. He is a very small person—something like five feet three inches tall—and can't weigh more than a hundred pounds."

After what the captain called "a long, legal harangue," the murder charges against Jeffrey Feltner were dropped, Feltner was found guilty of making harassing phone calls, filing a false report and trespassing. He was released from the Putnam County Jail after serving a total of four months.

Late in the summer of 1989, a man identifying himself as Paul Hendry telephoned a Daytona Beach television journalist to report that a self-described homosexual man named Tony said he had previously been involved in the death of several nursing home residents in Putnam County and had now committed two additional murders in Volusia County. He named the victims as Ruth Hamilton, killed at Bowman's Care in Ormond Beach in June, and Doris Moriarty, killed at Clyatt Memorial Geriatric Center in Daytona Beach in July.

The caller described Tony as having brown hair, bad teeth, long pinky fingernails and a mustache. "Tony does not want to go to the police . . . and he does not want his mother to find out," the caller said.

A few days later, Health Force, an Orlando-based company providing temporary employees to health-care and nursing home facilities, received a telephone call from a person identifying himself as Jeffrey Feltner's homosexual lover and roommate. "I'm calling you people," Feltner's roommate said, "because you're the ones who sent Jeffrey to jobs at both Bowman's Care in Ormond Beach and Clyatt Memorial Geriatric Center in Daytona Beach. I feel you should know that Jeffrey has told me he killed a patient named Doris Moriarty at Clyatt."

An official at Health Force immediately notified the Daytona Beach Police Department. Detective Bill Adamy took over the investigation.

At Clyatt Memorial Geriatric Center, Adamy learned from the administrator that Jeffrey Feltner had worked there for about a month. "He was a conscientious employee and he gave good care," the administrator said, "but he failed to show up for work on July sixteenth and seventeenth. You can't have that in a place like this, temporary employee or not. We rang him up at his residence and told him he was fired."

"What can you tell me about Doris Moriarty?" Detective Adamy asked.

The administrator described Moriarty as a retired registered nurse who'd been a patient at the center for three years. "She was eighty-eight years old at the time of her death and one very sick lady. There was absolutely nothing the least bit suspicious about her death. We found her dead in her bed on the morning of July eleventh and believe she expired in her sleep."

"Was she cremated or buried?"

"Cremated. Many people who die in nursing homes are cremated."

Adamy began his questioning of Jeffrey Feltner on August 11th. In the first interview, the then-unemployed nurse's aide admitted he'd telephoned the Daytona Beach television station under the name Paul Hendry and reported the killing of Doris Moriarty in Daytona Beach and of Ruth Hamilton in Ormond Beach. "But I didn't kill anyone," Feltner said. "I made the call to draw attention to the poor conditions in nursing homes."

"Don't you think you need some help?" Adamy asked.

Feltner said he was already receiving counseling on an outpatient basis at ACT, a mental health treatment center in Daytona Beach. "They know me there as Tony," he said.

74

Detective Adamy remembered that Tony was the fictitious name used for the homosexual man to whom
Feltner had attributed the two Volusia County nursing
home murders in his telephone call to the Daytona Beach
television station. He set about convincing Feltner to enter the mental health treatment center on a voluntary basis. "Why don't you let me take you to your residence
where you can put a few things together? Then I'll drive
you over to ACT."

Feltner agreed that he should voluntarily commit himself. Adamy drove to Feltner's home where the nurse's
aide packed a few of his belongings. The detective then
drove him to the mental health treatment center and
dropped him off.

A few days later, an ACT security guard found among
Feltner's belongings a sheet of paper listing seven names,
seven dates and three nursing homes:

Sonia Barnes, 78, February 7, 1988, New Life Acres.
Harry Towne, 82, February 8, 1988, New Life Acres.
Sarah Abrams, 75, February 10, 1988, New Life Acres.
Sally Tobin, 64, February 18, 1988, New Life Acres.
John Mallory, 73, April 6, 1988, New Life Acres.
Ruth Hamilton, 81, June 21, 1989, Bowman's Care.
Doris Moriarty, 88, July 11, 1989, Clyatt Memorial.

The guard turned the list over to supervisors who for-
warded it to Detective Adamy. Adamy recognized the
names as those of the seven people Feltner had reported
as homicide victims, only to maintain later that he'd fabricated the murder stories to draw attention to poor conditions in nursing homes.

A check with the individual nursing homes verified the
date in each instance as the date on which each resident
had been found dead in bed.

Adamy went to the mental health treatment center and
taped two additional interviews with Jeffrey Feltner—one
on August 15th and the other on August 16th. Feltner,
when confronted with the list of nursing home residents

he'd previously reported as murdered, again denied having anything to do with their deaths. Under Adamy's intense grilling, however, he finally broke down and confessed to murdering all seven of them "to relieve their suffering."

He explained that the killings began with Sonia Barnes at New Life Acres. "Sonia was in a lot of pain," he told Adamy. "Nobody would come visit her; her family turned against her. All they wanted was her money and her house."

"Exactly how did you kill Sonia?" the detective asked.

"I suffocated her, the same as I did all the others," Feltner answered. "I waited until they got to sleep, then I pulled their blankets up around their necks and got on top of them so they couldn't move. Then I'd hold their noses pinched with one hand while I cupped my other hand over their mouths. That cut off their airways. I always wore surgical gloves to keep a better hold. Then I just waited until they couldn't breathe any more. The whole procedure only took six minutes—sometimes, it was less."

"What about the others at New Life Acres? Why did you kill them?"

"Harry Towne, Sally Tobin and John Mallory were in a lot of pain and I felt sorry for them," Feltner said. "Everybody was against Mallory. The staff didn't like him. He had Parkinson's disease and couldn't walk very well, either. And he wasn't eating. He was always saying he wished he was dead."

"And Sarah Abrams?"

"She told me she wanted to die."

"Okay," Adamy said. "That takes care of the five residents at New Life Acres. Tell me now about Ruth Hamilton at Bowman's Care in Ormond Beach and Doris Moriarty at Clyatt Memorial in Daytona Beach."

"I can't tell you too much about Ruth," Feltner said. "She was in isolation when I went to work at Bowman's.

I asked why and nobody would tell me. The only thing they said was it would be a blessing if she passed away. Her suffering was really bad. I felt sorry for her. That night, I just closed her door and her curtains, pulled her blanket up to her neck, got on top of her and suffocated her like I did the others."

"And Doris Moriarty? She's the one I'm most interested in," Adamy said, "because her case comes under the jurisdiction of the Daytona Beach Police Department."

Feltner related that he'd been working at Clyatt Memorial for about a month before he realized Moriarty was in terrible pain. "She was really old—eighty-eight, or something like that—and she'd been a registered nurse. When I seen how bad she was suffering, I didn't just want to do nothing for her. Everyone was saying to just let her lie there and suffer, to just let her lie there and die. She had bedsores eaten right through to her bone. She was very contractive, she couldn't move much and she couldn't talk. I just couldn't stand to see her in any more pain. So I put on a pair of surgical gloves and suffocated her."

"Was Moriarty buried?"

"No. She was cremated the same as Ruth Hamilton."

Detective Adamy said he couldn't understand why Feltner worked in nursing homes if he couldn't stand to see the patients suffer.

"Actually, I enjoy working with the elderly," Feltner said. "I just don't like seeing them in pain. Killing them was the only way I could see to help them, to take the look of pain off their faces. I felt guilty doing it to all of them; I really didn't want to do it. I mean I didn't get no pleasure out of it. I didn't do it out of joy or just to see someone die."

"I still don't understand why you continued working in nursing homes if you couldn't stand to see patients suffer. You had to know from your experience at New Life

77

Acres that you had a propensity to kill patients to put them out of pain," Adamy said.

Feltner explained, "I guess it was because nursing homes were the only places I could find jobs. I tried Burger King, McDonald's, all those places. They accept your application, but that's it. Go to a nursing home and you're a male and you got your certificate, they hire you right on the spot. No questions, they just hire you."

On August 16th, Detective Bill Adamy obtained a warrant, returned to the ACT mental health treatment center and arrested Jeffrey Feltner for the first-degree murder of 88-year-old Doris Moriarty at Clyatt Memorial Geriatric Center in Daytona Beach on July 11, 1989. Feltner was then transported to a Volusia County branch jail. At his first appearance the following morning, Judge Darrell Carnell ordered the prisoner held without bail and appointed Public Defender Howard Pearl to represent him.

Detective Adamy, asked by the news media if he thought Feltner considered himself an angel of death, commented, "As far as I've been able to ascertain, Feltner doesn't have any delusions about what happened. He was sorry for the situation but not sorry for what happened. No, he is not an angel of death; he doesn't consider himself that at all. In his thinking, he believes these nursing home patients were being treated unfairly and that he was helping them when he put them out of their misery by suffocating them to death."

Jeffrey Feltner's confessions shocked authorities in both Volusia and Putnam Counties. Ormond Beach Police Department's Sergeant Ron Morgan immediately checked with the administrator at Bowman's Care Nursing Home where Ruth Hamilton had been a patient.

"This is unbelievable," the administrator told the sergeant. "I've checked the records and found we hired Jeffrey Feltner from Health Force in Orlando on a temporary, fill-in basis. He worked here exactly one shift. That was the night of June twentieth. We did find Ham-

78

ilton dead in her bed the following morning, but we had no reason to suspect she'd died from anything but natural causes. She was really in bad shape; we were expecting her to die. As per her wishes, her body was cremated."

Sergeant Morgan said he would get an arrest warrant, based on Feltner's confession that he had suffocated Hamilton.

Captain Cliff Miller in Putnam County expressed similar bewilderment when questioned by the news media. "We investigated Feltner a year ago when he claimed he killed five patients at New Life Acres Nursing Home outside of Melrose and had been thwarted as he was about to kill a sixth," Miller said. "We got absolutely nothing on him, except that he'd made some harassing phone calls, filed false reports and had stolen a few things from patients' rooms. We believed at the time that Feltner fabricated the stories to draw attention to himself. We closed the case.

"The next thing we hear," Miller continued, "Feltner's been arrested in Daytona Beach and he's still insisting he committed five murders up here. We've asked for copies of the Volusia investigation and are reopening the Putnam investigation. We are revisiting everything to see if it's possible any credence can be placed in Mr. Feltner's admissions. What I'm basically saying is: we're taking another very hard look at the situation here in Putnam County."

John Tanner, state attorney for Florida's Seventh Judicial Circuit, agreed there was a possibility that Feltner was seeking attention. "However," he told inquiring news reporters, "there are solid reasons for Jeffrey Feltner's arrest. When you have someone admitting to a series of murders and that person is in a position to commit those murders and the people are dead, I think you have pretty good probable cause.

"Nonetheless," the state attorney added, "the crimes

are going to be difficult to prove. Of the seven alleged victims, four were cremated—two of the five in Putnam County and both of the victims in Volusia County. On the other hand, it may be as difficult to prove Feltner did not kill these people as to prove he did."

On August 17th, Tanner released information to the press that Jeffrey Feltner had AIDS. "He was first diagnosed as being HIV positive, a possible precursor to AIDS, a couple of years ago. I believe the date was October of 1986. We will immediately arrange for him to start getting treatment," Tanner stated.

A Volusia County grand jury, on September 12, 1989, indicted Jeffrey Feltner for first-degree murder in the suffocation death of Doris Moriarty, 88, at the time she was a resident at the Clyatt Memorial Geriatric Center in Daytona Beach. Daytona Beach Police Detective Bill Adamy said there was now no reason for any other agency to be in a rush in its investigation or reinvestigation of Feltner. "He's been charged here and is being held without bail in the Volusia County Jail. He's not going to be going anywhere any time soon."

Captain Miller said he was pleased with the Volusia County indictment. "It will give Putnam County investigators more time to expand their probe into the five deaths Feltner has admitted to at New Life Acres. We've decided to concentrate our efforts on just one victim, rather than attempt to solve all five of the alleged murders at one time. We may exhume the body of one of the three deceased residents who were buried if pathologists say there is a chance foul play can be detected after this length of time."

Pathologists did believe examination of one of the buried patients' bodies would reveal how that particular patient had died. The body of Sarah Abrams was selected for exhumation because she'd been the healthiest of the five patients at the time of death and because family members, believing she may have been murdered, readily gave permission to have her body exhumed.

Following the exhumation on September 19th, a medical examiner determined Abrams had died violently of asphyxiation. That provided the evidence needed to substantiate Feltner's confession that he had suffocated her. But Feltner could not be charged with Abrams' murder right away. State Attorney John Tanner explained, "Under the prevailing circumstances, Feltner can be charged with the first-degree murder of Sarah Abrams only on an indictment from grand jurors."

Putnam County grand jurors convened on October 12th and, based on Feltner's confession and the autopsy report on the exhumed body, indicted Jeffrey Lynn Feltner for first-degree murder in the death of Doris Moriarty, for which he'd already been indicted a month earlier and scheduled to face trial in late November. Arraignment in the Putnam County case was set for November 8th.

On Monday, November 6th, Feltner was transported from the Volusia County Jail to the Putnam County Jail to get ready for the arraignment. Public Defender Howard Pearl said his client was going to plead not guilty to the first-degree murder of Sarah Abrams. "He seemingly has some kind of mental disorder that drives him to compulsive confessions to acts he has not committed," Pearl said.

At 7:50 on Wednesday morning, a Putnam County Jail corrections officer, who went to Feltner's cell to remind him to get ready for his scheduled court appearance, was unable to awaken the prisoner. The officer discovered Feltner was bleeding; he had slashed his wrists with the jail-issued razor given to him on entry into the general jail population two days before.

A rescue team rushed Feltner by van to the Putnam Community Hospital where doctors treated him for 27 superficial wounds to his wrists. Though Feltner did not respond to questioning by either the medical examiners at the hospital or counselors from the Bradford-Union-Putnam Guidance Clinic, his wounds were determined to be superficial and to have been self-inflicted in a feigned suicide attempt.

Following treatment, the former nurse's aide was taken back to the van and transported to the Putnam County Courthouse for the scheduled arraignment in the Sarah Abrams case. He refused, however, to get out of the van. As Feltner lay on a sheet in the back of it, Public Defender Howard Pearl tried to get him to accept a plea agreement offered by the state attorney's office. Feltner refused even to listen and, according to Pearl, appeared to be unconscious or in some sort of vegetative state. "He just couldn't bring himself to face the judge," Pearl said.

Accordingly, the public defender entered a written plea of not guilty for his client. Judge E.L. Eastmoore set a trial date for early January 1990. The Volusia County trial would follow. Pearl stated that, depending on Feltner's future conduct and psychiatrists' reports, he might be forced to ask that Feltner be declared unfit to stand trial.

Meanwhile, Jeffrey Feltner was put under a suicide watch at the Putnam County Jail. An inmate under suicide watch is in an isolation cell, is under the constant observation of a jail trusty and is checked at least every 15 minutes by a corrections officer. The corrections officers must document their findings.

Feltner remained unresponsive the rest of Wednesday afternoon and evening. He neither ate nor drank for the next five days and went for several more days without speaking. At times, he refused to get out of bed, remaining curled up in a fetal position on his jail cot. Pearl described his client as both troubled and ill. "He is miserable, withdrawn and deeply depressed," the public defender said. "Despite his confessions, he now denies killing anyone."

Jeffrey Feltner underwent two psychiatric examinations on November 14th. A psychiatrist found the accused murderer "too emotionally impaired and without sufficient psychic energy to challenge the prosecution. At this time, I do not believe Mr. Feltner can either testify relevantly or help himself in the legal process," the psychiatrist stated.

During Feltner's interview with a clinical psychologist, he would not respond directly to questions. "Therefore," the psychologist reported, "no conclusion can be drawn to determine whether he understood the nature of the acts which led to his arrest." The psychologist was of the opinion, however, that Feltner's mood disorders could be attributed in part to AIDS. "Therefore," he concluded, "it is my opinion that Mr. Feltner is incompetent to stand trial at this time."

On January 3, 1990, Circuit Judge E.L. Eastmoore held a hearing to determine Feltner's competency once again. In addition to the evaluations made by the psychiatrist and psychologist, he heard testimony from two jail corrections officers. They stated that Feltner understood directions, was able to take care of himself and functioned normally with other inmates. Both said the defendant was depressed but not in an abnormal way. "Just by the way he acts, you can tell he's depressed," one of the officers said. "But it's the I-don't-want-to-be-in-jail depression that everybody gets."

Judge Eastmoore handed down his decision. "Though Mr. Feltner suffers from bouts of depression—which are understandable considering the environment in which he finds himself—I do not believe he suffers from more severe mental disorders which would prevent him from receiving a fair trial," the judge said. He then explained that he based his decision on his own observation of the defendant during the hearing. "He has remained alert and has appeared to understand the legal proceedings. He himself has provided the best testimonial to his competency," Eastmoore said.

At a pretrial hearing on the Abrams case on December 28th, Eastmoore denied a request from the Public Defender Howard Pearl for more time in which to prepare for trial. He held fast to the January 8, 1990 trial date and set another competency hearing for Feltner, to be held before jury selection on the opening day of the trial.

Assistant State Attorney David Damore, named to represent the state in both the Putnam and Volusia County trials, said he would seek the death penalty against Feltner in both the Abrams and the Moriarty cases.

With opening statements in the Putnam County trial not scheduled to begin until one o'clock, Judge Eastmoore held a hearing with Assistant State Attorney David Damore and Public Defender Howard Pearl. The proceeding concerned the admissibility of the Feltner confessions which had been taped by Detective Bill Adamy of the Daytona Beach Police Department. Pearl wanted to exclude all parts of Feltner's statements not directly related to the death of Mrs. Abrams from evidence presented at the trial on the grounds they would be prejudicial to the defendant.

Eastmoore also denied that request, saying the confessions could be used by the prosecuting attorney as "similar fact" evidence.

Before the trial was to open, Feltner had indicated to his public defender that he would not accept any plea bargains. "I want a chance to tell the jury I am innocent," the accused murderer said. "I only confessed to the killings to draw attention to the neglect in the nursing home industry."

But Pearl, now convinced that admission of the taped confessions would bring a verdict of guilty of murder in the first degree and a recommendation of death in the electric chair from the jury, decided it was time for damage control. He talked with Assistant State Attorney Damore and worked out a plea bargain whereby Feltner would plead guilty to the first-degree murder of Sarah Abrams in exchange for a guarantee that Damore would not ask for the death penalty. In Florida, there are only two possible sentences for first-degree murder: death in the electric chair or life in prison with no chance of parole for 25 years.

Feltner agreed also to plead guilty to the murder of Doris Moriarty at the Clyatt Memorial Geriatric Center in Daytona Beach. Pearl said he would ask for a lesser charge than first-degree murder in the Volusia County case and would request that the sentence run concurrently with the Putnam County sentence.

Feltner's family stood firmly behind him throughout all proceedings and not one of its members believed he killed anyone. Background information given by his family disclosed that Jeffrey had been born in Miami in 1962 and lived there until 1979 when the family moved to Putnam County. He graduated from Interlachen High School in 1980 and in 1985 began working at New Life Acres where a family member was already employed as a nursing assistant. In 1988, Feltner passed a certification exam to become a nursing assistant and continued working at New Life Acres.

The relative said, "If anyone could have seen Jeffrey around those elderly people, they would never believe he could kill anyone. He was patient, kind and empathetic. We believe he invented the tale of killing patients to draw attention to the poor living conditions in nursing homes. He's told me he went about it all the wrong way," she said.

Another one of Jeffrey's relatives stated that Jeffrey had told him he had killed no one but had tried to devise a plan that would get officials to notice poor nursing home conditions. "Jeffrey said he knew he had AIDS and wanted to spend what time he had left to do something that would get officials to notice poor nursing home conditions. He said he wanted to do something everyone would be proud of but, like always, he'd messed up."

Circuit Judge Eastmoore accepted the plea bargain worked out by the prosecuting attorney and the public defender. He sentenced Jeffrey Feltner to life in prison with a mandatory 25 years for the suffocation death of Sarah Abrams, 75, at New Life Acres on February 10, 1988.

On January 12, 1990 Feltner pleaded guilty to the second-degree murder of 88-year-old Doris Moriarty at Clyatt Memorial Geriatric Center in Daytona Beach and was sentenced to 17 years in state prison.

Feltner is not expected to be charged in any of the other five deaths.

EDITOR'S NOTE:
Tony, Paul Hendry, Sonia Barnes, Harry Towne, Sally Tobin, John Mallory and Ruth Hamilton are not the real names of the persons so named in the foregoing story. Fictitious names have been used because there is no reason for public interest in the identities of these persons.

"DRUG-DEALING DOCTOR'S Rx WAS MURDER!"

by Bud Ampolsk

It is not without ample reason that Missouri has come to be known as the "Show me state." From the very beginning, residents of the area have been very special.

They've prided themselves on an inner toughness. It was this hardiness of body and mind which allowed their forebears to spearhead the move westward. The epics of their struggles against "The Big Muddy" have become American legends. Life has never been that easy for them. For many, a tenuous livelihood had to be scratched out of a harsh land which seemed to mock their best efforts.

Most of all, Missourians glory in their view of their fellow man. They do not give their trust easily. A neighbor must prove himself to earn that. But once that trust is given, it is not easily shaken.

Says one old timer, "We look a man right in the eye and we make a judgment. Once we give him our hand, that's it. It takes a hell of a lot to make us change our opinions about him."

This steadfastness of thought and loyalty is not limited to Missouri alone. It spills over state lines to nearby southern Illinois.

In recent days, it has been tested as seldom before. It has sent out shock waves which will not be forgotten easily. Some contend things will never be the same again.

The farmer who was driving down deserted Allen Road near rural Times Beach, Missouri, on December 13, 1984, was not preoccupied with philosophical thoughts about the attitudes of his neighbors. He had more immediate things on his mind.

There was the uncomfortable chill of the damp and misting morning. There were the thoughts of the waiting herd of cattle which had to be fed. There was a sense of urgency since it was already close to 7:30 a.m. Every minute counts when you are a farmer these days. Production is your only means of battling rising costs and falling prices.

In an instant, all of these problems would be driven from the farmer's mind by the immediacy of the situation which was right before him. That situation came in the form of the sprawled figure of a man lying beside Allen Road. What would somebody be doing out here in that position at this time of the morning?

Perhaps the sprawled man could be sleeping off a hard night's drinking. It wouldn't be the first time that had happened. And yet there was something about the stillness that was ominous.

The farmer shifted his foot to the brake pedal and brought his vehicle to a smooth stop. Ignoring the light rain, he walked the few steps to the prone figure. He bent over it just long enough to examine the wide, staring, sightless eyes and the ugly wound just behind the man's ear. Then he recoiled in stunned shock. Nobody had to tell the farmer that whoever it was who was lying at his feet was very dead, nor that the man had died violently.

Nor did anybody have to inform the farmer what his duty was. He knew that he must summon professional aid to the scene in the fastest time possible.

St. Louis County Police Detective Theodore Kaminski and Officers Jerry Warren and Don Blattner were among the first to answer the emergency call. They were joined by a paramedic who was also a firefighter.

Taking great care not to destroy any evidence at the crime site, the paramedic gingerly removed a covering which the police officers had placed over the man on the ground. Even a cursory inspection of the man's fixed pupils and the copious blood flowing from one, and possibly more, wounds to the head convinced the paramedic that he was dealing with a D.O.A.

After a short conference among the officers, it was decided that, since this wasn't a routine highway accident, it was a job for specialists. A second hurried call went out over emergency bands. In a matter of moments, Allen Road was swarming with representatives of the county medical examiner's office led by Warren Lucas, and numerous plainclothes police officers under the direction of Major Thomas P. Moonier. Moonier would become the ranking officer of the unfolding investigation.

The victim had been young, somewhere in his early 20s. He had suffered two wounds. In one, the bullet had crashed into the skull from a point behind the ear. There was a much larger exit wound under the left eye. A second slug had torn into the dead man's neck.

While the medical examiner's experts studied the physical condition of the corpse, detectives began a search of the victim's pockets. Their hope of finding some means of identification was dashed when they came up empty-handed. They remained that way after an exhaustive canvass of the area. No wallet, no scrap of paper, nothing at all turned up to tell them who the man had been.

Going over what little information was available to them in their primary findings, it appeared likely that the victim had not died by his own hand. This was indicated by the position of the two bullet wounds. The slug which had been fired into his neck had come from a point between 12 and 24 inches away from the man's body. The one which had been fired from behind his ear had been inflicted when the weapon had been held about an inch away from the victim.

Speculating on the fact that they were probably dealing with a homicide, the officers wondered whether robbery could have been the prime motive for the slaying. If a perpetrator had removed the victim's wallet to get at his cash, he could have taken the wallet with him.

However, this line of reasoning did not preclude other possibilities. All the detectives could be sure of at this point was that they were involved with something baffling.

On the instructions of Dr. Ronald Turgeon, a pathologist and deputy medical examiner for St. Louis County, the body was carefully removed to the morgue for a full autopsy.

The hours ticked by as Chief Warrant Officer Tom De-Priest of St. Louis County waited for word from the medical examiner's office. Fingerprints had been taken of the dead man in the hopes that they would serve as the means of his identification.

DePriest ran the prints through every possible check. Finally, approximately 12 hours after the original Allen Road discovery of the body, the authorities had something to go on.

The prints matched those of a man who had once been arrested in St. Louis on a minor charge. They were identified as belonging to Sean Cavaness, 22.

There was one other immediate development. Blood samples of the victim showed they contained .26 percent alcohol. This percentage indicated that the victim had been drunk to the point of having had his judgment and coordination seriously impaired at the time of his killing. Under Missouri law, anybody with a blood alcohol content of .10 percent is considered too drunk to drive a vehicle. Cavaness had more than two and a half times this amount in his system.

Now that detectives had a name and address with which to work, their probe fanned out.

It was recalled that, on December 12th, a day before

the discovery of Cavaness' body, a complaint had been registered by the victim's neighbors.

The complaining couple had told officers that an automobile had been in the area. It had been driven by a man who was acting in a suspicious manner. According to the informants, the driver had appeared to be "casing" the neighborhood.

Their suspicions and fears aroused by thoughts that the driver might be contemplating a house-breaking or some other crime, the man and woman had jotted down the vehicle's license number on a piece of brown paper and gave it to the cops.

A police check of the digits was quickly undertaken. It showed that the vehicle had been registered in the name of Dr. John Dale Cavaness.

Detectives felt that the presence of Dr. Cavaness in the area of his son's flat on the day before the young man's slaying could have some possible significance, although there was no suspicion that the elder Cavaness had been in any way involved in the crime.

John Dale Cavaness was a highly-respected pathologist and surgeon who was attached to Pearce Hospital in nearby Eldorado, Ill. He was also a gentleman farmer living on a large estate in Harrisburg, Ill.

In the days that followed, Sergeant Fred Foan, of the St. Louis County Police Department, and other detectives conducted a number of interviews with Dr. Cavaness in the hopes that the physician might throw some light on the case.

Aware of the doctor's standing in the community and the grief he might be experiencing as the result of his son's recent death, the authorities went carefully about their work. Days would go by with no reported new developments in the case.

Then, on December 19, 1984, less than one week after the discovery of the victim on the highway, the startling news broke. It hit St. Louis and the western section of Illinois like a bombshell.

Fifty-nine-year-old Dr. John Dale Cavaness had been arrested and was being charged with murder in the first-degree in the death of his son, Sean.

The gravity of the charge was punctuated by a statement of Chief Trial Attorney Steve Goldman of the St. Louis County District Attorney's office. Goldman said that he was prepared to seek the death penalty against Dr. Cavaness.

Outlining what their exhaustive probe had developed thus far, Sgt. Foan reported that a .357 caliber Magnum revolver, allegedly used in the killing, had been recovered from Dr. Cavaness' home on West Walnut Street. The gun had been hidden in Dr. Cavaness' garage.

In a joint statement, Foan and Jack Nolen, supervisor of the Illinois Division of Criminal Investigation office at Carmi, Ill., also reported that the victim's missing wallet and "other evidence" had been found hidden in a pile of bricks at Dr. Caveness' farm adjacent to the Lake of Harrisburg.

Dr. Cavaness was being held in the St. Louis County Jail as the ever-widening probe into his affairs continued.

Meanwhile, the reaction of the community was swift and incredulous. The charges which had been leveled couldn't possibly be true, they held. There had to be some tragic mistake.

The people of Missouri had put their trust into the revered physician. They could not and would not believe that the man they believed to know so well would have done anything to violate that trust.

Typical of their comments were these:

A licensed practice nurse: "It's not true. I've worked with him for over 25 years. I've seen him work all night to save a life, and even cry when he lost one (a patient). I don't believe it. Not murder. I've seen him work too hard to save lives."

Another hospital associate: "You couldn't find a better fellow. He is one of the best doctors in this part of the country, and his patients think that the sun rises and sets in him."

A civic leader: "A lot of people who have known Dr. Cavaness are convinced that the Dr. Dale Cavaness that we knew couldn't have done it. He has saved so many lives. The reason that I write with my right hand today is because he saved the use of it. In talking with people, one person even told me that, 'No way could he have done it. I hope and pray that he didn't do it, and if he did it, I hope and pray they can't prove it.' That's the way people who have talked to me feel about him. They all feel that something's wrong, someone's trying to set him up."

A merchant: "I've known Dale from day one. I went to school and grew up with him and I'm praying that he did not do this. I know him and his attitudes. If he did do something like this, he would be the first one to admit it. The community will miss him badly, and I feel he is one of the best doctors in Illinois. If I have any type of medical treatment, I would insist that Dale be present."

A book store employee: "I've known Dr. Cavaness all my life and I do not believe this. It's a frame-up and things like this should be investigated thoroughly before they are published."

A woman resident of the community: "I knew him very well. We went to the same church. I was completely shocked."

One friend of the embattled physician even went so far as to write an open letter to the editor of the Eldorado, Ill., Journal.

It read:

"For some time now, I've been visiting Dr. Dale Cavaness. Many of your readers are friends and patients of his and I would appreciate it if you would let me use your columns to share a few things about his state of being with them.

"First, let me say he is well and in a very good state of

93

mind primarily due to the great letters of encouragement he is receiving from many of you. We were talking about what a giving and loving town Eldorado is the other day, and he said he would never have believed that folk would care about a man enough to raise more than $30,000 for a defense fund. He then turned to the subject of those letters and said, 'and, oh, those letters, there is no way to express the value of the letters I have received.'

"Dr. Cavaness has also asked that I try to clear up some misunderstandings that some folk seem to have. He wants everyone to know that his office is being vacated at Pearce Hospital at his insistence. He realizes that the hospital can profit financially by the added available space. As everyone knows, a great part of Dr. Cavaness' life is Pearce Hospital, and he will not allow it to lose financially since it will be some time before he is able to be back to his practice.

"Someone had told me that he had said he would not be back to Eldorado to practice medicine anymore. When I asked him if that was true, he was shocked and dismayed. He said he never made such a statement and had never considered doing anything else but returning. 'I'm going to be cleared of these charges,' he said, 'and, if for no other reason, I would want to come back to Eldorado to try to repay those people who have donated and shown so much faith in me.'

"Dr. Dale shared with me in the strictest of confidence what had happened to Sean, since he had not even had any opportunity to tell his attorney the story. When I went back to see him the next week, his attorney had suggested that we not go public with this information until nearer the trial date. We believe that the attorney you have retained for him is the best and we decided that we had no choice except to do as he suggested. Both of us would like for you to know the whole story because that would end all those wild suspicions. Since that is impossible for now, I want you to know that I am convinced that Dr. Cavaness is innocent and I believe he will be cleared when given his day in court.

"A trial date will soon be set. I hope we will not forget about the defense fund and please continue to pray as well as send those letters.

"Thank you for your support and my thanks to the editor for printing this letter."

The "defense fund" the writer had referred to had been initiated by a number of community residents. It reached $37,000 by the time the Cavaness trial got underway.

Said a bank executive who was handling the fund, "Generally speaking, there are still a lot of people that believe he is innocent and there must be some extenuating circumstances."

Another leader in the drive said a committee was working hard to get Cavaness' patients to pay their back debts to the doctor. He described the physician as "a wonderful doctor but one of the poorest businessmen that ever walked the streets."

Meanwhile, the drive by authorities to nail down the case against the accused physician went just as relentlessly forward. More and more bits and scraps of Dr. Cavaness' life began to surface.

Attention was given to the death in 1977 of another Cavaness son under mysterious circumstances.

Mark Cavaness had been 22 years old on the afternoon of April 9, 1977. That was the day he had been found dead at his father's cattle farm. The case had been investigated by the Saline County Sheriff's Department.

County Coroner Wendell Lambert at that time had given the cause of Mark Cavaness' death as a single gunshot wound. A shotgun had been recovered from the Cavaness truck which had been parked near the body.

Foul play had not been listed as a probable cause of the death, but the case remained open under the investigation of county and state authorities.

Recently recalling the details of the discovery of Mark Cavaness' body, Saline Count Coroner Wendell Lambert noted that a determination had been made that Mark

95

had died of a shotgun blast to the chest.

He said the body had been found at the rear of a house at the family farm. Sean Cavaness, then a teenager himself, had gone to the farm in search of his older brother.

Lambert said Mark's corpse was lying a short distance from a truck and there was a shotgun in the cab. The shotgun was still in its gun case but the end of the gun case had been blown out.

However, the Saline County coroner said there was not enough evidence to establish if the vehicle had been booby-trapped or whether something had been set up to make it look like a booby-trap or even a suicide.

"There were too many unanswered questions," Lambert commented.

The case was still considered open on the books.

There were other sinister items in Dr. Cavaness' background, lawmen learned. One, of which there was no doubt, concerned the fine and three years of probation he'd received in Saline County following a fatal automobile accident.

In that case, the physician had copped a plea of reckless homicide following an automobile accident which took the lives of Donald McLasky, 28, of Harrisburg and McLasky's ten-month-old daughter. Dr. Cavaness had originally been charged as well with driving while intoxicated and with unlawful possession of firearms.

Of more recent vintage was a 1984 allegation made by a convicted drug dealer.

Stephen Vinyard was sentenced to eight years in prison on six counts of drug possession and delivery, including charges stemming from an incident on January 25, 1984. His cousin, Jerry Vinyard, was also sentenced to eight years in prison after having pleaded guilty to unlawful delivery of a controlled substance (morphine) on January 25, 1984.

The statements made in this case had not been brought out in open court since both men had copped pleas. (The

Vinyard cousins are currently serving their terms in the Vienna Correctional Center.)

In releasing information on the possible involvement of Cavaness with the Vinyard cousins, County Prosecutor Goldman said that he was aware that Cavaness had been named in the drug case. The implication had been that the doctor had supplied the cousins with some drugs which were later sold illegally. "I am aware of it and it may or may not be presented (at the Cavaness murder trial). I'm just going to wait and see how the trial develops."

Special Agent Nolen said his department was probing the Stephen Vinyard allegation, but at that point no other supportive evidence in the conspiracy had been developed.

"The information has surfaced and we are aware of it," Nolen said. "All of the allegations are being pursued by our department."

During a taped interview with police, Stephen Vinyard revealed information about the January 25th incident in which Jerry Vinyard had sold some purported pharmaceutical drugs — demerol, merperidine and morphine — to an informant. The interview was conducted on the day Stephen was charged with unlawful possession of merperidine and morphine.

Stephen told Illinois Division of Criminal Investigation Agent Ken Clore that Jerry had been behind in his house payments and needed some quick money and he had contacted Cavaness for a loan. His link to the physician was said to be through a relative who was the daughter of a woman Dr. Cavaness was dating.

Stephen said Jerry had obtained the drugs through Dr. Cavaness. When he was asked by Clore if he was referring to Dr. John Dale Cavaness, Stephen replied, "That's correct."

Clore then asked Stephen, "So, it's your understanding that Dr. Cavaness gave them to Jerry knowing that Jerry was going to raise some money by selling the drugs."

Stephen answered, "That's correct."

He had earlier told the agent that Cavaness had originally turned Jerry down on a monetary loan, telling Jerry that he did not have money available for a loan.

Now the police and prosecutors were zeroing in on the murder case against the famed physician. The key to the state's case would be a $140,000 life insurance policy taken out on Sean by his father. This policy, Prosecutor Goldman charged, provided the motive for the shooting of Sean.

The prosecutor was now ready to go before a St. Louis grand jury with an outline of the essential points of the case.

Cavaness was represented by Arthur Margulis, famed Clayton County trial lawyer.

Having heard the presentation, the grand jury acted swiftly. They returned an indictment of murder in the first-degree.

Said Goldman, "We're asking that no bond be set for Dr. Cavaness at this time. We are going to ask for the death penalty at this time, if the case goes to trial."

Margulis told reporters, "I anticipate that the arraignment will follow shortly, and I intend to enter a plea of not guilty on Dr. Cavaness' behalf."

The Dr. Cavaness Defense Fund, for its part, issued a written press release. It said:

"Meetings of the Dr. Cavaness Defense Fund are continuing to be held. In response to recent press releases from the St. Louis County Police Department, the committee would like to emphasize that Dr. Cavaness is innocent until proven guilty and the committee feels that the facts of the case thus far released have been strictly for the side of the prosecution and that there are undoubtedly additional facts that have been suppressed which will eventually come out. The fund drive is continuing and remains undeterred. Dr. Cavaness still needs your help. The monetary goals of the Fund have not yet been reached. Please help others show Cavaness we do appreciate and support him as he has helped and supported people in this area for many years."

With a trial date set for July 8th, Dr. Cavaness now decided to go public with the theme of his defense. He told police, according to Goldman, that he had actually been in the car at the time of Sean's death. Goldman added that this was the latest in a series of stories Cavaness had related to lawmen since his arrest.

Goldman said Cavaness contended that he'd been in the car with his son when Sean had asked for his father's gun and had shot himself in the head. The physician claimed that he had fired the second shot into his son's body to disguise the fact that Sean was a suicide in the interests of comforting the doctor's ex-wife and the boy's mother.

The prosecutor argued that authorities had not established any reason why Sean might have been driven to suicide. He charged that the physician's statements "don't make any sense."

Goldman also noted that Cavaness had granted an interview to a writer for a national magazine concerning the doctor's version of Sean's last minutes before death. (The writer refused to discuss the case with other members of the working press.)

For his part, Margulis reported that he had not authorized any interviews with the defendant. The defense attorney said he was busy preparing his case and felt confident concerning an acquittal at the July 8th trial.

"There'll be no plea bargaining. We have nothing to bargain with," Margulis said. "The doctor is not guilty."

Speaking of Cavaness' current morale, Margulis noted, "He's encouraged and wanting to go to trial. We feel we have a good defense." Margulis refused to deal in specifics of the coming defense, but added that Cavaness was anxious to have his side told.

Of the community support, Margulis said, "We're very impressed with the favorable reaction. People are supportive of the doctor, not only in these circumstances, but he is held in very high regard generally. I haven't come across one person who is against him."

The attorney said there was absolutely nothing to link Sean's death with that of his older brother. He also reported that Cavaness would definitely take the stand even though the move would allow the prosecution to introduce the doctor's previous criminal record as evidence.

The trial got underway as scheduled on July 8th in the courtroom of Judge Margaret Nolen of the First Division of St. Louis Court. The tension was palpable as the two legal giants—Goldman for the state and Margulis for the defense—prepared to hurl their heavy artillery at each other in the all-or-nothing legal battle.

A jammed courtroom sat on the edge of its collective seats as Goldman and Margulis outlined their opening arguments.

Now the moment of truth was at hand. At last the public would be let into the intimate and dark secrets which at best had barely been hinted at during the pretrial weeks.

They heard Goldman intone, "We, the prosecution, intend to prove that on December 13, 1984, on Allen Road, in an isolated area of St. Louis County, at about 6:30 to 7:30 a.m., the defendant, Dr. Cavaness, shot to death Sean Cavaness."

The prosecutor predicted evidence would show that Dr. Cavaness had taken his son out, got him drunk, proceeded to the secluded area and killed him, for over $140,000 in insurance money and because the doctor was also unhappy with Sean's life-style.

Step by step, Goldman reviewed which witnesses would take the stand for the state and outlined what their testimony would be. The lineup included the county medical examiner, Sean's girlfriend, the detective who had headed the investigation, the ex-wife of the defendant and insurance company representatives.

Margulis, speaking for the defense, promised revelations which would show "There is very much more here than meets the eye." He said he would dwell on Sean's physical condition and the state of his mental health, as well as the nature of the lethal wounds, to prove his contention that the young man had died at his own hand rather than having been a murder victim. He promised to put Dr. Cavaness on the stand to tell the jurors of the events of December 12th and 13th.

Said Margulis, "He will tell exactly what happened on that morning, the 'nightmare' he lived that morning and how he had altered the scene that morning and later told conflicting stories."

The defense attorney stressed Sean's history of alcoholism. He said he would introduce medical records which would attest to the extent the victim had, in the past, been affected by his drinking problems.

As the voices of the two courtroom adversaries held their audience spellbound, Dr. Cavaness added to the sense of drama in the case. Rather than appearing a man in a desperate struggle to save his own life, he was the picture of confidence. As he entered Judge Nolen's courtroom, the defendant was impeccably dressed. He waved and smiled to well wishers who called out words of encouragement to him. His actions reinforced their confidence that the defendant would prove his innocence to the satisfaction of the nine women and three men who comprised the jury.

There was a feeling that, at long last, a climax to the gripping and tragic saga of a family's fall from grace was now at hand.

The enormity of the charges were highlighted when the first witness, Dr. Ronald Turgeon, St. Louis County's medical examiner, gave a graphic description of the lethal wounds which he'd discovered in Sean's body.

Throughout the days that followed, Goldman called a number of witnesses who described the defendant as a man of two separate personalities — one which endeared him to his patients, and the other which caused his family to fear him.

The tension grew as the state neared the end of its presentation. Every one of Goldman's contentions was hotly battled by Margulis.

Then, just as it seemed that nothing could keep the final chapter from being written, there was a development which threw the courtroom into consternation.

At a Sunday session of the trial, it was revealed that the jury had viewed a document indicating that Dr. Cavaness had been given a polygraph test by the police. The problem was that the document had only been introduced at the trial by the prosecution and had been viewed by Judge Nolen as an exhibit. Because of this, the defense had moved for a mistrial.

In the interest of protecting the defendant's rights, Judge Nolen granted the motion.

Speaking to reporters, in the court corridors, Prosecutor Goldman said, "Results of the test were not indicated, but jurors' knowledge of it is still considered prejudicial.

"At the time evidence was presented, I was called out for instructions. When I came back and saw the documents, I thought there would be a problem. I took them to my office and looked them over and I knew we had a problem. It's very sad."

The prosecutor noted that his staff had talked to the jury following the mistrial decision and had learned that they had been leaning towards a conviction.

Margulis said of the motion, "It was the only thing I could do under the circumstances. I had to ask for a mistrial. I would say we will try it again this fall. In the meantime, I'm going to try to do something about getting bond set."

Detective Dave Barron of the St. Louis County Police Department, who'd played a key role in the case, stated, "I'm obviously disappointed. I think the evidence presented would have caused a conviction. However, our judicial system is set up to protect the rights of individuals, therefore assuring they have a fair trial."

With Margulis having a number of other legal commitments, the date of a retrial of the Cavaness case had to be set over until November 12th.

The move to arrange bond for Dr. Cavaness pending the retrial was blocked by St. Louis County Judge Bernhardt Drumm without comment.

However, Goldman said the judge's decision was based on the fact that one of the defendant's surviving children had reason to fear for his life should the accused physician be allowed to go free.

According to Goldman, the youth had testified at the bail hearing following his testimony at the original trial.

Said Goldman, "He testified if his father was released he would be in fear of his own life—for his own safety."

Asked specifically if that meant the witness believed his father would harm him, Goldman replied, "Yes.

"There was further testimony from him that his father threatened to kill him the week before Sean's funeral," Goldman added.

The second trial got underway in November, as scheduled. A jury of eight women and four men, who had been selected in Kansas City and would be sequestered in the St. Louis County seat, would judge the evidence presented. The out-of-county selection had been decided upon to guarantee the jurors would be disinterested. The move was considered more wieldy than a change of venue would have been.

St. Louis County Division 10 Judge Drew W. Luten, Jr., presided over the trial. Dr. Turgeon, the county medical examiner, was the first prosecution witness. He said that he believed a gunshot wound to the back of Sean's neck, with the bullet exiting just to the left of his left eye, had been the first shot fired into the body and had been inflicted at a range of about one inch.

He further theorized that, due to burns around a second wound just under the right ear, the shot had been fired at a distance of from 18 to 24 inches from the body itself and that either of the wounds could have been

103

fatal.

From pictures taken of the body, the medical examiner deduced how the shooting actually occurred. The wound below the ear was inflicted as the body lay on its back. (Lieutenant David Wendell of the Criminal Identification Bureau would later reconstruct the scenario, showing exactly how the murder was accomplished.) The pathologist's conclusions had been reached as a result of the study of blood flow patterns as represented in the pictures.

The forensic expert did not rule out the possibility of suicide entirely, but said that it was highly unlikely. He noted the .26 percent alcohol content of Sean's blood, saying that this amount of alcohol would have made the young man very drunk.

Margulis, in cross-examining the witness, established that the dead man had possessed "a fatty liver." This was consistent with the physical degeneration often seen in a chronic alcoholic. Turgeon also acknowledged that the amount of alcohol in Sean's body immediately prior to the young man's death would have impaired his judgment.

The defense strategy was outlined when Margulis questioned Turgeon on whether there wasn't a common practice of a suicide's family members altering circumstances around the scene to cover up the fact that a person had taken his own life.

Turgeon agreed to this but, under redirect examination by Goldman, said he had never heard of another family member firing a second shot into a body to conceal a suicide. He noted that he was positive the neck wound had been suffered first from a very close range.

Next to take the stand was the neighboring couple who had first spotted the suspicious car in the area of Sean's apartment. They said they had seen Cavaness' vehicle and that the doctor had been in the building from approximately 10:20 p.m. on December 12th until 1:00 a.m. on December 13th.

Attacking the suicide theory, the witnesses testified that Sean did drink occasionally, but that he was a happy drunk. The victim had been looking forward to the Christmas holidays when he would be spending time with his family in southern Illinois, they reported.

A girlfriend of Sean's testified that the young man had been in a happy mood from the time she had first met him in July, 1984, until his death. The couple had been considering marriage. She conceded there were times when Sean suffered bouts of depression, but said they passed quickly.

Turning to the relationship between father and son, she revealed that Dr. Cavaness had been paying the rent on Sean's apartment and had underwritten Sean's tuition at Meremac Community College until the son had dropped out in November, 1984.

The young woman testified that Sean had been running low on money in November and December. She added that the doctor had visited Sean at her house once in October. During that visit, Dr. Cavaness had purchased liquor and brought it with him. She said she had asked Dr. Cavaness not to get vodka, because she knew Sean would not drink anything else.

She testified, "At first he (Sean) didn't think his father loved him, then he (Dr. Cavaness) started coming around. He and his dad didn't get along too well."

Frictions between Dr. Cavaness and other members of the Cavaness family were outlined by another family member. She charged that the physician treated his friends and patients with much more consideration than he did his own relatives.

According to the relative, Sean had been in good spirits up until the time of his death. She stated that she did not in any way consider Sean a suicide risk.

She pointed out that Sean's drinking problem had improved markedly after he had undergone treatment for alcoholism in 1983 and 1984. She also confirmed that Dr. Cavaness had referred to Sean as "an embarrassment" a couple of days before the young man's funeral.

The other son testified that his father had paid for his education and that he had paid Sean's rent and tuition to school during 1984 up until Sean's death. But the witness said that payments were sometimes late and that the father's checks sometimes bounced.

He described Dr. Cavaness as "loud, boisterous, challenging and mean when drinking." He noted that Dr. Cavaness had claimed that he had no money to pay for a funeral when questioned about a $100,000 policy the doctor held on Sean's life. Dr. Cavaness had claimed the policy was void because of Sean's alcohol problems and asthmatic condition.

On the morning he had identified his brother's body, the witness reported having called Dr. Cavaness. His father had sounded drunk on the phone and kept repeating things. The son said Dr. Cavaness did not come up the next day until late in the evening after having received two subsequent calls from him.

Pivotal testimony was offered by Detective Barron. Barron said he first interviewed Dr. Cavaness at the son's home on the day the doctor arrived there. At that point, Cavaness told the police officer that he had not seen Sean in the last four weeks.

Barron said he had then returned to the apartment building where Sean had lived. In talking to the neighbors, Barron had been given the paper bag with the license number written on it. This had been the plate number of the car the neighbors had considered suspicious. When checked out, the number had proved to belong to a car owned by Dr. Cavaness.

The detective had attended Sean's funeral, which he described as having the atmosphere of "a family reunion." He said Dr. Cavaness had appeared to be happy and "slapping backs." Barron said that he had decided to wait until the day after the funeral before taking Dr. Cavaness into custody.

Barron told the court he'd apprehended Dr. Cavaness

at about 5:05 p.m. and had questioned the physician until 11:30 the next morning.

Early in that interview, the detective recalled, he told Cavaness that two witnesses had indicated they had seen him in town the night Sean had been shot. Cavaness said it was impossible and continued to deny the allegation even after having been shown the paper bag with the license number written on it.

However, some two hours and 20 minutes later, the doctor changed his story. Cavaness then admitted he'd been in St. Louis on the night of December 12th. He told the detective he'd arrived at Sean's apartment about 10:30 p.m. and stayed until about 1:30 a.m. He'd driven Sean to a store to get cigarettes, brought him home and had then left for Illinois. When asked why he hadn't made that statement in the first place, the doctor said he had been afraid he might be a suspect in the case.

During this interview, Cavaness noted the insurance company had refused to issue a policy on Sean because of the young man's medical problems.

Another interrogation was conducted on December 24th. At that time, according to Barron, the suspect had come up with still another story. Barron quoted Cavaness as saying, "It's not as bad as you think. Sean committed suicide and I covered the scene to make it look like a homicide to protect family members."

Dr. Cavaness then described having driven around with Sean all night and having stopped the car just about at dawn because they were traveling through an area which reminded his son of southern Illinois.

Said Barron, "They stopped so that Sean could look at some cows. Sean asked the doctor if he had a gun, and the doctor said he did and gave the young man a .357 magnum revolver. Cavaness said he got out of the car in order to get something from the trunk, and when he did, he heard Sean say, 'Tell Mom I'm sorry,' and looked up to see Sean fall from a gunshot wound. After realizing that the young man was dead, Cavaness told me he picked up the gun, stepped back a few feet and fired another shot into the body."

Barron testified that, when he had told Cavaness that the story would be easy to check because of the presence of powder burns on the hand of one who has fired a gun, Cavaness said he had taken a wet rag from his car and wiped Sean's hands clean. The doctor then said he'd removed Sean's personal effects and taken them to his own home in Harrisburg.

When the detective had expressed ignorance of the area's geography, Cavaness had drawn him two maps showing where to find the magnum and the other items.

The maps were marked as exhibits and entered into trial evidence.

On December 30th, in a subsequent interview, Cavaness changed details of this story, but continued to insist that Sean had shot himself.

Margulis cross-examined the detective strenuously, questioning procedures used in the investigation. The defense attorney charged Barron with having lied to the suspect during interrogations concerning the evidence which the state possessed. Barron contended that he had merely been testing Dr. Cavaness' reactions to statements the lawmen had made.

A representative of New York Equitable Life Insurance Company testified that the company had issued three separate policies on each of the lives of Dr. Cavaness' three sons for $100,000 a piece. The sale had been completed in 1984, with Dr. Cavaness being named the primary beneficiary and his ex-wife being listed as the secondary beneficiary to the sons, while the wife of one of them was the secondary beneficiary on his policy.

The representative pointed out that at no time had the company indicated to Dr. Cavaness that any of the policies were invalid. He said that a question about alcoholism in Sean's policy application had been answered in the negative. The policy had been signed by both Sean and Dr. Cavaness.

High points of the defense case were offered by a number of employees who had worked at Dr. Cavaness' farm. They cited Sean as "being down against everybody and feeling that everybody owed him a living." They cited the young man's drinking habits and said they had been growing worse prior to his death. They related that when Sean was drinking, he was hard to get along with and was subject to temper tantrums.

To a question concerning whether the doctor would be likely to give a gun to someone who had been drinking, the employees acknowledged that he wouldn't.

The defense strategy was to show Dr. Cavaness as a reasoning, caring family man, who was interested in the welfare of his relatives. It was designed to cast doubts on descriptions of him by his ex-wife, among others.

The former wife had agreed with other family members on her evaluation of Dr. Cavaness from the stand. She said, "My ex-husband was two different people, treating his patients with care, but being physically and verbally abusive with his family.

"His patients loved him, but Dale was always mean when he drank. Sean loved his dad: he didn't understand his dad's attitude toward him. Sean would say, 'I don't know why he hates me,' " the registered nurse told the court.

She noted that she and her husband had split when she was six months pregnant with her youngest son. She quoted Cavaness as saying, "I don't love you. I don't want you. I don't need you, and I'm sorry to tell you this when you're pregnant."

She cited Christmas, 1982, as an example of the relationship between the accused father and his dead son. The two had been arguing, and Dr. Cavaness chased the son out of the house. Then he said of Sean 'I'll kill him. I don't care if I go to prison."

However, the ex-wife did admit that the doctor had always responded to her calls for help in disciplining the sons.

109

Taking the stand in his own defense, Dr. John Cavaness pictured his family life as having been beautiful until the time he and his wife had undergone their divorce in 1972. He alleged that, following the divorce, he'd stayed in close touch with the family, acting as his sons' disciplinarian. He said Sean's problems with alcohol had begun to increase in 1978.

The doctor staunchly denied that he was experiencing any unusual financial problems during 1984. He claimed that oil had been discovered on his land and that gave promise of increasing the yield on his holdings.

In graphic details, Dr. Cavaness took the court through the last night spent with Sean. For the most part, his testimony here reflected that which had already been entered into the court record.

The defendant stressed the actions he took following Sean's having shot himself.

After hearing the shot, Cavaness said, "It was like a series of strobe lights. I was paralyzed for a second. I then said to myself, 'You are a doctor,' and I rushed over to him and surveyed the situation."

At first, the wound didn't look too bad to the physician. However, upon closer examination, Dr. Cavaness discovered Sean's pupils were fixed and dilated, indicating that his son was brain dead. At this point, Dr. Cavaness claimed he "tried to put it all together and decided what to do next."

Recalling that moment, Cavaness testified, "Perhaps in some self-serving form of denial, I determined that if he was killed by someone, then at least it would be gone and over."

At this point he said he turned Sean's body over and took the young man's wallet from his pocket and shot the body again in the back of the head to make it look like a homicide. Cavaness said that he then drove back to Illinois where he took care of some banking business and then proceeded to his farm.

Under a blistering cross-examination by Prosecutor

Goldman, Cavaness continued to hold to the psychological trauma he had suffered immediately after Sean's death.

"The human mind insulates itself in strange ways under stress," Cavaness said.

This brought a sarcastic response from the prosecutor. "You knew you shot your son in the head again. Obviously you know that, but that's not the point."

On Tuesday, November 19, 1985, the case of the People of Missouri vs. Dr. John Dale Cavaness finally went to the jury while an emotionally spent county awaited the final denouement. Over 11 months had passed since that fateful morning of December 13, 1984, when a farmer on his way to feed his cattle first came upon the corpse of 22-year-old Sean Cavaness.

Now there was nothing for the prosecution and defense to do but to await the decision of the eight women and four men from Kansas City who'd been charged with sifting through the evidence and rendering their verdict.

The jury acted with startling speed. In just two and a half hours, the panel returned to the courtroom, verdict in hand. They had found the defendant guilty of murder in the first-degree.

The following day, the same jurors were given the grim task of determining whether Cavaness should be imprisoned for life or pay with his own life for the murder of his son. This time the deliberations were concluded in just a little over three hours.

The decision was that Dr. John Dale Cavaness would join the 35 other death row inmates in Missouri awaiting execution in the state's gas chamber at the Missouri State Penitentiary at Jefferson City.

The death sentence is subject to a mandatory review by the State Supreme Court.

Perhaps the attitude towards the convicted murderer which had gripped southern Illinois for nearly a year were best expressed by the two opposing legal titans who had battled for Cavaness' life.

111

In their pleas to the jury concerning the severity of the sentence, they had said:

Goldman: "The death penalty is the only appropriate punishment for this horrible crime.

"He played God and ordained that Sean should die. You're sitting in legal judgment, but only God can sit in moral judgment. This is a rare instance when society has the right to protect itself."

Margulis: "I can't believe that Mr. Goldman has said to you that he welcomes the opportunity to ask for the death penalty. The stakes are a lot higher, and you better be sure.

"Consider his 30 years as a physician and his contribution to his community. I don't see what possible useful purpose could be served by the 12 of you deciding on execution in the gas chamber for Dr. Cavaness."

Throughout this last word by prosecutor and defense attorney, Cavaness remained impassive.

One close relative said he learned the doctor had found religion while awaiting trial. But the relative insisted such an epiphany would have been out of character for the physician.

"DEMENTED DOCTOR KEPT 3 SEX SLAVES!"

by John Dunning

"This," screamed the doctor, his lank, blond locks flying and his nickle-rimmed glasses flashing, "is the dream of unlimited male supremacy and female slaves without will!"

Twenty-two-year-old Susanne Wagner did not reply. There was no way that she could for she was nearly strangled from the apple which the doctor had forced into her mouth and she could not hear him anyway as the tape which he had wrapped over her face, nose, mouth and eyes, also covered her ears.

Otherwise, she was not covered at all. The first thing that the doctor had done after handcuffing her to the front of the kitchen range was to tear off her clothes.

He had then raped her twice in succession, easily achieving orgasm both times.

It was an impressive performance for a man of 36, but Susanne was not surprised. She knew full well the sexual feats of which Dr. Ulrich Koschwald was capable.

She had had a lot of time to gain her knowledge. It was now early in 1983, and she estimated that she had been the doctor's prisoner for more than a year. During that entire time, there had been few days on which the grotesque, immensely tall and thin doctor had not sated his abnormal lust on her defenseless body.

He was, she thought, totally insane, capable of anything. His threats to kill her if she attempted to escape were serious. After all, he had already beaten her within an inch of her life on countless occasions, and he had actually broken his right hand hitting her in the stomach with what he said were karate chops.

She did not know a karate chop from any of the other kicks and blows. All she knew was that they hurt terribly and left her terrified that she would die before she could get her breath back again.

The cellar was the worst. When the doctor took her down to the cellar, she never knew whether she would come out alive again or not.

Stripped naked, she would hang for hours, her wrists attached to the hook in the ceiling, her toes barely grazing the cold cement floor.

The doctor liked to fondle Susanne's body while she hung there helpless. First, the beating with the calf rope which left her entire body covered with green and blue stripes, and then the obscene touching and handling. Generally, this had such an effect on him that he raped her repeatedly as well.

Susanne was not taken down for the process. She was a small girl and the doctor was very tall. He could rape her while she was hanging.

Worst of all, perhaps, was when he brought his daughter to watch. Gretel Koschwald was 11. She knew very well what her father was doing to Susanne, but she said nothing, did not even change expression, as he tortured, manhandled and raped his victim. Silent, expressionless, she stood watching until it was over.

Gretel knew Susanne, of course. They had met frequently during the time that Susanne and Ulrich had been lovers. She had seemed a completely normal, little girl, a daughter from Ulrich's first marriage.

Susanne did not know why the girl was living with her father or where her mother was. Ulrich had told her that he had been divorced twice and that it had been over this

114

women's emancipation business, as he termed it.

Susanne had been emancipated too. She had not put up with any of the doctor's nonsense about male supremacy. Once, when they had quarreled, she had put him out of her car in the middle of the countryside and he had to walk nearly five miles home. Another time, she had hit him over the head with her hair brush.

It had been shortly after that when her martyrdom had begun. Ulrich had gone to a psychologist who advised on marriage problems. It was his own field at Regensburg University where he was carrying on research into the sexual problems of married couples, but he could not very well advise himself.

The psychologist, a Dr. Oswald Krecke, had recommended that they separate.

"Or," he had added, "fight it out openly."

That, reflected Susanne, had been the fatal advice. Ulrich, twice her size and, if he could be believed, a trained karate fighter, had, of course, chosen the open fight. It had been a Saturday in February of 1983, and when they arrived back at the isolated house at Am Eichelberg in the village of Pillnach on the Danube River, he had beaten Susanne so unmercifully that she thought he would kill her.

That had been the beginning. What the end would be, she could not imagine, did not want to imagine. She did not believe that she would ever leave that hideous house alive.

Chained to the radiator while the doctor was conducting his research in the university some six miles away, Susanne Wagner pondered her fate and recognized that she was, herself, largely responsible for it.

It had begun innocently enough. She had had minor problems with achieving orgasm and she had gone to consult the doctor. Like all Germans, she stood in awe of academic degrees and she accepted without question anything that the doctor told her.

He had told her that he wanted to make love to her.

115

Not directly, of course. He was, after all, trained in psychology and he knew how to approach women. He had been gentle, discreet indirect. Despite his near-revolting physical appearance, she had quickly found herself in bed with him.

There had been nothing remarkable about it. She had been a little flattered to find herself involved with a genuine doctor and scientist, but he was not her first lover and she did not think that he would be her last.

Or so she had thought until that psychologist had advised open combat.

How could he suggest a physical contest between a girl barely five foot four, and a trained karate fighter six feet four inches tall?

Of course, he could not have known that Koschwald was totally insane. He had probably been thinking of something on the order of a pillow fight. He could not know that the man would hammer on Susanne with his karate chops for over a half hour until he broke his own hand.

Would he think to check up on his patient and see how things were working out?

Certainly not. If Ulrich had not been back to consult him, he would assume that his advice had proven effective and that the problem was solved. There would be no reason for him to follow up.

And anyone else? Was there anyone else to save her?

Her terrified mind chased frantically around her brain like a caged squirrel in its wheel. Even after a year of torture, rape and humiliation, Susanne's spirit was not completely broken. With what little remained, there was still a trace of hope somewhere deep down inside her. One day, she would escape and the nightmare would be over.

But not through the help of anyone else. Regensburg, a charming city of 140,000 located at the junction of the Danube and Regen Rivers, was in the south of West Germany. Susanne came from Hamburg, far to the north.

116

She had neither relatives nor close friends in the area and she had maintained little contact with her family. She could be missing for years without anyone noticing.

Anything local, Ulrich would have taken care of. She had been living with him anyway so there was no landlord to report her missing. She had had only a part-time job at the university library and he could easily have eliminated any suspicion there.

No, she could expect help from no one. Unless she was to spend the rest of her life hanging from the hook in the basement or being raped over the kitchen stove, she had to save herself. Desperate Susanne Wagner bent her mind to the means of her own salvation.

It turned out to be easier than she would have thought. She had been too terrified of the doctor to really give much thought to escape, but now she was more frightened of the prospect of a future in captivity than she was of him. Although her mind was still numbed by fear, she realized that there were frequent opportunities for an escape if she had the courage to seize them.

Koschwald did not keep her chained all the time. It was true that when he went off to do his research at the university, he took away her clothes, but he did not always chain her to the radiator. If he was going to be absent for any length of time, he had to allow her access to the toilet. He, therefore, chained or handcuffed her to the lavatory drain pipe in the bathroom. This permitted her to sit on the toilet.

The drain pipe was, however, not galvanized iron like the pipes to the radiator, but light metal and secured on both ends with washer and screw fastenings which could be turned by hand if enough strength was applied.

Susanne applied all the strength in her body. Fortunately, she was still comparatively strong. Whatever else the doctor had subjected her to, he had fed her well and she had more than enough time for sleep, although usually under uncomfortable conditions.

Unscrewing the drain from the lavatory, Susanne

slipped off the chain around it and crept uncertainly out of the toilet. She could hardly believe that she was free and that she was now going to attempt to leave this horrible house.

Her heart beating so hard that she feared she would have a heart attack, Susanne scuttled on bare feet through the house searching for something to wear. She was not concerned with modesty, but the central heating was on, meaning that it must be cold outside. The house was nearly a half mile outside the village, and she was going to have to get a good deal further than that if she hoped to escape the doctor for good.

What would happen if she did not succeed was only too certain. He had repeatedly told her that he would kill her if she even tried to escape and she did not doubt his word for a minute.

She could not find her own clothes and was forced to dress in the doctor's long trousers and sweater of which she rolled up the arms and legs in feverish haste. She had no way of knowing when he would come back; she had to be out of the house and, if possible, out of Pillnach before then.

There was she knew, a bus service to Regensburg, although she had no idea how often it ran. In any case, she would need money for the bus and she hunted around until she found the equivalent of three or four dollars. She took it reluctantly, alarmed that the doctor might have her arrested for stealing.

It was 11:00 a.m. on Saturday, February 5, 1983, when Susanne Wagner slipped quietly out the back door of the house where she had been a virtual slave for over a year, and set off down the road in the direction of Pillnach at a jog trot. It was the very heart of the winter and the temperature was well below freezing. There was a six-inch layer of snow on the ground and sleet had frozen a crust over it which cut at Susanne's feet. She was wearing the doctor's slippers, but they were a half dozen sizes too large and she could not keep them on.

Suddenly, she heard the sound of a car motor and, panic-stricken that it might be the doctor returning home, Susanne plunged off the road and into the deeper snow and leafless bushes lining it.

It was not the doctor's car and she returned to the road, covered with snow and with her bleeding feet leaving red prints behind her. She had lost both slippers in her dash for cover.

Although the half mile to Pillnach seemed equal to the distance to the moon, Susanne finally limped, panting as much with terror as with exertion, into the village square and saw to her immense relief the bus for Regensburg waiting there.

Wild with joy at her freedom, she ignored the astonished stares of the bus driver and the two other passengers. Upon her arrival in Regensburg, she went directly to the social welfare department where she told an unlikely story of having been robbed of everything she owned. She was taken to the hospital and kept for two days, and then sent home to her family in Hamburg.

Susanne did not mention a word of what had happened to her nor did she ever once name Ulrich Koschwald. The doctor had convinced her utterly that he was capable of carrying out his death threats. It was only when she arrived in Hamburg that Susanne really began to feel safe.

In the meantime, back in Pillnach, Dr. Koschwald was angry and embittered at the escape of his slave. The relationship between him and Susanne had been, in his opinion, absolutely perfect. Now, with her gone, he was at loose ends and had nothing to occupy his leisure hours.

"I have always been attracted to the idea of holding a number of women as slaves under my power," he once told his psychologist. "Would you advise me to become mohammedan so that I can have four wives at once?"

Dr. Krecke said that he was doubtful of the legal position and he did not think that German women would adapt well to polygamy. They were, in his opinion, too aggressive and quarrelsome.

"They would probably sue for divorce and ask property settlements," he said, "and, as you have a high income . . ."

"I suppose you're right," sighed Dr. Koschwald. "I wonder what openings there are in sex research in the Middle East?"

He had not told Dr. Krecke any of the details of his experience with Susanne, but had only said that she had left him.

Dr. Krecke had no information on openings for sex researchers in the Middle East and Dr. Koschwald soon lost interest in the idea, his attention diverted through the discovery of a suitable and, in some ways, superior substitute for the faithless Susanne.

The young lady's name was Sabine Pauli and she was a little older than Susanne, 24, but prettier and gifted, with a generous build. Like most connoisseurs of women, the doctor liked to see a little flesh on a girl.

He did not, however, like to see it the normal color. Black, blue, red and green were more acceptable and he soon produced these effects on Sabine's originally pink skin.

Unlike Susanne, Sabine could not blame herself, for she had not been the doctor's mistress. She had merely come to ask him a question concerning his research, had been invited to tea, and found herself strung up naked in the cellar with what she took to be a total madman fondling her private parts.

A student at the university, Sabine was from another part of the country and had neither friends nor relatives in Regensburg. Koschwald, having obtained the address of the student room where she was living from her personal identity card, had gone around, collected her things and told her landlady that she was helping him with his research and would be staying at his house for a time.

The landlady had accepted this without question since

Koschwald was a professor at the university.

In a sense, Koschwald was telling the truth. Sabine was helping him with his research into sexual behavior. That it was his own sexual behavior and that she was not a volunteer were matters beside the point.

Sabine was going to help the doctor for nearly as long as Susanne, but unlike her, she was not to bear the burden alone. Taking a step further toward his dream of holding several female slaves simultaneously within his power, the doctor had kidnapped 19-year-old Beate Koch from the village of Pillnach on the same day that Sabine was installed in the cellar.

The girls were not to meet immediately. There was only one hook in the cellar ceiling and, like many German academicians, Dr. Koschwald was not only incapable of installing one, but would have spurned the menial task as being beneath him.

Beate was, therefore, chained to the radiator in the spare bedroom, which was better than the cellar for it was not as cold and she was not subjected to the agony of being suspended by her wrists with her toes barely touching the floor. On the other hand, the bedroom was not as sound-proof as the cellar and she was constrained to wear a gag, which cut into the corners of her mouth and made her feel as if she were choking, night and day.

It was all that she did wear, of course. Dr. Koschwald wanted his slaves naked and ready to be raped at any moment.

He did not torture Beate quite as much as he did Sabine, but he raped her more. Beate had been a virgin and she obviously hated every obscene thing that was done to her. The doctor found this stimulating.

Things were progressing nicely for the doctor. His dream of many female slaves subservient to his will was already partially fulfilled and, despite the misgivings of Dr. Krecke, German girls were proving to be highly suited to polygamy, provided, of course, that they were dealt with in a firm manner. The trick was to teach them to know their place.

And yet, even an academician with a doctorate in sociology can make mistakes. Although he did not know it, Dr. Koschwald had made one when he carried off the thunderstruck, unbelieving Beate Koch.

For Beate, unlike Susanne and Sabine, was a local girl and her parents were conservative farmers who did not believe in letting girls run wild even if they were 19 and, under German law, adults.

Moreover, Beate, a pretty but hard-headed girl, had never shown any tendency to run wild and had but a few dates with boys, all of them neighbors known to her parents.

So when Beate failed to turn up for dinner that evening of May 4, 1984, they telephoned around the village to her girl friends, determined that she was, apparently, not in the village at all and called the police in Regensburg.

A plainclothes officer from the Missing Person Section came out that evening, took statements from Beate's parents, collected a recent photograph and returned to Regensburg.

A circular, bearing the girl's picture and the details of her age and appearance was made up, posted at bus stops and in the post office and distributed to all police units in the area. It produced no results.

It was, of course, only by the following week that the circular was distributed. By then, the officers from the Missing Person Section had held many interviews in Pillnach and what they learned was ominous.

Normally, the disappearance of a pretty, 19-year-old girl meant a romantic fling with someone of the opposite sex, but this appeared to be ruled out in the case of Beate Koch. Her best friends were quite certain that they would have known if she were in love and equally certain that she had not been. As a matter of fact, there were not many persons with whom she could have been in love. The village was small and the number of available males in the right age group was extremely limited.

Nor had Beate had contact with young men outside the village. She rarely went in to Regensburg and, with the exception of two cousins who lived there, knew no one in the city.

An accident was out of the question. Beate had been on foot and the land around Pillnach is relatively flat and without ravines that a girl can tumble into. The Danube ran along one side of the village, but the banks were safe, and in any case, Beate was a first class swimmer.

"The indications are," said the sergeant in charge of the Missing Persons Section, handing over the Beate Koch file to Inspector Walter Schreiber, "that the girl was picked up in a car and taken away. On the basis of the statements of her relatives and practically everyone else in the village, it seems unlikely that she would have gone willingly."

The inspector laid the file carefully on the desk in front of himself, but did not open it. He was a man in his late 50s, gray-haired, clean-shaven and with that quiet, assured air which civil servants approaching retirement often display.

"White slavers?" he suggested tentatively, lifting his head to look the sergeant in the face.

"I doubt it," replied the sergeant. "Granted, the villages are the preferred hunting grounds but she was a bit old for it and the wrong coloration. Nearly all of them go to North Africa or the Middle East and they want blondes."

"And as young as possible, the bastards," said Detective Sergeant Julius Karstens, the inspector's rock-jawed, hard-faced assistant. "Twelve is an old woman for them."

"And you're sure that she's not simply snuggled up with some lover somewhere?" asked the inspector.

"As sure as we can be," responded the sergeant. "We've been on it over seven months now and we've run out of possibilities."

123

"All right," said the inspector, "We've got it."

He handed the file to Sergeant Karstens.

"Read it and let me have it back," he said. "You can start setting up the detail immediately after you have familiarized yourself with the case."

That same afternoon, a new contingent of detectives arrived in Pillnach and began their investigations and interrogations. They were criminal investigations men and their approach was quite different from that of the officers from the Missing Persons Section. There was no certainty that Beate Koch was dead, but there was no certainty that she was alive either.

She was, though, feeling better than she had felt in some time. This was not because Dr. Koschwald had stopped torturing and raping her, but because the shock of the experience had begun to wear off.

During the months that had passed, Beate had learned a number of things. She knew, of course, who Dr. Koschwald was and she assumed that she was being held in his house, although she had never been in it before.

Beate also knew that another girl was being held captive in the house and even had occasion to speak briefly with Sabine when she was brought up to use the toilet.

The encounter had not produced much in the way of information. Both girls were convinced Koschwald was mad. But there was a certain comfort in knowing that she was not alone and gradually, country girl common sense began to reassert itself. The problem, she realized, as Susanne had realized before her, was to escape.

Beate did not know how Susanne had solved the problem or even that she existed, and the solution would not have been available to her in any case. Dr. Koschwald had learned his lesson. He no longer went off leaving his slaves chained to the toilet fixtures.

Instead, she was attached with a heavy link chain and padlocks to the radiator in the bedroom and the only hope appeared to be some way of breaking the chain. This was, however, impossible, so Beate turned her attention to the pipe entering the wall. It was a new house and it would be, she thought, probably no more than copper tubing.

She was quite right and the chain, once she had dug away some of the plaster, easily tore the soft copper tube in half. Hot water from the central heating system sprayed over the room, but it was not hot enough to burn her and Beate ran to the cellar where she tried unsuccessfully to free Sabine.

"Don't stay! He could come back any minute!" shrieked the terrified girl. "Run for help! Get the police!"

Beate did not stop to look for clothing, but tore down a curtain, made herself a sort of toga and ran out of the house and down the road to Pillnach as fast as her legs could carry her.

A half hour later, a detachment from the Regensburg police smashed down the door of the doctor's house and rescued Sabine Pauli.

They also had to rescue the doctor. The villagers already knew enough of what he had been doing from Beate Koch that they were preparing to burn him at the stake.

Two days later, on March 12, 1985, Dr. Ulrich Koschwald made a full confession to the torture and rape of the three girls. He repudiated it before his trial on May 22, 1986, but the court allowed it to stand. He was sentenced to five and a half years imprisonment, to be followed by psychiatric therapy which the court felt certain would make him a normal, useful citizen.

There was violent disagreement from the spectators and the judge was forced to clear the court.

"HER SKULL WAS CRUSHED BY 'DR. EVIL EYES'!"

by Andrew Lowen

The wind, barbed-edged and lacerating, was shifting snow with the force of a plough.

On the bleak Great Orme mountain range in North Wales, a blizzard had swaddled the rugged landscape in a soft white coat.

Such velvet virgin beauty was nothing more than a wicked trap of nature.

The howling wind that February 3rd night of 1984 drowned most of the familiar noises—the braying of the wild dogs and the squawking of the seagulls as they sought refuge from the nearby raging Bristol Channel.

Not surprisingly, then, the banging on a window of a mountain cabin was at first mistaken for rattling shutters.

"That's someone knocking," said Mrs. Maggie Parsons, a crofter's wife, as the tap-tapping became more demanding and urgent.

There was no fear in her voice. Mountain folk don't scare easily. Every day is a grim battle for survival.

"It's your imagination," her husband, Harry, disputed. "No one's daft enough to be out on a night like this." Years of practice had enabled Harry Parsons to speak

126

clearly with his curled wooden pipe still wedged in the corner of his mouth.

Neither had his wife stopped knitting for one second during their terse conversation.

A log fire crackled in an open hearth, glowing with a soporific warmth. Maggie swayed to and fro in her rocking-chair as she retaliated: "There it is again. I tells you it's someone a-knocking on our window."

"And I tells you, it's the wind," Harry insisted stubbornly, refusing to give ground, reaching for his flagon of home-brewed, frothy ale.

There were no television voices or images in the cabin: neither of them believed in "them newfangled gadgets."

"Invention of the devil," Harry had often commented to other crofters when they'd let it be known that they could keep the modern world at bay no longer.

They did possess a radio of sorts, but it had remained muted for three years or more. And the out-of-the-Ark telephone was there for emergencies only and was never used more than five or six times a year.

There was no mistaking the origin of the third rap on the window. It could have been made only by a human knuckle.

"I'll go," muttered Maggie, already on the way.

"It's too late for normal folk to be calling," Harry called after his wife as a sort of warning. It was a little after nine o'clock—time for the Parsons couple to be preparing for bed.

Through the frosty, snowflaked window, Maggie saw the wraith-like, ashen face of a middle-aged man.

It took her several seconds to open the front door. Bolts, latches and chains had to be unfastened, and keys had to be turned.

As the door was pushed open by a puff of spiteful wind, Brian Harris almost collapsed into the cabin. At that moment, he looked a cross between a snowman that had been blessed with the basic signs of life and a human being perilously near to death.

127

"I need help," he blurted out. "It's my wife. They've got her. They're wild. They're mad. I don't know what they'll do to her."

By this time, Harry Parsons had left his chair by the fireside and had joined his wife. The pipe was still between his lips. He'd exchanged his flagon of ale, though, for a double-barrel shotgun, loaded and cocked.

"Have you a phone, please?" Harris inquired in a lathered state. "I must call the police."

"Help yourself," Harry said laconically, leading the way to the old-fashioned, upright phone under the straight timber staircase. "Lines could be down on a night like this," he warned. "We've had no cause to use it since before Christmas, as far as I can recall."

It took the cops a good two hours to reach the log cabin. There was only one road up the mountain range, which was blocked in numerous places by its twisting, zig-zagging curves. It was a nightmare drive for the advance party, led by Sgt. Bill Norris, a member of the uniform division, stationed at the nearby seaside resort of Llandudno.

With Sgt. Norris were three rookie police constables. When they arrived at the cabin, they found Harris sitting beside the fire, wrapped in a blanket and sipping whiskey.

The story Harris poured out to Norris was the most sensational the sergeant had ever heard.

Harris, a high society optician, had been driving with his wife, Edna, from their home in Blackpool, a holiday town on the English northwest coast in Lancashire County, when they had been flagged down on the mountain road by a motorist who seemed to have had a breakdown.

"We were making for the Great Orme Mountain Inn for the weekend," Harris explained frantically. "The road was really treacherous. We'd almost gone off it several times, so I stopped.

"My wife was saying: 'You must help him, Brian. We

128

could be the last people to come along this way tonight. He could freeze to death out here on a night like this.' We acted the way any Samaritans would.

"I pulled up and got out . . . and that's when I saw the sawed-off shotgun. He pressed it into my stomach and said: 'Make one sound and I'll blow your guts all the way down into the valley.'

"I asked him what he wanted. I said he could willingly take all the money I was carrying and my credit cards, just as long as he didn't harm me or my wife, but he just laughed. He kept poking me in the stomach with the shotgun, saying: 'Shut your mouth! Stuff your money! We know exactly what we want and we're going to take it.'

"That's when I saw the other man. He must have been hiding round the other side of their vehicle, because he'd been out of sight when I stopped. Next thing I knew was the second man was pointing a shotgun at my wife's head through the front passenger window of my car."

Harris paused to drink some more. Mrs. Parsons busied herself in the kitchen, preparing coffee and sandwiches for everybody.

Sgt. Norris decided not to ask questions until Harris had finished his story or ran out of steam.

"I was ordered to get into the front passenger seat of their car," Harris continued. The whiskey was beginning to find its way to his brain. He was less shaky and the color was coming back to his thawing cheeks.

"I protested, but it was no use. He said if I didn't do as he said he was going to blow up me and Edna. My wife was becoming hysterical, but there was no way I could get to her to try to calm her.

"The other guy had climbed in my car beside Edna and I don't know what he was doing to her, but she was shouting her head off.

"I was driven for about 15 minutes, then literally pushed out of the car on a bend. Luckily I fell into a

129

snowdrift, and it was just like landing on a waterbed. I didn't feel a thing.

"There was no way I could find my way back to my car and Edna. I had no idea where I was. The snow was falling and I was lost. I just started trudging through the snow and, quite by chance, I stumbled across this cabin.

"I'm certain they were going to rape my wife. They may have even kidnapped her. If they know who I am, they'll also know I'm not exactly poor. I think we could be in for a ransom demand. I'll be guided by the police, though. I promise not to do anything without having police approval."

Sgt. Norris used the phone and spoke with the night inspector at Llandudno police station. The sergeant was told to wait with Harris while the inspector contacted Detective Chief Inspector David Madoc at home.

When the phone rang in the cabin, it was the chief inspector calling to tell Sgt. Norris that he (Madoc) was about to leave home to head for the Great Orme mountain range and wanted precise directions.

Madoc also explained that a large team was being rounded up so that a full-scale search of the area could be launched at first light in the morning.

Norris asked if he should take a formal statement from Brian Harris, but the chief inspector did not think that a good idea.

"I shall want to question him first," Madoc stated gravely. "There's nothing more you can do now until I arrive."

It was almost three o'clock in the morning when Madoc and his partner, Detective Sergeant Larry Hurd, finally made it through to the log cabin. By then, it had stopped snowing, but the roads, shimmering and slippery, were probably more treacherous than ever.

The senior cop introduced himself and gratefully accepted a mug of steaming black coffee, generously sweetened, from the matriarch.

Before turning his attention fully on Harris, Madoc

consulted with Sgt. Norris. They were huddled together in the corner of the room for a minute or so, with inaudible whispers floating into the rafters above their heads.

When Madoc crossed the floor and positioned himself directly above Harris, he asked him: "I believe that you mentioned to Sergeant Norris that you had been driving a Volkswagon?"

"That's right," Harris replied, looking up anxiously, his hands still wrapped around a tumbler, the whiskey almost gone.

"Can you give me the registration number, please?"

"Of course," answered the optician, quickly adding: "Have you found the car? Did you pass it? Is it still there by the roadside?"

Madoc didn't answer the barrage of questions. Instead, he waited for Harris to reveal the registration number of the Volkswagon.

As soon as Harris had dictated the car registration number, Madoc stated severely: "I'm afraid we're going to have to go for a drive right way, Mr. Harris."

"You have found the car, haven't you?" the optician pressed, shaking violently now.

"Yes, we have," Madoc admitted. "We came across it on the drive up here, slightly off the road."

"What about Edna?" Harris demanded. "Did they harm her? Is she all right?"

Inspector Madoc tried to place cushions around his words as he warned Harris: "You must prepare yourself for a shock, I'm afraid. We have found a woman in the car. She's dead. I want you to tell us if that woman is your wife."

It was some 15 minutes before Harris was in a state fit to leave the cabin. Half an hour later, he was confirming that the body in his car was indeed that of his wife, Edna, aged 47.

There was nothing much that could be done that night. Madoc ordered that nothing should be touched until a medical examiner and forensics could be brought to the scene at dawn.

Brian Harris was driven to police headquarters in Llandudno, where a doctor treated him for shock. The cops made arrangements for him to be booked into a hotel.

In the meantime, Madoc wanted a description of the man who had flagged down Harris and his wife and of the second man who climbed into the Volkswagon with Mrs. Harris.

"Can you recall what sort of car they were driving?"

"I should think so!" Harris retorted emphatically. "I was in it for long enough. My God, I was." He went on to describe a white Rover saloon car.

"Can you recall the registration number?" Madoc inquired.

Harris shook his head violently, almost spitting out the words: "Dammit, no! I could kick myself, but I didn't have a chance to see the number.

"I wasn't looking at the car when I was flagged down. My eyes were on the guy in the middle of the road. And when I was made to climb into the Rover, there were no lights to show up the license plate."

"Okay, what was the color of the interior?"

"Black, I think," the distraught optician answered thoughtfully. "It's hard to say in the dark. It could have been something like a dark-green, but I reckon it was black."

"Leather?"

"Yes, leather."

"Anything special about the car?"

"Such as?"

"I don't know, Mr. Harris . . . perhaps a certain smell to it, or a collection of books or tools that might give us a clue as to the occupation of the suspects . . . some article?"

Harris again shook his head, this time more thoughtfully and with less vigor. "I didn't see anything. Sorry,

132

but I wasn't really alert to those kind of incidentals."

Madoc understood and didn't labor the point. Now he concentrated on a description of the two men. He looked at the doctor.

"They were both big," Harris said, his voice still very shaky.

"How big is big?" Madoc pressed, seeking greater detail.

"Both well over six ft. tall, I'd say, and thick-set, sort of beefy, but I can only really talk about the one who took me. I didn't get a close-up of the other guy."

"The man who took you . . . how old was he?"

"Perhaps thirty-five. No older."

"Any accent?"

"Yes, Welsh."

"So you think he was local?" Madoc queried.

"I'm sure he was Welsh," Harris responded, refusing to be drawn any further with his conclusion.

"Any distinguishing marks?"

"I didn't see any."

"What were they wearing?"

"Overcoats and boots."

"Boots?"

"Yes, sort of Army boots. The overcoats were fully buttoned up. I couldn't see what they were wearing underneath. The guy who took 'em was also wearing woolen gloves, that I do remember."

Madoc rested for a couple of minutes while Det. Sgt. Hurd caught up with his note-taking. The inspector used this natural break as an opportunity to gather his thoughts, before going on: "You must be able to describe the face of the man who forced you into the Rover?"

Harris obliged, giving a detailed description of a long-faced man with a curled down mustache, a cloth cap pulled low just above his eyes and two tufts of hair on both sides of his head that gave the appearance of ear-phones.

"Later today I'll get one of our artists to do a sketch

133

of the suspect from your description," said Madoc. Harris simply nodded.

Breakfast for Madoc and Hurd that morning was a take-away carton of coffee and buttered toast, which was consumed on the drive back to the murder scene. Also during the drive, they shared a battery-operated electric shaver. Madoc's breakfast was slightly more extensive than his sergeant's. In addition to the toast and coffee, he also had a couple of aspirins for a headache that was pole-axing his skull.

Dr. Marvin Grossman followed in his own car. A team from forensics was already there, having begun their search operation some 30 minutes earlier.

Meanwhile, all police forces in Wales and the west of England had been warned to be on the look-out for a white Rover saloon car with two men, one of them answering the description graphically drawn with words by Brian Harris.

Naturally, the body hadn't been moved. It was on the floor in the rear of the car, one arm resting on the seat, her frilly red panties around her knees and her woolen skirt pulled up around her waist. There were several tears in her black stockings and one of the suspenders had snapped. She had also been wearing frilly pink garters and a quarter-cup bra that matched her silk panties. Her purple patent high-heel shoes were under the body.

Nothing appeared to have been touched in the trunk. The suitcase was still there, containing the clothes that had been packed for the weekend.

It was not easy for a preliminary medical examination to be conducted under these circumstances, but Dr. Grossman did his best, taking almost 45 minutes.

"All the evidence points to her having been battered to death," he reported to Madoc. "The skull is severely depressed in many placed. Crushed, in layman's terms. A solid, heavy weapon—hammer or cosh or lead piping, that sort of thing."

"Was she raped?" Madoc inquired.

"Oh, I should think so," the doctor stated. "Her pants have been pulled down, but there's no bruising around the vagina or thighs, but that isn't significant. But you'll have to wait for the autopsy report to be sure."

Madoc then inquired about the time of death, but it was impossible for the medical examiner to be helpful on that score because of the weather conditions. All Dr. Grossman could really do was confirm death and give an indication of the injuries that caused the fatality.

Police photographers took pictures of the body from all sides of the vehicle before the dead woman was handed over to the agents from the coroner's department.

Police pathologist Max Browning was ready to commence the autopsy at Llandudno General Hospital the moment the coroner's wagon arrived with the body.

Two hours later, Madoc was listening to the pathologist's findings. Firstly, there was no doubt that the victim had died from the beating to the head. There were no other injuries. Neither was there any evidence of rape: no semen had been found in the vagina and no sign of forced sexual activity.

Secondly, Edna Harris had eaten a substantial meal no more than half an hour before death. The digestion process had only just begun and most of the meat and vegetables were still in the stomach.

Thirdly, the pathologist was convinced by certain aspects of the lividity and blood formation that the body had been moved after death.

Early that evening, Brian Harris was again further questioned at his hotel. Madoc wanted to know how long they'd been driving from their home before being flagged down.

Harris answered: "A couple of hours or more."

"Did you stop at any other time during the journey, except when flagged down on the mountain range?" Madoc probed.

"No," Harris replied. "We kept on going because we

135

wanted to reach the hotel before the weather closed in completely."

This answer didn't match with the pathologist's report that the victim had eaten "a substantial meat and vegetable meal shortly before death."

What's more, despite the cold weather which made determining the time of death slightly precarious, the pathologist felt that Edna Harris had been dead longer than the husband's testimony suggested.

Something else had been bothering Madoc right from the moment he'd first seen the body.

Why was the woman not wearing an overcoat when she knew she was going to go out in a snowstorm on one of the coldest nights of the year and would be away for a whole weekend in a mountain range? Why was there not a woman's overcoat anywhere in the car? The sums did not add up.

The time had come to make inquiries about Edna and Brian Harris with the cops in Blackpool, their hometown.

The cops quickly discovered that in April, 1983, Brian Harris had been convicted on a drugs and sex charge, which resulted in his being given an 18-month suspended jail sentence.

The case had attracted enormous local press coverage, in which he'd become dubbed "Doctor Evil Eyes."

Reading about the case in 1983, Edna, at the time a divorced woman, had phoned the oversexed optician, although they'd never met before.

It seems that she offered him comfort and sympathy, saying that she believed in him and was disgusted by the way the media had persecuted him. A tryst was arranged and, within six weeks, they had decided to marry.

From police and medical files, Madoc learned about Brian Harris's psycho-sexual problems, which dated back to 1962 when he suffered brain damage in a road accident.

After the wedding, Edna and her teenage daughter had

moved into Harris's mansion-style house in Cottesmore Place, Blackpool. This was Brian Harris's third marriage.

During the next couple of days of the investigation into Edna Harris's homicide, the cops concentrated on the husband. Madoc asked the suspect: "Why didn't your wife take an overcoat on the worst night of the winter?"

"She must have forgot," was the instant reply. "We packed in a hurry. She didn't feel cold in the car because we had the heating on."

"You said you didn't stop for a meal, yet we know that your wife had eaten a full meal a few minutes before her death."

"The pathologist must have made a mistake. That's all I can say," Harris responded.

"Why should your wife's underwear have been pulled down and yet she was not sexually assaulted in any way?"

"Don't ask me; ask the killer."

The manager of the hotel where the couple apparently were going to stay on the night of the murder revealed that the booking had been made the same evening.

Inspector Madoc then told Harris that he intended to search the suspect's home and that a warrant for this purpose had already been obtained. "I shall want you with me," Harris was informed.

In a waste disposal unit in the kitchen the cops discovered the left-overs of the last meal eaten in the house before the couple had left for the weekend. That was immediately dispatched to the forensics laboratory for analysis.

In the garage, the detective scientists discovered pale stains on a wall that could have been caused by blood. Similar marks were also detected on a hammer and a length of lead piping in a tool-box.

Complicated scientific tests established that the left-overs taken from the kitchen waste-disposal unit matched the food in the dead woman's stomach. So, Edna's last meal that evening had been consumed at home just be-

137

fore she died. The marks on the garage wall and the hammer were confirmed as human bloodstains. Further detailed research finally established conclusively that the blood had come from Edna Harris's head wounds.

Faced with all the indisputable scientific facts and the considerable substantial evidence, Brian Harris confessed to the killing of his wife.

In a signed statement, he told of the stormy relationship, right from the first day of the marriage. There were rows over money, property and jealousy. In particular, Mrs. Harris resented her husband seeing his two young daughters from his second marriage.

On the day of the homicide, Harris tried to visit his daughters, but there was no one at home. When he returned to his own home, he had a ferocious argument with his wife and claimed he tried to commit suicide in the garage with fumes from his car, but failed.

After again failing in a bid to see his children, he alleged he took Edna for a drive and they fought verbally about "matters of property" and he decided to kill her and commit suicide, but he couldn't "find a suitable place."

After eating a quick meal on their return home, his wife was standing in the garage "with a smirk on her face," and that's when the death-attack took place.

It was after she was dead that Harris made a booking at the hotel and then set out with his wife's body in the back of the car. The story of the two attackers was complete fabrication from beginning to end.

But when he appeared before Judge Sanderson-Temple at Preston Crown Court in July, 1985, the defendant was informed: "It was not murder. It was manslaughter because you were then, as I am satisfied you still are, a man of diminished responsibility."

Nevertheless, 49-year-old Brian Harris was jailed for life and will probably never be released in view of the medical evidence which made it clear that he could always be a danger to women.

139

"BIZARRE CASE OF THE BED-HOPPING DENTIST"

by Ann Fish

Everything seemed normal when Jimmy Dale Hudson, a 38-year-old dentist, eased his car into the driveway of his home in an affluent neighborhood in the small military-school community of Oak Ridge, North Carolina.

He thought little of the fact that his wife's car was not in the drive. Kay often took their three-year-old adopted daughter, Wilma Dale, for rides or shopping.

Hudson frowned as he thought of the little girl whom he and Kay had adopted in April of 1983. The Hudsons had seemed to be ideal prospects to the social workers from the North Carolina Children's Home Society. Both were well-educated. Hudson had a thriving dental partnership and Kay, the daughter of a Baptist minister, worked side by side as a dental hygienist with her husband while guiding his career.

To help them breeze through the adoption process, a friend who worked for the Guilford County Department of Social Services coached the couple about questions they would be asked and the best answers for them to give during the interviews to determine their suitability as parents.

For a while, after bringing the baby home from the hospital, Hudson was happy with the new addition to his

140

family, but then Wilma Dale began having medical problems. She suffered respiratory and ear problems, frequent sore throats, and dizziness.

Kay spent more and more time with her daughter and less with her husband, who had grown accustomed to the undivided attention of his wife during their dozen years of marriage.

He often complained to Kay about their deteriorating relationship. As the child approached her third birthday, Hudson gave Kay an ultimatum: "Kay," he said, "you've got to find a way to get rid of Dale."

Always a traveler, Hudson started spending less and less time at home. His dental practice began suffering from his absences. His partners soon forced him out of the Greensboro, North Carolina practice.

Kay persuaded her husband to continue as a part-time dentist. But Hudson preferred traveling—enjoying cross-country train trips, jaunts to the Caribbean and especially to resorts where vacationers sunbathed in the nude.

A graduate of the University of North Carolina's Dental School in Chapel Hill, Hudson spent many Saturday afternoons during football season in Kenan Stadium, cheering on the Carolina Rams with fellow members of the prestigious Rams Club.

Now, Hudson shook himself from his reverie and went into his house. The silence was ominous. Something was wrong. Furniture and other things were missing, he told police later.

He reported that he saw a letter with his name on it. He tore it open. Kay had gone with the child and the letter contained no indication as to where she was.

He read and re-read the pages, he told the cops, while growing more frantic with each passing minute. In her parting letter, Kay wrote: "This is not a rejection of you, but a realization that I have caused you to give up two dental practices, be miserable and not want to come home.

"I have tried to work, provide a home, support, and

sex, but something that I do just seems to create a very unhappy, independent response in you. I have tried to be tolerant of your girlfriends.

"I have loved you for 17 years, but I cannot continue to watch you in pain. You are free of a dental practice now and you should be free of Dale and me as well.

"When you have signed the (separation) agreement, you are free to date whomever you wish. I want you to be happy. It is all I ever wanted.

"However, every decision I have helped you to make . . . has just made you sink further into quicksand and misery . . .

"It seems that over the last two weeks, you have been psychologically pushing me away, by pulling me and then kicking me. I do not want to cause you any more unhappiness.

"If you think of being violent to yourself or to others, remember that life is a precious gift and not yours to take away.

"The pain you were in last Sunday seemed like gangrene caused by our relationship and amputation is the only healing process available.

"Always know that I care very much about you and that is why I am not here."

Hudson said he made several quick phone calls to acquaintances to find out Kay's whereabouts, but either they honestly did not know or they would not reveal her secret. He could not find out from anyone where Kay was living.

Since completing her master's degree at the University of North Carolina at Greensboro, Kay had taken a job at Moses Cone Memorial Hospital. She was not working when Hudson said he called the hospital — the switchboard operator said she could not give out Kay's new telephone number.

He reached for the phone again and dialed police headquarters. He told the dispatcher that Kay was mentally unstable and that she had deserted him. He said he was afraid that harm would come to his wife and asked the dispatcher if the police could help locate her. When the dispatcher told him he would be unable to assist him, Hudson hung up the phone in despair, he told police.

A short time later, Hudson again called the police department and said that he was having a heart attack. His request that the police call Kay and bring her to the hospital succeeded. Kay arrived at the hospital and the couple talked. That was when Hudson learned the location of Kay's apartment.

Kay persuaded her distraught husband to seek psychiatric help. He agreed. When Kay arranged for Hudson to see a Greensboro psychologist, Dr. John Edwards, she warned the doctor that Hudson could become violent. "If he kills himself, he won't go alone," she told the doctor.

Dr. Edwards had several meetings with Hudson and his wife separately. At one point, Hudson told the doctor, "I'm just whipped, I need help."

Kay told the doctor that Hudson needed help.

On March 13th, she said that Hudson talked about "mass murder" after he lost his dental practice. She also told the doctor she was afraid Hudson might hurt himself, but she did not think he would harm her. She indicated that her husband had no prior history of violence.

Dr. Edwards also learned from Kay that she was happy with her decision to "rid" herself of her husband. "I have no intention of moving back," she told the doctor. "I fully intend to start dating."

On March 24, 1986, a blood-spattered man approached Greensboro Police Officer Greg J. Dean in the police department parking lot and said, "I think I killed my wife and daughter."

Although he told the officer he could not remember details of the slaying, in a calm voice and showing almost no expression, Jimmy Hudson told Dean that his wife had attacked him with a butcher knife. He said he had wrestled the knife away from her but could not remember what happened after that.

Hudson claimed that the next thing he remembered was standing at the sink, washing blood from his hands.

When Dean asked him how his daughter was killed, Hudson stated that "the child got in the way somehow." He did not refer to Kay or Dale by name nor did he show any remorse about their deaths.

When Hudson showed Officer Dean the wounds he claimed he had received from his wife, he was taken to Wesley Long Community Hospital for treatment of the slashes to his neck, chest and hand.

He asked Dean to check on his family, then gave police written directions to Kay's apartment. When police arrived at the apartment, they found the bloody bodies of Kay Hudson and her daughter.

Kay's body was sprawled face-up in the living room between a recliner and an antique bar. The body of the little girl, who was dressed in a pink nightgown and winter coat, was in a pool of blood near the front entrance. The throats of both had been cut and slashed.

Police charged Hudson with two counts of first-degree murder.

Hudson continually asserted that he could remember little of what happened. While housed at the Eastern Correctional Center at Maury, he underwent hypnosis in an effort to recall the events that led up to the deaths of his wife and child. He also underwent psychiatric tests to determine whether he was competent to stand trial. The reports indicated that he was.

His attorney, Michael Schlosser, began considering the use of the insanity defense after Hudson announced to police and psychiatrists that he hoped to receive a death sentence.

In August, as he prepared for the trial to begin in the fall, Assistant District Attorney Gary Goodman said he would seek the death penalty because of the atrociousness of the crime. Under North Carolina law, a jury could consider the cruelty of the attack — and the fact that it involved two victims—when deliberating life or death.

Hudson "deserves to be tried on a capital basis," Goodman said. "It's my opinion that the evidence will support findings of two aggravated factors for capital punishment."

The trial was delayed until February, but then Raleigh attorney Thomas C. Manning, who had begun representing Hudson, became embroiled in an argument in the courts over the fact that the prosecutors, in June, had offered Hudson a 100-year prison term but then withdrew the offer weeks later.

The defense attorney said that Goodman, who became "overly involved" in a wrongful-death civil lawsuit filed by Kay's father against Hudson, improperly used the criminal-plea negotiations in an effort to settle the suit.

Manning, who called the negotiations "unethical," filed a legal motion in an effort to force Goodman to honor the plea bargain that would allow Hudson to plead guilty to two counts of second-degree murder in exchange for two-consecutive 50-year prison terms.

During the hearing, Richard M. Greene, who represented Hudson in the civil case in which Kay's father sought $2.2 million from Hudson, testified that Kay's parents would be satisfied with a long prison term. When they wrote to tell Goodman of this, he replied that a double homicide warranted capital punishment consideration and that other prosecutors and police described the case as "one of the most brutal and heinous" in Guilford County history.

When Kay's family met personally with Goodman in October, they again requested that he not seek the death penalty. But, a week later, the family received a letter from Goodman saying that Hudson would be tried for his life. "The law and our duty are clear," the letter said.

After two days of testimony, Guilford County Superior Court Judge Thomas Ross ruled that the prosecutors did not have to honor the earlier plea bargain.

Assistant District Attorney Rick Greeson may have prompted Ross's decision.

"I'm not proud of what I've heard," Greeson said of Goodman's action.

"I don't know whether he did right or whether he did wrong. The facts of this case do not show any agreement. Like it or not, conditions were not met. I guess when you get two criminal attorneys playing contracts, this is what you get."

Five days after Ross's ruling, Jimmy Hudson went on trial for his life.

Selection of the jury took a full two weeks, with the attorneys for the state and the defense questioning 96 people before seven women and five men were finally seated. Four alternates—three men and a woman—were also selected.

The jurors would be asked first to determine if Hudson were guilty or innocent of murdering his wife and child. Then, if they returned a first-degree verdict, they would decide whether to imprison Hudson for life or sentence him to death.

In opening statements, Defense Attorney Manning said the tests which Hudson took from a psychologist the same day he murdered his family would show that the defendant had a personality disorder which could cause psychotic behavior. He emphasized that Hudson was not guilty of killing Kay and Dale because, at the time, he was insane. Manning noted that Hudson had visited the psychologist just three hours before Kay and Dale were killed.

But, Prosecutor Goodman counter-argued the fact that Hudson had all but confessed to the murders when he went to the Greensboro Police Department and said that he thought he had killed his wife and child.

The prosecutor told the jurors to look closely at the photographs they would be shown during the trial. "I know that those photographs are gruesome, are horrible, and I know that you're not going to like them. . . . I ask that you look at those to appreciate the horrible deaths they suffered at the hands of the defendant."

For the first time, it was made public that the mother and daughter had been beaten before they died. Goodman said that facial bruising was clearly evident in the photographs.

The first state's witness was Officer Dean, who told of Hudson approaching him in the parking lot. He said that Hudson's wounds seemed superficial and that he remained calm while talking about his family's death.

As the trial moved into its second day, the jurors were shown a gruesome videotape of the crime scene. Wilma Dale was lying just inside the front door, her pink nightgown hardly visible because of a large pool of blood. The child's throat was slashed all the way to the spine.

An Easter-egg dye kit was scattered about the living room where Kay's body was located. Her throat, too, was slashed, completely around the neck to the spinal cord. A handkerchief was stuffed in the wound.

Except for a set of car keys at the mother's elbow and the egg-dye kit, very little else in the apartment appeared disturbed or broken.

The television set was still on when police arrived and they found muffins cooling on the kitchen counter. They also discovered a butcher knife on the blood-spattered kitchen floor.

Although Defense Attorney Manning objected to the jury's seeing the entire tape, his objections were overruled by the judge after A.D.A. Greeson argued that the jury should see the crime scene as police found it.

Manning said he felt that one scene, showing that rigor mortis had set in, in the child, would turn the jury against Hudson, since it was so grisly.

The 45-minute video, which was shown on two telephone sets as Detective J.R. Ballance described the crime scene, emphasized the distance between the bodies of the two victims.

The jurors saw the video several times as attorneys pointed out the location of bloodstains, scuff marks, and other details about the crime scene.

Dr. James D. Kindl, the emergency-room physician who treated Hudson at the hospital, testified that the lacerations on Hudson's chest and hand were relatively shallow, and suggested a slashing rather than a stabbing motion.

The doctor also testified that Hudson was calm throughout the examination and did not mention his wife and child.

The jurors viewed color photographs of the victims as the police had found them in the apartment and during an autopsy in Chapel Hill. They also watched as police evidence specialists used a diagram to show where dozens of individual bloodstains and blood patterns were found in the living room, kitchen and foyer.

Prosecutors then began introducing various pieces of evidence, including the bloodstained coat little Dale was wearing. When officers revealed that a toy car and Valentine cards were in the coat pocket, the child's grandfather left the courtroom weeping.

Two .38-caliber pistols were introduced into evidence. A loaded one, stained with blood, was found in a shaving kit in Hudson's car. The other was found in Kay's apartment. Officers also said that numerous bloodstains were found in Hudson's car.

Other bloodstains were on a rolling pin and a spatula discovered in a closed kitchen drawer in the apartment.

When officers showed the jurors the coat and T-shirt Hudson wore when he was arrested, they indicated that there were no cuts or slashes on either, although Hudson claimed to have been cut on his neck, chest and hand during a struggle with his wife.

The key to Kay's car was missing from her set of keys, which were lying near her body, but officers later found it in Hudson's possession. A handkerchief Hudson was carrying at the time of his arrest also matched the one which was stuffed into Kay's neck wound, officers testified.

Another factor brought into court records was that men's clothing discovered in Kay's apartment did not belong to her estranged husband.

FBI expert Mike Malone testified that one of the hairs found on Wilma's clothing and body was forcibly removed, and experts surmised that it had been yanked or torn from Hudson's head, since the hair samples matched those of the defendant.

But another factor to which Malone testified was that none of Hudson's hair was found on Kay's body, and none of Kay's hair was on the child's body.

The hair on the butcher knife found in the kitchen matched samples of the child's hairs and Malone testified they had been sliced or cut.

As the trial moved into the second week, pathologists said that Wilma was probably conscious and might even have staggered after a knife had severed one major artery and sliced halfway through her backbone. Her mother had been beaten so severely that she might not have been conscious when she was slashed with a knife, severing major arteries and cutting into her neckbone.

During cross-examination, Defense Attorney Manning suggested that the child might have been in the arms of her father and was cut when Kay attacked him with the knife. Although the Chapel Hill pathologist, Dr. Robert L. Thompson, agreed that the child's injuries might have been "accidental," he said he was uncertain exactly how the wound was inflicted.

But, again Prosecutor Goodman brought out the photographs of the child's body to illustrate that Wilma was slashed rather than stabbed and that Thompson's medical opinion did not support the possibility of an accidental stabbing. He stressed that a large amount of force was essential to cut into a backbone, and the nick to Wilma's spine indicated two or more cutting-slicing motions.

According to Dr. Thompson's testimony, evidence that the child defecated indicated she might have been in an upright position and aware of her attacker. He also said she might have taken a step or two after she was cut.

At Defense Attorney Manning's suggestion that the child's neck wound was caused by only one incision, Dr. Thompson replied, "I believe there would have to be two strokes."

Another time, Manning contended that the bruises on the child's face could have been caused by a fall, but evidence entered by the prosecution showed that she would have had to have fallen three times to sustain the facial wounds found on her body.

Hudson listened solemnly to the testimony, but when the pathologists described the condition of the child's body, he slumped into his seat, then dropped his head into an open Bible.

Further testimony from the doctors revealed that neither of the victims had wounds on them which would have been indicative of those found on persons involved in a struggle or attempting to ward off blows.

In the middle of the second week of the trial, Detective Ken Brady read into evidence the statement that Hudson had given officers about the slaying.

He said he had kept Wilma Dale all day on March 24th, and dropped her off at about 6:00 p.m. When Kay asked him to leave, Hudson said he refused to do so until he kissed the child goodbye, since he did not think he would see her again for a few days.

The child came down the steps in her nightgown but said she was cold, so she put on her winter coat. Hudson said he picked her up and "Kay started insisting I leave," the statement indicated.

Although he said Kay was afraid he might take the child out of the house, Hudson said he was not trying to do so.

According to the statement, Kay "started cursing and hollering. (Wilma) Dale got upset and started crying. I sat down on the floor at the foot of the stairs and was holding Dale. Then, all of a sudden, Kay slapped me two or three times. Then she hit me with something, and the next thing I knew, Kay had a butcher knife.

"Kay aimed at me with the knife. That's when I got cut on the hand.

"That's when, I guess, two people got crazy and violent at the same time," the statement went on.

Hudson said he did not remember what happened next, but his first recollection was when he was washing blood off his hands in the kitchen. "I remember seeing Dale in the foyer and Kay in the living room. When I was washing my hands, I took my shirt off and dropped it on the kitchen floor."

Hudson had described his marriage as "normal . . . with a few rough spots here and there," in the statement. But as the officers delved into the background, the statement began revealing more facts about Hudson's personal life.

"On approximately six or seven different times, I have had affairs with different women, but Kay probably only knew about two or three of them," the statement continued.

Several weeks before she was killed, however, Hudson's wife had found several letters he had written to some women. "One letter was current and the others went further back than a year of more," the statement continued. "My affairs were also with out-of-town women, as I never saw any women here in Greensboro, due to my position in the community.

"At one point in our marriage, I suggested we go to a nudist colony, but she didn't want any part of it. She finally just told me to do my thing, but don't bring home any pregnant women or diseases. As far as I am aware Kay never had any affairs with anyone," he told the officers.

"I have been under a lot of stress lately and I am not a violent person. I love them so much I can't believe this happened," he said.

As soon as the statement was completed, co-prosecutor Greeson began tearing it apart, citing several discrepancies between it and evidence at the crime scene.

He said that Hudson's shirt had no cuts or slashes on it, although he claimed he had been stabbed by Kay. And the shirt was found on the stairwell, rather than in the kitchen, as indicated in the statement.

A.D.A. Greeson also noted that Hudson had never explained why it took him two hours to get to the police station after the attacks occurred.

Under cross-examination, Detective Brady said that four years earlier, he had investigated death threats to Hudson for sleeping with another man's girlfriend. During that period, Hudson had been excited and shown genuine fear, Brady testified.

Another of the state's witnesses was a relative of Kay's who lived in California. She testified that Hudson called her often, seeking her help, and that just prior to the murders, she had acted as an intermediary between Hudson and his wife.

"He said he knew he had done wrong by not loving (Wilma) Dale, but he was going to change that," the relative testified. She said that Hudson was bitter over Kay's abandonment of him in an effort to start a new life.

"I used to think Kay was a warm, loving person," Hudson told the woman in one telephone conversation. "And now, I see that she's a cold, calculating woman."

The relative testified that Hudson told Kay to "find a way to get rid of" the child.

"I did," Kay told her kinswoman. "The only thing is, I went with her."

The state rested its case against Hudson on March 19th. Hudson was the first witness called by the defense in an effort to show that he had mental problems.

As Hudson read the letter from Kay in which she blamed herself for their marital problems, he broke into tears and sobbed. He repeatedly told the jurors that he could not recall the murders, but told them that prior to going to the police station, he held a pistol to his head and contemplated suicide.

He said he was not sure at that point if the deaths of his wife and child had been real or a "nightmare," but he said he remembers thinking, "If they are (real), I don't want to live. If it's not real, I don't want to die."

As he told how his adopted daughter "interfered" with his marriage, he testified that Wilma Dale "kept hanging on to Kay's coattails. All I said was, "You got to do something to Dale so I can talk to you."

As he began cross-examining Hudson, A.D.A. Greeson introduced into evidence records from the Central Prison law library which revealed that Hudson had spent much of the past year learning about the history of the insanity defense in criminal trials and how the defense could be applied. Minutes earlier, Hudson had testified that he knew very little about the insanity defense, except what his attorneys had told him.

The accused claimed that his research about the defense, the appeals process and the information about the state's criminal defense attorneys was part of his "self-psychotherapy. It has in no way influenced me in telling the truth as I remember it."

When Hudson continued to declare that he could not remember details of the slayings, Greeson asked how he could recall trivial information but forget significant facts and events which might explain the murders.

The prosecutor noted that Hudson could remember the following:

Kay's attacking him with a butcher knife, but not what she had used when she supposedly beat him.

That he had been stabbed and slashed by his wife, but could not explain why there were holes in his shirt.

153

As Greeson quizzed Hudson, the defendant would often sit as if he were in a trance and reply that he chose not to remember unpleasant details or facts which he did not consider important.

"When you're fighting a fire, you don't take notes," he repeated constantly, adding, "It became like a darkening, sinking, maddening, psychedelic nightmare."

Another part of the evidence about which the prosecutors questioned Hudson extensively was the boxes and bags of love letters and sexually explicit photographs and books they had confiscated.

"It's just sad that all this material has to be discussed," Hudson maintained.

He admitted that he had often advertised in "swinger" magazines and engaged in group sex with men and women across the country, but he said his wife had also participated. And yet some of the letters introduced into evidence revealed that Hudson complained that his wife would not become involved in the "swinging" scene.

At one point, Hudson testified that the child's adoption was the second most important day in his life, but A.D.A. Greeson immediately brought out a letter which he had written four days later to a girlfriend in Chicago, telling her that he appreciated the nude photograph of her so much that he had masturbated in his office.

"I want you to tell the jury just what you were doing just three days after that young girl came into your life," Greeson shouted at Hudson. "Tell them what you were doing in your office with Kay's photograph and Dale's on your desk."

After Hudson left the stand, Dr. Bob Rollins, a psychiatrist at Dorothea Dix Hospital, painted Hudson as a selfish, manipulative man who could not cope with his wife's leaving him and went into a violent rage. Rollins declared that although Hudson had a mixed personality disorder, he was legally sane.

"In my opinion, he would be responsible for his actions . . . you can have a mental disorder and still be

154

responsible," Rollins said. But the defense attorneys said they believed that Hudson was psychotic at the time he killed his family.

Dr. Edwards told of his meetings with both Kay and her husband, and said that Hudson's fragile mental health might have become a deadly catalyst when his wife left him.

Describing Hudson as "almost whiney at times," Dr. Edwards said that his testing showed Hudson to be a "severely disordered personality" who was "very dependent" on his wife, who made all the important decisions in their lives—including the funeral arrangements for Hudson's parents.

Another psychiatrist, Dr. Selwyn Rose of Winston-Salem, said that Hudson's strong emotional bond to his pampering mother, with whom he slept until he was 15, was directly responsible for Hudson's psychotic behavior.

He also revealed that Hudson suffered his first episode of amnesia when he found his mother dead on the floor and tried to revive her. He remembers nothing of the incident, the doctor testified.

He described Hudson as a fragile, narcissistic, dependent, flaky wimp. Dr. Rose said that Hudson's two personality disorders caused him to feel depressed and insecure and to have no regard for the feelings of others.

The doctor said the fact that Hudson could not remember all the events that occurred on the night of the murders "is consistent with his being psychotic. It's tantamount to shock, emotional shock," Rose testified, adding that amnesia "is another repressive mechanism."

Following the testimony from the mental experts, the state brought a surprise witness to the stand—a fellow prisoner of Hudson's who had been convicted of murder and was now a prison librarian.

The prisoner had helped numerous men prepare their cases, he testified. When Hudson came to him, he also helped him.

Hudson admitted to the librarian that he had murdered Wilma Dale so he could make Kay's murder and crime scene "fit" his contentions of insanity.

Hudson also studied the novel *Fatal Vision*, the story of the Green Beret physician who was convicted of killing his wife and two daughters. The book details how the doctor killed his family, then created evidence—including self-inflicted wounds—to make it appear that they had been killed by a group of "hippies."

When the prosecutors first approached the librarian about helping them, the man said he agreed to furnish them information on Hudson, but said he would not testify, since a prisoner's life is endangered if he testifies against another prisoner.

But then, the prosecutor showed the librarian photographs of Kay and Wilma Dale.

When the man was shown the autopsy and crime-scene pictures of the little girl, prosecutors said he broke down and cried. He agreed to testify. "I'm still not over it," he solemnly told the jurors.

Of course, the defense lawyers tried to shake the jurors' belief in the librarian's testimony by telling them that he had put a pistol to the heads of two Fayetteville, North Carolina prostitutes and cold-bloodedly pulled the trigger.

They asked the jurors why the man would come out of prison and endanger his life by testifying "for the enemy" against another prisoner for the first time in the 20 years of his incarceration.

They argued that conscience could not possibly be the factor for the prisoner to turn "traitor," since he himself had killed three people in his lifetime.

"What's the difference?" one of the defense lawyers shouted at the prisoner.

"The little girl," the man answered quietly, bowing his head.

During closing arguments, Prosecutor Goodman informed the jurors that Hudson had told the prison librarian of killing his wife, then waiting almost 20

156

minutes before slaying his daughter "to make it fit."

He also referred to a neighbor's testimony that he had heard nothing unusual on the night of the murders, although Hudson claimed that screaming, cursing and other noises occurred during his struggle with Kay.

The prosecutor asked the jurors to think about the two hours it took Hudson to go to the police.

What happened during that period of time? he demanded.

"What took time was the defendant thinking about the next one (the child's murder) and also what he was going to tell police when it was all over," Goodman maintained, adding that the prisoner's testimony was consistent with "what the evidence shows."

The jury deliberated for 13 hours on Friday, and on Saturday, April 11, 1987. When they returned, they had found Hudson guilty of first-degree murder in killing his daughter and second-degree murder in killing his wife.

Although the courtroom was heavily guarded with deputies from the Guilford County Sheriff's Department, Hudson sat quietly and showed no response as the verdict was read.

A few days later, the jury sentenced Jimmy Dale Hudson to life in prison for murdering his daughter. Then, Judge Ross sentenced him to 50 years for the murder of his wife.

"PERVERSE SEX PLEASURES OF THE SADISTIC DOCTOR"
by John Dunning

On the night of August 1, 1974, the moon was full and the air over southern Germany was as soft and warm as milk. Through the clover fields along the shores of charming little Lake Langwied, some three miles to the northwest of Munich on the great Stuttgart-Munich Autobahn, a gentle breeze, no more than a current of air, whispered as softly as the hidden words of lovers, sweet with the scent of clover blossoms.

In the center of the field lay a beautiful young woman, her lovely face smashed out of all resemblance to humanity, the dark marks of strangulation on her slender throat, her body seeping blood from 13 deep knife wounds, her dress pushed up around her waist and her legs wide spread to expose obscenely her naked genitals and, most grotesque of all, a large, carefully hollowed out cucumber thrust deep into her vagina from which it protruded like some ghastly, unnatural growth.

Throughout the night, the corpse lay among the clover blossoms, the limbs stiffening and contracting as rigor mortis set in, the slow trickle of blood and body liquids congealing from bright red to dull, dusky brown and the black death patches building on the buttocks and shoulder blades as the no longer circulating blood sank into stagnant pools beneath the skin.

Dawn comes early in summer in Europe and it was barely five when the great, golden sphere of the sun rose above the lake and shone down on the body of the dead woman.

With it, came the flies and the ants and all of the other little creatures of the fields who feed upon whatever chance brings them. Here was food for a great many tiny mouths, mandibles and sucking tubes.

There was, therefore, a great cloud of flying insects which rose into the air as Willi and Ursula Franke came running through the clover field, the picnic basket swinging gaily between them.

Willi and Ursula had only been married two days earlier and they were spending their honeymoon in the south of Germany, far from the chilly shores of the North Sea which was their home.

The warning cloud of flies had not, however, gone up until the couple were almost upon the corpse and the two young people were subjected to the full impact of the hideous scene.

Ursula screamed, let fall the picnic basket and, in a purely instinctive action, turned and raced off across the field as if the devil were at her heels.

Willi hesitated, made a sort of gesture at the corpse as if he would like to help, but could not because of more pressing matters, and ran after her. A quarter of an hour later, they arrived in their little Fiat 500 at the first police substation on the edge of Munich and, while Ursula wept quietly in the car, Willi went in and reported.

Unfortunately, the police would not let them leave until a patrol car had been dispatched to the scene and had reported back that there was, indeed, a dead woman lying in the clover field.

This was unfortunate, because Ursula was well on her way to a nervous breakdown from which she did not recover until the couple had got back to Hamburg. Although she had only seen the corpse for an instant, it was one of those searing experiences where some terrible

159

sight is so vividly burned into the brain that it is never really forgotten again.

Such sensitivity in a young bride was easily excusable when even such a hardened police officer as Inspector Joseph Biedermann of the Munich Police Department of Criminal Investigations turned almost pale and averted his eyes from the horrible spectacle.

The inspector was not a man who turned pale easily. Stout, jolly, bull-necked and normally red-faced, he had spent over half of his 56 years in criminal investigations and he had seen a great deal, but never anything like this.

"Very worse kind of sex pervert, I suppose, Guenther?" he said to the tall, dark and polished-looking police medical expert who was kneeling beside the corpse and carrying out his examination while Detective-Sergeant Sepp Meier, the inspector's assistant, swung a towel to ward off the flies.

"A very unusual kind in any case," said Dr. Brockmuehle, who was not known to have any emotions whatsoever other than a sort of mild scientific curiosity. "I've never heard of such a case."

"You mean the cucumber?"

"Not only the cucumber," said the doctor. "Before it was inserted into her vagina, she was subjected to vigorous and consummated intercourse. Her vaginal passage is flooded with ejaculate."

"And?" asked the inspector.

"Normally," said the doctor, "if I may use the term, a person sufficiently perverted to have done this with the cucumber would not have been capable of conventional intercourse. In addition, she has been very severely beaten about the face, her throat has been strangled enough to rupture the larynx and she has thirteen stab wounds from what looks like a butcher knife. I suspect that these were the actual cause of death, but I can only say for certain after the autopsy. However, the strange thing is, they seem to be arranged

160

almost in a pattern, particularly over the breasts."

"And your conclusions from all this?"

"This was not a simple sex murder," said the doctor. "There are elements of a ritual murder here, but not any ritual murder that I have ever read about."

He got to his feet and stripped off his rubber gloves.

"You can have them put her into the coffin now, Sepp," he said, "unless there's something the lab wants to do first."

The huge, rawboned sergeant with his short-cut stubble of reddish-brown hair looked questioningly at the technician in charge of the squad from the police laboratory who shook his head.

"All right, boys," said the sergeant, signaling to the stretcher bearers waiting beside the police ambulance with the coffin used for transporting murder victims to the police morgue.

"It happened last night," said the doctor as the inspector watched unhappily the struggles of the stretcher bearer to force the stiffened legs together enough to permit placing the body into the coffin. "Between eleven in the evening and two this morning, say. I'll try to get you a preliminary report by this evening."

Whereupon, the doctor walked across the field to his car, got in and drove away.

The stretcher bearers shoved the feet of the corpse down into the coffin and clapped on the lid as if they expected that it might spring out. It was a rather grisly action to witness.

The inspector gave himself a little shake and reached for one of his short, thick, black cigars.

"All right," he said brusquely. "What have we got?"

"Identification," said the sergeant, holding up a woman's handbag. "According to her personal identification papers, she was Mrs. Freya Talabani, aged thirty-five, born Debusmann and married in 1969 to Dr. Fouad Talabani, aged thirty-five and resident at one ten Goethe Street."

"Talabani?" said the inspector. "What kind of a name is that? Goethe Street in Munich?"

"In Munich," said the sergeant. "Sounds like some kind of an Arab or Indian name to me. Otherwise, there's nothing of significance in the bag. Money, personal things like lipstick and the usual gear that a woman carries around with her."

"And you, Max?" said the inspector to the technician whose men had just completed an inch-by-inch search of the scene in a radius of 150 feet from the body.

"One murder weapon," said the technician, holding up a plastic sack containing a blood-smeared butcher knife. "And one hand print."

He held up a second sack containing a woman's shoe. There was a bloodstain across the heel.

"That's the print," said the technician. "Good enough for a positive identification just as soon as you catch him."

"That may take a little while," said the inspector. "Is that it?"

"With the exception of the cucumber," said the technician. "It may be traceable."

"You're kidding," said the inspector

"No," said Max.

He was not kidding, either. By the following day, he was able to tell the inspector where the cucumber which had been thrust into Freya Talabani's vagina had been bought.

"In a fruit and vegetable store in Wartenberg," he said. "Unfortunately, they do quite a business and nobody knows who bought it. It was bought on July thirty-first."

"Wartenberg?" said the inspector. "Where in hell is that? I never heard of it."

"Village about forty miles to the northeast of here," said the technician. "The closest town is Moosburg."

"But, Christ! That's close to forty miles from where she was found," said the inspector.

"Right," said the technician. "So my suggestion would

162

be to take a hard look at the residents of Wartenberg. Your man should come from somewhere right around there, unless, of course, he was so sneaky that he deliberately picked some place that had no association with him to buy his cucumber."

"I wouldn't think there would be that much planning to the thing," said the inspector. "The print on the shoe turn out all right?"

"Just fine," said the technician. "Nothing on the knife. Common make of butcher knife you can find in any kitchen. It's not new."

"All right, Max," said the inspector, and as the technician started to leave the office, "hold it a minute. Just out of curiosity, how in the devil did you trace that pickle?"

"The vegetable wholesalers don't use the same packing materials," said the technician. "We get the general area from that and then it's a matter of taking samples of the dirt and dust from the individual shops. We can't always do it."

"But you're sure this time?"

Max was sure, but, although a squad of detectives was sent to Wartenberg and spent the best part of a day checking out the residents, no connection to Dr. or Mrs. Talabani could be found.

"Mrs. Talabani comes from a distinguished family here in Munich," said Sergeant Meier, who had notified the bereaved husband, arranged for the formal identification of the corpse and discreetly looked into the background of the family.

"Her father is the pediatrician Dr. Max Debusmann, her mother is the lung specialist Dr. Ernestine Debusmann, one brother is the gynecologist Dr. Peter Debusmann and the other is the dentist Dr. Siegfried Debusmann. Not surprisingly, she married a doctor. Surprisingly, however, he's not of German origin. He's a Kurd from Iraq. Lived in Germany since 1959, took his degree here and is very successful and also very popular. He was King of the Marksmen last year."

King of the Marksmen is a title given to members of the target shooting clubs who achieve the highest scores at the annual contest. The title carries a certain amount of social distinction and the sport itself is inclined to be somewhat snobbish.

"How did he take it?" said the inspector.

"Completely broken up," said the sergeant. "The Talabanis have a reputation for being unusually happy."

"Had," corrected the inspector absently. "And the family?"

"As bad as the husband," said the sergeant. "They haven't told her father yet. He's sixty-three and he just got out of the hospital. Had some kind of a nervous breakdown due to overwork, as I understand it."

"But none of them have any suggestion as to how this might have happened or who might have killed her?" asked the inspector. "All those doctors, they could have had some dangerous nuts among their patients."

"No suggestions," said the sergeant, "and I don't think they are that kind of doctors. None of them are psychologists. Anything in the autopsy report?"

"Nothing concrete," said the inspector. "He narrowed the time down to between eleven and midnight. However, it's what he isn't sure about that bothers me. He thinks that the big sex bout that she had just before her death was voluntary. He says he doesn't think she was raped."

He held out a sheet of paper. "Here, read this."

The sergeant took the autopsy report and read half aloud. "No laceration or reddening of the labia major. Extensive secretion of lubricating fluids in addition to male ejaculate. Vaginal passage distended . . ."

He handed the paper back to the inspector.

"Couldn't the distension of the vagina be due to having that cucumber shoved into her?" he asked.

"Apparently not," said the inspector. "Guenther says it was put in shortly after she died and that the passage was already relaxed at that time making insertion easy.

164

Otherwise, there would have been lacerations."

The sergeant looked thoughtful. "That could mean that she went out there with her murderer voluntarily," he muttered. "But all the information I had was that the Talabanis were happy with each other. Not a word of any affairs involving her or him either."

"You're going to have to take a closer look," said the inspector. "If Guenther is right, the man who killed her was someone she knew well, well enough to enjoy sex with in any case."

"It still doesn't make sense to me," said the sergeant. "All right. The woman had a lover. They went out to the clover field beside the lake for a little loving. Normal enough. They had intercourse. Also completely normal and enjoyed by all parties. Then, all of a sudden, this completely normal lover turns into a homicidal freak. He strangles his mistress. He smashes her face in. He stabs her thirteen times with a butcher knife which he must have brought along for the purpose. And he carefully hollows out a cucumber, also brought along expressly for the purpose and shoves it up her vagina. I don't see how the man could be so normal at one minute and so crazy the next."

"No," agreed the inspector. "You're right. It just isn't possible. But what then? Were there two men? One with whom she came out to have and did have intercourse and another who then jumped on her, smashed her face, strangled her, stabbed her and so on? And, if there were two men, then how would the second man know that Mrs. Talabani and her lover were coming out to the clover fields to frolic under the full moon? Or are we to assume that this was a coincidence? This complete raving lunatic was sitting out in the clover field with a cucumber and a butcher knife in his pocket waiting for the first woman to come along?"

"It couldn't be that, either," said the sergeant. "The grass isn't long enough that a man could hide in it, even at night. They'd have seen him. And, even if they didn't because they were, say, having intercourse, there would still be the question of what happened to the lover. He might have been such a coward as to run off and abandon his mistress to a madman, but I think he'd have at least tried to get help."

"Well," sighed the inspector, "it could be that he feared exposure of his association with Mrs. Talabani, but as a matter of fact, that didn't happen. All those people running around the clover field would have left tracks and the only tracks that Max found were those of Mrs. Talabani and a man coming in and the man going out. Then, there were the tracks of Mrs. and Mrs. Franke who found the body and the tracks of the patrolman from substation Kater who checked it out. And that was it. There was no madman sitting in the field with a butcher knife and a cucumber in his pocket."

"In short, we always come back to the same thing," groaned the sergeant. "The man who murdered her was the man who she willingly accompanied to the clover field and with whom she had enthusiastic intercourse. The exasperating thing is, with that handprint on the heel of her shoe, we'd have him dead to rights if we just had any idea of who it was."

"It's got to be someone she knew," said the inspector, "and, unless she was a much different woman than we have any reason to believe, someone that she knew well. That's the only possibility and that's the angle we're going to work on."

Logical as the inspector's reasoning was, it did not produce any results. Even the most exhaustive investigations failed to turn up the slightest evidence that Freya Talabani had had any relations with men other than her husband aside from the normal, casual social ones.

She had, it seemed, been quite satisfied with her husband, more than satisfied, as a matter of fact, for she had often spoken enthusiastically to her girl friends of Dr. Talabani's prowess as a lover.

166

"If they and she can be believed, the doctor is a seven-day wonder in bed," said the sergeant. "It's hard for me to believe that she could have had a lover on the side. Somebody would have noticed something."

"You would say, then," said the inspector, "that the only person that she would really have enjoyed sex with would have been her own husband?"

The sergeant grunted with surprise.

"I see what you're getting at," he said. "But why? Talabani is a doctor, not a mad sex freak. And, if he faked it, why? He hasn't the hint of a motive in so far as I've been able to determine."

"You're sure he hasn't a girl friend?"

"Dead sure," said the sergeant. "It would have been even harder for him to cover up something like that than for her.

"He has no girl friend. And he doesn't stand to collect a nickel from his wife's death. She wasn't even insured. So why?"

"I don't know why," said the inspector wearily, "but if the only person she would enjoy sex with was her husband and the person who killed her was one with whom she enjoyed sex, then the one who killed her has to be her husband."

"We could take his handprint," suggested the sergeant.

Dr. Fouad Talabani, however, refused to have his handprint taken.

"This is an outrage!" he exclaimed. "My wife is murdered and, instead of you making any serious effort to detect her murderer, you come to me with all sorts of silly requests!"

"Hmm," muttered the inspector upon hearing of the doctor's reaction. "Very interesting. Get a warrant and search his place from top to bottom. Don't miss a thing."

The sergeant may have missed something, but he did not miss much. What he and Max and the technicians from the police laboratory found made an impressive list, that was for sure.

167

First, there was a brand-new butcher knife in the Talabani kitchen. It had been bought the day after the murder.

Secondly, blood spots were found on a pair of trousers in Dr. Talabani's wardrobe. The blood was Group A-2, the same as Mrs. Talabani's.

Thirdly, a partially burned, blue polo shirt belonging to Dr. Talabani was found in the incinerator behind the house. It was also heavily stained with Group A-2 blood.

Finally, Dr. Fouad Talabani was taken into custody and, despite his objections, his handprint was taken.

It matched exactly the print in blood on the heel of his dead wife's shoe.

Although Dr. Talabani continued vigorously to protest his innocence, he was taken before the examining judge, who in Germany serves in the place of a grand jury, and formally indicted for the murder of his wife Freya Talabani.

During the year that passed, Dr. Talabani never once admitted to his guilt in the murder and in this he was supported by the entire family of his dead wife. None of the Debusmanns believed that he had committed the crime nor did any of his many friends and patients.

It was, therefore, with a curiously lopsided case that Prosecuting Attorney Ernst Hilger began the trial in October of 1975. He had clear evidence in the form of the blood spots on Talabani's clothing and his handprint on the heel of the shoe, but he had no confession and, worse yet, no motive of any sort. The police investigations had only gone to confirm that the Talabanis had been unusually happy as a married couple and that neither had been involved in any affair with a third party.

Represented by famous defense attorney Rolf Bossi, Dr. Talabani was called to testify in his own behalf and gave for the first time his own, startling version of the murder.

His wife, he said, had been killed by the Iraqian Secret Service in order to discredit him in Germany.

This claim was refuted by the prosecution, Dr. Hilger pointing out that, first of all, Dr. Talabani had been in Germany for over 15 years and was a German citizen, secondly, he had never had anything to do with the Kurdish independence movement which had produced so much bloodshed in Iraq and, thirdly, there was nothing that the Iraqian Secret Service, if indeed there was any operating in Germany, would stand to gain from such an action.

For the next two days, the prosecution pressed the material evidence, the blood spots and the butcher knife which it had now been possible to positively identify as coming from the Talabani kitchen. There was, moreover, a tentative identification by one of the sales clerks in the vegetable store in Wartenberg of Dr. Talabani as the person who had bought the cucumber on July 31st which was later found thrust into Mrs. Talabani's vagina.

The defense countered with denials of the evidence and, under cross-examination was able to weaken the statement of the sales clerk who admitted that she could not really tell one foreigner from another.

The blood on Dr. Talabani's clothing was admitted to have come from his wife, but several days prior to the murder when she had suffered a nose bleed. In staunching it, Dr. Talabani had got blood on his trousers and polo shirt. The shirt had been deemed too badly stained to save and had been thrown in the incinerator.

As for the bloody hand print on the heel of Mrs. Talabani's shoe, the defense questioned the accuracy of the police observations, pointing out that a handprint was not the same as a fingerprint and producing expert testimony to the effect that such evidence was not acceptable as proof positive.

At this point, having thrown doubt on all of the material evidence presented by the prosecution, the defense went over to the matter of motive, producing psychological testimony to the effect that Dr. Fouad Talabani was sane and normal and that the murder carried out upon

Mrs. Talabani could not have been performed by a man who was either one or the other.

"You are asked to believe," said Dr. Bossi to the jury, "that this successful, happily married physician took his wife, without the slightest motive, to a clover field outside the city, there made passionate love to her and then beat her savagely about the face, strangled her, stabbed her thirteen times with a knife from their own kitchen and then inserted a cucumber, which he had gone forty miles to buy the previous day, into her vagina.

"You have heard the testimony that Dr. Talabani is a sane man. Would these have been the actions of a sane man?"

The jury obviously did not think so.

And then, the prosecution launched its counterattack.

An expert on Middle Eastern customs and civilization identified as Dr. Ludwig Graesslich was called to take the stand.

"Would you tell the jury, Dr. Graesslich," said the prosecuting attorney, "what in Iraq is the significance of a hollow cucumber placed in the vagina of a dead woman?"

"Well, the placing of a hollowed-out cucumber in the vagina of a dead, that is to say, murdered woman is a Kurdish custom still practiced today," said the doctor. "It signifies intense hatred for the woman on the part of the person who places the cucumber there and is intended as a sign of degradation and humiliation even after death."

"Thank you, Dr. Graesslich," said the prosecuting attorney.

The defense waived cross-examination of the doctor who was recognized in his field, but pointed out that this supported Dr. Talabani's theory that the Iraqian Secret Service had murdered his wife.

"The intent was clearly to degrade and humiliate Dr. Talabani," said the attorney for the defense, "for only he would have known the significance of the cucumber. Such an act would be pointless, if no one knew what it meant. What possible motive could Dr. Talabani have had to wish to degrade and humiliate his own wife and thus, by extension, himself?"

The argument was convincing, but the prosecution was not finished.

The next witnesses were psychologists from the clinic where Dr. Max Debusmann, the father of the murdered woman, had been undergoing treatment.

According to their testimony, Dr. Debusmann had not suffered his nervous collapse as a result of overwork, but rather due to a crisis within the family. There had, it seemed, been violent quarrels involving all of the family members and Dr. Talabani as well. These had taken place during July of 1974, the month before the murder of Freya Talabani.

"Before, however, that we go into the cause of these quarrels," said the prosecuting attorney, "it might be well to examine the relationship of Dr. Talabani to his father-in-law. We shall attempt to show that this was a warm relationship filled with admiration by the younger man for the older doctor who he regarded as a model of everything that could be expected of a German physician."

The defense objected on the grounds that Dr. Talabani's relations with his father-in-law were not pertinent to the case, but was overruled.

Witnesses were then brought who testified that Dr. Talabani had, indeed regarded his father-in-law with something approaching hero worship. Like many persons who change their nationality, Fouad Talabani was a far more enthusiastic German than are most native-born Germans and Dr. Max Debusmann was his ideal.

Talabani, who had been called back to take the stand admitted this.

"But," said the prosecuting attorney, "your admiration for the Debusmann family was abruptly shattered at the beginning of July, 1974, when you learned that the man who you so admired had been associated with the

171

euthanasia program of the Nazis prior to and during World War II. At that point, your love for the Debusmann family abruptly turned to hate. Is that not correct?"

Dr. Talabani did not answer.

The prosecuting attorney then presented his version of the events leading to the death of Mrs. Freya Talabani.

There had been, he suggested, monumental family quarrels following the disclosure of Dr. Debusmann's part in the Nazis' execution programs and there had been a break between Talabani and his wife.

Dr. Debusmann had gone to the mental hospital and there had been efforts, possibly by other members of the family, to effect a reconciliation.

Freya Talabani had apparently believed that her husband was in agreement with this and had accompanied him willingly to the clover field where they had had sexual intercourse, following which Dr. Talabani had killed her.

"The act," said the prosecuting attorney, "was premeditated. Otherwise, how did Dr. Talabani happen to have the family butcher knife and a cucumber, bought the day before, with him?"

Dr. Talabani now attempted to change his statement, saying that he had been passing the clover field when he suddenly saw his wife fighting violently with a strange man. It was, he said, the strange man who had killed her.

At this point, Dr. Bossi asked for a recess for consultation with his client.

Following the recess, the defense asked to change the defendant's plea from not guilty to guilty but with reduced responsibility due to severe mental stress.

The plea was accepted and on October 10, 1975, Dr. Fouad Talabani was sentenced to 10 years imprisonment, the sentence requested by the prosecution, but considered lenient by many observers in view of the premeditated nature of the act.

It has been announced that the sentence will be appealed.

"THE DOCTOR PRESCRIBED SEX ORGIES"
by Randall Shanley

The affair of the lecherous psychiatrist caused surprise and wonderment among the foreign press corps stationed in West Berlin and other parts of West Germany. None of them ever expected it would become a scandal of such epic proportions. None of them ever expected that the overwhelming majority of decent citizens throughout free Germany would react with such universal shock, horror and outrage.

During a discussion of the case after a trial session at the Court of Justice in July, one correspondent for a leading London newspaper, groping for some familiar frame of reference to bring it all into perspective, observed: "My God, it's as though the Prime Minister had been caught buggering little boys in Trafalgar Square at high noon!"

There was good reason for the surprise and wonderment in the press corps. Those who had any substantial length of service in the country had come to accept the fact that some of the most bizarre crimes in the world occurred in Germany with remarkable frequency and were accepted by the public with little more than passing interest. Sensational sex crimes, in particular, seemed to burst into the German press weekly, sometimes even more frequently, but few became anything more than journalistic three-day

174

wonders before they were replaced by more current sensations.

In short, the Germans seemed to accept with relative equanimity sex murders involving mutilation, decapitation, dismemberment — heterosexuals and/or homosexual — committed by members of any of the sexes of ages from eight to eighty.

Yet in the present instance, public outrage and shock had swept the whole country over a case which, by any standard of reference, should have been considered far less serious — in most countries — than any of the examples cited. It did not involve the murder of anyone, for one thing. No irreparable physical injury had been inflicted by violence perpetrated on any victim, for another. No sensational theft was involved, either, as, for example, a successful raid on the national treasury.

What, then, was the crime which had become a national emotional issue to every decent German?

It was a crime which in the United States, to cite one country only, probably would have been reported briefly on the back pages of all but the most sensationally-oriented newspapers.

It was "the corruption of public morals." To the orderly German mind, with its traditional respect for authority, this was a crime of the highest gravity. And in this instance, the gravity of the alleged offense was compounded many fold by the character of the man accused. He was one of free Germany's best-known and most highly regarded psychiatrists.

Dr. Hermann Tillmann was charged specifically with the seduction of eight girls who had not yet reached "the age of consent."

Dr. Tillman was charged further with inducing them by dire threats to engage in sexual encounters with a number of his friends. These friends, coincidentally, were men of high standing in the business, industrial and professional community of West Berlin, an element which added fuel to the wave of public indignation.

And there were still more charges lodged against the eminent psychiatrist. Dr. Tillmann was also accused of raping a 21-year-old girl.

As if that were not enough, the concluding count in the roster of crimes alleged to the handsome doctor was that he had forced his former wife to commit various sexual acts with a 16-year-old youth as he watched like a common degenerate voyeur.

The published reports of these charges pointed out that if Dr. Tillmann was found guilty of all of these charges—a very strong possibility—the court could sentence him to spend the remainder of his life in prison.

The shock engendered by publication of all these charges stemmed largely from the character of the accused. For Dr. Tillmann was a man who, in many ways, enjoyed a large degree of public trust, not only as a physician privileged to receive the confidences of his patients, but because of other things. He was one of West Berlin's leading psychiatrists and neurologists. His academic accomplishments were of the very highest; he had written and published learned books. He held membership on a wide variety of committees dedicated to the public welfare.

One of the Berlin newspapers compared the office which he maintained in his luxurious apartment on Olivaer Platz, just off the Kurfurstendamm—the Fifth Avenue of Berlin to a movie set. Court testimony given later would emphasize this comparison with the revelation that the entire "set" was bugged, not only electronically, but optically, with secret peepholes; two-way mirrors to permit surreptitious surveillance of activities in other rooms; a device which permitted the doctor to stand at his control console, throw a switch, and lock every door in every room of his fiendish layout, thus making prisoners of whoever happened to be occupying the rooms at the moment.

Physically, Dr. Tillmann certainly did not look anything like a monster who would be guilty of such actions. A tall, handsome man of 40 with a charming manner and the trim build of an athlete, he had built up a thriving practice among the wealthy. He enjoyed a very special popularity with middle-aged women in the upper strata of Berlin society.

According to published reports, it was estimated that he probably earned as much as $5,000 a week.

Once the charges against the handsome psychiatrist had been announced, the press went all out to dig up every scrap of information they could unearth about the man. The newspapers reported that according to associates and friends who knew him well, Dr. Tillmann's most conspicuous traits were his amazing energy and his efficient use of same. In order to take care of all his patients, he frequently worked as much as 16 hours a day, from around eight in the morning until midnight.

Yet despite this demanding schedule he still found time to give lectures at various universities and, from time to time, to give testimony in court cases as a state psychiatrist.

It was something of a mystery, when one considered the doctor's heavy schedule, how he also managed to pursue leisure time social activities as a man about town, but the fact that he did so was beyond dispute. Divorced from his wife, he was often observed driving his expensive Italian sports car—a custom-built Alfa Romeo which reportedly cost around $25,000. The sporty red two-seater was upholstered in genuine tiger skins. Rarely was Dr. Tillmann seen abroad in this spectacular vehicle without an equally spectacular young fraulein in the seat beside him.

He also was a frequent patron of the theater and the city's art galleries. And quite often he was seen with a party of friends at one of Berlin's more expensive night clubs.

One of his hobbies which endeared him to his women patients was his fondness for animals. He kept three cats and three large dogs, and he delighted in demonstrating how he had trained them to do whatever he told them. Some of these feats were reported to be extraordinary and

177

many of the people who had witnessed them declared the animals "understand every word he says to them."

"I seem to have some hypnotic power over them," they quoted the doctor. "I don't entirely understand it."

He also had an intense interest in rare and colorful tropical fish, and kept several hundred of them in tastefully appointed aquariums all over his luxurious apartment, and his office area as well.

This was the side of Dr. Tillmann's personality which was known to the public, and to most of his patients. By all outward appearances, he was a highly intelligent, charming, urbane man, a man who stood at the very pinnacle of his profession, a man full of zest for life.

Revelations which surfaced in the aftermath of the charges lodged against him, however, would indicate there was a startlingly different side to his character, a side known only to his closest friends. The details of that hidden side of Dr. Tillmann would be laid bare, in all its intriguing sordidness, at his trial.

These revelations would make it abundantly clear that Dr. Tillmann avidly pursued yet another hobby. He trained young girls to do whatever he told them, and in this, as one of the prosecutors would tell the court, "he had the same sort of hypnotic power which made it possible for him to command animals to do his bidding without question!"

The West Berlin police gained their first hint of what went on at the doctor's cocktail parties when they received a telephone call from the mother of a beautiful girl who was only 19 years old. The case was assigned to the Morals Squad, and Inspector Kurt Baumann drove to the apartment of the woman caller to investigate the complaint.

The veteran police officer was admitted by a rather frail-appearing middle-aged woman with an air of genteel desperation about her. She told the inspector that she was a widow and worked as a librarian to support her daughter.

"Erika has always been a problem to me," the woman

178

said sadly when they were seated in the modestly furnished living room. "I raised her from childhood without a father, and she grew up a highly emotional girl, restless and unhappy.

"Two years ago, when she was seventeen, she began running around with a wild crowd of young people. I saw trouble ahead for her and realized that she needed professional help, so I sent her to Dr. Hermann Tillmann."

The worried woman paused to wipe away the tears beginning to trickle from her eyes. Then she shook her head and said sadly, "I realize now that it was the worst mistake I possibly could have made."

Inspector Baumann recalled vaguely that Dr. Tillmann had been involved in a divorce action several years previously, but he knew very little about the man at this point. That was a temporary condition, however; very shortly he would make it his business to learn everything there was to learn about the prominent psychiatrist.

"Then the doctor was unable to help your daughter?" he asked the woman.

She bristled with bitterness as she replied: "He didn't even try! He took my money and began his treatments by seducing her!"

The inspector interrupted to remind her she was making a very grave charge, and he hoped she had proof of what she was alleging. She assured the detective she did.

"I had no idea what was going on," she continued, "because I don't get home until after the library closes at nine o'clock every evening. But Erika has just admitted that for nearly two years she has been attending a series of wild parties at his (Dr. Tillmann's) apartment, where perfectly disgraceful things went on."

As the angry woman paused to recover her composure, Inspector Baumann said gravely, "If he seduced your daughter while she was a minor, and under his professional care, then he is guilty of a very serious offense . . . What sort of things went on at these parties?"

"Well, Dr. Tillmann invited his friends over—other doc-

179

tors and businessmen. According to Erika, he persuaded the girls to go around his apartment in the nude, and to be intimate with the men."

"Were the other girls his patients, too?" asked the inspector.

"A few of them were," the mother replied. "Others were girls he had met through friends, or in bars and nightclubs. His own office girls also attended the parties and took part in the shocking behavior.

"Erika came home from one of his parties last night, drunk and crying her heart out. I finally persuaded her to unburden herself to me. She's waiting in her room now, and I want you to hear her story just as she told it to me."

The widow disappeared for a few moments and returned with a slender, sultry-eyed girl with honey-blonde hair done in a fashionable coiffure which made her appear older than the 19 years her mother said she was. She wore a shapeless black sweater which did little to conceal the splendid maturity of her bustline. She also wore skin-tight slacks and flat-heeled shoes.

The young blonde seemed self-conscious and a little afraid of the police inspector as she told him — with gentle prodding from him — of her experiences with the prominent psychiatrist, a man who was 21 years older than she was.

Erika said that at first, when she began seeing the doctor, they had had a normal doctor-patient relationship. She would lie on the couch in his consulting room and attempt to talk out her problems while he took notes and offered occasional comments.

But that didn't last long. One day as she lay there on his couch, she said, Dr. Tillmann began to fondle her breasts and tried to make love to her. She grew angry and resisted him, she added.

Then, quite candidly, she admitted that Tillmann was so handsome and pleasant, she was strongly attracted to him. The very next time he made advances, she yielded to him.

"I became his mistress," Erika said. "From then on,

180

when I came for my usual appointment, he would lock the door of his office and we would make love."

"Did you ever see him outside office hours?" the inspector wanted to know.

"Yes," the girl answered. "He took me out in the evening sometimes—to the theater and to night clubs. He even promised to marry me, but I didn't take him very seriously. I was very happy in those days."

"Mother noticed the change in me, although she didn't know what had caused it. She was pleased that she had sent me to Dr. Tillmann."

Despite her happiness during that period, Erika went on, there was one problem—she had fallen hopelessly in love with the brilliant, charming psychiatrist—and that was why she suffered such a shock when he first invited her to one of his cocktail parties.

"When I arrived, everyone was sitting on the floor, drinking and having a gay time," the blonde beauty said. "A record player was blasting, and somebody was beating out the rhythm on the bongo drums, while a pretty girl with long golden hair was doing a dance in the middle of the room. She didn't have a stitch of clothing on.

"She was completely nude!"

Erika went on to say that as the party progressed, the men induced other girls to strip naked. After a while, pairs of men and girls began disappearing into the bedroom together.

At one point, Dr. Tillmann came over to her and asked her if she was having a good time. When she told him testily that she wasn't having a good time at all, he seemed disturbed.

"It's good for people to forget their inhibitions once in a while," he assured her. "You'll get used to it soon."

"From then on," the girl continued, "he insisted that I come to all his parties. They were impromptu affairs. He just called up people and invited them over. Sometimes he excused himself to see patients and returned later. The girls

181

from his office always kept things going."

Erika said Tillmann persuaded her to serve drinks to his friends in the nude. They would be nude, and so would she. Then, one night, he insisted that she go into a bedroom with one of his friends.

As if she was reading the inspector's mind, she hastened to explain: "Dr. Tillmann has a very strong personality, and by this time I seemed to be completely under his influence. I did as he told me and submitted to his friend's advances when we went into the bedroom. Both of us were nude."

During the following months, the girl continued, the doctor forced her to engage in sex relations of various types with other men on many occasions. She said she hated herself for the life she was leading, but she seemed powerless to break the emotional hold that Dr. Tillmann had over her.

"Then last night I made a discovery," Erika continued after a brief pause to light a cigarette. "I found out that the doctor had a special 'see-through' mirror between his office and the master bedroom, so that he could watch his guests as they made love.

"He had been sending me into that room with his friends *so that he could watch us from his office!*

"I realized then that Dr. Tillmann was a depraved monster. When I came home last night, I told mother everything, and I never intend to see that man again."

Inspector Baumann asked her for the names of Dr. Tillmann's friends, and she recited as many as she could recall. She also provided him with the names of some of the girls, but there were many she knew only by their first names, or by nicknames. Some of the girls she didn't know at all.

Inspector Baumann assured Erika and her mother that the police would launch an investigation at once. Returning to police headquarters, Baumann went directly to the chief inspector of the Morals Squad and made a full report. It was decided to begin an undercover inquiry into the private life of the fashionable psychiatrist. Inspector Baumann was assigned full charge of the investigation.

"Track down the under-age girls and attempt to get full statements from them, implicating the men," the chief inspector instructed him. "Also get inside Tillmann's apartment yourself and see what goes on there. Try to attend one of his parties."

The inspector began by assigning two research men to dig into the psychiatrist's background. He instructed another officer to look up the court records of Tillmann's divorce action.

"As I recall, his wife charged him with infidelity," he told the detectives. "Try to locate her and bring her to headquarters. She could prove to be a very valuable witness against Tillmann."

The inspector assigned other detectives to locate the party girls and take statements from them. Then he telephoned Dr. Tillmann's secretary and made an appointment with him for late that afternoon. As he saw it, the best way to get into the psychiatrist's apartment was to become his patient.

Arriving at the doctor's office, Baumann was shown into a spacious waiting room furnished in expensively impeccable taste. The walls were decorated with valuable bronze bas reliefs. Gaily-colored tropical fish of improbable shapes swam about in glass tanks. The floor was richly carpeted and the doors were covered not with paint, but with gold leaf.

The waiting room was filled with patients, mostly expensively dressed women in their forties and fifties, and Inspector Baumann had to wait his turn. At last he was shown into a lavishly decorated office where the handsome doctor sat behind a massive desk of highly polished ebony.

The inspector noted that Dr. Tillmann, with his suavely professional manner and his conservatively styled London-tailored clothes, appeared to be a sort of Hollywood version of a successful German psychiatrist. He had a "Heidelberg scar" on his left cheek, the result of a saber wound which was a reminder of the blood sport which used to be very popular among certain German men as a badge of their courage and virility.

Some of the Berlin newspapers later would hint that in Dr. Tillmann's case, the scar was not the result of a duel for sport or honor, but had been self-inflicted for effect. No conclusive evidence of this charge was ever produced, however.

Inspector Baumann described himself to the psychiatrist as a harried businessman with jangled nerves, an unruly digestion, and chronic insomnia.

"Those are common complaints here in Berlin, with the Communists practically breathing down our necks," Dr. Tillmann said sympathetically. "Aside from the political factor, though, they are typical of what we call the 'executive syndrome.'

"Fortunately, the trained neurologist can usually treat such cases very effectively. I'm a busy man, sir, but I believe I can fit you into my schedule."

Inspector Baumann said he was grateful for that, and after some discussion about fees, it was arranged that the doctor would see him twice a week, with evening appointments at eight o'clock.

It was very close to that hour right now, and as the inspector left the office he could hear the muffled sounds of faraway voices and gay feminine laughter.

Instead of leaving the building and proceeding to the street, Baumann slipped through a hall door leading into the doctor's apartment.

The voices grew louder, to the background accompaniment of the steady beat of American rock and roll music coming from a powerful stereo player. In the living room ahead of him, the inspector could see dignified looking middle-aged men dancing with slim-bodied young girls. Two couples were locked in close embrace on a studio couch.

But then Baumann heard someone coming so he ducked through the nearest doorway. He found himself in a thick-carpeted bedroom, the principal furniture of which was an oversized bed covered in cloth of gold. The walls were hung with heavy draperies, and the ceiling appeared to be sound-absorbent. The inspector realized he was in a sound-proofed room.

Then he noticed a small round mirror on a wall. He recognized it at once as the "see-through" mirror Erika had described. Anyone in the adjoining room would have a full view of the bed and whoever was occupying it.

The inspector then left the apartment, afraid that if he should be discovered there the doctor would suspect at once that he was under investigation.

Late the following day, Baumann's research team brought him information on the psychiatrist's background. Dr. Hermann Tillmann was a native of Bonn, the capital of West Germany. He had been born of a very old and distinguished family which in recent generations apparently had gone to seed.

Tillmann's grandfather had been a prosperous merchant but an eccentric; he had committed suicide while still only in his forties. The psychiatrist's father had been a gifted surgeon, but he had developed an acute nerve condition which ultimately led to his suicide at the age of 65. One of Tillmann's uncles had become mentally unbalanced early in life. He was committed to an institution and eventually died there.

Apparently untouched by the mental instability in his family background, Tillmann had been a bright student in the local schools and at medical college. He had interned in Berlin hospitals, and then had gone on to specialize in neurology and psychiatry. Within a very short time of entering private practice he had built up a large and extremely lucrative clientele.

The researchers had been able to learn very little about the doctor's present pattern of living or his cocktail parties, but during the next few days, detectives interviewed a number of teenaged girls whose names had been supplied by Erika. One of these girls was a patient; the others were girls the doctor had met through friends or possibly had picked up in bars or nightclubs.

Their stories were similar to Erika's. The doctor had been a perfect gentleman at first. Then, after winning their confidence, he had seduced them, sometimes promising them marriage to overcome their resistance to the idea of yielding to his sexual advances. After that, his pattern was consistent.

When he had made each of them emotionally dependent on him, he threatened to break off the relationship unless they attended his parties and took part in the promiscuous sexual activity. All of them, eventually, had yielded to his wishes.

It seemed clear to the investigators that Dr. Tillmann seemed to derive a perverse, unnatural pleasure from the deliberate, systematic degradation of young girls.

The detectives had not attempted to talk with the three girls employed in Tillmann's office because of the fear that they would tip off the doctor to the ongoing investigation. From a doorman, however, they learned about a young receptionist who recently had left Tillmann's employ after being with him for nearly five years. Like Erika, apparently, she could no longer stomach the doctor's cocktail parties and the promiscuous hi-jinks that went on at them.

This girl provided the investigators with a wealth of information about Dr. Tillmann's bizarre menage. Among his other peculiarities, he was a veritable kook about electrical devices of all kinds. In his car he had an electric coffee maker, an electric perfume sprayer, and another electrical device which rang a bell when the car was in danger of skidding on ice.

His apartment was a network of electrical wiring. He had sensitive microphones concealed in fireplaces and lamps, behind pictures, and under chairs and tables in every room. He even had microphones under the chairs in his waiting room.

186

By pushing one of 25 buttons on a console in a drawer of his desk, Tillmann could eavesdrop on anything being said by his employees, his patients, or his guests, anywhere in the apartment or his suite of offices—and by flicking another switch he could record every word of their conversations!

The doctor also could listen in on all calls received on the telephones in his offices and apartment, and these too could be recorded if he wished. He also had installed a device by which he could lock and unlock, separately or all together, all the doors in his establishment.

Dr. Tillmann's former receptionist said that because of his extravagant tastes in clothes, cars, interior decorating and electrical gadgets, the doctor was about 100,000 marks in debt. This, she said, was largely responsible for his compulsive work habits. Constantly dunned by his creditors, he worked himself almost to the breaking point, taking many more patients than he could do justice to.

He had not taken a vacation in 10 years, nor had he found time to read medical journals or books. Actually, it appeared, he was behind the times in his profession, but he had been able to disguise the fact by his quick intelligence, his eloquence and his persuasive personality. The constant strain under which he lived had driven him to increase his drinking, however, according to the secretary, and to seek escape in the world of uninhibited sex practices.

At this point in the probe, detectives located the psychiatrist's former wife, who was living obscurely in Berlin and working to support Tillmann's daughter, born shortly after her divorce from him. When brought to headquarters, the slender, attractive brunette, still only 24 years old, proved to be a willing witness against her former husband. The young woman, who came from a highly respected family, had gone to work as a stenographer in the doctor's office at the age of 16. In due course he had proposed marriage, after which he seduced her.

"He kept postponing the wedding date until I threatened him with a breach of promise suit," she said. "Then he married me in a hurry. He was worried that the publicity of a lawsuit would ruin him professionally."

For several years their marriage had been a fairly ordinary one, the young woman said. Then the doctor, working under constant pressure, had begun drinking every evening, and the wild parties had begun. He had insisted that his wife take part in them, and she did so reluctantly, she said. But then she began to drink, too, and soon she came to accept the parties as a normal part of the hectic life they were leading.

"One night he asked me for 'proof of my love,'" Tillmann's ex-wife told detectives. "He insisted that I go to bed with a sixteen-year-old boy. I didn't realize how twisted his mind had become, and I did as he asked me. But this was only the beginning. He forced me to have relations with many other men. He seemed to get some special thrill out of that. I learned later that when I thought I was alone with a man — or that young boy — he was watching us through his see-through window and recording every word we spoke on a hidden tape recorder.

"At last I became so disgusted with him that I sued for divorce. He knew I could ruin his practice if I told everything I knew, so he didn't contest the divorce. But I still despise that man, and if he's been ruining the lives of other young girls as he did mine, I'm ready to testify against him in court."

Inspector Baumann took a long statement from the psychiatrist's former wife which described many shocking details of the doctor's sex parties.

It was formidable evidence indeed, but Baumann was anxious to get a witness who could provide evidence about the doctor's criminal activities in the more recent past. His men found one witness who provided a small measure of what he wanted, a former nurse in residence at the Tillmann apartment. Her name was Angela Neubauer, who said she had refused to be seduced, and had successfully guarded the door of her room when some of

188

Tillmann's male guests tried to gain entry in hopes of having sex relations with her.

But Inspector Baumann wanted more than that. He was still visiting the psychiatrist regularly as a patient, but thus far he had been unable to crash one of the doctor's parties. Hoping for a break, Baumann took to keeping the apartment-office under surveillance in the evenings after his sessions with Tillmann. The break he was hoping for finally came one snowy evening as he saw a young couple leave the building hurriedly. The girl, a lovely brunette, was sobbing and her young male escort had his arm around her, trying to comfort the girl. Baumann caught a scrap of their conversation and heard the young man say they'd catch a taxi to the police station "to report your doctor friend for the sex maniac he is."

Baumann approached them at once, identified himself as a police officer, and said he would drive them to the police station himself. At headquarters he took the couple before the chief inspector.

Dabbing her eyes with a hankie, the 21-year-old girl, whose name was Inga, told a shocking story. She said that she had met the doctor at the home of a friend and he had invited her to a party. She had accepted on the condition that she might bring along her fiancé to the affair.

"I had no idea what kind of a party it was to be," the girl said. "When we arrived a girl was dancing in the nude while the men made lewd remarks. Other girls took off their clothes later. A fat, middle-aged man asked me to dance with him, then led me into a dark room and began taking shocking liberties. I slapped him and broke away from him."

Later, Dr. Tillmann asked her to dance, Inga said. She had liked him when they met and felt no hesitation about dancing with him.

"He asked me if I would like to see his apartment, and I said I would," the girl continued. "He took me into a bedroom that was hung with heavy drapes and had a big bed with a gold cover on it. Then he pressed a button some-

189

where in the wall and the door closed behind us and I heard the lock click. The next instant he had his arms around me. 'Your boy friend needn't know anything about this,' he told me."

Inga said that when she realized his intentions she struggled free of him and ran to the door. But she found that it had no knob on the inside, and she could not open it. She pounded against its padded surface and screamed, but Tillmann only laughed.

"It's a soundproof room," he told her. "Go ahead and scream. Nobody will hear you."

Then he seized her again. She tried to fight him but he was much too strong for her. He dragged her over to the bed and raped her.

"Then he told me again that I must not tell my boy friend what had happened," Inga said. "He threatened to do something even worse to me if I ever told anyone. Then he pressed the secret button again and let me out of the room."

The girl said that she told her fiancé at once that the doctor had raped her. He wanted to give Tillmann a beating, but she persuaded him that they must leave at once and go to the police and report.

When the girl had finished her story, Inspector Baumann asked her: "Would you be willing to testify in court to what you've just told me?"

"Yes!" the girl said vehemently. "I'll do anything I can to help put that man in jail!"

When he had arranged to have the couple driven to their homes, Baumann discussed the case with the chief inspector. They decided that they now had sufficient evidence to turn the matter over to the prosecutor's office for further action.

On the heels of this, Inspector Baumann and a group of officers went to Tillmann's office the next day and placed the psychiatrist under arrest. Tillmann, taken completely by surprise, protested his arrest indignantly, but offered no resistance as he was led through a waiting room full of astonished patients and out of the building to a police car.

Other police contingents, meanwhile, were rounding up a score of the doctor's men friends who had attended his parties. All were taken before a judge. The men, most of them prominent figures in business and professional circles of West Berlin, were assured that their identities would not be disclosed, and then all were released on bail. Dr. Tillmann, charged with a wide range of serious offenses, was denied bail and ordered to prison.

The case came to trial some six months later, in early July, before a woman judge, Magistrate Yorck von Worthenburg. By this time the prosecutor, a brilliant and vigorous 34-year-old woman, Hilda Vierlich-Muller—had built the strongest possible case against the accused Dr. Tillmann, who sat pale and silent before the court as he heard himself charged with a shocking variety of offenses against the under-age girls, against his own wife, and against the 21-year-old Inga, who claimed he had raped her.

For eight days, Dr. Tillmann's pretty young victims testified against him on the witness stand as a battery of journalists from all over Europe jammed the press section. By order of the court only the first names of the victims were revealed.

One of the high points of the trial, from which the public was excluded, was the testimony of a lovely brunette beauty contest winner named Marthe, who had gone to Dr. Tillmann in desperate need of psychiatric help. The stunning 20-year-old girl had attempted suicide over a broken romance. Failing in this, she had begun to drink heavily.

Instead of helping her back to mental health, the eminent psychiatrist had allegedly gotten her drunk, seduced her, and then led her into a life of debauchery. Marthe told the court that the doctor, when accepting her as a patient, had told her she need not worry about money.

"How often were you with him?" Judge von Worthenburg asked the witness.

"Nearly every night the first three weeks," the girl replied.

"And what happened?"

"I told him about my childhood, my youth, and my whole life. When I said I wanted to get away from drinking, he asked me how much drinking I could stand, and he said he wanted to test me. He insisted that we drink together. It was then that we first became intimate. I was too drunk to resist him."

"And did you come home very late that night?"

"Yes," the witness replied to the judge's question, "and drunk. My parents were furious with me and my father ordered me out of the house. So I went back to Dr. Tillmann and he took me in."

Responding to another question, Marthe said she attended the doctor's parties many times. The magistrate then asked her what she did at them.

"Well, some of the girls walked around with hardly any clothes on," she answered hesitantly.

"*Hardly* any clothes?" the judge echoed sharply. "We have already been told that the girls were nude, and *you* must have been nude, too."

Marthe then admitted this was so. She went on to testify that the doctor, to whom she had come for help with her drinking problem, had encouraged her to drink at his parties, and then had induced her to have intimate sex relations with his male guests at the very bawdy parties he hosted regularly.

The lurid testimony of Marthe and the other witnesses left little doubt of Tillmann's guilt. In the psychiatrist's defense, his attorney, Dr. Otto Weyer, could only plead that Tillmann had worked so long under a severe strain that he had succumbed to the mental illness present in his family strain.

"He is one of Berlin's leading psychiatrists," Attorney Weyer said to the court, "but he himself finally needed a psychiatrist more than his patients did."

The jury of eight men and two women was unimpressed

by this defense, however. To them, it seemed that the doctor was in sufficient command of his faculties to plot the deliberate seduction and rape of innocent girls with the help of soundproof rooms and doors without doorknobs.

After listening to the witnesses and viewing all the evidence presented in the 10-day trial, the jurors deliberated and returned a verdict which pronounced Dr. Hermann Tillmann guilty on all counts.

The doctor's co-defendants were convicted only of contributing to the delinquency of minors, and they were let off with fines of varying amounts. As for the chief defendant, Dr. Hermann Tillmann, the court decreed that his punishment would be a sentence of six years in the penitentiary.

Inasmuch as he could have been sentenced to prison for life, many Germans, still outraged by Dr. Tillmann's corruption of public morals, expressed indignation that he should have been let off so lightly. Some, however, took comfort in the thought that his prison cell would be barred by a door which could not be opened by pressing a secret button.

EDITOR'S NOTE:
Erika, Inga and Marthe are not the real names of the persons so named in the foregoing story. Fictitious names have been used in order to comply with German police regulations.

"12 VICTIMS FOR THE ANGEL OF DEATH!"

by Jack Goulding

Four days before she died, Mrs. Florence Gibbs, 66, walked into Centinela Hospital in Inglewood, California, complaining of nausea and stomach pains. It was a weekend and most doctors' offices were closed so her family took her to the hospital for an examination.

The diagnosis was high blood sugar. She lapsed into what appeared to be a diabetic coma and was placed in an intensive care unit at the hospital.

After treatment, the woman soon appeared to be on the road to recovery, and her family was told she would be able to return to her home the following day and would be placed on a liquid diet.

But the elderly woman never left Centinela Hospital alive. Hours after she had been told she was well enough to go home, Florence Gibbs was dead. Her relatives and friends, including the family doctor, were absolutely stunned by the suddenness of her death.

There was a notation in the death report filed by the county coroner's office which read tersely, "A daughter said someone gave her mother poison." It was dated March 5, 1981, the day the woman died. Nonetheless, the cause of death was officially listed as "hypertensive arteriosclerotic cardio vascular disease." However, previous examinations did not indicate that the woman had ever suffered heart disease.

No autopsy was performed on Florence Gibbs, and her death still remains a mystery.

Mrs. Gibbs' family were convinced Florence met with foul play. One relative told a newspaper reporter that someone had killed her. "I feel it in my mind, and it just keeps boiling up in me . . . She told me to take her out of that hospital. I didn't."

Often in the case of elderly persons who die of apparent heart conditions autopsies are not performed unless there is good reason to suspect foul play. Coronary ailments in elderly persons are not unusual.

And there the Gibbs case rested.

With the benefit of hindsight, an autopsy should have been done shortly after her death. It might have helped save the lives of a number of elderly hospital patients.

On April 21, 1981, two months after the death of Mrs. Gibbs, a deputy coroner in San Bernadino County received an anonymous phone call from a woman shortly after midnight. She informed him that 19 sudden and mysterious deaths had occurred in the Community Hospital of the Valleys near Perris in a period of two weeks.

Actually, it turned out that there were 11 such deaths in the 36-bed Perris hospital and one in the 68-bed hospital in nearby Banning.

The unlucky dozen men and women who fell victim to an unknown killer were identified by the Riverside County Sheriff's Department as:

Irene Anne Graham, 89, of Perris. She was admitted to the Perris Hospital on March 29th and was pronounced dead on March 30th.

Bernard Vernon-Lee Kean, 52, of Perris. He was admitted to the hospital on April 4th and died the same day.

Beatrice Roberson Cline, 79, of Perris, admitted on April 4th and died the following day.

Minnie Lee Dampsey, 89, of Sun City. Admitted to Perris Hospital April 4th and died the following day.

195

Gertrude I. Bryant, 63, of Perris. Admitted April 6th and died the 11th.

John W. Rainwater, 95, Mead Valley. Admitted April 9th and died on April 11th.

Kenneth Lancelot Silvera, 82, Perris. Admitted April 13th and died April 14th.

Marian E. Stewart, 80, Sun City. Admitted on April 10th, died April 14th.

Henry Castro, 65, Mead Valley. Admitted on April 17th and died April 20th.

Virginia Bayless, 78, Perris. Admitted April 19th, died April 20th.

Bertha Mae Boyce, 74, Homeland. Admitted April 20th, died April 22nd.

J. Clifford Swanson, 79, Cherry Valley. Admitted April 21st, died April 25th. He was the only Lidocaine victim to die at the San Gorgonio Pass Memorial Hospital in Banning.

All these deaths occurred in March and April of 1981. And every one of them was a mystery. The victims were elderly men and women. The symptoms were the same in every case, and there was no apparent motive in any one of them.

All expired at the same time of day—one a.m., four a.m. or seven a.m. and all died in critical care wards in the hospitals.

The Riverside County Sheriff's Office came down hard on the Perris Hospital for not informing the office of the unusually large number of deaths under what appeared to be the same set of circumstances.

Detectives began their investigation by questioning staff members in both hospitals.

When the Los Angeles county coroner learned of the increasing number of elderly people dying in the intensive care units in Riverside and San Bernadino County hospitals, he told newsmen that the bodies of as many as 30 patients who died under somewhat unusual circumstances in Los Angeles County may have to be exhumed.

Autopsies performed on several elderly patients who died in Riverside County hospitals detected lethal doses of Lidocaine, a powerful heart medication, in the body tissue.

In one case the amount of Lidocaine found in tissue samples was 50% higher than the lethal dose. In four cases Lidocaine was found in patients for whom no Lidocaine had been prescribed.

Authorities in Riverside County said that some of the Lidocaine retrieved from the Perris Hospital had been adulterated . . . why or by whom had not been determined. Nevertheless, it was still deadly.

Officials at Perris Hospital suspected someone had been tampering with the Lidocaine. Most of the hospital's supply of the drug was returned to the manufacturer in Chicago.

Investigators in Chicago found that, in some cases, the samples contained an unusually low concentration of the drug. But in at least one case, the concentration of Lidocaine recovered from syringes used at the hospital "was much higher than the stated concentration on the ampule package."

The manufacturer checked its own supplies of Lidocaine from the same lot used by Perris Hospital but found no irregularities.

An intensive examination of some of the bodies did determine that Lidocaine, a powerful drug used to stabilize heart rhythms, had been detected. The drug also has a tendency to remain undetectable after it has been in the body for long periods of time. It also has the tendency to accumulate in the body after a series of normal doses.

Then came the case of Raymond A. Palmer, 58, who died in Centinela Hospital on Feb. 1, 1981, the same hospital in which Mrs. Gibbs died under mysterious circumstances a month later.

Palmer had a long history of chronic lung disease. (Mrs. Gibbs did not.) Palmer had been kept alive on a respirator. Mrs. Gibbs was not in this category.

Suddenly Palmer developed low blood sugar. So, later, did Mrs. Gibbs.

A lung specialist said Palmer responded to the standard treatment for insulin overdose—a solution of water and sugar. He responded, then died after he developed an uncontrolled heart rhythm followed by a complete heart stoppage, as had Mrs. Gibbs.

Given the patient's past medical history, the lung specialist at first believed his patient died of natural causes but qualified that by saying that Palmer might have been given an unnecessary injection of insulin—or an injection of Lidocaine. He said he doubted an insulin injection would be detectable at the time of the autopsy.

The doctor said Palmer was so ill that there was an informal agreement with the family that no heroic measures were to be taken to sustain his life. Any illness would have killed him.

The death of Bertha Mae Boyce, 74, of the community of Homeland, was another strange one. She was admitted to the Perris Hospital on April 17, 1981. On April 22nd she died and her body was sealed in a casket, loaded into the back of a station wagon at a mortuary in Riverside and taken to a crematorium where sheriff's officers seized it before it could be disposed of.

Sheriff's detectives saw no deliberate coverup attempt in this move but rather the result of administration confusion between the hospital, the mortuary and the crematorium.

Batteries of sophisticated toxicological tests later showed that Mrs. Boyce died of a massive overdose of Lidocaine—the drug that was linked to 10 other deaths at Perris Hospital and one at the San Gorgonio Pass Hospital in Banning.

Despite the fact that the investigation into the deaths had been going on for some time, detectives had been unable to get a handle on it. It seemed that the best approach would be to focus on the work schedules of hospital personnel. They felt certain that the anonymous woman who

198

had first reported the unusual number of deaths was herself a member of the staff. She knew the names of the dead, the filing numbers of the medical reports of the victims, and the working habits of most of the staff members.

At this point, a member of the medical staff told detectives that some of his notes had been taken from one of the intensive care units. And he identified the person he suspected of the theft. The detectives obtained a search warrant and staged a late night raid at the home of a male nurse at Perris Hospital.

But what interested the detectives more than the theft of the notes was that the nurse's work hours coincided with the hours the murders were committed and he worked in the same section of the hospital—the intensive care unit.

They found no stolen notes in his home but what they did find were two vials of Lidocaine and a quantity of morphine, a syringe, and a small amount of heart medicine.

The nurse said he inadvertently brought the Lidocaine home some time before. Frequently in emergency situations, he said, nurses and doctors put medications in their coat pockets and forget them.

The nurse said he found the half empty vial of morphine in the hospital and was going to report it to the director of nursing but, by then, he was no longer working in that hospital. The nurse said the syringe was given to him by a friend to treat a pet cat.

While the man was being questioned by newsmen after the raid on his home in Riverside, the family of the late Florence Gibbs was watching TV in Los Angeles. They recognized the male nurse at once and recalled that he had cared for their mother shortly before her death at Centinela Hospital in March, 1981.

But neither the male nurse nor anyone else had been charged with the murder of the Los Angeles woman because of lack of evidence. As a matter of fact, the male nurse denied any unethical connection with the patients who died under mysterious circumstances in the two Riverside County hospitals over a period of two years when he worked there.

He said a combination of misdiagnoses by doctors in the hospitals, the possible contamination of drugs, administered to patients and inadequate supervision by the nursing staff could also have contributed to the deaths.

He told detectives that some nights, he was the only registered nurse on duty in the 36-bed hospital in Perris. He said records available to him lacked medical histories, and notes on changes in the condition of patients were not left in his care. He said he would have to use his best judgment in emergency situations.

The nurse told officers he tried unsuccessfully to persuade his superiors to determine whether the hospital's supply of Lidocaine was contaminated and that he was "scared" by the high number of deaths that occurred during the 11 days he worked in the hospital.

He said that on his first night at the Perris Hospital, two patients died on his shift. He said he felt that the district attorney's office was trying to railroad him and hinted he was a prime suspect in the murder cases.

He said one patient died on his shift on April 23, 1981, at the San Gorgonio Pass Hospital in Banning. He said he did not minister to that patient but a doctor did.

It was not until Nov. 23, 1981, five months after his home was searched and the drugs found that the male nurse, Robert Diaz, 42, was taken into custody, and booked on 12 murder charges.

This was the first time Diaz was actually named in direct connection with the murder counts. An earlier charge of drug possession against him had been dropped.

The warrant for his arrest charged him with the deaths of 11 patients at the hospital in Perris and one in Banning.

Riverside County Assistant District Attorney Thomas Hollenhorst said that Diaz's arrest came after several exhumations and a study of hospital records, which showed a "common plan and design" in all 12 deaths.

Hollenhorst said all the murders occurred at hospitals while Diaz worked in them. The victims died on the early morning shifts while Diaz was working on coronary and intensive care shifts.

D.A. Hollenhorst, who is now a municipal court judge, said it seemed unusual that all the victims died at specific times — one a.m. and four a.m. — when Diaz was working and shortly before seven a.m. when he left the hospital and went home. "There almost appeared to be a time for dying," Hollenhorst said. Diaz was on duty on 10 of the shifts in a 12-day period when patients died.

Diaz's arrest on the murder charges came after nearly seven months of intense efforts to unravel the case.

Hospital records showed that Diaz had been linked in one way or another with every one of the murder victims. Before they died, all had complained of dizziness, violent seizures, high blood acid contents, and an unusual blueness of the body from the chest up.

Diaz fought back by filing a multi-million dollar suit, charging the County of Riverside with defamation of character and violation of his civil rights. He complained that his life had been ruined by the charges and pointed to the fact that he had been under a cloud of suspicion for months, and no charges had been filed against him for nearly a year. And even at that stage of the investigation, the evidence was admittedly circumstantial.

Hollenhorst declared, "The evidence is complex and requires testimony from medical experts. This is going to be a difficult case to prosecute."

Who was Robert Diaz? He admitted that he always wanted to be a doctor but thought he was too old for medical school and settled for nursing school at Purdue University at Calumet, Indiana. He had earned his way through school by doing astrological forecasts and charts for his friends and other students.

Diaz described himself as an Egyptian mystic who had really lived in another life in the body of King Tut. For the most part his fellow students considered him to be a good nurse but something of a crackpot.

He also claimed to be the great, great, great grandson of El Cid, the Spanish national hero who conquered Valencia from the Moors in 1094.

"He was a big talker," recalled a classmate who asked that her name not be used. "He drove everyone crazy. He always wanted to tell everyone else in the class about nursing studies, but he was a very poor student himself. We just didn't see how he was ever going to make it, but he really persevered."

One relative of Diaz said he once insisted on having his pet dog put to death by having someone hold he animal while he gassed it with a hose linked to the kitchen stove. Diaz seemed to enjoy telling his family of gory medical procedures he participated in and chose the dinner hour to relate them, the relative said.

Diaz was one of 13 children of a family in the steel town of Gary, Indiana. He joined the marines at age 18, but he deserted and was discharged as unsuitable for military service. One person told authorities that, while Diaz was studying nursing, he always insisted that he be introduced to guests as "Doctor Diaz."

After a two-month long preliminary hearing, the murder counts lodged against Diaz had been lowered to 12 from the original 27. Some of the victims were killed directly by Lidocaine poisoning; in other cases Lidocaine intoxication contributed to their deaths.

Diaz's trial finally got underway in early 1984. Superior Court Judge John J. Barnard heard it without a jury. It dragged on for nearly five months. Not once during that period did the prosecution ever offer a motive in the multiple killings.

During the trial, a number of nurses in the hospitals where the crimes took place testified that Diaz seemed to "enjoy playing doctor for critically ill patients during medical emergencies."

It wasn't until the trial got under way that the public became aware of the enormity of the crime. Twelve elderly persons, many of whom were clinging to life by a thread, had it snatched away from them by a cold-blooded killer who used them as puppets for his amusement.

The trial, largely a joust among medical experts, consisted of 71 witnesses for the prosecution and 12 for the defense.

Some medical experts testifying for the defense argued that the patients could have died from heart disease or other ailments of old age, not necessarily from illicit injections of drugs.

They said, for example, that therapeutic doses of the drug in question can accumulate in patients suffering from heart problems, thus accounting for the high level found in the bodies of the victims. Among the 71 witnesses called by the prosecution, the testimony varied. Some said he liked to "play doctor," that he often behaved in bizarre ways, sometimes predicting that patients who appeared to be in stable condition would soon get into trouble and die—and some did.

One nurse recalled that she was once talking to Diaz when he told her that Lee Jones, a patient, was "going to have some trouble" that night. Then on March 25, 1981, during Diaz's 11-to-7 shift, Jones died—just as Diaz had predicted.

Diaz also told nurses that he often carried Lidocaine on his person just in case an emergency arose. Prosecution testimony showed that an 82-year-old patient fought desperately to keep from taking a Lidocaine shot. Fortunately, a nurse stepped in and took charge and the shot was not administered.

Several hospital nurses recalled they had seen Diaz "flitting" from room to room in the dark stillness of the night administering shots that had not been authorized by doctors.

Diaz was on the stand for six days testifying that he gave life saving injections only when it involved a life and death situation.

As for his uncanny death predictions, the defense argued that Diaz predicted difficulty for some patients only after noting that their physical condition was deteriorating. And in every statement he made from the witness stand, Diaz insisted that he had never injected a single patient with a fatal overdose of Lidocaine.

During his testimony, Diaz recalled the case of 79-year-old Beatrice Cline who was admitted to the hospital on her birthday, April 4th. He said, "She came in wearing a bunny suit (pajamas)." He recalled how she held his hand and how he tried to comfort her.

"That one got to me," he said, but he did not elaborate. That patient died on April 5th. Diaz eventually was accused of her murder.

Diaz also testified that one night one of his patients was reeking of alcohol, was very combative and died the day after he was admitted. Diaz said valium, morphine, and Lidocaine were ordered for that patient but none had any effect. The defendant said he could not recall who ordered the Lidocaine for the patient but insisted, "I did not give that patient any medication that night."

In his cross-examination of Diaz, Deputy D.A. Patrick Magers emphasized discrepancies between Diaz's testimony and that of previous witnesses but Diaz refused to change his position. Another doctor testified he left his notes on the case in the intensive care unit where Diaz worked but the notes were missing from the patient's medical history and were not found.

Diaz denied he had ever seen such notes, but it was this incident that led to the police search of Diaz's home where the drugs were uncovered.

Much of the testimony offered by Diaz, about the quantity of Lidocaine administered to patients, was contradicted by the testimony of other witnesses. Diaz said it always was within the bounds set by the hospital when he administered it.

The suspect denied he ever referred to himself and another nurse as "the deadly duo" because a number of their patients died, as one witness had testified. He also denied an allegation that he flitted in and out of the patients' rooms "like a butterfly."

Asked if he had ever injected a patient with a gram of Lidocaine "and watched what happened," Diaz denied it. He did admit that he sometimes played the role of a physician during emergency medical procedures for some patients because doctors on duty did absolutely nothing.

In any case, on Friday, March 30, 1984, little more than three years since the first death was reported, Judge John J. Barnard returned a guilty verdict against Diaz of murdering 12 elderly patients by giving them overdoses of a heart regulating drug at two Riverside County hospitals where he had been employed.

No sooner had the verdict been returned against Diaz than he turned to his attorneys at the counsel table and began discussing his upcoming penalty trial. Because of the "special circumstances" in the multiple murders, Diaz faced either death in the gas chamber or life in prison without the possibility of parole. But since the trial was a capital case, an appeal of the verdict is automatic.

Public Defenders Michael B. Lewis and John J. Lee told reporters, "We are satisfied we got a fair trial from the judge." Lewis said he hadn't yet decided what approach he would take on the pending appeal.

Asked how he felt about the verdict, Public Defender Lewis replied tersely, "Disappointment." Deputy D.A. Magers, who prosecuted the case, commented, "I feel wonderful."

Earlier, Magers had called Diaz "nothing but a killer." He said that the prosecution's case was designed to be all or nothing. Either Diaz had to be found guilty of all 12 murders or acquitted of all of them.

Magers said, "If I had to point to one piece of evidence that stands out in my mind it would have to be the syringes."

He was referring to three syringes containing traces of Lidocaine. When full, those syringes would have contained one gram of the drug, 10 times more than standard doses used for therapeutic purposes.

The syringes were recovered from the hospital in Perris where 11 of the patients died between March 30th and April 22, 1981.

Two of the syringes had been hand-labeled by Diaz with the name of the patient who had received the drug.

They had been placed in a box the hospital used to collect Lidocaine syringes after the coroner's office began investigating the mysterious deaths there. Testifying as one of 12 defense witnesses, Diaz explained the syringes introduced into evidence were not the same ones he had placed in the box.

Two weeks after the guilty verdict was returned, Diaz was sentenced to death in the gas chamber.

Handing down the death penalty, Judge Barnard said he chose the capital penalty because "aggravating circumstances in the case outweighed the mitigating circumstance." But he did not elaborate.

Prosecutor Magers said, "Just the gravity and nature of the offense were the primary factors the judge was guided by. Mr. Diaz murdered 12 people in cold premeditated, and deliberate fashion by poisoning."

Defense Attorney Lewis told a reporter, "I am very disappointed and unhappy about the sentence. I thought there was serious, reasonable doubt about his guilt. Because of that I didn't think the death penalty was warranted."

One of the mysteries surrounding the five-month trial was the question of motive for all the killings. During the penalty phase of the trial, Prosecutor Magers answered that question succinctly when he declared that Diaz committed the murders for his "amusement and entertainment" in the game of a nurse playing doctor.

"WERE KILLERS LOOSE IN ANN ARBOR'S V.A. HOSPITAL?"

by Peter Oberholtzer

The tension was almost tangible in the United States District courtroom of Judge Philip Pratt in Detroit. At about 10:35 a.m. on Wednesday, July 13, 1977 word had been sent from the jury room that a verdict had been reached at long last in what was believed to have been the longest trial in any federal district court in the United States. The trial had begun on March 28th after six months of procedural hearings and a month required to select a jury of nine women and three men.

Before selection of the jury had started, Judge Pratt had announced that the jurors would be sequestered for the duration of the trial. Undoubtedly this had caused a delay. The trial lasted 13 weeks before going to the jury. The panel deliberated for 94 hours over a period of 15 days before a verdict was reached.

During the long trial, 100 witnesses testified and 6,500 pages of trial testimony were typed for jury use. There were 78 witnesses for the prosecution and 22 for the defense. The jurors made notes on each of the 100 witnesses. In addition, medical records, charts and graphs which had been introduced into evidence were available to the jury.

Of the 12 members on the jury, 10 were white and 2 were black — a circumstance that would be made a big issue by the three defense attorneys.

However, unlike jurors in many other trials, not once during the 15 days of deliberation did the sequestered jurors complain or send word to the judge that they were hopelessly deadlocked, or that they had no hope of reaching a verdict — despite the fact that the members of the panel were away from their families for about 20 weeks.

Day after day the uncomfortable wooden benches serving as the only seats in the federal courtroom were jammed with spectators. Many of them were relatives of the defendants.

More than $100,000 was raised by friends and sympathizers of the defendants, but this sum soon dwindled to nothing as the defense costs mounted. By federal law, the government had to pick up the tab after the defendants became destitute. The amount reached more than a million dollars.

This was the background of the spectacular trial when word was received that the jury had reached a verdict after its long deliberation.

Now came the usual courtroom noises — the scraping sounds as the spectators took their seats and some of these talking excitedly in anticipation of the nature of the verdict.

Finally, the courtroom was jammed by members of the media and the spectators, a majority of whom were relatives and friends of the defendants. Some had come from overseas specifically to attend the trial.

All had to rise as Judge Pratt came from his chambers and took his seat behind the bench. After he had sat down, the spectators again took their seats.

Judge Pratt surveyed the crowded courtroom and waited a few moments for the murmurs of the spectators to subside. Then he addressed them.

"You are to maintain decorum, regardless of what the verdict is," Judge Pratt instructed the spectators. "There is to be order in the court."

The spectators took him at his word and even the whispers subsided. Then all heads turned in the direction of the box, where the jury had sat patiently for weeks listening to the long trial. The jurors filed in quietly and took their seats. The foreman handed a sheet of paper on which the jury's verdict had been written to the clerk of the court.

He turned, walked a few steps and handed the sheet to Judge Pratt. He read it but his features remained impassive, giving no hint of what he had read. Then he handed the sheet of paper to the clerk.

The clerk faced the audience, many of whom were craning forward, anxious to hear what the jury had decided. Then the clerk began to read . . .

This was the culmination of a spectacular, complex case that had started for federal law enforcement officers on Friday, August 15, 1975. That afternoon, the Federal Bureau of Investigation received a call from a man who identified himself as Dr. Duane T. Freier, Acting Chief of Staff of the Veterans Administration Hospital in Ann Arbor.

Ann Arbor, about 30 miles west of Detroit, is probably best known because in this growing city of about 110,000 population, in addition to the V.A. Hospital, the University of Michigan with almost 50,000 students is located. It is the center of a prominent educational community, with Eastern Michigan University and its student population of about 2,000 located about eight miles to the southeast.

Dr. Freier told federal agents that in his institution there had been 56 cases of respiratory arrest — that is, breathing failures — since July 1st. A normal number of breathing failures for this period would have been 8 to 10. At a meeting of staff physicians it had been decided to seek help because it was now believed that a killer might be at large in the hospital.

He was asked, how many patients were in the hospital?

Dr. Freier replied that there were approximately 300; the capacity was 311.

How many employes did the hospital have? The agent on the line wanted to know.

Normally, the doctor said, the number of paid employees ran around 700. The actual number at any given time depended on such factors as resignations, retirements and transfers, as well as an occasional death.

209

There was another group of workers, usually numbering about 400, he added. These were all volunteers who donated their services. Some worked part of a day once a week, others full days once or more each week.

Essentially the duties of the volunteers were to assist regular employes in a wide range of activities. Their work was loosely supervised by regular VA employes. The group that was most valuable were those who, when the weather permitted, wheeled patients out onto the grounds to sit in the sun or, if it was too hot, in the shade of a tree. These volunteers served coffee and doughnuts or other pastries to many of the patients.

This was generally known as the entertainment group. Some patients had failing eyesight and the volunteers read newspapers, books, or stories from magazines to them. These were all things that reasonably intelligent people without any special training could do.

The other group pushed patients on litters from their rooms to an operating room, to X-ray or to some other place in the hospital. Sometimes an employee accompanied the volunteers, but at other times, the volunteers passed nursing stations and checked with regular employes.

Others helped in the various offices — to do filing or to dig out a file on a patient who had been in the hospital previously and was being admitted again. Still others in this group were competent typists. How did the hospital recruit volunteers?

They were recruited, said the doctor, mostly by veterans' groups and other reliable organizations. These included the American Legion, the Veterans of Foreign Wars and various reliable civic clubs. Only occasionally was a volunteer who came directly to the hospital accepted.

The agent probed further. Were these volunteers screened?

The screening was done by the organization that recruited the volunteers. The VA facility accepted only those who came through sources that were known to be reliable and who had a genuine interest in the welfare of

210

the hospital's patients.

Did the hospital have a record of all the volunteer workers, their names and addresses?

Dr. Freier replied that the hospital had this information, but no evidence had been turned up to indicate that any of them could have been responsible for what hospital officials had reluctantly decided were crimes.

Why? the agent asked.

Dr. Freier replied that the volunteers worked only until about 3:30 p.m., when the evening shift came to work. He said that most of the respiratory arrests — breathing failures — had occurred on the evening shift. The hours the employes worked on this shift were from 3:30 to 11:00 p.m. The volunteers didn't work during those hours and they could be eliminated as possible suspects.

The doctor said, because the suspicious breathing failures had occurred on the 3:30 p.m. shift, he believed whoever was responsible for the respiratory arrests worked on that shift.

How many were employed on that shift?

Dr. Freier replied that the number varied between 300 and 400. But these were all paid employes and there were no volunteers on this shift.

Who, the agent asked, are these employees?

He was told that they ranged from cleaning women to some of the hospital's top physicians. However, Dr. Freier said if he had to narrow it down to one group, he would say there were more nurses than any others. Asked about his own position, Dr. Freier said that he was Acting Chief of Staff because the Chief of Staff, Dr. S. Martin Lindenauer, was in England. He had been in London for several months on a working Sabbatical. He was expected to return to the United States the last week in August.

Did he know about the suspicion that a murderer was at large in the hospital?

He didn't, Dr. Freier said, because he had been out of touch with the hospital for several months.

The special agent on the line suggested that Dr. Freier

start at the beginning and tell what he knew of the puzzling case. The doctor agreed.

He said the wave of respiratory arrests had been going on since July 1st. When the top men of the hospital staff met the next morning to read a summary of what had gone on during the 24 hours since they had last met, they noted there were more than the usual number of breathing failures.

Respiratory arrests are not uncommon among patients — usually those who have had surgery. In any given month, the number of breathing failures ranged from five to eight. These were seldom fatal — they were in the intensive care unit and were closely watched by the competent staff of nurses. Respirators, machines that force oxygen into the lungs of the patient through small tubes inserted through the nose — were always close at hand and, at the first signs of a respiratory arrest, nurses, who frequently were assisted by doctors, saw to it that the breathing machines were put to work and kept connected to the patient until he was able to breathe normally again.

At first, it was believed that the increase in the number of respiratory arrests was coincidence. Normally the patients most susceptible to breathing failures were the aged or the very sick. But the pattern gradually changed after July 1st.

Some of the victims were not very sick and after what was regarded as minor surgery — mending a broken arm or elbow or repairing a hernia or similar operations — they were expected to recover in a few days and be well enough to be discharged from the hospital.

As one of the physicians on staff at the VA Hospital described the situation, one minute the patient in question would be fine and the next he would stop breathing. Medical people attending the patient couldn't determine the reason for this occurrence.

As Dr. Freier described it, there was no let-up in the abnormal number of breathing arrests. They continued to mount. And senior staff surgeons and physicians — a group of a dozen high-level doctors — began what they called Death and Complications Conferences.

At these conferences, they tried to convince themselves that the respiratory arrests were normal, that it just happened that the number of breathing failures were five times the previous average.

But as daily reports continued to show the number of respiratory arrests were not diminishing, the senior doctor began to worry about the sharp rise.

During the first four weeks in July, from the 1st to the 28th, there were 22 breathing failures. Normally, there should have been five during this period.

A short time before July 28th, two nurses who knew of the respiratory arrests went to see the senior physicians. They said they were concerned about the increased breathing failures and they wondered if there was some kind of contaminated medication in the operating rooms that was causing them.

This was possible, of course, and an immediate investigation by specialists was ordered. The medications in the operating rooms were sent to the pharmaceutical laboratory at the University of Michigan in Ann Arbor.

While the outcome was awaited, the number of breathing failures continued to mount. The 22 in the first four weeks of July were at least 14 above normal. But from July 28th, when there were three respiratory arrests, the number climbed. A report came back from the University lab. No contamination had been found in the medication from the operating rooms.

Meanwhile, interns and residents who were just beginning their careers decided that the patients should know what was going on. They began telling the patients they attended of the wave of respiratory arrests and advising them what to do to survive.

While no definite cause for the deaths had been determined, it seemed probable that the increasing number of victims were being viciously injected with a specific type of muscle relaxant. There are 10 or more drugs that are used as muscle relaxants. Many are derived from curare, a drug discovered by Spaniards in South America in the Sixteenth

Century. It is derived chiefly from the plant, strychnos toxifera. How it was extracted and prepared was developed by South American Indian witch doctors, who closely guarded the secret of its preparation for more than two centuries.

In South America, the Indians used curare on the tips of their arrows. The liquid drug was always lethal to anyone unfortunate enough to be struck by one of the poisoned Indian arrows. The drug, curare, in its raw form is fatal almost instantly: it paralyzes all the voluntary organs of the body — that is, the organs over which an individual has control. This includes breathing and the muscles of the arms and legs, as well as those of the abdomen.

Injections are given by anesthesiologists most often to relax the abdominal muscles of nervous patients just prior to the beginning of an operation. It takes effect within 30 to 40 seconds and within a minute, the patient would stop breathing. But at the same time that he is given an injection of a muscle relaxant descended from curare, he also is hooked up to a respirator, which enables him to breathe.

Now, the interns and young VA doctors told their patients how to protect themselves. The moment they had the beginning of a numbing feeling, whether or not they had had an injection, they should cry out and if possible wave their arms. The interns stressed the importance of moving quickly. Unless they moved or cried out at once, they might not be able to.

The young doctors did this without orders from the senior physicians: they didn't want anyone to lose his life if it could be saved and they didn't want the stigma that might go along with losing too many patients.

If anyone on the hospital staff suspected that a potential killer was at large in the hospital — probably an employe of the hospital — it was not voiced. This was to come later.

The senior physicians wondered if there had been a medical mistake that could account for the wave of respiratory arrests. But the original investigation failed to turn up any evidence of medical mistakes.

On August 4th there was a meeting of senior physicians

and surgeons. Dr. Freier had attended many of these meetings in the past. His normal position was assistant chief of surgery. But that day he was Acting Chief of Staff—the hospital's head man—filling in for Dr. Lindenauer.

"I just put it to them," he said, "I said: 'I'm new at this and I need some advice. Should we go head with a formal investigation of all this?'"

The senior doctors had already considered that. The VA Hospital in Ann Arbor had a reputation as one of the finest in the Veterans Administration system of hospitals. In fact, it was considered one of the best hospitals of any kind in the United States. They were reluctant to call in outside help because it would bring bad publicity. Dr. Freier accepted their advice.

The respiratory failures, meanwhile, had continued, but at least five times the normal pace. In fact, there were so many emergencies in which the breathing failures were involved that nurses and doctors began to expect the call, which was Code Seven. The calls occurred nearly always at night on the 3:30 to 11:00 p.m. shift, two to four times a night, almost every night.

Somehow, for a reason nobody could account for, a young nurse, Denise Nichol, 22, happened to be close by when one of the alarms sounded. This occurred so frequently that other nurses began to joke about it. But it wasn't funny to Denise.

"Maybe I should get out of nursing," she told a friend. "I feel like a jinx."

Her friend tried to reassure her, telling her it was nothing to worry about. But Denise continued to fret about it; especially when the number of breathing failures seemed to increase.

Then on August 7th, Denise failed to come to work. Her telephone was not answered and an investigation was made. In her apartment in a building across the street from the hospital, her body was found in a chair facing the television, which still was turned on. A cigarette had burned down to her fingers.

A comprehensive autopsy was performed but the pathologists could not determine the cause of her death. Her blood showed a high level of Darvon, a pain-killing drug, but it was not high enough to be lethal. There was no suicide or farewell note and suicide was ruled out. Nor was there any sign of violence.

She might have thought she was a suspect, but her death had no effect on the breathing failures. They continued at a rate of five times over normal and in some cases higher.

The breathing failures became so frequent that nurses would stand out in the hall on the third floor — where the Intensive care unit, the scene of most of the failures, was located — and wait for the next alarm, sure it would be sounded.

VA headquarters in Washington had been notified and a team of five medical investigators, headed by Dr. Lawrence Foyt, came to try to solve the mystery. The doctors still didn't want to ask for outside help and the bad publicity that inevitably would follow.

The medical investigators looked for some common denominators and found two. Although one physician said that the breathing failures occurred all over the hospital, the majority of them were in the intensive care unit. Also, it was determined that virtually all the respiratory arrests occurred on the 3:30 to 11:00 p.m. shift.

This narrowed the work of the investigators considerably. The arms of the patients who had suffered breathing failures were examined and no needle marks, except on the patients for whom injections had been ordered — a comparative few — could be found.

Nevertheless, it was believed that the victims had received dosages of a muscle relaxant. There are more than 10 different brands of these descendants of curare, manufactured by highly reputable pharmaceutical firms. Anesthesiologists at the hospital used three brands, but two of the three used only occasionally. The brand generally used as a muscle relaxant was Pavulon. While Pavulon was suspect, there was no evidence that it had been the drug causing the breathing arrests. Pancuronium is the technical name of the drug.

At the latest Death and Complications Conference, the day before Denise Nichol died, the subject of one patient was brought up by one of the doctors. While a few of the breathing failures were normal because of the conditions of the patients, the doctors could think of no reason why this particular patient should suffer a respiratory arrest.

Many of the doctors had become extremely worried. "It was just one of those deep-seated uneasy feelings that you don't have things under control," Dr. Freier said. The only persistent common denominator that applied to all the victims was that all were receiving nutrients or medication through IVs (intravenous devices). But they already had checked the patients on IVs, who had experienced respiratory arrests. They had found no needle marks where none should be.

Yet it was most probable that the drug causing the breathing failures was administered through the IVs. But how? The only answer to that seemed to be that the drug had been put into the IV solution.

If only one nurse had handled the IVs, the answer might be simple. There were a number of ways she might have been checked. But it wasn't that simple. It seemed quite improbable that every nurse handling IVs had put a drug into the solution.

It was a serious problem and it was growing worse, but Dr. Freier decided he needed more evidence before he called in the authorities. He and other senior surgeons wanted to exhaust all the possibilities before the situation was exposed to the pitiless light of publicity, which could conceivably give the hospital a bad name, possibly even wreck its fine reputation.

But publicity is not always bad. There was a case in Chicago in 1966 when eight nurses were slaughtered in one night. One nurse survived to help the police artists make a sketch. The drawing was recognized by some veteran

217

officers as a likeness of Richard Speck.

A picture of Speck was found in the files of mug shots and the surviving nurse positively identified Speck as the killer. But where was he? How to find him?

The police superintendent decided on publicity. Speck's picture was published in all the papers and broadcast on all the TV stations. A young doctor saw the picture in a Chicago paper and he studied it. Not that he expected to come into contact with Speck, but he was curious as to what a mass killer looked like.

Later that day, he was summoned to a ward in the Cook County jail where he worked. A tall young man who had rented a small cubicle in a West Madison Street flop house had slashed his wrists with a razor blade. He had bled some but the wound was not serious.

The doctor looked at his face and recognized the patient as Richard Speck. He stepped out of earshot momentarily and sent a nurse to find the policeman assigned to the hospital. He arrived in a few moments. He nodded in agreement that it was Speck and called headquarters. While the doctor was still putting bandages on the slashed wrist, reinforcements arrived and Speck, who was not seriously injured, was taken to headquarters.

He was later convicted and sentenced to the chair. But by the time his appeals had been exhausted, the Supreme Court had ruled that the death penalty laws, as written, were unconstitutional. Speck went to court again and got a sentence of 400 years. He is still in prison.

As the doctors at the VA hospital were to learn, publicity was their most powerful weapon. If the law had been called in late in July, when the doctors first became worried, many respiratory arrests might have been avoided. But it was decided to wait another week.

Without any regularity but on a random basis, doctors had begun examining IVs late in July. But they had found nothing that could be considered suspicious.

Then came the night of August 12th, one that Dr. Freier and the two doctors who were on duty that night probably never will forget. The first breathing failure occurred at about 6:00 p.m. Doctors and nurses rushed to the patient and began the now familiar routine of restoring his breathing. Soon this had been accomplished.

The nurses hoped for a little rest, but this was not to be. About 10 minutes later there came an alarm from the intensive care unit. Doctors and nurses rushed to the bedside of a patient who was awake and alert but unable to talk. His hands still were moving and he was pointing to his throat. A respirator was attached and the patient began breathing again.

The next call came in about 15 minutes after the second patient was back to normal. His breathing ability was restored and soon he was breathing normally.

The doctors and nurses were perhaps more exhausted than the patients. They fervently hoped there would be no more emergencies. Their hope was in vain.

The fourth victim that night was an elderly man who had been operated on for a broken hip. He was quite elderly and he died before the doctors and nurses could get him to breathing again. Staff doctors said later it was possible that he had died from natural causes because of his age.

In the room next to this elderly man, a nurse found a man in his 30s who had stopped breathing. His face was beginning to turn blue, as often happens with a respiratory stoppage. By quick action the doctors and nurses restored his breathing.

(Parents of recalcitrant children will recall that a child sometimes holds his breath until his features begin to turn blue if he doesn't have his way.)

The tired doctors and nurses had a respite but it was short. The next three breathing failures that night were on the fourth floor, just above the floor on which the intensive care unit was located. In a period of three hours, from 6:00 to 9:00 p.m., the doctors and nurses had attended eight patients with respiratory arrests. One elderly man had died, possibly of natural causes.

After that, for several hours, things seemed to settle down to the normal routine of a 311-bed hospital. That was enough to keep the limited staff busy.

Then at about dawn, a 53-year-old disturbed patient on the fifth floor ripped out the screen on the window in his room and jumped. He landed on a grating that covered a window well on the ground-floor level. Every vital organ in his body was crushed. He was the first suicide at the VA Hospital since 1971.

That was the story that greeted Dr. Freier when he sat down at his desk on the morning of Wednesday, August 13th. "It suddenly occurred to me that somebody was doing this on purpose," said Dr. Freier.

Evidence of that had been mounting with each passing evening, but Dr. Freier and the other senior members of the staff couldn't bring themselves to believe that a mad killer was at large in the VA Hospital.

The motive for trying to kill patients in a manner that was nothing short of horrible just wasn't apparent, any way it was considered. There seemed only one possible motive — the potential killer must be mad.

Before he had fully digested the events of the most horrible night in the hospital's history, Dr. Freier was visited by Dr. Anne Hill, the hospital's chief anesthesiologist. Dr. Freier quoted her:

"She said 'I had this horrible feeling — what if someone was doing this?' And I said, 'I've had that feeling for past couple of days.' "

But despite the evidence presented that morning, the two doctors were not sure. Dr. Freier decided that there would have to be more evidence before he would call in the FBI. The hospital had five men making their own medical investigation and Dr. Freier decided to wait for the results of their probe. He expected those results in about a week.

But he didn't have to wait a week. Two days later brought

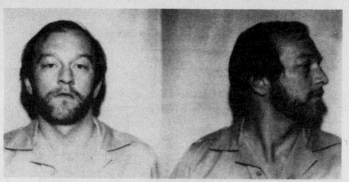

Dr. Kenneth Z. Taylor

The dumb bell handle with which Dr. Taylor beat his wife Teresa to death.

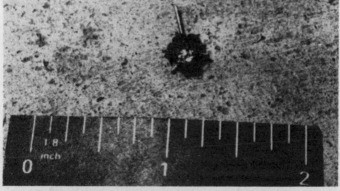

Earring discovered by investigators in Taylor's garage matched the one found on the victim's corpse.

Donald Harvey

Dr. Glennon Engleman

Robert R. Diaz (left) at his sentencing.

**Dr. Richard Boggs as a promising
medical student.**

**Dr. Richard Boggs at his arraignment for the murder of
Ellis Greene.**

Dr. Klaus Wietfeld and his wife Monika at their wedding.

Dr. James Klindt and his wife Joyce.

Pharmacist Steven H. Oken

**Dawn Marie Garvin,
Steven Oken's first victim.**

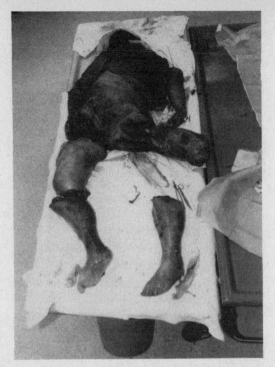

The mutilated body of Ruth Nedermier

Inge Lemont

another wave of breathing failures. The investigating doctors were now convinced that someone was deliberately causing the breathing failures and they were ready for some tests, which were suggested and supervised by Dr. Hill.

The four doctors witnessed the tests run by Dr. Hill that night in the intensive care unit. Two patients were injected with the suspect drug, Pavulon. Their reaction was what was to be expected from the drug.

The patients were hooked up to respirators immediately and within two minutes were breathing normally. The investigating doctors were convinced.

The FBI had been called in and a dozen men arrived on the evening of Friday, August 15th. Dr. Freier told them that 56 patients had suffered breathing arrests between July 1st and August 15th. There were 22 the first four weeks in July but, in the next three weeks, the number increased sharply to 34. One frightening thing about the statistics was that only 22 persons had been involved in the 34 breathing failures. Some of these had been attacked twice, others several times.

Was that the reason the FBI had been called in? Dr. Freier was asked after he had completed his narrative.

Only partly, the doctor replied. He had intended to wait five more days, but the firm evidence he wanted showed up before that. One of the patients, a 49-year-old man of Coloma, Michigan, who had open heart surgery and who had been a breathing failure victim more than once, handed a note to a doctor.

Although the note was not made public, the gist of it was that the patient had seen a Filipino nurse, Miss Filipina Narcisso, going out the door just before one of his attacks.

Miss Narcisso had come from the Philippines in 1971 and had worked at the VA Hospital since 1973. She had been generally regarded as a very competent nurse. Thirty-one years old she had considerable experience as a registered nurse, both in her native Philippines and in the United States.

Just what her motive could be, if she indeed were responsible for the breathing failures, was one of the biggest riddles of what at best was a very puzzling mystery.

Another item of substantial evidence was furnished by Dr. Bert N. LaDu, head of the university lab. Dr. LaDu had taken urine and blood samples from the patients and had his technicians do a series of complicated tests.

The lab report showed that the blood and urine samples reacted as they would have if Pavulon had been used. But there were eight other drugs that would react in a similar manner. Pavulon, however, was used at the VA Hospital and the others were not. If one of the other eight had been used, it would have had to come from outside the hospital.

On the basis of the heart patient's note, Miss Narcisso became a suspect and remained one throughout the long investigation.

Dr. LaDu was a specialist in the field of relaxing drugs. He had been called as an expert witness in one of the trials of Dr. Carl Coppolino.

Dr. Coppolino was an MD who specialized in anesthesiology. One of the drugs he had used was succinylcholine chloride. He knew that up to 1964, pathologists had been unable to detect the presence of this drug, a muscle relaxant similar to Pavulon. A comparatively new brand, succinylcholine chloride was also a descendant of the powerful South American poison curare.

Announcing that he had suffered four coronaries, Dr. Coppolino was no longer able to practice at a hospital. He had studied hypnosis and had become quite good at it, listing himself in the yellow pages as an MD-hypnotist who made house calls. He said his condition was so bad that he was unable to drive a car.

The Coppolinos had moved into a plush house in the exclusive Fox Run section of Middletown Township in New Jersey, less than an hour's drive from New York City. A year before, an army colonel and his attractive brunette wife had moved into a house across the street. The colonel was retired and drove into New York every day to his insurance office.

One day in 1964, the colonel didn't feel well and stayed

home. He was attended by Dr. Carl, who gave him an injection. Carl's wife, Carmela, was also an MD and worked in the research department of Hoffman-La Roche, a well-known and reputable pharmaceutical firm in nearby Nutley, New Jersey. She, too, was acquainted with the colonel and his wife.

After Dr. Carl had given the colonel the injection, his wife went to sit in the Coppolino backyard, leaving a note for the children: "Don't disturb Daddy." But the oldest daughter, then 15, went into the colonel's room.

Suddenly she came running to the back yard of the Coppolino home and cried: "I don't think Daddy's breathing." Dr. Carl confirmed that the colonel was dead, then called his wife in Nutley and asked her to come home. She did and, after examining the body and listening to what her husband told her, she signed the death certificate, attributing the death to a heart attack. The colonel was buried with full military honors in Arlington National Cemetery.

Before and after the colonel's death, the colonel's widow had been driving Dr. Carl to keep appointments — house calls to treat patients with hypnosis, at which he had been quite successful. He had also written 14 scientific papers and one book, "Billion Dollar Hangover," that made the best seller lists.

The Coppolinos decided to move to Florida, where Dr. Carl could devote himself to writing in a milder climate. They bought a swank house on Longboat Key, a suburb of Sarasota. The doctor already had started his next book, "Welcome to the Coronary Club," when they moved in 1964. The colonel's widow bought the adjoining lot and had a house built on it. She moved later, promising her children they would try it for at least a year. Her house was not quite completed and the widow and her children moved into an apartment temporarily.

The widow and Dr. Carmela Coppolino became good friends. On August 28th, she called the Coppolino home and Dr. Carl answered. He said: "Carm is dead." She had died of a heart attack, he said. He phoned a woman doctor in the north section of Sarasota. He had become slightly acquainted with her in what had appeared to be a casual meeting.

When she came, Dr. Carl told her that Carm was complaining of chest pains. From her examination and from what Dr. Carl told her, the woman doctor signed a death certificate, attributing Dr. Carmela's death to a coronary occlusion, a form of heart attack that almost always is fatal.

Less than a month later, Dr. Carl got a license to marry a wealthy divorcee who then lived in Sarasota. In December, 1965, the colonel's widow blew the whistle on Dr. Carl Coppolino. She said she had become a close friend of Carmela Coppolino and she didn't believe the young woman died of a heart attack. She said she was stunned when she heard that he had married the wealthy divorcee.

She told Sarasota County Sheriff Ross Boyer that she herself had expected to marry Dr. Coppolino. When he married the divorcee she realized that he had been interested in only money rather than in her—it was said that the divorcee was quite wealthy. She thought about it and said that both her husband and Dr. Carmela had been in good health.

It was clear that Dr. Carl had killed them both so that he could marry the colonel's widow—for her money. But before that had occurred he had met the wealthier divorcee.

Her charges were serious and Sheriff Boyer went to New Jersey. Authorities there consulted the late Dr. Milton Helperin, New York City Chief Medical Examiner, and he agreed that no way to find traces of succynoline chloride had been found. His chief toxicologist, Dr. Charles J. Umberger, heard the story and, after the widow had said, "This man is capable of murder," agreed to help try to find a way to detect the relaxant drug.

With an exhumation consent signed by her father, also a doctor, Carmela Coppolino's body was exhumed and an autopsy performed. It showed conclusively that she didn't die of a coronary. Specimens of tissue from the vital organs and other parts of the body were taken for pathological study, while Dr. C. Malcolm Gilman, Monmouth County medical examiner, carried on animal experiments with the help of Dr. Umberger.

With the consent of the widow, the army colonel's body was exhumed and an autopsy was performed, Dr. Helperin and some of his staff assisting. They announced that the injection hadn't killed the colonel but that he had died of manual strangulation, probably from a pillow held over his head to cause breathing failure.

The Monmouth County Grand Jury indicted Carl Coppolino and a fugitive warrant was sent to Sheriff Boyer, who had kept Coppolino under surveillance by plainclothes detectives. The doctor was arrested and held for transport to New Jersey. The next day, the Sarasota County Grand Jury indicted him for the murder of his wife.

But New Jersey had first call and he was taken there, with the understanding that he would be returned to Florida after the trial. This turned out to be a wise move, because Dr. Coppolino was tried and acquitted. He had engaged famed lawyer F. Lee Bailey, who added another win to his string of victories.

Apparently Bailey expected the trial in Florida to be easy. But he had reckoned without State Attorney Frank Schaub (now a Circuit Judge). Schaub persuaded Dr. Helperin and Dr. Umberger to come to Sarasota to testify. They suggested that Dr. LaDu of the University of Michigan be summoned, and he testified also. Dr. Umberger and Dr. Gilman had found a method of detecting the presence of the muscle relaxant. The Florida jury wasn't impressed by the flamboyant Bailey and he lost the case. Dr. Coppolino was convicted of murder and sent to prison for life. As this was written he was still there, having long ago exhausted his appeals.

Now, in Ann Arbor, with two dozen agents assigned to the case, the FBI set up headquarters in the VA Hospital and began an intense investigation. They obtained the names of more than 300 persons who had been in the hospital on the evening shift when practically all the breathing arrests oc-

225

curred. These included doctors, nurses and other employees, patients who could be questioned and visitors on the evenings the incidents were recorded.

On August 29th, two more patients died. They had suffered respiratory arrests before August 15th. After this, only emergency cases were admitted to the hospital. Only emergency operations were performed. All patients who were not too sick were sent home. The number of patients in the 311 bed hospital eventually dwindled to 188.

Most of these were questioned by the FBI special agents, but only two facts emerged. Miss Narcisso and another Filipino nurse, Mrs. Leonora Perez, had been seen near the patients or near the IVs in rooms where breathing failures occurred.

Miss Narcisso was transferred to a section of the hospital where she didn't come in contact with patients. She was assigned duties where she had nothing to do with such things as medication or IVs. At her own request, Mrs. Perez was transferred to a VA Hospital in Detroit, but she was not allowed near patients or medication. She was given duties similar to those of Miss Narcisso. Mrs. Perez had also been seen near IVs or patients who soon afterward suffered breathing arrests.

So far, nobody had told of seeing either nurse do anything unusual. Nobody recalled seeing either nurse with a syringe in her hand, although syringes were plentiful in the hospital and easily available to any nurse.

The federal officers were not at all sure that Miss Narcisso and Mrs. Perez were involved in the breathing failures, but both had become prime suspects.

The agents called on Dr. Derek H. Miller, professor of psychiatry at the University of Michigan, for a psychiatric profile of one who might try to kill patients by causing the breathing failures. He agreed to study the case and come up with the profile as soon as possible.

Meanwhile, the agents had been astonished at the ease with which various medications, including Pavulon, were available to anyone who cared to look for them. Different

226

types of medicines were available on most floors and were not locked up.

The agents knew this was contrary to the practices at most hospitals, where medications prescribed by doctors are doled out by employes called medical nurses. They knew that in many hospitals, a patient couldn't even have an aspirin tablet without the approval of his doctor.

They looked in the refrigerator in the intensive care unit and discovered a quantity of Pavulon. When he was asked about this, Dr. Freier said that the refrigerator was not locked and almost anybody, whether or not he was a hospital employe, might open it and remove the powerful drug.

When Dr. Freier was told of the discovery of Pavulon in the intensive care unit refrigerator he said it was "not an appropriate place" for the drug to be kept.

After that, all the Pavulon was gathered up and put under lock and key. Dr. Hill, the chief anesthesiologist, and his assistants were notified and given the keys. But other personnel, including the nurses, were not told where it was kept.

In addition, other potentially harmful drugs were collected and, with the advice of the doctors as to who would be using them, these specific doctors, as well as the nurses, were given the keys. This is a procedure that is used in hospitals that don't have nurses assigned especially to doling out medicines.

Before the entry of the FBI in the investigation, a number of tests had been started by investigating doctors and now the results of the tests began to come in.

One doctor who had examined all the IV tubes in an effort to determine how the Pavulon was injected into them found a blue substance he couldn't account for inside one of the tubes. This had been sent to the university lab for analysis.

The report came back that the substance was a mild cleaning fluid used to clean the IV tubes. Lab doctors said that the fluid was harmless and even if some of it had gone into a patient's arm through an IV tube, it wouldn't have hurt the patient and certainly couldn't have caused a respiratory failure. So that lead was discarded.

Meanwhile, Dr. Martin Lindenauer, 42, had returned from London and shortly after the FBI entered the investigation, returned to his post as Chief of Staff at the hospital. The reports were delivered to him.

A second report was on the examination of the blood and urine of two patients who survived after they had been given muscle-paralyzing drugs and had been revived by respirator. Inasmuch as Pavulon was the main drug of this type in use at the hospital, it seemed almost certain that the weapon was Pavulon.

"It fits with the clinical evidence and it's good evidence — not in the legal sense, but it's good medical evidence," said Dr. Lindenauer.

The two patients whose blood and urine were tested were two of the last of the unexpected breathing failures. They had occurred on August 15th, the evening the FBI was called in.

Then on September 2nd, another patient who had suffered three unexpected breathing failures before the FBI was called in, died. He was only 41 and there were "grave suspicions," according to Dr. Lindenauer, that his death was a delayed result of the respiratory failure.

However, his death could have been from normal causes. He was suffering from diabetes with complications and other symptoms and had been in the VA Hospital off and on for the past two years.

With the number of patients down to 188, Dr. Lindenauer was disturbed about the future of the hospital. He told a news conference that "the hospital can't go on like this." He said it had been decided to reopen the hospital to regular admissions within a month."

One feature that pointed strongly to the two nurses was that in the three weeks since the FBI had entered the investigation, there had not been a single unexpected breathing failure. This was a great relief to the doctors and the rest of the nurses who had worked on the breathing failures.

"I just can't even describe how terrible it was," said one

young nurse.

Meanwhile, Dr. Miller finished the psychiatric profiles he had drawn up for the FBI, but refused to divulge what was in them; the FBI was equally silent. But some other psychiatrists were not so reticent.

A Detroit psychiatrist, Dr. Emanuel Tanay, who had testified as an expert witness in many cases involving the criminally insane, said of the type of person possibly involved: "We would have to assume that he is someone medically knowledgeable — somebody who has been a medical corpsman or somebody who is on the staff." Dr. Tanay, who had also done a great deal of writing on violence, added: "Obviously, the individual is not a disorganized person because he is committing a skillful act."

Dr. Tanay went on that the killer is a person who is "fairly well functioning," and who "would not impress you as someone sick."

The theoretical suspects as defined by Dr. Tanay would include nurses, technicians and non-profession staff members, but doctors could not be ruled out, nor could medical students.

Most of the psychiatrists who studied the known facts of the case agreed that the killer was highly disturbed and perhaps carried a grudge of some kind against the Veterans Administration, the hospital itself or the medical profession in general.

One doctor suggested that the killer's motive was to embarrass the hospital to the extent that it would not have enough patients and be forced to close.

Investigators came up with two theories. One was that the killer was a young doctor in his twenties, probably a Vietnam Veteran who was then a technician at the hospital. The other suggested that the killer was a nurse who hated men, possibly one who had recently had a disagreement with one of her superiors.

These theories were pure speculation but they were the

closest the doctors, the FBI or anybody else ever came to a motive for the killer's actions.

The psychiatrists said they believed that either of the theoretical suspects would have been sufficiently disturbed to need the services of a psychiatrist and had encountered the police at some time.

Dr. Irwin Perr, a professor at Rutgers, a New Jersey University, said: "Nobody is an expert on mass murders because there are not enough of them, thank God."

There is a special sickness that drives people to multiple homicides, Dr. Perr added and in these cases, psychiatry doesn't help much. Dr. Perr is a specialist in the legal aspects of psychiatry.

Two Chicago specialists gave their views, Dr. Charles Wepman, a psychology professor at the University of Chicago, said the Ann Arbor killer might be similar to Charles Manson, who was convicted in 1971 of the murders of Sharon Tate, a movie starlet, and six other girls who were members of what they called the "Manson family."

"He could be an old patient or employe who says to himself, 'These people are never going to be any good; we might as well get rid of them and at the same time get even with the U.S. government.'

"He's going to show how badly the government treats these people who have given their all for their country," Dr. Wepman added.

"I can outline about forty-five good reasons for murder," the doctor said. "One man I studied did it because of ennui. He was just sick and tired of his wife, so he shot her one day.

"Murder is just an extension of all the rest of our behaviors," Dr. Wepman said. "It's an ultimate one, however. Where else can you go after murder, except suicide. And suicide is murder."

Miss Narcisso was questioned extensively and she accused the FBI agents of harassing her. She remained a prime suspect, although no motive was apparent.

Trying to bring order out of chaos, Dr. Lindenauer did some rearranging. Intensive care remained on the third floor, but all patients needing IVs were moved to the third floor. Pavulon and similar drugs were locked up.

If the hospital was to return to a semblance of normalcy, it would need patients.

"That's why I fear the bad publicity," Dr. Lindenauer said, "because if patients don't trust this hospital, they won't come here. I just hope there will be patients out there still," in the days ahead.

"When you get right down to it, a hospital runs on trust." Everyone in the hospital must trust everybody else.

Dr. Lindenauer said: "This is a first-rate hospital . . . It has to go on."

He decided that the hospital would begin normal admissions on the second Monday in September. But he said temporarily the number of patients would be limited to about 250.

Only about half the usual number showed up the first day, but admissions became normal as time passed.

Meanwhile the FBI had stepped up its investigation. They talked to one patient, a comparatively young man from Detroit who had an injury but nothing wrong with his heart and lungs. The doctors could find no reason for his breathing failure.

"It feels like instant death," he said. "It's like somebody grabbed hold of your throat real quick and it's just how long you can hold your breath—thirty, maybe sixty seconds. Then your whole body becomes numb."

In describing one of the attacks, which he believed was similar to that suffered by more than 50 patients, the young man continued:

"It hits the vision first. Your right eye goes way to the right. Your left eye way to the left. Then you feel nausea. The first time every thing just slowly stopped. But the last time was really bad."

He had been one of the less fortunate ones in that he had been attacked by the breathing failure several times. but he

231

had been lucky enough to survive. The worst effect was that he had difficulty in breathing when he tried to stand, because of a collapsed lung.

"I have a bad case of nerves," he said. "I asked for protection. They haven't caught whoever is running around the hospital. I don't get much sleep." He was well enough to go home, but personal and medical reasons kept him in the hospital. "This is supposed to be one of the best hospitals in the country," he explained.

The federal investigating officers used every tool at their disposal, but they didn't have the luck they had hoped for. After specimens had been analyzed in the university lab, the FBI lab in Washington and a toxicology lab in Denver, it was decided that the medication used to try to poison—some successfully—more than 50 patients was Pavulon. Three of the latest victims who had suffered breathing failures before the FBI stepped in were exhumed with the consent of their widows or next of kin. Tissues for analysis were removed from vital organs and other parts of the body, and within two hours each exhumed body was back in its burial place. The tests confirmed that the fatal drug was Pavulon.

The FBI questioned more than 300 persons and in late fall closed up shop. The agents didn't disclose all they had learned, but the two Filipino nurses remained the prime suspects. The FBI turned over its information to Richard Delonis, chief of the criminal division of the U.S. Attorney's office in Detroit.

In addition to the testimony of several witnesses that they had seen Miss Narcisso and/or Mrs. Perez near the patients who suffered breathing failures, there was the further fact that there had not been a single suspicious breathing failure since August 15th, the night the FBI had appeared on the scene.

However, the G-men failed to come up with a solid motive. All they had were theoretical motives, none of which had been proved. Nor had the federal officers found a witness who had seen either nurse with a syringe in her hands prior to the attacks. However, doctors had decided that the deadly drug had been injected into the IV tubes of the patients who had almost suffocated.

A federal grand jury was summoned and the two nurses along with other witnesses were subpoenaed. Miss Narcisso was questioned as second time by the jurors. But the grand jurors decided there was not enough evidence and the two nurses were not indicted.

The FBI renewed its investigation, questioning the entire fifth floor of the VA Hospital. But security was tight and questioning of witnesses, mostly former patients, was tight. One of those questioned was the patient who had put the finger on Miss Narcisso. But he changed his story several times and finally said he believed the person he saw leaving the room was a man. He said he saw only the man's back as he went out the door.

This patient's open heart surgery apparently had been a success. He recovered and was allowed to go home, but in June, 1976, he died of heart failure.

During its second session at the hospital, the FBI used hypnosis on some witnesses in an effort to refresh their memories. The additional material gained by the officers was turned over to the U.S. Attorney's office.

Another grand jury was summoned and a few of the survivors of the breathing failures testified before the jurors. On June 16th the jury returned a 16-count indictment against the two nurses. There were five charges of first-degree murder, one charge of conspiracy to commit murder and 10 counts of attempted murder by introducing Pavulon into the IV tubes of patients who survived.

Both women were arrested and were later released on $70,000 bonds each. The trial actually started on March 28, 1977, although more than six months were devoted to disposing of pre-trial motions and a month to selecting a jury.

Mrs. Betty Jakin, 51, who had been a supervisor at the VA Hospital, left a letter claiming responsibility for the deaths. But at the time she made the statements she was confined to a mental hospital in Ann Arbor. Doctors testified that she was suffering from terminal cancer, acute guilt feelings, hallucinations and severe depressions. She committed suicide after writing the letter. The jury was out of the room and the letter was not admitted in evidence. Nor was the note left by the patient who had originally pointed the finger at Miss Narcisso, because of the several times he changed his story before his death.

Assistant U.S. Attorney Richard Yanko headed the team of prosecutors; his chief assistant was Delonis. Very little that was new came out at the 13-week trial during which the jurors were sequestered.

The original 16-count indictment had dwindled to eight charges. After nine weeks of the trial, Judge Pratt dismissed one of the murder charges, which was against Perez, leaving two poisoning and one conspiracy charge against her. One murder, one conspiracy and two poisoning charges against Miss Narcisso.

The jury convicted Mrs. Perez on all three charges, but found Miss Narcisso not guilty of two poisoning and one conspiracy charge.

The defense attorneys said they would begin the long appeals routine in the next week. That already has started and it may take months or even years. Meanwhile, Judge Pratt allowed the convicted nurses to remain free on the same bond.

On September 19th an Illinois court ordered that the two nurses submit to further psychiatric testing before a final decision was made on their sentencing.

As this was written, that was the status of what most consider the most bizarre case in medical history, as well as one of the most unusual in criminal history.

"12 SLUGS ENDED THE MARRIAGE ON THE ROCKS!"

by Jaye Fletcher

The year was 1967 and, at age forty-one, Donna Brown Branion had everything. She was the daughter of a wealthy and influential family, she was married to a noted and charming physician and she and her husband had a beautiful, healthy four-year-old son.

Donna Branion and her husband, Dr. John Branion, lived with their child in a lovely home in Chicago's Hyde Park. With their wealth and social graces, the Branions enjoyed a lifestyle that most blacks during that troubled time could only dream of. But in the City of Chicago in 1967, Hyde Park was perhaps still the only neighborhood where blacks, even wealthy and socially advantaged blacks like the Branions, could have lived with harmony and complete acceptance alongside their white neighbors.

For Hyde Park, a southside neighborhood snuggled against the shores and beaches of Lake Michigan, was the home of the University of Chicago. The atmosphere of that prestigious institution, renowned worldwide as the birthplace of atomic reaction, pervaded the entire neighborhood. Hyde Park was, and remains today, an area where people's daily lives are lived in the shadow of those long blocks of old, dark brick halls. Cocktail party talk in Hyde Park is less likely to center around sports than around aero-

235

nautical physics and recent breakthroughs in the fields of genetic engineering and cancer research.

The Branions, John and Donna, had been members in good standing of this quietly gracious community for some years and, with Donna's social skills and John's notable credentials in the field of medicine, they were eagerly sought after as dinner party guests.

On December 22, 1967, Donna Branion had finally completed her small family's Christmas preparations. The decorations were all in place, the tree was standing, fragrant and glittering, near the front windows of the Branions' huge, expensively furnished front parlor. Over her morning coffee, Donna was planning her guest menu for the sumptuous dinner she and her husband were planning. Dr. John Branion had left the house at 9:00 a.m. and had taken their son to the nearby nursery school. He would go from there to the Ida Mae Scott Hospital for his morning rounds, after which, he would return to pick up the boy on the way home. This was a routine they often followed, and Donna planned that all of them would be together again in time for lunch. She was wrong.

At 11:05 a.m. on December 22, 1967, one of Donna Branion's neighbors was just returning home from grocery shopping. She had been putting the groceries away for five to ten minutes when she heard something that sounded like gunshots. She particularly remembered the time because her grocery shopping had taken longer than she'd expected and she'd been annoyed to realize that it was already 11:05 a.m. when she returned home. Some few minutes later, that same neighbor woman, looking out her window, saw Dr. John Branion running out of his front door and dragging his four-year-old son alongside him. The doctor appeared nearly hysterical and was shouting at the top of his voice for various neighbors to come out.

Dr. Branion thrust his son into the arms of the man who lived next door, gasping: "Keep an eye on him. Something's happened to Donna!"

He then turned and ran back inside his home. Several

236

neighbors, after a moment or two of shocked hesitation, followed.

Donna was lying face-up in the laundry room just off her large, sunny kitchen. She was wearing her favorite beige sweater and a brown-and-white plaid skirt. Her arms were sprawled akimbo and her legs were pressed together and bent slightly to the right, as though preserving her modesty to the last. Twelve large-caliber bullet holes punctured her head, face and neck.

Donna Brown Branion, the woman who had everything, was dead.

Dr. John Branion could only stare at his wife's body in shock and horror. His hands shook and the only sound he made was a low, continuous moan. Several neighbors attempted to console him, while others ran to call the police. The next-door neighbor called for his wife, who was also a physician. Within a few moments, the woman doctor arrived and knelt down next to Donna's body. Her examination took only seconds and merely confirmed what everyone already knew. Donna Branion was beyond medical help.

In response to the various neighbors' emergency calls, uniformed patrol officers were the first to arrive at the scene. Once they viewed the situation, they immediately radioed for detective teams and supporting laboratory technicians. Meanwhile, they began taking down names of everyone who was on or near the scene, and the times and exact sequence of events. The sleuths arrived shortly thereafter, and behind them, a small army of fingerprint technicians, forensic photographers and microanalysis specialists swarmed across the Branions' home to collect their samples, their photos, and their bits of hair, lint, blood samples and fibers that so often prove crucial many months later in the prosecution of a murderer.

Once the technicians were finished and Donna Branion's body was removed, the detectives' real work began. They had to interview everyone who was in any way connected with the crime, establish whereabouts, relationships, time sequences and corroborating witnesses for each. It was, and

237

usually is, tedious work.

Dr. Branion was nearly incoherent with grief at the brutal murder of his wife, but detectives were able to establish from him that he'd arrived home about 11:45 with his son. He told the detectives that he'd walked through the house, calling out several times for his wife. When he'd finally seen her lying, covered with blood, in the laundry room, his first thought had been to get his son out of the room. He'd run out, calling for help from his neighbors, before returning to his dead wife.

Had he, Dr. Branion, examined his wife to check whether she was actually dead or whether she could perhaps have still been alive?

Dr. Branion shook his head, saying that the moment he'd looked at her, he'd known she was dead, because of the lividity in her legs. (Lividity is the settling of blood to the lowest point in a dead body. Since the heart is no longer pumping the blood through the circulatory system, gravitational force causes the blood to sink, creating blotchy and mottled purplish discoloration of the skin. Hence, the term lividity. The longer the body lies, the more pronounced the lividity.)

Over the next few days, detectives made the rounds of the neighborhood, asking questions, requesting that people try to remember anyone or anything suspicious they might have seen — something that would give the police a lead in this seemingly inexplicable murder. No one recalled seeing anyone suspicious hanging around the Branions' home on the day of Donna's death. But little by little, almost reluctantly, the neighbors began to drop bits and pieces of information that the Branions' "ideal" marriage was not what it should have been.

There were often fights at the Branion home, according to neighbors. Not ordinary fights, like most married couples had on occasion, but real knock-down, drag-out brawls. And the Branions seemed to fight far more often than most people as well as more violently. Sometimes, the battles continued every single evening for days on end. They were not deliberately eavesdropping on the Branions, each of the neighbors assured the detectives, but such noisy shouting and screaming was difficult to ignore.

The detectives listened to these revelations and asked whether the neighbors had any sense of the reason or reasons behind the Branions' domestic eruption. Donna Branion had, for some months now, been regularly accusing Dr. Branion of seeing another woman, or even more than one woman. He, in turn, vigorously denied any infidelity but often countered that, should he seek the comfort of another woman's arms, the fault would lie with Donna herself.

The investigating detectives listened intently to these inside views of the Branions' personal life and they took notes on whatever they learned. But experience had taught them that, no matter how elegant and peaceful the exterior of a couple's life may seem, internally there was often turmoil, discord, even domestic violence. It was a sad pattern they'd seen many times before and did not, in and of itself, necessarily point an accusing finger at Dr. Branion. Only facts could do that, and thus far, no such accusatory facts had come to light. Nevertheless, having heard essentially the same disquieting commentary from some of the Branions' neighbors, the detectives began to pay particular attention to the somewhat differing versions of the doctor's movements on the day of his wife's murder.

According to Dr. John Branion, he had left his home at 9:00 a.m. on the morning of December 22, 1967. He'd dropped his son off at the nearby nursery school and continued on to the Ida Mae Scott Hospital, which was only a few blocks from his home. He made his hospital rounds until about 11:30 a.m., then left the hospital. On his way to the nearby nursery school, he'd stopped to pick up an elderly woman friend of the Branions who was to have lunch with them, but the woman wasn't feeling well and had decided to cancel the luncheon engagement.

He'd continued to the nursery school where, he said, his son was waiting outside for him. He picked the boy up and continued home, arriving at approximately 11:45, and upon

239

entering his home, he discovered his wife's body.

Each of the doctor's destinations—the nursery school, the hospital, the elderly friend's home—was only a matter of blocks from his own house, so the detectives saw nothing amiss in his having left the hospital at 11:30, picked his son up, visited the elderly friend, and arrived home all in 15 minutes.

Although they had no particular suspicion of Dr. Branion's movements, which seemed able to be easily verifiable all along his route, the detectives asked the doctor if he could remember at what time he arrived at the elderly friend's home after leaving the hospital.

Yes, the doctor remembered quite well because he'd been running just a few minutes late. He'd told the friend he would be there to pick her up at 11:30, but when he arrived and she wasn't waiting for him, he'd glanced at his watch and noted that he was two or three minutes late. He'd gone to the door and was told that she was canceling the luncheon because she wasn't feeling well.

Did he remember what time he'd arrived at the nursery school? Certainly. The school was only a block or so from the friend's home, so it was probably exactly 11:35 when he pulled up in front. He usually picked the little boy up at exactly 11:30, which was probably why the child was waiting outside for him. School officials dressed him in his warm coat, hat and gloves and then, when the doctor was a few minutes late, they'd had the boy wait outside so as not to become sweaty and overheated by waiting inside the school.

During their ensuing investigation, the detectives encountered discrepancies in the times various people remembered hearing the shots and recalled seeing Dr. Branion running from his home dragging his son alongside and shouting for help. The woman who had been grocery shopping and had come home at 11:05 thought that it was only five or ten minutes later that she'd seen the doctor running across the lawn. But, the detectives decided, she was obviously mistaken in her estimate of how long she'd been unpacking groceries before seeing Dr. Branion. Had it really been five or ten minutes after she'd arrived home, that would have placed the time at 11:10 or 11:15.

As part of their re-tracing everyone's movements on the morning of Donna Branion's death, the detectives already established that Dr. Branion had not completed his hospital rounds until shortly before 11:30. They had interviewed the last patient Dr. Branion had seen that morning, a young man who was suffering with a minor chest ailment. The patient reported that Dr. Branion had come into his room at 11:25 a.m. He remembered the time precisely because, like most hospital patients, he was lying in bed bored and looking forward to the doctor's visit to break the monotony. The patient reported that Dr. Branion seemed distracted and eager to conclude the visit. He had stayed with his last patient less than a minute, then he was gone.

This discrepancy in the time of that morning's events as related by the grocery-shopping neighbor seemed odd, but the detectives knew it was not unusual. When people have no particular reason for noting the exact flow of time, their later impressions are frequently way off base. Unless, like the patient in the hospital, one had a particular and specific reason for mentally imprinting the exact moment of an event, time itself could steal away the seconds and minutes like a surreptitious thief. Thus, having established that Dr. Branion was actually making his rounds in the hospital at the exact same moment his grocery-shopping neighbor reported seeing him running out of his house, detectives almost immediately discounted that neighbor's version of that fatal morning.

This discrepancy of witness testimony and actual fact excluded some potentially vital evidence.

Not so easily disposed of, however, was an account given by another of the Branions' neighbors. This man, who happened to be the very same neighbor who had later taken the boy from Dr. Branions' arms, and whose wife was the doctor who examined and pronounced Donna Branion dead, this same man had been expecting and eagerly awaiting a long-distance telephone call from a friend. They had arranged that the friend was to call exactly at 11:30 a.m. The man remembered glancing at the clock the moment the phone rang, and feeling pleased that the call was right on time.

While he was talking on the telephone, Dr. Branion's neighbor had kept his eye on the clock because of the fees involved in long-distance telephoning. When the hands on his clock had just moved to 11:36, according to this neighbor, he heard what sounded like shots. He told his caller to hang on a moment and listened intently, but nothing further was heard so he continued with his conversation. His telephone call had lasted just under 15 minutes, bringing the time to 11:45. After hanging up, he recounted the highlights of the conversation to his wife for a few minutes, until their conversation was interrupted by Dr. Branion's shouting for help.

If this neighbor's version of the time of that morning's events was to be believed, then the exact time of Donna Branion's death had been fixed — 11:36 a.m., give or take a minute. And again, if this version was proved to be accurate, as telephone records would later show, then Dr. Branion could not be considered a suspect in his wife's murder, since his own statement indicated he had been at his son's nursery school at that exact same moment.

The detectives now went to the nursery school to confirm and double-check the doctor's account of the time and circumstances of his arrival there on December 22, 1967.

"Oh, my word, no! That is simply not true! Absolutely not! Good heavens, how could you even think such a thing!"

This was the reaction the detectives got when they repeated to the nursery school supervisor Dr. Branion's statement that his four-year-old son was bundled up and waiting outside when he pulled up in front of the school to pick the child up. The nursery school supervisor was appalled, her years of training and dedicated child-care seemingly brought into question. Under no circumstances, she now told the detectives, under *no* circumstances would she let a four-year-old child to be dressed up and set outside to wait

242

for a parent. Why, the very idea was abhorrent! Did the detectives, with all their years of police experience, not realize how dangerous such a practice could be to the health and welfare of a small, helpless child?

The detectives assured the outraged woman that they did, in fact, realize the dangers facing a child who was left waiting outside alone along a busy thoroughfare, but reiterated to her that Dr. Branion had specifically mentioned in his statement to them that his son was outside on the sidewalk alone, when he pulled up in front of the school at 11:35 a.m. to pick him up. They were merely repeating to her exactly what the doctor had said to them.

The woman snorted her contempt. She told them either they couldn't get their witnesses' stories straight, or Dr. Branion had taken leave of his senses, to even have suggested that she would bundle a four-year-old into his winter clothing and then shove him outside to wait for a tardy parent. Did the detectives realize that some parents, without any regard for the nursery school personnel, would arrive *hours* late at times? Were the detectives suggesting that she should wait only until the appointed time of the parents' arrival and then begin flinging her helpless charges out onto the sidewalk until their parents saw fit to pick them up?

The detectives attempted to soothe the woman's professional pride, but she would have none of it. Besides their outrageous intimation that she would turn out a helpless four year old onto the sidewalk, she sniffed, they were quite wrong in trying to convince her that Dr. Branion had arrived to pick up his son at 11:35. She knew very well what time the doctor had arrived. She should, since he was 15 minutes late. He had arrived at 11:45 a.m.

The detectives' internal alarm bells went off. Dr. Branion had stated clearly and without any hesitation whatsoever that he'd gotten to the school at 11:35, that he'd found his son already outside waiting for him, and that he'd gone home from there, arriving at 11:45 to find his wife murdered.

In order to be certain, the sleuths sat down with the nur-

243

sery school mistress and carefully went over the entire sequence of events on the day of December 22, 1967, as best she could recall them—which was very well, indeed. Her version of the timing coincided exactly with Dr. Branion's insofar as the start of the day's events.

She agreed that the doctor had dropped his son off at just about 9:00, which, she added, was his usual time. But from there on, her version and the doctor's version differed wildly as to how and when that morning at the nursery school ended. According to the school mistress, Dr. Branion usually arrived for his son somewhere between 11:30 and 11:40 a.m. But this one particular morning, December 22nd, he arrived a few minutes late, actually at exactly 11:45 a.m.

And how was she so certain of the time? sleuths pressed. Surely, she had other children to look after and could not be expected to recall the exact arrival time of each parent, they reasoned. She agreed, but added that her second class of pre-schoolers was due at the school at noon, and she'd kept glancing at the clock, worried that something at the hospital would be keeping Dr. Branion. When she saw his car pull up in front of the school, she glanced at the clock and was relieved to note that she would still have 15 minutes to tidy up in preparation for her next batch of students. She also told the detectives that the doctor had rushed into the school, apologizing for being late, and that he seemed incredibly rushed for time—so much so that he knelt down beside her and helped to put on the little boy's winter outer garments. She went on that while she helped the child pull on his boots, Dr. Branion was busy thrusting gloves onto the boy's hands and tying the child's woolen hat around his head.

Then, once the child was dressed for outdoors, a matter of a minute or so after the doctor arrived, Dr. Branion scooped the boy up in his arms and left. The school mistress had been somewhat flustered at this whirlwind behavior and she stood and watched as the doctor put his child into the front passenger seat and then ran around to get behind the wheel of his car. She said that he'd made a hurried U-turn and sped off—in the direction of his home.

244

If the nursery school mistress' recollection of the times and circumstances involved was accurate, and she seemed an extremely accurate woman, then the detectives realized the case was beginning to point very incriminatingly toward the doctor himself as the murderer of his wife. If he had, in fact, arrived at the school at 11:45, and not at 11:35 as he had said, then there were ten minutes unaccounted for in his movements on that morning. Moreover, if the shots heard by the neighbor who had been making a long-distance telephone call had occurred at 11:36, give or take a minute, then where was Dr. Branion at the time those murderous shots were fired?

In an effort to double-check the doctor's whereabouts, the detectives next went to interview the elderly woman who was supposed to have had lunch with the Branions that day. She told the detectives essentially the same thing Dr. Branion had told them.

He arrived at her apartment just moments after 11:30 to pick her up, but she hadn't been feeling well and had begged off. She said the doctor had been very solicitous, hoping she felt better soon, and then he left immediately. But she added something at this point, something the detectives hadn't heard before and which intrigued them. She said that the arrangements for her lunching with the Branions had been made by the doctor himself just the night before. She had already been in bed, since it was after 10:30 p.m. when the phone had rung. It was Dr. Branion, inviting her for lunch the following day with him and his wife.

She told the detectives that she had been extremely surprised at the invitation, first of all because she was not in the habit of lunching with the Branions, and secondly because of the lateness and the gentle insistence on the doctor's part that she come for lunch the very next day. The elderly woman said she had tentatively agreed, but added that if she wasn't feeling any better on the following day than she was now, she would have to cancel. The doctor agreed wholeheartedly.

Detectives now had a pretty damaging circumstantial case

245

against Dr. Branion, but they wanted to be thorough before confronting such an influential and well-respected member of the community with their suspicions.

They re-interviewed the woman doctor who'd examined Donna Brown Branion's body and pronounced her dead. During this re-interview, they mentioned that Dr. Branion had said that he hadn't examined his wife upon discovering her body because he knew for a fact that she was dead, having noted lividity in her legs. The woman doctor immediately shook her head. Impossible. She examined the body only moments later and found it to be still warm, a sign that death had occurred only shortly before. And she would stake her professional reputation on her statement that no lividity whatsoever had yet taken place. Dr. Branion was mistaken, maintained the woman physician.

But detectives knew it was more than that. He hadn't been mistaken — neither in time sequences he'd given to the detectives nor in his estimation of the condition of his wife's body. He hadn't been mistaken at all. He'd been lying.

The detectives went to the states attorney's office with their case and, on January 22, 1968, at 11:00 a.m., they placed Dr. Branion under arrest for the murder of his wife. It was exactly one month, less six minutes or so, since her death.

On June 12, 1968, Dr. John Marshall Branion, Jr. was convicted of the premeditated murder of his wife, Donna Brown Branion, and sentenced to serve 20 to 30 years in the penitentiary. His attorney immediately appealed the decision, and Dr. Branion, due to his prominence in the community, was freed on a $5,000.00 appeal bond.

What happened next in the case of Branion v. Branion reads like a novel, but is true. From June of 1968 until early in 1971, Dr. Branion continued his appeals of the murder conviction. His attorney used every technicality, every loophole to attempt to have the conviction overturned. But, in early 1971, Dr. Branion's last appeal was exhausted when the Illinois Supreme Court upheld the original conviction, requiring that Dr. Branion turn himself over to the marshall's office and begin serving his 20 to 30 year sentence. But that did not happen, because Dr. Branion disappeared.

The murder case and trial had received wide publicity, but Dr. Branion's complete disappearance received even more. Friends and acquaintances were brought in and questioned, bulletins were sent out with the doctor's photo and description. But Dr. Branion seemed to have vanished into thin air, and eventually, other news, other murders, consumed the public interest and Dr. Branion's mysterious disappearance vanished from the front pages.

Nothing further was heard in the matter until October 22, 1983, when, under the direction of the U.S. Department of State, two Cook County Sheriff's deputies flew to Uganda, Africa, and took Dr. Branion into custody, 20 years after the murder of his wife.

Much of John Branion's experience during those missing 20 years remains a mystery, and probably always will, but some of his activities are known. Authorities have established that after fleeing the United States, Dr. Branion went to the Sudan and from there to Uganda. From 1972 through 1979, Dr. Branion served as Ugandan dictator Idi Amin's personal physician, and was probably one of the few doctors involved in the care and treatment of Ugandan troops wounded during the Israelis' 1976 raid on the Ugandan airport at Entebbe. After Amin's fall from power, Dr. Branion disappeared, but it is known that he turned up some time later in South Africa and then in Malaysia. It was when he returned to Uganda in 1983 that he was taken into custody and turned over to U.S. State Department officials.

The official State Department version of these events recounts that Uganda's decision to expel Dr. Branion was reached at "diplomatic levels" between Washington, D.C. and the Ugandan capital of Kampala. But unofficially, authorities involved in the matter feel that Dr. Branion simply ran out of money, that he'd been sheltered and even welcomed by these various governments while he had money to spread around, but that once he could no longer pay his own way, he was taken into custody and turned over to United

States justice.

Dr. Branion has been remitted to an Illinois penitentiary to begin his 20 to 30 year murder sentence. He will face escape charges at a later date.

"'ANGEL OF MERCY' WAS A DEADLY BACKSTABBER!"

by Bob Carlsen

Peter Stodolka was so thrilled about getting a new leg he told his neighbors that he was going to dance a jig. Considering the spunk the old fellow had, that wouldn't have surprised them too much. Peter was an outgoing, friendly, 78-year-old single amputee who required frequent nursing and custodial assistance. But his handicap was strictly physical. Mentally, he talked as if he had two good legs. He was a character who would be missed after July 28, 1986.

Peter also was an excellent judge of character. He could size up the nurse's aides who cared for him within a short period of time. As a diabetic, Peter didn't want just anybody administering care to him. In June, he told one of his neighbors that he didn't trust one of the aides who'd shown up at his home.

Consequently, he gave his neighbor $1,000 for safekeeping before he made a final decision on whether he was going to continue with that particular aide from the home health care service. Peter, a widower, lost his leg at the beginning of 1985 to diabetes. In the middle of 1985, he sought assistance from a health service company. The company didn't provide home health care, so it sub-contracted the work to another health care company which could provide Peter with nurse's aides so he could continue to function in his home. He lived in the 9900 block of Old Highway 99, which at one time used to be the main corridor between Olympia and Tacoma, Washington, before Interstate 5 was constructed.

Between the summer of 1985 and July 1986, Peter Stodolka received care from a variety of nurse's aides who came to his home. Some of them he liked, others he couldn't get along with, and still others didn't like their jobs and quit. Consequently, Peter didn't have just one aide during the period of time he was being cared for. He had several, and talked about them with his neighbor who'd known him for years.

If he liked the nurse's aides, he'd praise their work. But if he had misgivings about an individual, he confided this to his neighbor, and that's why Peter gave her the $1,000 for safekeeping.

It was July 29, 1986, when the nurse's aide rang the doorbell to Peter Stodolka's home and got no response. This was not unusual, for often if a client is in the bathroom or a back bedroom, the nurse's aide can't hear the client's verbal response. Since it was her regularly scheduled visit, the nurse's aide let herself in to Peter's home. She was expected and knew that Peter wouldn't mind her intrusion.

Peter, as it turned out, wasn't in a position to object to anything. What should have been a routine visit for the nurse's aide turned out to be the beginning of a murder investigation for the Thurston County Sheriff's Department in Olympia.

The nurse's aide called out Peter's name as she moved through the modest house, but she got no response. This puzzled and alarmed her, for even if Peter was occupied at some task, he should have responded verbally by that point. He wasn't in the kitchen, living room or bathroom. When the aide got to the bedroom, she saw Peter lying prone on the bed. He was completely still and failed to respond when she called his name.

The aide had seen death before. She felt remorse for Peter as she approached the bed to routinely check for a pulse. She figured he probably had a heart attack.

But as she approached, she spied the ugly wound in his

chest. The blood saturated the shirt around the wound and that's when the nurse's aide realized this was no heart attack. Peter Stodolka had been murdered.

The nurse's aide went to the kitchen and dialed paramedics and then the county sheriff's office. She had ascertained that Peter didn't have a pulse, but regulations required her to follow a certain procedure to relieve herself and the firm for which she worked of any liability. That is why she notified the paramedics and the sheriff's office.

Paramedics confirmed the victim was dead and the scene was turned over to investigators from the sheriff's department. A deputy county prosecutor and a medical examiner arrived at the home along with sheriff's deputies.

The investigators determined the crime scene was limited to the victim's bedroom. Although the house appeared untidy, this was not unusual or surprising for a man who had only one good leg. To expect such a handicapped person to keep an immaculate house was unreasonable. Although untidy, the house didn't appear to be ransacked.

The victim was found lying on his back on his bed. A blanket was wadded up and at the left of his head. Both his arms were bent at the elbow with his hands, resting on his chest, partially covering the two severe wounds. The victim was completely clothed.

There was no sign of a struggle, which didn't surprise detectives. A man with only one leg and not wearing his artificial limb wouldn't have been able to put up much of a fight other than kicking with his one good leg and warding off blows with his arms. But as far as being able to get up and move around the room for a fight, that was impossible.

Neighbors later would tell detectives that Peter was still getting used to his prosthesis and was using a walker to get around the house.

Detectives questioned the nurse's aide who'd discovered the body to find out as much as possible about the victim's habits, requirements and routine. The nurse's aide told them the front door was unlocked when she'd arrived. This wasn't unusual, she explained, since many clients requiring

251

home health care often leave the door unlocked when they know an aide is coming.

Detectives noticed that the blood around the two chest wounds was coagulated and this caused them to theorize that the victim had been dead for quite some time. The medical examiner concluded that the time of death was probably on July 28th, the day prior to the body's discovery.

The fact that the victim was fully clothed and not in his pajamas also hinted that he was murdered the day before rather than during the night.

Peter sometimes took naps while fully clothed, the nurse's aide explained, but in the evening he'd get into long underwear or pajamas to sleep.

The victim's long underwear, which he often used in lieu of pajamas because they were warmer, were hanging on the shower curtain rod in the bathroom, detectives discovered. A dirty shirt lay in the bottom of the bathtub.

Investigators discovered that the victim had been stabbed a total of three times. The two chest wounds were apparent to detectives upon viewing the body, but it wasn't until the body was rolled over for removal that they found a third stab wound in the victim's back.

"To attack a cripple when he's in bed is the work of a real lowlife," commented a deputy at the scene. "But to stab him in the back had to be the height of cowardice."

Investigators surmised the victim may have been lying on his side or stomach sleeping when the assailant struck his first blow, that being to the victim's back. Then the assailant struck his next two blows, one being the fatal blow, to the victim's chest.

It didn't appear as if the victim put up any type of fight. There was no flesh or blood under his fingernails, nor were there defensive wounds on his palms or forearms.

"He probably didn't even know what hit him," one officer said. "If he did know, he couldn't do a damn thing about it."

The body was bagged and taken to the county morgue for autopsy. All of the activity around the victim's normally quiet home did not go without notice from the neighbors, many of whom gathered outside to learn the horrible truth about the fate that had befallen their friend.

"How could anybody do such a thing to a harmless soul like Pete?" one neighbor cried unashamedly as the body was removed from the scene. "He never did anything to deliberately hurt anyone. In fact, until his leg was amputated, he'd always gone out of his way to help people. I just don't understand it."

Detectives Conrad Riedl and John Bowen, assigned to the case, had a hard time understanding it, too. The place wasn't ransacked, the crime wasn't sexually motivated and, from what they'd been told up to that point, Peter Stodolka had no enemies, and in fact was well liked by many. The detectives shuddered to think that the crime was a thrill killing by somebody who got a rush out of picking on a helpless amputee who couldn't adequately defend himself.

The victim's home was dusted for fingerprints. A welter of prints was found. Many of them would turn out to be the victim's and others would turn out to belong to nurse's aides and friends. It was a case in which there were too many fingerprints to do the investigators any good. A lot of people legitimately had reason to be in Peter Stodolka's home, and to link them to the crime because their prints happened to be there would be an injustice.

None of the fingerprints found were bloody, which would have been a different situation altogether.

The murder, as murders go, was rather tidy compared to some the detectives had seen. There wasn't blood spattered all over the place. The victim's blood got on his shirt, the bedsheet, the mattress and pillow.

The bloody pillow was found stashed in a paper bag elsewhere in the house. The detectives thought this was quite odd. Why would the killer make an attempt to hide a pillow? It wasn't as if the pillow was some damning piece of evidence which could point an arrow directly at the murderer.

"Maybe it's more important than what we think," Detective Bowen told his partner. "We're assuming all of the blood on the pillow is the victim's. Maybe old Peter was able to put up more of a fight than we're giving him credit for."

But if some of the blood on the pillow belonged to the killer, wouldn't the killer have taken the paper bag and pillow with him and dumped it at another location? Perhaps he intended to do just that but in his or her haste left it behind, the detectives speculated.

The sleuths weren't ruling out the possibility that the killer was a woman. A woman could just as easily have gotten the drop on the sleeping amputee, plunged the blade into his back and then twice into his chest. They knew it was a possibility that had to be considered.

Also, the detectives had to look closely at the fact that during the past year, a lot of people, friends, and nurse's aides particularly, had access to the victim's home. It would have been an easy matter for any one of them to make a duplicate key to the house, slip in while Peter was sound asleep, and murder him. But what was the motive?

The detectives conducted a thorough search of the house and discovered that apparently only one thing was missing — but it was a very significant item. They could not find the victim's billfold anyplace.

Probers cogitated on that long and hard. If a stranger had slipped into the home with the purpose of swiping the amputee's billfold, couldn't he have done so without having to murder the old man? It certainly seemed so. Would a stranger commit murder just to steal a wallet when he or she had no idea what was in it? A stranger would have looked at the amputee, would have looked at the modest home and furnishings and figured the victim had very little worth stealing. Would it be worth committing murder to get his wallet? Somebody exercising common sense probably wouldn't commit such a murder for an amputee's billfold. But if the killer was doped up and had no sense of judgment, then he might commit such a crime for a stipend, sleuths reasoned.

"That's the problem with dopers," one detective said. "You never know what they'll do just to get one fix."

That's all a drug addict lives for — his next fix. A doper,

254

even though a stranger to the victim and knowing his chance of being caught would be quite slim, could have committed such a crime, the detectives figured.

That was one theory—that Peter Stodolka was killed by a stranger. The second theory, that he was killed by somebody he knew, also was closely considered.

Detectives questioned Stodolka's friends and neighbors. Those who hadn't been home to see the ambulance arrive and the body removed were shocked when they learned of the murder.

In questioning neighbors and friends, the sleuths were deliberately vague about details of the murder. They didn't reveal to anybody, especially the local newsmen, that the victim was stabbed three times, twice in the chest and once in the back. Even the best newsmen, who eventually learned the cause of death, believed the victim was stabbed three times in the chest, and reported such. It wasn't until the trial that the public learned the killer was a backstabber.

In questioning the victim's friends and neighbors, the detectives got, for the most part, the expected reactions of surprise and remorse. But when they talked to Peter's closest friend, the woman who lived nearby, they learned some very interesting things about one of the victim's nurse's aides.

"Pete said he didn't trust this guy," the friend recalled. "He didn't trust him at all. That's why he gave me his money to keep for him. He said he heard the guy walking around his house at night. That's when it started. That's when Pete got suspicious."

The nurse's aide whom Pete didn't like appeared on the scene in June of 1986, the neighbor explained. "Pete told me he didn't like the guy." The friend told detectives that she thought the nurse's aide was congenial and trustworthy.

"I told Pete he was just imagining things," she said. "I just sort of dismissed his fears. But I took the thousand dollars he gave to me for safekeeping."

Sleuths were curious about why the victim had that much money around the house. The friend told them that Pete sometimes kept as much as $1,800 at the house.

255

"When was the last time this nurse's aide was at Mr. Stodolka's house?" Detectives Riedl asked the neighbor.

She said it was June 24th. That would have been a month and four days prior to the July 28th murder. The nurse's aide had stayed at the victim's house overnight on June 24th because Stodolka required overnight care. The next day, he was relieved by another nurse's aide, the woman told detectives. That was the last time he came to Stodolka's house in the capacity of a nurse's aide, but he did return to visit Stodolka as a friend after June 24th, the detectives learned from the neighbor. Other neighbors confirmed the story.

When detectives learned that the one neighbor had received $1,000 of Stodolka's, they had to consider the possibility that she was a suspect. But after talking to her and other neighbors, and learning of her sterling character, they dismissed that possibility as nothing but folly. She never could have done such a thing, of that they were convinced. Thus her story about the nurse's aide whom Stodolka especially disliked took on even more credence.

Meanwhile, the autopsy on the victim confirmed what detectives had suspected, that he'd been stabbed once in the back and twice in the chest. One of the chest wounds had pierced his breastbone. The second chest wound had broken a rib and punctured his heart, thus being the fatal wound. The killer had plunged the knife in so deeply that the hilt of the knife left marks where it hit the chest.

Detectives learned that the nurse's aide whom the victim disliked was Nicholas R. Giesa, born June 5, 1956. Probers went to where Giesa lived and talked to his neighbors. They learned that Giesa had moved to the apartment complex the previous winter with a woman.

They'd come from California. It was clear to neighbors that Giesa and the woman, although living in the apartment together, were nothing more than roommates, and there was no romantic relationship between them.

When the woman lived with Giesa, he was friendly and outgoing, and the drapes in the apartment always were open.

256

But at the end of March, Giesa apparently wanted their relationship to evolve beyond the platonic stage and the woman didn't. They argued frequently. One day she packed everything and moved out. She moved in with her boyfriend.

That was a blow to Giesa, neighbors said. After that he changed. He did a 180-degree turn as far as his personality went. The drapes in his apartment were, for the most part, always kept closed, and he had little to do with his neighbors.

One day when he did have the drapes open, the apartment manager happened to be walking past. The manager glanced in the window and saw that Giesa was absorbed in something. When the manager took a closer look, he observed that Giesa was knitting.

About that same period of time, Giesa started looking for work as a nurse's aide, detectives learned. Giesa's work record was spotty. After graduating from high school in Torrance, California, he worked at a hamburger joint before joining the Navy. Upon leaving the Navy, he pushed hamburgers again in South Carolina, attending school at times.

He eventually moved back to California to work for a computer software company. He left that job to travel to the Pacific Northwest with the woman who became his roommate during the winter of 1985 to 1986. It was in the spring of 1986 that he sought work as a nurse's aide.

The first company he tried turned him down flat. His job skills didn't impress the potential employer. Said the firm's manager: "He was so obnoxious. That sticks in your mind. He was turned down on the interview alone. He was pushy and aggressive and said he had all these skills. He was such a no-hire situation all the way around."

After being unsuccessful at that firm, Giesa made an effort to improve his job interview presence, and eventually he found a job paying a stipend of $600 per month, which barely enabled him to support himself.

In June of 1986, Giesa was given the task of taking care of

Peter Stodolka. According to Giesa's neighbors, Giesa's odd behavior continued through June.

The death of Giesa's father bothered the nurse's aide. Also during the summer of 1986, two of Giesa's other patients died, detectives learned.

Said one of Giesa's neighbors: "He was weird. He was talking to himself, looking around. He was giving me the creeps. He never talked about his job. He just said he was going downtown."

Detectives learned that the day after Stodolka's murder, Giesa had made a substantial payment on a van he was in the process of purchasing. The sleuths estimated the murder victim may have had as much as $800 in his wallet when he was killed and robbed. This figure was arrived at because the neighbor said Stodolka was known to have as much as $1,800 at his home, and he had given her $1,000 of that because he didn't trust Giesa.

Detectives also learned that after Giesa finished with the victim as a client on June 24th, Giesa told the apartment manager he'd lost his job. That being the case, where did he get the money to pay his July rent and make the next payment on his van? detectives wondered. Perhaps he'd resorted to murder.

Detectives next contacted the woman with whom Giesa had lived in Olympia for a period of about six weeks. She told them that when she met Giesa in California, she felt sorry for him and suggested that he move up to Washington where he might find more opportunities. The woman, described by those who knew her as a good Samaritan, suggested that Giesa accompany her to Olympia, where she was moving so she could be near her boyfriend. It was clear from the beginning, she told detectives, that she was trying to help Giesa as a friend, and didn't want to get involved with him romantically.

Apparently, Giesa misinterpreted her actions, and after sharing an apartment and nothing more for six weeks, he wanted the relationship to develop into something more than just friendship.

258

"So I left," she said, concluding her story to detectives.

Without a roommate to help share the expenses, Giesa diligently sought work and eventually landed the job as a nurse's aide. But during this period of time he became even more introverted. By the time the murder occurred, he was knitting and crocheting, something he hadn't done before, and had reverted back to calling his mother "momma," when he wrote to her.

"He's reverted back to his childhood," said one person who assessed Giesa's personality change.

Detectives got search warrants for Giesa's apartment, van and surrounding premises. They found an athletic tote bag which contained a sheathed hunting knife, 10 inches in length with a five-inch blade, one side of which was serrated. The medical examiner had expressed the opinion that such a blade could have made the stab wounds found in the victim.

Also found was the victim's stolen wallet and some money. The victim's driver's license and other personal items were in the wallet. Sleuths noticed Giesa's hand was cut.

Nicholas Robert Giesa, 30, was arrested without incident and taken into custody. He made two statements to sleuths, one to Detectives Bowen and Riedl, the second to detective Joe Vukich. The first statement was tape recorded.

"I remember I just wanted to go for a ride," Giesa told the detectives. So he decided to stop by Stodolka's house for a visit. "I thought I'd just go up and say hello."

Giesa claimed he found Stodolka in bed, where Stodolka often stayed because he was an amputee. They chatted. He said he gave Stodolka a back rub, and Stodolka fell asleep.

Something caused Stodolka to awake, Giesa claimed. "When he rolled over, he thought I was someone else," Giesa said. "He stated, 'What the hell are you doing in my house?' "

Giesa said Stodolka was very angry and picked up a knife from a bookshelf and lunged at Giesa.

Detectives later would be told by one of Stodolka's neighbors and also other nurse's aides that Stodolka didn't keep knives around, but Giesa stuck to his story.

"We fought. Next thing I know is, the knife was in his back. We were fighting. I was trying to hold back the knife. We fell on the bed and we rolled and that's when I saw the knife in his back."

Then in the heat of anger, Giesa said, he stabbed the victim in the chest.

Giesa claimed Stodolka cut his hand with the knife. Detectives suspected Stodolka was able to ward off Giesa before the death blows were struck and, by so doing, caused Giesa to cut himself with his own knife.

Giesa went on to say in his confession that after stabbing the victim, he realized what he'd done, and merely took the wallet to make it appear to be a robbery.

Giesa repeatedly emphasized that he didn't go to the house to kill, burglarize or rob Stodolka. In a second statement to Detective Vukich, Giesa's story changed.

After Stodolka woke up and demanded, "What in the hell are you doing in my house?" Giesa and the victim started to argue. Giesa started to have delusions that he was arguing with his father, with whom he had a very stormy relationship because of childhood treatment. His father had just died that summer and, at the time of the murder, he was alive again in his mind, Giesa said.

Giesa didn't see Stodolka at all. He saw his belligerent dad. He grabbed from the desk what he thought was a flashlight and hit his father. The flashlight, really the knife, caused the back wound. Upon seeing this, Giesa claimed he snapped back into reality. He saw Stodolka writhing in pain and felt sorry for the old man. He thought it would be most merciful to put Stodolka out of his misery by stabbing the amputee twice in the chest.

Detectives noticed that in this second version of events, Giesa told about the delusions of Stodolka as father and knife as flashlight. This story (which they didn't believe) differed considerably from his initial version. Probers couldn't help but wonder if he was laying the groundwork

260

for some type of mental disorder defense.

Nicholas Robert Giesa was charged with first-degree murder, and in October of 1986, that charge was upgraded to aggravated first-degree murder after the county prosecutor became convinced the motive was robbery.

Aggravated first-degree murder, if the defendant is found guilty, carries either a death penalty or life in prison without possibility of parole. In this instance, the county prosecutor didn't try for a death penalty sentence, so the maximum sentence Giesa faced was life without parole.

While in prison awaiting trial, Giesa penned the following letter to his deceased father:

"If Dad were alive today—6-18-86.

"Dad, you are a son of a bitch, you keep telling mom and I you love us, but by your actions tell us you don't care.

"You cut me down saying I couldn't learn anything but when asked questions of you who is it who never had time for me. Who always shoved me away?

"Who was it that wouldn't listen to his own family or doctor?. . . Even though the doctor told you it was OK to go back to work but take it slow. Did you listen?

"Hell NO!

"We all love you. Even mom whom you abused for so many years with your damned drinking.

"You don't even know how many times I have heard mom crying in bed because she was afraid of you having an accident hurting you or someone else.

"Even though your attack is in 80 you seem to listen for a while but not long.

"Between your damn drinking and excessive working you are killing yourself.

"Why don't you listen to anyone who cares about you?

"You never listen to anyone but yourself. We all love you and care about you."

Giesa left the letter to his dead father unsigned. It later was admitted into evidence in court.

The trial began in mid-October 1986. Superior Court Judge Carol Fuller, in a pretrial hearing, determined that the jury couldn't be allowed to hear testimony or know that the murder victim was an amputee. The defense attorney successfully argued that this, although true, would unnecessarily prejudice the jury against the defendant. The judge agreed, much to the chagrin of the prosecution and courtroom spectators who didn't realize how much evidence is routinely withheld from juries, through no fault of investigators, but rather, through legalistic machinations.

The fact that the jury couldn't learn the victim was an amputee was a boon to the defense, for it lent credence to Giesa's story that the victim lunged at him with a knife. This story of Giesa's was plausible, but only if the victim had two good legs, which the jury members were led to believe he did because they heard or saw no evidence to the contrary.

But during the trial, the woman who'd briefly lived with the Giesa testified that Geisa was a liar who told grandiose stories and couldn't be believed. She believed he told these stories in a misguided effort to win her love.

The prosecution contended Giesa murdered Stodolka for the money. The defense contended Giesa thought he was really arguing with his father and couldn't form the intent to murder. Both sides presented psychiatric testimony to support their respective contentions.

On October 24, 1986, a five-woman, seven-man jury returned its verdict of guilty to the charge of aggravated first-degree murder. Judge Carol Fuller scheduled sentencing for December 3, 1986. During the interim, she received two letters from Stodolka's friends. The first read thusly:

"What an experience these last six months have been for me and my family and friends. I have probably experienced every emotional feeling there is and God has given me peace beyond my understanding through the whole situation.

"On the last day of the session I was so pleased with your response to not be in a hurry so you could think the case through. This is when the defense attorney tried to rule out first-degree aggravated murder for the jury to consider. I was so upset in hearing this that I really started praying for you. You then stood firm against the defense's request.

"I want to thank you for taking time to allow justice to happen."

A second letter went like this:

"Judge Fuller, I rejoice that justice was done in the case of the State of Washington versus Nicholas Giesa! Unfortunately, I was able to attend the trial only on Friday the 17th and Monday the 20th, but this one thing stood out: any information about Peter's physical capabilities was suppressed. I appreciate the fact that you have a duty to see to it that nothing is brought to surface which would prejudice the jury against the defendant, however, I believe it was necessary for the jury to know how really helpless Peter Stodolka was. There was no way in the world that he could have lunged at anyone—with or without a knife and in my opinion, this needed to be brought to light to prove that Giesa was a liar.

"Providentially, a lady did testify to that fact anyway—that he was a liar and was known for it. There were other things which were suppressed also, but this one thing seemed to be intended to prejudice the jury in the opposite direction: to elicit sympathy for Giesa.

"Fortunately, Our Lord saw to it that justice was done according to His Word."

On December 3, 1986, Nicholas Robert Giesa, 30—a man who spent his last free days knitting, crocheting and stashing unwashed dirty dishes in his apartment cupboards and reverting back to his childhood, in the opinion of some—was sentenced by Thurston County Superior Court Judge Carol A. Fuller to life in prison without the possibility of parole.

He is now serving his sentence and has appealed.

"THE CASANOVA WAS A CHAINSAW KILLER"

by Jack G. Heise

It was a chunk of meat, about the size a butcher might slice off the hind end of a small calf, minus the legs.

A couple of fishermen hauled it out of the Mississippi River, upstream from Davenport, Iowa. They were wide-eyed when they discovered it to be a portion of woman's body, a section from the belly button to the buttocks.

For weeks, police agencies used skin divers and officers in boats with grappling hooks to comb the river bottom and banks, but that was all they came up with: no head, no hands or arms, no feet or legs and no upper part of the body.

A dozen or more forensic pathologists examined the carefully preserved portion of the torso. They reached a consensus that it came from a white female in her mid 30s or early 40s and, from the pubic hair, they determined she had either light red or auburn hair.

They figured the part of the body had likely been in the water for about a month and had become hung up on the bottom until the fishermen snagged it. Because the section had been gutted, no body gasses had formed to bring it to the surface.

The rest of the corpse, pathologists reasoned, might

264

have been consumed by scavenger fish or rolled on down the Mississippi to almost anywhere between Davenport and New Orleans.

They weren't able to make a positive identification from just the flesh and skin, nor to hazard a guess as to how she may have been slain prior to being butchered. They did reach a conclusion, however, that whoever did the butchering had a knowledge of anatomy and had used a chainsaw to hack up the corpse.

A number of persons around Davenport, and eventually the police, claimed they had a pretty good idea who the victim might be, but there's a long stretch between a pretty good idea and proof, particularly if you have to go to court with it . . .

Close friends and relatives of Joyce and Dr. James Klindt weren't too surprised when the couple split up. They figured it was a shame because they had been considered the ideal married couple who came together in a story-book romance.

Jim Klindt had been an all-star high school athlete and had the looks to go with it so that he had been crowned "King of La Mer" at the high school graduation spring dance in 1966.

He followed the family medical tradition and went on to the Logan College of Chiropractics in St. Louis, Missouri. That's where he met Joyce Monohan from nearby Granite City, Illinois. A strawberry blonde, Joyce had been a beauty queen, so they became one of the most handsome couples on campus.

They were married before Klindt graduated and then, when he got his degree, they moved to Davenport for a waiting practice.

From the start, Dr. Klindt did well for himself. He had a $100,000 plus home built in a fashionable neighborhood, drove around in a silver Cadillac Seville, and Joyce had a blue Mercedes. James enjoyed his money and went for rich man's toys, purchasing, among other things, a luxurious

265

motor home and three expensive boats.

Considered a civic leader, Dr. Klindt sponsored a ladies bowling league team with Joyce as a team member. Joyce did all the things expected of a wealthy man's wife and devoted much of her time to charities.

But as the years rolled along, all was not as perfect with the "ideal couple" as might appear on the surface. Close friends knew that Dr. Klindt had a "roving eye" and, when it stopped roving and came to rest upon a woman considerably younger than Joyce and apparently more sexually aggressive, friends suspected there might be trouble.

Unlike the proverbial wife who is last to know, Joyce confided in her friends that she knew what was going on and was biding her time.

"I'm giving him enough rope to hang himself," Joyce told a close friend. "And when I'm ready, he's going to be lucky if he comes out of it with a spare pair of socks."

Joyce said that she not only knew all about her husband's romantic escapades, but she had other things to insure that, when the time came, she would get just about everything she wanted in a divorce settlement. She did not confide what "the other things" might be.

The friends weren't surprised when the split came on March 18, 1983, but what did surprise them was that Joyce moved out of the house instead of booting out her philandering husband as she had so often said she would do.

When questioned by friends and relatives of Joyce as to where she had gone, Dr. Klindt told them in no uncertain terms that it was none of their business. Furthermore, he didn't know and didn't care. He said they had one of their frequent spats, and he had given Joyce $4,000 in cash and she had decided to go on a vacation and let things cool down.

The relatives became concerned when they learned that Joyce's car had been found abandoned in the parking lot of a motel across the river from Davenport in Moline, Illinois. She hadn't registered at the motel, and none of the employees could recall having seen the attractive blonde.

A week after she left, and with no word from Joyce, the friends and relatives went to the police. They expressed concern because they felt certain that, if Joyce had gone somewhere, she would have contacted them.

The officer they talked to said he would take a missing person report and check into the case. The fact was, however, that with burglaries, armed robberies and various other crimes to investigate, a missing person report on a 34-year-old woman who allegedly left home after a quarrel with her husband doesn't create much of a stir in police activities.

The police officer did contact Dr. James Klindt. He wasn't any more cordial to the officer than he had been with Joyce's friends and relatives. He suggested that there were probably better places into which the officer could stick his inquisitive nose and to leave the dispute between himself and his wife up to them to settle.

After a couple more weeks without any word from Joyce, the friends and relatives returned to police headquarters. They let it be known that they weren't very pleased about the way the police were handling the case and, to put it bluntly, they thought it was more than just a missing person case. They were of the opinion that Joyce finally had her fill of her philandering husband's activities and had pulled the string on him. They figured that rather than let Joyce take him to the cleaners, he had gotten rid of her.

Theory is one thing and fact another. However, at the insistence of the friends and relatives, the case was assigned to the department's ace homicide investigator, Lieutenant Ted Carroll.

Carroll went to Dr. Klindt and laid it on the line for him. Relatives were saying they suspected he had killed his wife, and if he had any idea where she might be, it would be a good idea to locate her and calm down the relatives.

267

Dr. Klindt pooh-poohed the suggestion that he could possibly have killed his wife. He said, however, that he wasn't surprised at the charge because he and some of his wife's friends and relatives weren't on the best of terms. He said he still didn't know where his wife had gone, but if he heard from her or she returned home, he'd notify Lieut. Carroll.

Things really heated up a short time later when the frustrated friends and relatives learned that Dr. Klindt had moved the woman they called his paramour into his home, giving her the title of housekeeper.

"Housekeeper," one of the relatives snorted when he gave the information to Carroll. "The only housekeeping she'll do will be in the bedroom."

Carroll admitted that it was unusual, possibly even defiant, for Dr. Klindt to move the woman into his home prior to a divorce and while his wife was still missing.

He explained, however, that legally there wasn't much he could do about it until there was some definite information as to the whereabouts of Joyce.

"Why don't you guys get off your duffs and go out to the house and see what you can find?" a relative insisted. "If he killed her, it was probably there and then he took her God knows where and then left her car at the motel."

Carroll had another job of explaining to do. It might sound reasonable to check out the house, but legally it was impossible. It would require a search warrant and without a probable cause, a judge would not issue it. Dr. Klindt was regarded as a reputable physician and, if the police made any overt moves, the chances were that he'd slap them with a fat lawsuit.

Promising what action he could legally give the case, Carroll took the information to Lieutenant Jim Van Fossen, head of the Criminal Investigation Division. "You know the law," Van Fossen told him. "You make a false move at this point and you could blow the whole thing if a case should develop."

What looked to be a possible break in the case came when a friend of Joyce, who had been out of town, returned and learned she was missing.

The friend explained that shortly before Joyce disappeared she had been discussing with her the possibility of obtaining a divorce from her doctor husband. Joyce had given her some things to keep, which she said she didn't want her husband to know about.

The things Joyce had turned over to her friend for safekeeping were a cassette tape recording, a diary and some photographs.

When a relative and the friend brought the things to Lieut. Carroll, the relative said, "You just listen to that tape and you'll know damn well why I've been insisting all along that he killed Joyce."

The tape apparently had been secretly recorded during one of the heated quarrels between Joyce and Dr. Klindt. The voices, identified by the friend and relative as being those of Joyce and her husband, began with Joyce accusing him of being unfaithful, and his response, which did not deny the charges.

At one point where they were discussing property settlements and the values of the home, furniture and other property, Joyce suddenly shouted out, "You spit all over my face!"

Klindt's voice taunted, "And I'll do it again!"

There was a muffled response from Joyce and then Klindt's voice, "I don't give a damn about you anymore. You hire a lawyer and I don't want you around me again."

It went on, "I hate you. I hate your guts." In an outburst, he shouted, "You are horse shit!"

There was a muffled sound of Joyce's voice and she apparently had her head stuffed against a pillow and accused Dr. Klindt of trying to smother her.

He responded, "I was trying to kill you, yeah."

There were more muffled sounds as Joyce's head was again thrust against the pillow and then Klindt's voice threatening that he would cut her into small pieces and flush her down the toilet.

Carroll listened to the tape that lasted for 45 minutes and, when it was finished, he commented that while it held threats during a violent argument, it could hardly be considered in any way, shape or form a confession of a crime.

"People often say things they don't mean when angry," Carroll pointed out. "They say they are going to kill somebody, but they don't actually contemplate doing such a thing."

The diary and photographs, however, were something else.

In the diary, Joyce wrote that she had evidence that all of her husband's income wasn't from his clinic and chiropractic services. She stated that he was dealing in drugs and dispensing them out of his motor home. She threatened that if Dr. Klindt gave her a bad time in the divorce, she would turn the information over to the police and see that he was sent to jail.

The photos were of secret caches in the motor home where the drugs were kept with closeups of various illicit drugs and marijuana.

"We've got something here," Carroll said. The diary and the photos could be used as evidence to furnish probable cause for a search warrant, not only for the motor home but the house as well.

Carroll took the information to Scott County Attorney William Davis with a request for a search warrant. Davis suggested that it might be best to wait on serving the warrant. He advised planting an undercover officer to watch the motor home and catch Dr. Klindt in an actual drug deal that would result in a more severe penalty than only possession of drugs.

"I'd like to go for it right now," Lieut. Carroll told him. "This drug stuff is peanuts if he actually killed his wife like her relatives and friends believe. I'd like to take a lab team and give that house a real workover."

270

Davis said he would prepare a search warrant and have it issued by the court.

Before the search warrant could be served, the fishermen hauled the portion of a woman's torso out of the river.

Carroll was eager to serve the search warrant. He went to the big house, known locally as "The Castle" because of a turret-like structure in the center that housed a circular staircase around a huge fireplace leading to the upstairs rooms.

The detectives and technicians went over the house with a fine-tooth comb. The search was disappointing. They were unable to find any visible indications of bloodstains in the rooms, basement or garages.

They did, however, find a chainsaw. It was taken as possible evidence and turned over for a microscopic examination in the lab.

Drugs were found in the motor home in the places revealed by the photos Joyce had taken. A charge of illegal drug possession was filed against Dr. Klindt.

The tall doctor did not appear to be disturbed when the detectives showed up at his clinic and took him into custody on the charge.

"I suppose Joyce's relatives put you up to this," he was quoted as saying. "They've been bugging me ever since she left. I know they think I killed her, and they've openly accused me of it, but they're off their rockers.

"Joyce is out there somewhere probably laughing her head off because of the trouble she's causing me and probably thinking that I can't get a divorce while she's missing."

As proof of his statement, Dr. Klindt said that he discovered that Joyce had taken $34,000 in cash from a secret compartment in an air duct in their home. He said she had plenty of money to stay away as long as she wished to make his life miserable.

Booked on the drug charge, Dr. Klindt immediately made bail and was released. At his trial, he entered a guilty

271

plea to the misdemeanor charges of illegal possession of amphetamines and marijuana. He was fined $300.

In the meantime, the lab crew was unable to locate any traces of blood, skin, bone or hair on the chainsaw. Either it had been thoroughly cleaned or it wasn't the instrument used to hack up the corpse. The chainsaw was returned to Dr. Klindt.

Nevertheless, Carroll continued his investigation into the strange disappearance of Joyce. He was convinced the partial torso found in the river was that of the missing woman. However, a number of forensic pathologists who examined the remains were unable to state positively that it could be that of any particular individual. And without any proof that Joyce had been slain, while Dr. Klindt continued to insist that she was alive, no legal action was possible.

Four months after the disappearance of Joyce Klindt, Carroll took some of the new evidence he had collected to Prosecutor Davis. He had learned that the week following Joyce's disappearance, Dr. Klindt had purchased $800 worth of women's jewelry. It couldn't have been for his missing wife.

Carroll had also located two witnesses who were positive they had seen Dr. Klindt in his airboat on the river the day following Joyce's disappearance. It had been a cold, drizzly, foggy day and the witnesses recalled that it was the only boat on the river that day. The doctor had been seen cruising about 18 miles upstream from where the woman's torso part had been found.

"So he bought some jewelry for his girlfriend and went out for a boat ride," Davis commented. "That doesn't place him as a murderer. You may think he killed her, and I may think he killed her, but we have to convince a jury she's actually dead to get a conviction."

"What do we need?" Carroll asked.

"Teeth, fingerprints, something for a positive identification," Davis replied.

"Fat chance of coming up with that now," Carroll said. "So, where do we go from here?"

"Possibly nowhere at all," Davis responded. "There's just the chance that he may have committed the perfect crime."

"No way!" Carroll said explosively. Then he vowed, "I'll chase that guy all over hell barefooted until I nail him."

As more months passed it appeared that if Joyce had been slain, it was the perfect crime and would eventually be relegated to the unsolved file.

Then, almost a year to the day after Joyce was reported missing, a report came in from the Southwestern Institute of Forensic Sciences in Dallas, Texas. The report stated that from examinations of the specimens sent to them from the torso, they could be 98.8 percent certain that the remains were those of Joyce Klindt.

The technical procedures used, boiled down to layman's language, explained that the genetic markers to identify a body is much like using blood typing but more sophisticated.

The test that was conducted by Benita Harwood, comparing genes and enzymes from relatives of Joyce with those in the partial torso, revealed that it "is 107.8 times more likely two individuals (relatives) would produce the genes found in the torso than a random couple."

The genetic markers, or genetic fingerprints as they are sometimes called, are a comparison of 70 substances found in human tissue, with most of the enzymes and genes inherited.

What made the test so positive, the report stated, was that the rare enzyme in the partial torso had also been found in the blood of the relatives.

When Prosecutor Davis was shown the report, he said, "Okay, let's go to trial. I'll file the murder charge today."

Davis was well aware of the tremendous task ahead of him. Not only did he have to prove a murder with only a portion of a torso to identify the victim, but he would face

273

a formidable opponent in the attorney who had been hired by Dr. Klindt.

Lawrence Scalice is considered to be an outstanding criminal defense attorney in the midwest. He has handled numerous cases in which he has won an acquittal for his clients, including a recent case in which the defendant was identified by two witnesses as being hired to do the murder. Davis and Scalice are good friends, but have entirely different courtroom manners.

Scalice, a graduate from the University of Iowa, served as an assistant Polk County attorney when he came out of law school. He became one of Iowa's youngest attorney generals in 1965 at the age of 31. He lives in a $200,000 plus home in Des Moines, has an annual income in excess of a hundred thousand dollars and a net worth of over one million dollars.

In the courtroom, he displays a "folksy style" that appears to be casual and relaxed, but his opponents say he's a "sly old fox" and throws his witnesses and the jurors off guard by his "country boy" appearance and style.

It is well known that he puts together a book on every case he handles so there will be no surprises once he's in court. He spends a great deal of time questioning prospective jurors and often uses a consultant to study the body language of the jurors.

Pros. Davis presents quite the opposite appearance and demeanor in court. A slender, former basketball star and honor student, Davis worked days as a fry cook in a fast food restaurant to put himself through school. He graduated from the Drake University law school in 1970 with the award of being the top student in the class. When he ran for Scott County Attorney, he was considered to be an underdog without much chance of winning. He was elected in what was termed an upset. When he filed for his second term, because of his reputation, there was no one to oppose him.

Known to be a 60-hour-a-week man in court, Davis is

termed a "bull-dog," firey and fist-pounding with a shrill voice, and like Scalice, he goes into court prepared to win his case.

Both Davis and Scalice have said they are happy to practice criminal law and agree that most criminal attorneys are "frustrated actors." They both enjoy the theatrics and drama of a well fought trial.

Both the prosecution and defense attorneys were well acquainted with the judge who would preside over the hearing. Judge James Havercamp had been a classmate of Scalice when they graduated from law school in 1958.

Judge Havercamp is known to his legal colleagues as "King James" because, when he sits on the bench, there's never any doubt as to who is in command.

A man with a sharp tongue and dry wit, Judge Havercamp has been known to chastise any attorney in open court who is not properly prepared to present his case. He has won the respect of the legal profession by insisting that a trial proceed as rapidly as possible and makes prompt, often correct, decisions on procedure and evidence.

The trial for Dr. Klindt, because of the pre-trial publicity in Davenport, was moved down river to Keokuk.

The sensational case in which the wealthy doctor was accused of killing his wife and hacking up her body with a chainsaw, plus the legal giants who were to prosecute and defend in the action, packed the courtroom to SRO daily. Spectators arrived hours before the courtroom doors opened and often carried their lunches so as not to have to vacate their seats during the lunch recess.

To add to the drama, the trial opened on the 15th wedding anniversary of Joyce and James Klindt.

It took nearly a week to select seven men and five women who could swear that they had not formed an opinion on the case.

Pros. Davis' opening statement took two-and-a-half hours to acquaint the jurors with the 80 witnesses and 160 items offered into evidence. He stressed that Dr. Klindt had the motive and the opportunity to murder his wife and that there was no other person who would wish her dead. He emphasized that, although only a part of the torso of the victim had been found, it could be established beyond a reasonable doubt that it was that of Joyce Klindt.

Scalice addressed the jurors with his usual casual and friendly style. When he sat on the edge of the counsel's table during his remarks, he was chastised by Judge Havercamp as to proper courtroom decorum.

Scalice did not deny that his client might have been guilty of philandering and that he and his wife had engaged in bitter quarrels. The admission was made because Davis was allowed to introduce the tape recording made by Joyce as evidence. Scalice, however, pointed out that if all unfaithful husbands who quarreled with their wives were guilty of murder, the country would soon be decimated.

His strongest contention was that there was no possible way the state could prove the partial torso taken from the river was that of Joyce Klindt. Scalice made a point of the fact that the torso had been found a month after Joyce disappeared and the condition of it did not indicate that it had been in the water that long. He read off a list of 10 women who had been reported missing in the Davenport and Chicago areas and stated that the torso might well belong to any one of them.

"Joyce is alive," he told the jurors. "She is voluntarily keeping her whereabouts a secret to punish her husband for his indiscretions."

The trial lasted four weeks, with each day delivering the promised drama with the testimony of the witnesses, the gruesome photos of the hacked torso, the startling tape recording and the theatrics of the attorneys.

The courtroom resonated with the booming voices of both attorneys, with impassioned pleas from Davis to find the defendant guilty, and equally as impassioned pleas from Scalice to not find a man guilty of a crime that had never been committed.

When the jurors were sent out to deliberate a verdict, the spectators and news reporters who had written and broadcast voluminous accounts of the trial, were almost evenly divided on their opinions as to whether Dr. Klindt would be found innocent or guilty.

The pivotal point, they agreed, was whether or not the state had been able to positively prove that the torso was that of Joyce Klindt.

After four days of deliberation, the panel returned, stating they were hopelessly deadlocked. And like the spectators, they were almost evenly divided in their opinions as to whether Dr. Klindt was innocent or guilty of the charge.

Judge Havercamp, after polling the jury and satisfied that additional time to deliberate would not result in a unanimous verdict, ordered the venire dismissed and stated there would be a new trial.

Both Davis and Scalice were disappointed in the result, but not dismayed.

Pros. Davis confidently told the investigators who had gathered the evidence and the reporters, eager for a statement, "We convinced half of them this trip. We'll convince all of them next time around."

Scalice held to the same philosophy. He said he was confident, now that he knew the state's case against his client, that he could win without much trouble an acquittal at the next trial.

The site selected for the new trial was Sioux City. It was held in a massive brick building that is a post office and has a single courtroom on the second floor. The ornate Woodbury County Courthouse is on the National Registry of historic buildings.

The old building has a huge stained glass dome in the middle and the courtroom has a V-shaped stained glass ceiling with stained glass along one wall. There are two marble fireplaces in the room, dating back to when there was no central heating system, and there is a black marble-covered railing in front of the elaborately carved oak bench and wall.

Prior to the trial, Davis informed the news media that the second trial would not be a rerun of the first. He and investigators had spent every possible moment going over the testimony in the first case to find the flaws. He felt the state's case had failed to convince the jurors that the torso taken from the river was that of Joyce Klindt.

Scalice felt that his case had failed because the six-foot-six Dr. Klindt had appeared too arrogant at the first trial. His appearance apparently convinced some of the jurors that he might be capable of such a crime.

Taking a tip from the first trial, Prosecutor Davis employed an associate professor of psychology at the University of Iowa to help him in the selection of a jury.

When the panel was completed, it varied from the first trial in that there were 10 men and only two women.

During the questioning of the prospective jurors, Pros. Davis hammered home the point that they must be capable of making a decision and that, in order to return with a guilty verdict, they only had to be certain beyond a reasonable doubt, and not beyond all doubt.

Scalice spent much of his time questioning the witnesses by asking them to look at his client and to tell him whether or not he appeared to be arrogant.

The new trial began as sensationally as the first, with the young woman with whom Dr. Klindt was alleged to be having an affair coming into the courtroom prior to the arrival of the judge and jury and planting a kiss squarely upon the lips of the defendant.

The new strategy to present the state's case by Davis was evident from the opening. He concentrated upon establishing proof that the torso was that of Joyce Klindt, confident that if he could prove that, it wouldn't be difficult to convince them that Dr. Klindt was the only person with a motive and opportunity to commit the crime.

He called as a witness Benita Harwood, the laboratory technician from Dallas, who had been responsible for his having originally filed the murder charge. The witness revealed that, from an examination of the genes and enzymes in the torso as compared to those of Joyce's relatives, it was 107.8 times more likely to have been produced from her relatives than from a random couple.

The next witness was a professor of genetics and pediatrics at the University of Iowa. He confirmed that his findings were similar to those of Ms. Harwood.

Dr. Mark Stolorow, a forensic serologist, testified that his findings confirmed those of the two witnesses who had preceded him.

Next to take the stand was a world famous anthropologist from Oklahoma City. He was qualified as an expert from the numerous cases in which he had been able to reconstruct the identities from body parts found in major plane crashes around the world.

He stated that from the flesh and bones he had examined, he would place the torso as having come from a white female, 27 to 40 years old, five-foot to five-foot six-inches, weighing 125 to 145 pounds, with reddish light brown hair.

At the time, Joyce disappeared, she was 33 years old, five-foot four-inches, 125 pounds with what had been described "dishwater blonde" hair.

To take care of the question about the hair, Davis called to the stand a hairdresser who testified she had taken care of Joyce's hair for a number of years. She stated that the natural color of Joyce's hair was a light brown with reddish tint, but she had it frosted to that of a grayish-blonde.

Pros. Davis next called to the stand a dermatologist. There had been testimony at the first trial concerning what appeared to be a birthmark and a mole on the hips of the torso. The defense had established that no one could recall that Joyce had either a birthmark or a mole on her buttock. The testimony from the dermatologist was that what appeared to be birthmarks or moles in the photos of the torso might well have been bruise marks, created at the time she was slain or after the body had been placed in the water.

Expecting a challenge by the defense, Davis called as witnesses two members of the United States Corps of Engineers, who testified that, during the time the torso was in the river, it was at flood stage. Other body parts could have been carried down river, but the torso, for some reason, was hung up on the bottom, 18 miles below where Dr. Klindt had been seen in his airboat on the day following Joyce's disappearance.

With his technical witnesses finished with their testimony, Davis called to the stand a professor of Statistics and Actuarial Science at the University of Iowa. He testified that from the statistics he had received, there was a 99 percent probability that the torso was that of Joyce Klindt.

Davis followed the testimony with that of two additional statisticians from the Loras College in Dubuque. They stated that, based upon the assumptions, from their actuarial tables there was a 98.82 percent probability that the torso was that of Joyce Klindt.

Scalice immediately scoffed at the testimony and told the jurors that it was the first time he had ever heard of anyone attempting to prove a murder by statistics.

During a recess, Davis confidently told Carroll and Van Fossen, "I think we've got them this trip. I think those statisticians did the trick. I've stressed from the start that they only had to decide upon a reasonable doubt and not beyond any doubt. We'll throw that tape recording and diary at them next and that will provide the motive."

The rest of the trial was pretty much the same cast of characters and props that had been used during the first trial, with Davis showing motive and opportunity for Dr. Klindt having committed the murder, and Scalice arguing that Joyce was still alive and the jury could not convict a man for a crime that never happened.

When the prosecution and defense had completed their cases and given their closing arguments, the spectators and press were not as evenly divided in their opinion of the outcome as they had been during the first trial.

"Scalice is one of the best in a courtroom," one reporter commented. "But I think Davis got to him this time. He sure did his homework to identify the torso as that of Joyce Klindt. The rest was just gravy with the tape recording."

The jurors returned with a verdict on Tuesday, November 20, 1984. It wasn't all that Davis had hoped for, but it was a long way from what Scalice had in mind.

The panel found Dr. James Klindt guilty of murder in the second degree. The conviction could carry a maximum penalty of 50 years in prison. However, Scalice immediately gave notice of appeal, so Judge Havercamp delayed setting a sentencing date.

"I'd have liked it better if they came in with first-degree and I could have argued for the death penalty," Pros. Davis was quoted as saying. "But I'm not worried about an appeal. They'll have to show errors in the trial, and 'King James' simply doesn't allow any errors in his court."

"CHILLING CONFESSION OF CINCINNATI'S CYANIDE KILLER"

by William K. Beaver

Pathologist Lee Lehman continued his methodical examination on John Powell's 44-year-old body. Powell had been critically injured in a July 1986 motorcycle accident and had laid in a deep coma in Drake Memorial Hospital for nearly eight months.

When Powell died on March 7, 1987, the Hamilton County coroner was required to perform an autopsy since Powell had been admitted as the victim of traumatic wounds sustained in a motor vehicle accident and had died later.

As the pathologist worked with his usual surgical precision, he became aware of a curious odor—the bittersweet smell of almonds. Immediately his suspicions were aroused.

The smell of almonds can sometimes indicate the presence of the class-six supertoxin, cyanide, a poison so toxic that a very small dose can immediately kill an average-sized man. But why would cyanide be present in the body of an accident victim? the pathologist wondered.

Lehman was well aware of how the deadly poison worked. The substance when introduced into the body prevents the cells from utilizing already available oxygen. As the cells become oxygen-starved and start to shut down, brain functions also cease, including the operation of the lungs. The lungs stop working, oxygen already in the body is not used, and death is almost instantaneous.

But another fact troubled Lehman. He knew that only about one person in five could even detect the odor, so it was crucial that he be absolutely certain. To be sure, he submitted several of Powell's tissue samples for testing.

When the test results came back, Lehman's suspicions were confirmed. There were positive traces of cyanide in Powell's body.

When Lehman reported his results to Hamilton County Coroner Frank Cleveland, Cleveland immediately ordered autopsies for any deaths occurring at Drake Hospital since March 7th. No evidence of other poisonings was found and no other suspicious deaths were uncovered.

Cleveland reported the results of the autopsy to Drake Hospital's chief executive officer and hospital administrator. This man had an already difficult job running the county-owned, tax-supported, 446-bed facility. Drake Hospital had been the subject of controversy before and the administrator knew that even though a board of directors ran the hospital, any foul play would be his responsibility.

The administrator called a meeting to plan what steps the hospital should take. The people present attested to the case's importance for the hospital and the city of Cincinnati.

Lieutenant William Fletcher of the Cincinnati Police Department's Homicide Division was accompanied by the four officers assigned to the case—Detective Sergeant Paul Morgan, Detective Sergeant John Jay, Detective Ronald Camden and Detective James Lawson. All were experienced investigative professionals.

Also present was Jack Leach, spokesman for the coroner's office, coroner Frank Cleveland, pathologist Dr. Lee Lehman, Drake Hospital's administrator and a woman who was second in command at Drake Hospital.

As representatives of Drake Hospital and the coroner's

283

office outlined the facts, the detectives understood both the gravity and the difficulty of the case. Drake employed over 750 people. Every person who had contact or access to John Powell would have to be interviewed, which included three shifts of hospital employees, medical staff, nurses, nurse's aides, and maintenance people. Powell's relatives and visitors would also have to be investigated.

As the detectives began the awesome task to polygraph interviews, Sergeant Morgan searched for information concerning where and how someone had obtained cyanide.

As a powder, cyanide is generally found in two common forms—sodium cyanide and potassium cyanide. Cyanide is used for several different chemical uses, but more significantly it is also employed for many illegal purposes. Medical experts explained to Sergeant Morgan why this is so.

When cyanide is used to murder someone, unless the examining physician can smell its telltale almond odor, the poison is not detected. When the embalming process is completed, most signs of murder disappear as the embalming fluid breaks down the cyanide.

Destroying evidence of murder is not the worst thing about cyanide, but rather, the ease with which it can be purchased off the record. Unless the cyanide is obtained from someone who keeps detailed records, as in the case of few scientific supply houses, there is no means of identifying a purchaser.

The disappointing information seemed to fit with the general flow of the investigation. As the work of uncovering leads continued, the polygraph interviews provided no clues. John Powell's wife agreed to an interview, but after a long session with detectives, the investigators decided she knew nothing about Powell's death.

On Saturday, April 4th, one of the nurse's aides at Drake, Donald Harvey, came to the homicide squad's office for questioning. The police had become suspicious of Harvey when he had called the detectives and asked to reschedule his previous appointment.

They learned in the interim that Donald Harvey had worked for Cincinnati's Veteran's Administration Hospital, but was forced to resign following a confrontation with the VA hospital's security.

Harvey had worked at the Veteran's Administration Hospital as an autopsy assistant from 1975 through July 1985. According to reports from the VA hospital, police learned that Harvey had been stopped by hospital security after an undercover agent witnessed him putting a gun into his gym bag.

The VA hospital administrator reported that when security personnel searched Harvey's bag, they found a .38 snub-nosed revolver, some syringes, needles, anatomy textbooks, surgical scissors and gloves, a cocaine spoon, the morgue's floorplan and several books about the occult.

The police detectives began questioning Donald Harvey without yet putting him on the polygraph machine. During the course of their interrogation, Harvey admitted killing John Powell. Sergeant Morgan asked him to make a statement. Harvey said he would.

The Cincinnati police had long made a practice of videotaping suspects' statements and as the expensive equipment was readied, Sergeant Morgan felt somewhat relieved that Harvey had confessed to Powell's murder, but his experience made him apprehensive about what Harvey might say in his statement.

As the electronically recorded statement progressed, Harvey admitted murdering John Powell by poisoning him with cyanide which had entered his body through a gastric tube.

When Harvey finished with his statement, Sergeant Morgan placed him under arrest and charged him with aggravated murder in the death of John Powell, 44, a General Electric welder who left behind a wife, four daughters, and a son.

Morgan and the other detectives felt there might be other victims, but who they were and how they had died would be nearly impossible to discover unless Harvey told them. He only admitted to the death of John Powell, but the evidence was strong enough that the prosecution could convict Harvey on an aggravated murder charge.

A transcript of the videotapes were sent to Prosecutor Art Ney, Defense Attorney William Whalen and the four police detectives. Lieutenant Fletcher reported to the press that Powell's death appeared to have been an isolated incident. The lack of any credible evidence other than people's suspicions would allow the police to draw no other conclusion. It would be a matter of time before conclusions were reached.

On April 28th, Donald Harvey pleaded not guilty to the murder of John Powell by reason of insanity. The judge ordered that he undergo a psychiatric evaluation.

Sergeant Morgan and his team of detectives still considered it possible that Harvey had killed others. But they were stymied by the fact that no evidence existed to support their suspicions. Some members of Drake Hospital had also raised concerns about suspicious deaths but no eyewitnesses had seen anything, nor did any of them have evidence to substantiate their claims.

Sergeant Morgan knew that little else could be done with Donald Harvey except to concentrate on helping the state convict him. But the six o'clock news on June 23, 1987, changed all that.

A local television station devoted their entire half hour to what they claimed was significant evidence that warranted further investigations at Drake Hospital. A two-month investigation led by their anchorman, according to the newscast, revealed that hospital personnel remained convinced that as many as 23 suspicious deaths had occurred while Donald Harvey had worked at Drake Hospital. In addition to this, the newscast claimed that a statistically higher number of deaths had occurred on the ward where Harvey worked than had occurred in the other hospital wards.

On June 25th, Prosecutor Art Ney announced that he would launch an investigation into the allegations made by the news broadcast. On July 6th, a special grand jury convened to investigate those cases in which patients had died while Harvey worked at Drake Hospital.

Between July 14th and July 18th, the bodies of 10 people were exhumed by the Hamilton County Coroner's Office and reautopsied for signs of poison or anything else suspicious. Tissue samples were sent to the FBI laboratory in Washington, D.C., and when the results came back only two showed traces of arsenic poisoning.

The judge ordered Harvey's trial, originally scheduled for July 27th 1987, to be postponed until January 25, 1988, in order to continue the investigation of possible other homicides.

Near the beginning of August 1987, Sergeant Morgan and his team were informed of some interesting developments by the prosecutor. Harvey, knowing that he would face the death penalty if found guilty of other homicides in addition to Powell's, wanted to give information on other deaths if a plea-bargain arrangement could be made.

Attorneys for the prosecution and defense finally reached a complicated plea-bargain arrangement. Harvey would be required to give details of all the crimes he had committed in Hamilton County. He would plead guilty to all the crimes and would agree to never appeal his conviction. If Harvey would appeal, or if other crimes were found outside his confession, the prosecutor could reindict him with the intention of seeking the death penalty.

Donald Harvey was brought to the homicide division's office and a plan was made to videotape the sessions. During nearly 16 hours of questioning, the Donald Harvey story began to appear far worse than Sergeant Morgan or anyone else had imagined.

Harvey, an admitted homosexual since his teenage years, was born in Hamilton, Ohio, but was raised in the impoverished area of Island Creek, Kentucky. He had grown up in an old farmhouse surrounded by Kentucky's familiar tobacco fields and was educated in an eight-room schoolhouse.

Harvey claimed that during his childhood, he was sexually abused by family members and neighbors. When Harvey turned 18, he moved to London, Kentucky, and with the help of a friend, he got a job as an orderly at Mariemont Hospital in London, where he worked from May 11, 1970, through March 31, 1971.

According to Harvey, 1971 was also the year that he first attempted suicide, by breaking into one apartment, stealing clothes and then breaking into another apartment and setting it afire. He was arrested and the charges were reduced on the stipulation that he seek mental treatment. He pleaded guilty to petty larceny and was fined 50 dollars.

After being examined by a court-ordered psychiatrist, Harvey was declared satisfactory by mental health personnel and he joined the Air Force in June 1971. He was stationed near San Francisco, where he became familiar with the large gay community there.

He was honorably discharged in March 1972, but his discharge also mentioned a character/behavior disorder. Harvey claimed that after he was discharged he soon had problems with his family and took an overdose of pills. He was in the Lexington Veterans Administration Hospital for four months and then was treated as an outpatient for another 18 months.

Harvey began drifting through several hospital jobs. He found a job as an orderly in the mental health ward and later was a ward clerk on a surgical floor at Good Samaritan Hospital in Kentucky from June 1973 through January 1974. From August 1974 through February 1975, Harvey worked as an orderly at another Kentucky facility, Cardinal Hill Hospital.

He then worked at Saint Luke's Hospital in Kentucky as a ward clerk from March through September 1975, when he joined the Veterans Administration Hospital in Cincinnati. He worked there as an autopsy assistant for nearly eight years and was then transferred to the cardiac catheter unit. He was transferred back to the morgue where he stayed until he was forced to leave in 1985.

Harvey then joined the staff at Drake Memorial Hospital where he worked until his arrest in April 1986.

Harvey claimed that he committed murders which were not connected with Drake Hospital, but were related to his own personal life.

Harvey shared a first-floor apartment with his homosexual lover in a duplex owned by his lover on Colerain Avenue in the Mount Airy section of Cincinnati. Harvey had started his relationship with his lover in 1979. After four years, the relationship began to sour and Harvey claimed that he wanted to protect his relationship from the people who he felt threatened it.

The second-floor apartment was rented to a Helen Metzger, a loyal employee of the same insurance company for 45 years. On April 4, 1983, Harvey put arsenic in a small piece of pie with whipped cream topping. Helen Metzger became Donald Harvey's victim.

A vice-president of the insurance company later noted that at Helen Metzger's funeral, the pallbearers included himself, Harvey's roommate, another insurance company employee and Donald Harvey.

Harvey's next victim was Henry Hoeweler, his lover's father. Hoeweler had been admitted to Providence Hospital and during one of his visits, Harvey had sprinkled arsenic into Hoeweler's pudding. Henry Hoeweler died of arsenic poisoning on May 1, 1983.

Harvey attempted to murder Hoeweler's wife more slowly by giving her smaller dosages of arsenic over a two-year period, but did not kill her.

Harvey had a friend who worked in a beauty salon. In January 1984, Harvey attempted to kill her by putting stolen hepatitis serum into her coffee. The woman was hospitalized but did not die.

In 1985, Edgar White lived upstairs in the apartment formally belonging to Helen Metzger. White, 81 years old, began an argument with Harvey's roommate in March 1985, claiming that he was paying the hot water bill for both apartments.

Harvey decided to kill White and when White complained of a stomachache, Harvey mixed arsenic in a bottle of Pepto Bismol and gave it to White. White suffered several severe symptoms, but did not die.

Harvey then put more arsenic in a second bottle of stomach medicine and also gave it to White. This time White became much sicker and was admitted to Providence Hospital where he died on March 22, 1985. Harvey also confessed to killing White's dog by poisoning the animal with arsenic.

When Harvey admitted to killing Edgar White, a second autopsy was impossible because White's body had already been cremated. Police did find the second bottle of medicine untouched after two years. Highly specialized tests indicated the presence of traces of arsenic.

Another personal victim was James Peluso, a member of a prominent Newport, Kentucky, family and an acquaintance of Harvey's. Peluso was also killed by arsenic sprinkled in pudding. The prosecution later claimed that Harvey confessed to another murder of a woman who lived above him by poisoning her and her dog. The only evidence was Harvey's confession which, under Ohio law, was not enough to convict him.

Sergeant Morgan and his team of detectives listened in disgust as Donald Harvey confessed to the killings. But his confession became even more gruesome as Harvey recounted a growing list of death and murder.

Harvey claimed that the homicides at Drake Hospital were committed because "he felt sorry for them." Sergeant Morgan and the prosecutor both highly doubted the claim, especially in light of the murders of his neighbors.

The victims at Drake Hospital began with Leon Nelson

who had worked for the same company for 36 years and was a deacon in his church. When he was admitted to Drake Hospital, Nelson had a wife and a very large family. Harvey murdered Nelson on April 12, 1986, by placing a plastic bag over Nelson's mouth and nose and then placing a wet towel over the bag, suffocating him. Virgil Weddle was murdered next on April 19, 1986, after Harvey mixed rat poison in with Weddle's dessert.

Harold White was poisoned with arsenic while at Drake Hospital, but died in June 1986, after being transferred to another facility.

Edward Shreibels died on June 20, 1986, after Harvey mixed arsenic into Shreibels' orange juice.

Robert Crockett died on June 29, 1986, when Harvey mixed cyanide and water than injected the solution into Crockett's intravenous tube.

Donald Barney, a hero of World War II, had been admitted to the hospital in a coma, but had come out of it. He died on July 7, 1986, when Harvey put a similar cyanide mixture into his gastric tube and then injected cyanide into his buttocks.

James Woods died on July 25, 1986, from cyanide that had been injected through the gastric tube.

Earnest Frey, an accountant, died on August 16, 1986, by the same means.

Milton Cantor died on August 29, 1986, after cyanide was injected into the gastric tube.

John Oldenkirk died in the summer of 1986, after Harvey poisoned him with arsenic.

Roger Evans had been married to his wife for 37 years. He died on September 17, 1986, from a fatal injection of cyanide through the gastric tube.

Claborn Kendrick practiced law and favored the death penalty. His wife was vacationing in Hawaii and Donald Harvey waited until she returned to murder him. Kendrick died on September 30, 1986, from cyanide through the gastric tube.

Albert Buehlmann died on October 29, 1986, after Harvey mixed cyanide into a cup of juice and then helped Buehlmann drink it.

William Collins died on October 30, 1986, also from cyanide mixed with orange juice.

Mose Thompson had a feeding tube injected directly into his stomach. He died on November 22, 1986, after Harvey put cyanide in the tube.

Cleo Fish died on December 10, 1986, after drinking cyanide mixed with orange juice. Harvey admitted having a conversation with Fish shortly before Fish finished the juice.

After Harvey broke off his relationship with his roommate/lover in late 1986, he started giving him small doses of arsenic to make him sick, allegedly for revenge.

Odas Day was a retired Cincinnati policeman. He died on December 10, 1986, after Harvey injected cyanide into his feeding tube.

Leo Parker worked at a restaurant and liked to play cards. He died on January 10, 1987, from cyanide injected into his feeding tube.

Margaret Kuckro was killed on February 15, 1987, by orange juice mixed with cyanide.

Joseph Pike died on March 6, 1987. Harvey was running low on cyanide, so he used a petroleum distillate used to clean tubes and colostomy bags.

The next day, March 7, 1987, Harvey poisoned John Powell using the remainder of the cyanide and injecting it into his gastric bag. The same day, Harvey killed Hilda Leitz by using the same petroleum distillate he had used on Joseph Pike.

Stella Lemon died on March 16, 1987, from an earlier injection of cyanide.

Harvey admitted that he tried to kill one victim by feeding him AIDS-infected blood, but the tactic did not work. The man later died because of Harvey's use of cyanide.

The investigation team sat in stunned silence as the suspect's 16-hour confession ended. Harvey also confessed to another 10 murders at the Veteran's Administration Hospital during his employment there. He could not, however, give satisfactory evidence of the methods of murder and the victims. He also confessed to killing eight other people at hospitals outside Hamilton County.

To corroborate his story, Harvey told investigators that he had kept a list of some of the victims. After a careful search, the investigators found a list, containing the names of 17 victims, neatly folded and stashed behind the mirror in Harvey's trailer.

On August 13th, Judge William Mathews revoked Donald Harvey's $200,000 bond after rumors surfaced that Harvey had suggested a deal—he would give an exclusive interview to the first person who posted the bond money. Reports suggested that a New York paper was prepared to accept Harvey's terms.

Before the grand jury decided to indict Harvey, he testified before them for two very brief periods. The grand jury had already endured several marathon sessions of viewing Harvey's videotaped confession.

The grand jury also heard testimony from a court-appointed expert who testified as an expert witness in the Florida trial of serial killer Ted Bundy.

This witness, a physician, reported that Harvey was not mentally ill, but instead had a character flaw, a character disorder which caused Harvey, like Bundy, to have a compulsion to kill, a compulsion which had to be satisfied. The witness said that the problem lay at the core of Harvey's personality, stemming in part from his childhood, and could not be reversed.

When Harvey appeared in court on August 18th, the courtroom overflowed with families of the victims, reporters, television cameras and the legal staffs. Harvey appeared calm as he sat with two law enforcement officials standing directly behind him.

Defense Counsellor William Whalen, a veteran of both

the city and county prosecution staffs, appeared ready to proceed with the guilty pleas.

Prosecutor Art Ney had constructed an elaborate four-by-six-foot white board with the charges, dates and names of all 28 victims.

As the trial proceeded, the facts of each murder were read aloud by the prosecution, and after each count, the defense rose, pleading guilty. The same continued 28 times.

As a hushed crowd looked on, the judge began pronouncing sentences — 20 years to life for each murder charge, three of which would be consecutive terms and the rest would be concurrent; seven-to-25 years for attempted murder; and eight-to-15 years for felonious assault. Harvey would have to serve 60 years in prison before being eligible for parole at age 95.

Many people believe that Donald Harvey killed others, and if any evidence is located supporting these allegations, he could be reindicted and possibly face the death sentence. For these reasons, Harvey may have decided to confess to other murders.

On Friday, January 20, 1989, Prosecutor Ney called a press conference and revealed that he and an assistant visited Harvey in the Southern Ohio Correctional Facility in Lucasville, Ohio. Harvey allegedly informed his defense attorney by letter that he wanted to confess to as many as seven other murders.

When Ney saw Harvey, Harvey decided he did not want to talk. Ney acknowledged that Harvey could be also retried if he is caught deliberately lying to the prosecution.

The strange case of Donald Harvey may one day reveal more murders, but it all started because one keen-eyed pathologist could do what 80 percent of the population could not — smell the bittersweet odor of almonds!

"THE DENTIST EXTRACTED INSURANCE MONEY FROM HIS MURDER VICTIMS"

by Joseph L. Koenig

By day, 27-year-old James S. Bullock was a clerk for the Union Electric Company of St. Louis, Missouri. Nights he spent at St. Louis University, where he was taking his degree in business.

Just before the start of the Christmas break, early on the bitterly cold Monday evening of December 22, 1958, the slender, bespectacled young man kissed his wife of just a few short months good-bye and hurried out the door to his car. Although classes did not begin for nearly an hour, it was never very easy finding a parking space near the crowded inner city campus and so he was in the habit of arriving early at school. It was not quite 7:00 when he twisted the key in the ignition and pulled away from the curb.

Less than half an hour later, a motorist driving past the St. Louis Art Museum was forced to stamp down hard on his brakes to avoid hitting a young man who had staggered into the street directly in front of his car. When the stranger, who was evidently not well, collapsed on the pavement, the motorist threw his car into park and rushed to his side. As he knelt over the man, whose life blood was pouring out of three well-placed bullet wounds, he happened to glance over his shoulder at a stocky man in an overcoat standing in the shadows of the closest building with what looked like a gun in his hand. As soon as the gunman saw his eyes on him, he darted around a corner and vanished into the early darkness.

Before medical help could arrive, the youthful gunshot victim succumbed to his wounds. The first St. Louis police officers to reach the scene removed from his pockets identification for 27-year-old James S. Bullock of Richmond Heights. The young man's body lay in a pool of blood at the end of a crimson trail which the lawmen backtracked nearly 100 yards to a spot behind the museum in Forest Park. There they found his car, its engine still running.

"The front seat is soaked with blood," one of the investigators said. "Apparently, he was shot here, at least the first time. I just wish I knew what he was doing in an out-of-the-way spot like this."

When homicide probers broke the sorry news to her, Bullock's young widow could offer no motive for his killing. She had no idea of what took her husband away from his usual route to school and to the fatal detour into Forest Park. However, under the unstinting efforts of a diligent young prosecutor, Thomas F. Eagleton — later to become a United States senator from Missouri — the detectives delved aggressively into Bullock's personal history, hoping to find a clue to his slayer's identity.

Barely two months before he died, they found out, Bullock had sought the help of a local private eye in following a man who worked at the same elementary school where his wife taught kindergarten. Even more interesting was the fact that only four days before he was shot to death he had asked the administrator of the St. Louis County Sanitarium if he could be admitted for a period of about two weeks.

"His request was most unusual," the administrator would recall. "He said he wanted to know if he could stay in the sanitarium without anyone knowing. He made it plain that he didn't want treatment, only that he wanted to hide. He was told that he could be admitted only on a doctor's order, however."

In time, the focus of the homicide probers' attention turned to Mrs. Bullock's ex-husband, a 31-year-old St. Louis dentist, Glennon Engleman. Lawmen learned the couple had been married about two years before the young woman divorced him and married Bullock. When they learned that Engleman had a part-time job as a dentist with Union Electric and was also rumored to have continued seeing his ex-wife after her subsequent remarriage, their interest in him soared.

Although the stocky, moon-faced dentist could not come up with an alibi for the time of Bullock's murder, detectives could not link him to the brutal crime. Engleman adamantly refused to submit to a lie detector exam and when he was brought before a coroner's jury and, later, a grand jury, he clung to the Fifth Amendment.

Soon after her husband's death, Mrs. Bullock moved to Kansas City, Missouri, and married again. Despite repeated appeals from St. Louis lawmen, she refused to return to their jurisdiction to make herself available for questioning.

When, at the end of a prolonged legal battle, James S. Bullock's estate finally was settled, his widow received $64,500 in insurance money. Not long after, she reportedly invested $15,000 of this sum in a Pacific, Missouri drag strip owned by Dr. Glennon E. Engleman.

Less than five years later, Engleman's interest in the drag strip came to the authorities' attention when a 23-year-old factory worker, Eric L. Frey, was killed there while using dynamite charges to plug an old well. The man who pulled Frey's tattered remains from the bottom of the well was Dr. Engleman. One day later, after a brief inquiry, the death was ruled an accident, and the young man's body was cremated.

It was some time after that before authorities found out that Frey, who was making $78 a week, had taken out a $25,000 life insurance policy barely two weeks before his death. He also was covered by a $12,000 group life policy at the drag strip. The person who seemed to have profited most by Frey's death was his wife's step-uncle by marriage, Dr. Glennon Engleman, who received $16,000 of the insurance money from the grieving widow.

For nearly 13 years, until September 5, 1976, Dr. Engleman managed to keep a rather low profile with the law. Early that afternoon, however, a 26-year-old telephone lineman, Peter J. Halm, and his 24-year-old bride, were exploring some limestone caverns near Pacific, Missouri, when a shot rang out and Peter fell to the ground.

"I've been shot!" the young man cried. "Get help!"

Halm's wife raced out of the woods and hastily called for help at the nearest phone. But by the time police and ambulance attendants arrived, her husband was dead. Barely 50 yards away from the body, investigators found a rifle mounted with a telescopic scope.

During the investigation which followed, detectives learned that in the 18-month period preceding her husband's death, Peter Halm's widow had worked as a dental assistant for Dr. Engleman and that her brother once had been employed at the drag strip near Pacific. After receiving $90,000 from the insurance company and refusing to take a lie detector test, the young woman moved to California to be near her brother.

Little more than three years later, on January 14, 1980, Mrs. Sophie Marie Barrera started up her 1975 Ford Pinto and died in a dynamite explosion which rocked the entire neighborhood. Investigators were told that the murder victims had owned a dental laboratory on South Grand Boulevard and that one of her most frequent customers was Dr. Engleman. He was also one of her most outstanding debtors and she recently had filed a lawsuit against him to collect $14,504 he allegedly owed her.

A hearing on the suit had been scheduled for January 21, exactly a week after Mrs. Barrera was killed. When detectives interviewed Dr. Engleman about the slaying, he refused to submit to chemical tests which would show if he had recently handled explosives such as dynamite.

Although no charges were filed against him and he was released from custody, investigators refused to believe it was sheer coincidence that the doctor had been on the fringes of so many violent deaths. Looking into his background, they found that Engleman, who was now 53, was a St. Louis native who had attended Washington University Dental School. He had been married three times and all of them ended in divorce. His patients described him as mild-mannered and pleasant.

But there was another side to Engleman's personality, one which the homicide probers began to learn about a few weeks after Mrs. Barrera's death, when they were contacted by a woman purporting to be an ex-wife of the dentist. On Thursday afternoon, February 14, 1980, by pre-arrangement, Engleman's ex-wife — wired with a hidden police microphone — met the dentist for lunch at a South Lindbergh Boulevard, St. Louis, restaurant. During their conversation, Engleman allegedly admitted murdering Peter Halm and just 10 days later, on Sunday, February 24, homicide probers took the dentist into custody at the home of his sister. The following day, Monday, he was formally charged with the slaying of the telephone lineman.

Although St. Louis police brass were reluctant to comment on the information that had led to Engleman's arrest, Lieutenant Richard O'Connor admitted to newsmen that it had come from an "informant" whom he refused to identify. He went on to say that this informant linked the dentist to at least three other unsolved slayings and that the motive for the Halm slaying was money.

Over the next few months, Engleman was indicted on both state and federal counts stemming from the death of Mrs. Barrera. Before he could be brought to trial on those charges, though, he first faced 16 federal counts of mail fraud and conspiracy in the Halm case. As a result of extensive publicity, the August trial was moved to St. Paul, Minnesota.

The highlight of the proceedings came on Saturday, August 9, when the prosecution played the tape of the conversation Engleman had with his ex-wife in the St. Louis restaurant ten days before his arrest. Although the conversation was difficult to follow at times because of loud background noise and disco music blaring from a jukebox, the jurors clearly heard the defendant tell his wife such things as, "There's no compulsion, no driving urge on my part to keep getting rid of my fellow man."

When his former wife asked him what the purpose of the Halm slaying had been, Engleman answered, "Babe, you're experiencing it right now—money. Money, money, money.

"It's not that I'm not willing to work for it . . . Look at me. That $10,000 I got from [Halm's wife]. Where would I be now? Take that $10,000 away from me . . . and where would I be now?"

When the former Mrs. Engleman said that she was worried about the mental state of Halm's wife, Engleman answered, "When I saw [her] the last time, she was . . . I tell you what, you can be sexually intimate with another person . . . and you can be homicidally intimate with another person."

At that point, his ex-wife asked him if he had had sex with Mrs. Halm.

"No," the dentist replied. "You've had to keep a secret between yourselves for weeks, months. You finally get back to your partner. You know what it amounts to, what a relief it is. The camaraderie you've had . . ."

Engleman later complained that the St. Louis newspapers were conducting a smear campaign against him by linking him to the other deaths in which insurance money was collected. He said that he could envision his attorney in court, shouting, "Smear, smear, smear," to convince a jury that the charges had been trumped up against him.

When the former Mrs. Engleman said that she agreed the newspapers were conducting a smear campaign, he

300

replied, "See, and you're even prejudiced against me. You know we're guilty as hell."

During the conversation Engleman went on to say that, along with Mrs. Halm, he had planned Halm's murder for insurance money. He specifically ruled out any involvement by Mrs. Halm's 39-year-old brother.

"Was this an afterthought with you and [Mrs. Halm]?"

"Afterthought?" Engleman asked.

When his ex-wife explained that she wanted to know if the slaying was plotted before or after Halm's 1975 marriage to his wife, Engleman muttered something which the microphone did not pick up.

Earlier in the trial, it was noted, Mrs. Halm had told the court that she had agreed to pay Engleman $10,000 after the murder, but Engleman told his ex-wife that he was supposed to receive $20,000.

Engleman told his ex-wife that Mrs. Halm "got a lot of dough. We figured we'd make $100,000" on her marriage and the subsequent murder.

Testimony at the trial indicated that Mrs. Halm had received about $75,000 in insurance money and proceeds from the sale of their house after her husband's death. Some $45,000 of that sum was spent by Mrs. Halm and her brother between the summer of 1977 and the spring of 1978, much of it for living expenses and to finance the brother's theatrical promotion business in California.

Taking the stand for the defense, Engleman's sister-in-law said the dentist was at a friend's home on Washington Terrace in St. Louis at the time of the slaying. Her story was backed up by the friend and a neighbor. In the end, though, the jury did not buy their story and on Thursday, August 14, 1980, Dr. Glennon E. Engleman was found guilty of 15 counts of mail fraud and a single count of conspiracy to murder Peter J. Halm, Jr.

"That's life," Engleman told his attorney upon hearing the verdict.

United States District Court Judge William L. Hungate set sentencing for September 12. Engleman received a maximum penalty of 80 years in jail and a fine of up to $25,000.

The prosecutor, Federal Attorney Robert D. Kingsland, told reporters that he was very pleased with the outcome of the trial.

"I think it was a very conscientious jury," he said. "They were trying to do a good job. I admire them for that. They had a lot of evidence to consider."

Three weeks later, on Monday, September 8, in the Jefferson City, Missouri courtroom of Cole County Circuit Court Judge Byron Kinder, where it had been moved on a change of venue, Engleman's trial for the murder of Peter Halm got underway. In his opening remarks to a jury of ten women and two men, Prosecutor Gordon Ankney said that Halm's widow, testifying as she had in St. Paul under a grant of immunity, "will tell you Dr. Engleman said, 'Why don't you marry someone and I'll kill him.'"

Ankney went on to say that the state's key witness would testify that Engleman had told her that he killed Eric L. Frey to obtain a share of his insurance money. At the mention of Frey's name, defense counsel rose angrily to his feet and motioned for a mistrial, but was overruled by Judge Kinder.

The first witness for the prosecution was Police Sergeant Gregory J. Moore, who told the court that when he investigated the scene of the Halm slaying he discovered two pieces of silver tape in the shape of a cross near the victim's body. About 15 yards away, suspended from a tree with the same kind of tape, was a beer can. Ankney indicated that Mrs. Halm had been told by Engleman that the area would be marked so that she would know where to stand when he shot her husband.

On the second day of the trial, Halm's widow, an attractive, dark-haired woman of 28, speaking in a low, almost inaudible voice, testified that Engleman first had suggested the murder plot just a couple of months after she went to work for him.

"He suggested I marry someone and he would kill them for insurance money," she said. "He told me how to fill out insurance forms and how to change beneficiary forms.

"He told me who would be good to marry and who would be bad. A person working for a large firm would be good, because they would have good insurance benefits. Professional people would be bad, because their deaths would be more thoroughly investigated."

Peter Halm was nominated, she said, because he had been her boyfriend when they were students at Kirkwood High in St. Louis. After they broke up, she had not seen him again until he was chosen as the victim in the murder plot. Engleman regarded him as an ideal choice, she added, because his job with the Southwestern Bell Telephone Company provided generous insurance benefits.

Asked about the actual slaying, the woman told the court how she and Engleman drove to the scene near Pacific to rehearse it. At this point in her testimony she broke into tears.

"I'm sorry," she whispered. "I can't think. I can't think."

After a brief recess called to enable the woman to regain her composure, she returned to the stand.

"He took me down a path," Mrs. Halm continued, "and told me it would be marked with a black X, or a white X, I can't remember . . ." she said. "He told me to take Peter down the path. He said he would be off to the left."

"When did this rehearsal occur?" Ankney asked.

The woman replied that it had taken place about a month before the slaying. She explained how on September 5, 1976, she drove her husband to the caves near Pacific and they walked to the spot which Engleman had marked. "We came away from the pond a few feet and I heard a gunshot," she told the court. "I don't remember if I was looking at Peter.

"Peter fell to his knees. Then he fell on his face. He

said, 'Get help! I've been shot.'

"I just started screaming. Dr. Engleman came out of the bushes. He grabbed me and told me to shut up, to be quiet. He had the gun in his hand. He then grabbed my arm and told me to shut up."

Then Engleman dropped the weapon on the ground and kicked some dirt and leaves over it, she said.

"All right," Ankney said. "What happened after the murder?"

The woman said that she moved to California to be with her brother. Visiting Engleman's office on her first trip back to St. Louis, she testified, she was asked if she had been contacted by the insurance companies and warned not to appear too eager to receive the money or to cause any suspicion.

When it was defense counsel's turn to question the witness, he implied that she had wanted her husband out of the way because she had fallen in love with another man. Her motive, the lawyer said, was not the "murderous, outrageous, atrocious concept of killing someone for money."

Under cross-examination the woman admitted that her marriage "was hell," but insisted that after her husband was dead "the money wasn't important."

"You shot your husband. You physically shot your husband, did you not?" the attorney asked.

After a long pause, the woman answered, "No."

"Then is it your testimony that from 1973 or 1974 until September 5, 1976, you cold-bloodedly, on a day-by-day basis, plotted to kill for money?"

"Yes," the woman cried as she buried her face in her hands.

"Mrs. Halm, you shot your husband, did you not?"

"No, I didn't."

"But you knowingly and willingly participated in a plan to murder an innocent man?" the attorney asked.

"Yes."

"Is it your testimony that when this man [Engleman]

304

told you of the atrocious suggestion, you didn't run screaming out of his office?"

"Yes."

"Tell the jury your reaction when he told you he was going to butcher some innocent boy for money."

"I can't recall," the woman said.

After moving to California, she continued, her brother tried to convince her not to give Engleman the $100,000 they had agreed upon.

"My brother wasn't going to pay Dr. Engleman," she added. "I told him to, because Dr. Engleman would kill us, too."

Under re-direct examination, the witness said that Engleman had told her of arranging the 1963 murder of Eric Frey at the drag strip in Pacific. The doctor, she testified, told her that he was an expert in the use of dynamite and that the slaying of Frey was similar to his plan to kill her husband because he had received a share of the insurance benefits in the earlier slaying.

Following the woman to the stand was her brother, also testifying under immunity that he had given the defendant $10,000 in the parking lot of a Kirkwood church in March of 1977. The funds were part of the insurance settlement his sister had received upon her husband's death.

While the witness remained on the stand during a brief recess, Engleman, who was seated barely ten feet away, reportedly mouthed the words, "I'm going to kill you."

"What did you say?" the witness asked.

"You heard me, fatso," Engleman answered out loud.

Defense counsel shrugged off the exchange, saying, "It's about as truthful as anything else the witness has had to say."

Under cross-examination, the witness said that he had spent most of the money his sister received from Halm's death financing an unsuccessful theatrical venture in Los Angeles. He also admitted that he had not paid income taxes in the last four years, despite driving a Mercedes-

Benz, paying for an apartment in Los Angeles while supporting a family in Missouri and frequently flying from St. Louis to Los Angeles.

"I plan to file very shortly," he said.

The prosecution's next witness was the defendant's former wife. After the tapes from the St. Louis restaurant were played for the jury, she said that on the day Peter J. Halm was shot her husband left their Mehlville condominium in the morning and returned in the late afternoon.

"When he came home," she said, "he went back to the laundry room and put his clothes in the washing machine."

In March of 1977, she said, accompanied by another man who had since been linked to the murder, her husband came back to the condominium one day with a paper bag containing $10,000 in $100 bills. After she counted the money with the other man, she testified, she went to a number of neighborhood banks and exchanged the $100s for smaller bills. Almost $7,000 of the sum, she said, was used to pay back taxes.

Taking the stand in his own defense on Thursday, September 11, Dr. Engleman denied taking part in the four-year-old murder.

"Did you ever discuss a scheme with Halm's wife in which she would marry some person and that you would kill him and then you would get the insurance?" his attorney asked.

"Never."

"Did you ever murder anyone?"

"Never."

Asked if he ever had seen Peter Halm alive, Engleman again answered, "Never."

"Did you ever see him dead?" the attorney asked.

"When he was lying in state at the funeral home, I attended the wake."

Under cross-examination, Engleman was asked if he had threatened to kill a male witness the day before.

"Did you say it?" Prosecutor Ankney asked.

"If I did, he qualifies for it, doesn't he?" Engleman answered.

Engleman insisted that the incriminating statements he had made on the tapes were a "cock-and-bull story" he had given his wife in an attempt at regaining a valuable coin collection she had taken when their marriage broke up. He explained that he was trying to frighten the woman who was holding the collection in exchange for sole custody of their 11-year-old son.

"Well, that cock-and-bull story just happens to be true," Ankney said. "Is that not correct?"

"Look, my wife has taken my life savings. She has my boy. There is no way I can get my money back from this female. I made the biggest mistake in my life [by pretending to have killed Halm]. That's why she took advantage of me, to tape me.

"I'll go to the penitentiary for life before giving up my son," he shouted. "One day he is going to be an adult and he's going to say, 'Mom, what happened to my father?'

"I'd tell my wife anything to get my son back. Is that too unreasonable to believe? I never knew I was being set up. She lets that lousy bug in our bedroom. She took [my son] out of my life, my flesh and blood. My God, don't I have a right to have my son?"

At one point, Judge Kinder told Ankney and Engleman to stop arguing when the witness insisted that he was lying when he told his wife that he had expected Mrs. Halm to receive $100,000 in insurance payments and give him $20,000.

"How would I know about that?" Engleman said about the $100,000.

As for the money he did receive, Engleman explained, "All I've heard is $10,000, $10,000, $10,000. I've never heard $20,000 come up before. Where do I get these figures? I suck them out of my thumb."

When the jurist asked the men to "please" end their

argument, defense counsel tried to calm his client and told him, "Just answer the questions or we'll be here until midnight."

"I can be here for 50 years. Where am I going from here? I'm 53."

When the defense attorney again tried to calm his client, Engleman snapped, "Damn it, they're trying to put me in prison for 50 years. This isn't a traffic ticket."

In his final arguments to the jury, Ankney termed the defendant a "Dr. Engleman and Mr. Hyde. You saw two sides. The gentle dentist, Dr. Engleman, the father figure. But you saw another side when he got mad. That was not Dr. Engleman. That was Mr. Hyde.

"I think he killed for the thrill of it. This is a man who compares killing with sex. A man who enjoyed it. That tape is a confession to a murder, a confession that you heard. It was no cock-and-bull story."

Ankney denied the defense counsel's contention that it was Halm's wife who had committed the slaying because she was in love with another man.

"Is there anyone here with a soul, a soul who thinks that the moment she saw him killed that she knew what it was going to be like. Don't you think it's possible that she didn't want the money anymore?

"She's not being punished adequately, but every night, when she goes to bed, she thinks about it. She had a conscience about it. He does not. And that's the big difference between them."

Defense counsel countered by reiterating his claim that the woman had committed a crime of passion and had never conspired with his client to collect insurance money.

"If her motive for killing Peter Halm was money, do you honestly believe that she would cold-bloodedly, for one and a half or two years, plot on a day-by-day basis to marry him for his money . . . and then not want the money? Is that the kind of testimony that the state would have you believe in convicting this man?

308

"This angel of death, this poisonous fruit, the embodiment and personification of evil, the banshees cried out on that Halloween night when she married her husband," he continued. "Would you convict anyone on the testimony of . . . the angel of death, that immunized killer?"

Referring to a pathologist's report which stated that the slug which struck Halm's spine entered his body at an upward angle, the attorney said, "I suggest to you that when that five-foot-three inch murderess fired that rifle at her six-foot, one-inch husband, the path of the bullet went upward into his body."

At 11:30 on Friday morning, after receiving the charge from Judge Kinder, the jury retired to the deliberation room to debate Dr. Engleman's fate. Just 77 minutes later, they returned to the courtroom to announce that they had found the 53-year-old dentist guilty of capital murder, which, under Missouri law, carries a minimum sentence of 50 years in prison.

"I don't relish a verdict of guilty," Engleman declared. "I'm only 53. In 50 years I'll be 103. There won't be anything but dust."

Little more than two weeks later, again in St. Paul, Dr. Engleman's run of bad luck continued when he was convicted in federal court on a charge of using an explosive in the death of Sophie Marie Barrera. A November attempt at trying him for the capital murder of a woman in Missouri failed when a sheriff failed to keep the jury properly sequestered and a mistrial was declared. It was not until January of 1981 that the state of Missouri was ready to try again, this time in the Gasconade County Circuit Court of Judge John C. Brackman in Hermann.

Once again, the most damaging evidence against Dr. Engleman were the tapes of the conversation he had had with his former wife, particularly a section in which he talked of having a person do "simple little killings for a thousand bucks." At another point, the defendant was heard to speak of his personal dislike for Mrs. Barrera and her attorney and to brag of his proficiency with explosives.

Engleman's beleaguered defense attorney attempted to discredit the former Mrs. Engleman and suggested to the jury that she wanted to see her ex-husband behind bars because of the disagreement concerning the coin collection and their son. The incriminating statements on the tapes, he said, were "merely clever" attempts at trying to scare the woman into returning the coin collection. The attorney added that Engleman had not benefitted financially by Mrs. Barrera's death because the suit against him was still being pressed by her corporation.

The prosecutor, Assistant St. Louis Circuit Attorney Thomas E. Dittmeir, was quick to point out that Mrs. Barrera's lawyer had stopped handling the case soon after his client was slain and that the Barrera family did not hire another lawyer to proceed with the suit until after Engleman was arrested.

On Thursday, January 29, 1981, after three hours and 15 minutes of deliberation, the jury returned a verdict of guilty against Dr. Engleman and immediately the penalty phase of the trial began with Judge Brackman presiding.

Testifying for the defense was a long-time family friend who said that when she first met Engleman she walked into his dental office and said, "I have a bad tooth and I only have two dollars." She began to cry as she said, "He wouldn't even take my two dollars."

In an emotional appeal for his client's life, defense counsel quoted generously from the Bible.

"Do not judge and you will not be judged yourself," he told the jurors. "Do not condemn and you will not be condemned yourself. Grant pardon and you will be pardoned."

As he picked up the Bible he said, "I thought I would turn myself to another source. The law books have given out."

Dittmeier, in asking for the death penalty, told the jury "to have some compassion for Sophie Marie Barrera, for her family and for other potential bombing victims."

Mrs. Barrera's family, he said, was not allowed "to bury her in one piece. Her feet and her left hand were in a bag in the coffin with her. This isn't a time for mercy. This is a time for justice," he declared.

When the case was returned to them, the jurors debated for an hour and 20 minutes before reporting to Judge Brackman that they were unable to arrive at a decision. As a result, Brackman, under the law, will be required to assess Engleman's punishment of life in prison. The jurist held off setting a formal date for sentencing until defense counsel decided whether or not he would file a motion for a new trial.

"A year ago, when I started on this," Engleman's attorney said, "I sat in the kitchen of [Engleman's sister's] home and I told her, 'There's only one thing I can do and that's to save his life.' To that extent, I've done my job."

"I knew I wouldn't be on death row," a tired, subdued Glennon Engleman told reporters. "My sister [an astrologer] told me I wasn't going to be on death row."

The dentist's only other comment was to apologize "for the cosmopolitanites from St. Louis bringing their dirty laundry to wash in the streets of Hermann, Missouri."

"FLOATER IN THE
PINK NIGHTIE"

by John Dunning

It was a sad Wednesday morning for 11-year-old Andree Wietfeld and her nine-year-old sister, Nicole. When
they came down to breakfast, their mother was not there
and their father told them sorrowfully that she had run
away.

"Run away?" asked Andree. "Why?"

"We had a quarrel last night after the guests had
gone," replied Dr. Klaus Wietfeld. "She wanted me to do
the dishes last night, but I was tired. She'll be back."

Andree did not say a word, but she later told Nicole
that there could not have been that many dishes to do.
The evening before had been her mother's birthday and
there had been a party, with not too many guests, only
close friends of the family.

"Will Mommy come back?" asked Nicole.

"She wouldn't go off and leave us," responded Andree
stoutly, but she was worried too.

Monika Wietfeld did not come back on Thursday and,
on Friday, Dr. Wietfeld went to the Bad Salzuflen police.

"I'm afraid there may have been an accident," he said.
"I've heard nothing from my wife since Tuesday evening,
March 29th, and none of her friends or relatives have
seen her. She was very upset when she left. She shouldn't
have been driving."

The desk sergeant on duty respectfully took down the details. Monika Wietfeld: aged 39; born in Frauenfeld, Switzerland; wife of Dr. Klaus Wietfeld; head of the Bad Salzuflen Orthopedic Clinic; and resident at 46 Langenberg Strasse in the extremely expensive residential suburb of Wuesten. She had been driving a white Opel Kadett, license number DT-LX 663.

The desk sergeant's manner was deferential because he was speaking with a doctor, a title regarded with reverence in West Germany. He showed more respect because he knew very well who the 46-year-old man with the expensive clothes and the almost boyish appearance was.

Bad Salzuflen 50 miles to the southwest of Hannover, is not large. The year-around population numbers only slightly more than 50,000. It does, however, have an efficient and disproportionately large police force. This due to its fashionable spa, which visitors come to enjoy. They bring a great deal of money with them and it has to be protected.

Since Dr. Wietfeld was an important man, the Bad Salzuflen police spared neither effort nor expense in their attempt to locate his missing wife, but without the slightest success.

Police found Monika's car on April 18th, exactly three weeks after she disappeared. It was parked in a rest area off the highway near the town of Exeter, roughly five miles from Bad Salzuflen.

The car was locked and there were no signs of violence on or in it, but Inspector Boris Hummel, the chief of the Bad Salzuflen Department of Criminal Investigations, considered the find ominous. There was, he reasoned, no cause for Monika Wietfeld to abandon her car at a place where she would have had a minimum three-mile walk to any form of public transportation.

"If she'd intended to leave her husband, she'd have taken the train, assuming she didn't want to drive all the way to Switzerland," he told Sergeant of Detectives Walter Kamp, a tall, handsome man with a rather expressionless face. "I'm afraid we have to consider the possibility of a criminal act."

"It wasn't kidnapping for ransom," said the sergeant. "They'd have contacted Wietfeld by now."

"Perhaps they have," said the inspector, "and he's not coming to us because he's afraid they'll harm her. Of course, there may be some other explanation besides kidnapping or murder. You didn't find any indication of a lover?"

"None," answered Sergeant Kamp. "Model wife and mother and too busy to have fitted in a lover if she'd wanted to."

Inspector Hummel, a heavyset, dark-haired man with worry lines across his forehead, sat for a moment in deep thought. "We'll see what the lab finds on the car," he said finally, taking his cigar out of his mouth and looking speculatively at the end which was burning very unevenly. "If her prints aren't on the steering wheel . . ."

They were, but . . .

"Smeared," said the identification specialist. "Someone wearing gloves drove the car after she used it. Her prints are elsewhere on the dashboard, but not on the gear shift lever. That's assuming that the prints we took from her toilet articles are really hers."

"No reason to doubt it," said Inspector Hummel. "Well, I think we're justified in opening a formal homicide investigation."

"Motive?" asked Sergeant Kamp.

The inspector shrugged. "She could have picked up the wrong hitchhiker," Hummel said. "I don't know. We haven't enough information."

"Would a woman running away from home after a fight with her husband pick up a hitchhiker?" asked Kamp.

"A woman of that class wouldn't normally pick up a hitchhiker at all," replied Hummel. "I just can't think of anything else."

The change from missing person to homicide had no

effect on the investigation which continued without progress for nearly another week.

It was, by then, April 24th, a Sunday. On this day, a rather athletic girl named Herta Obermeyer decided to take a walk.

Herta did not live in Bad Salzuflen, but in Muenster which was a sizeable city 50 miles to the west. Among its many other attractions, Muenster boasted a fine, large body of water known as Lake Aa on the southwestern edge of the city's center and it was along its shores that Herta decided to walk. It was a reasonably good day for one. The spring was advanced and many trees were in bloom. Although the sun was shining brightly, there was a brisk west wind which swayed the tall reeds along the shore, giving glimpses of muddy, gray water between them.

And of something else.

A long, cylindrical pinkish-gray object caught Herta's eye. She could not identify it, but it inexplicably made the fine hairs on Herta's forearms stand straight up and her mouth turn suddenly dry.

Abruptly aware that she was very much alone, Herta began to back slowly away, but then stopped.

Whatever the thing lying amidst the reeds was, it had to be investigated. She was doubtful that, if she left now, she would be able to find the place again in the featureless reed beds.

A girl not lacking in courage, Herta Obermeyer found a stump on which she could sit. She took off her hiking boots and socks, rolled up the legs of her slacks and waded into the water far enough to see what the object was.

Then, with a rapidly beating heart, Herta returned to the stump, put on her boots without the socks and set off on a run for the nearest house.

What she had seen lying in the water among the reeds was a human corpse, but in such frightful condition that Herta could not tell whether it was a man or a woman.

315

"She's been in the water for some time," said Dr. Adelbert Hortig, the specialist in forensic medicine attached to the Muenster Police Department of Criminal Investigations. "I doubt that we'll be able to obtain fingerprints."

The body had been lifted carefully out of the water and brought to the police morgue where attempts were being made to identify it.

"Can you give us any physical characteristics so that we can run a check in the missing person files?" asked Inspector Hummel who had taken provisional charge of the case.

"Female," replied the doctor. "Late thirties. About five-feet-six in life. Weight around a hundred and ten pounds. Dark hair, shoulder length."

He probed with rubber-gloved fingers in the rotting mass of the victim's belly.

"She has probably had children, but that's not entirely certain."

"Right," said the inspector. "That with what she had on her should be enough."

The corpse had been clothed in the remains of a pink, silk nightdress. A gold ring with a sapphire and six diamonds adorned the ring finger of her right hand. She was wearing a good, but not expensive wristwatch which, being waterproof and quartz, was still showing the correct time. She also had a gold earring in her left ear.

Monika Wietfeld's facial features, after nearly three weeks in the water, was not recognizable by anyone, but her jewelry was, since it had been noted in her description at the time she was reported missing. Inspector Hummel requested the jewelry be sent to Bad Salzuflen for possible identification by Monika's husband. There was no point in sending the body since he would not be allowed to view it in any case. As for the autopsy, that was being performed in Muenster by Dr. Hortig, a small man, with a dark, narrow face and a large, wide mustache. The doctor was highly qualified, but in

316

this case he was able to determine little.

"The body has been in the water too long," Hortig said. "There are no serious wounds or injuries to vital organs. The skull is not fractured. She could have been strangled, or smothered. She might have been poisoned, or maybe she drowned. She could even have died of some disease. I cannot give a cause of death."

"Or a time?" asked Inspector Hummel who had driven over from Bad Salzuflen to view the corpse.

The doctor shrugged. "Only within days," he said. "The end of March, beginning of April."

"Corresponds to the time of the disappearance," said Hummel. "The husband has identified the jewelry, but the commissioner wants something more. Were you able to get an impression of the teeth?"

"Good ones," replied the doctor. "Upper and lower jaws. Her dentist should be able to recognize them easily."

Monika Wietfeld's dentist did recognize the impressions and the identification of the corpse was regarded as complete.

The rotting remains were sealed in a metal coffin which was sent to Bad Salzuflen where the metal coffin was placed inside an expensive wooden one and buried. The weeping Dr. Wietfeld and his two little daughters followed the hearse to the cemetery.

Inspector Hummel did not attend the funeral. As head of the Department of Criminal Investigations, he was also head of the homicide squad.

While the funeral was in progress, Hummel was sitting with Sergeant Kamp in his office and trying to decide what kind of a case he was investigating.

"We can't sustain a homicide charge on what we have," Hummel said. "The Muenster medical expert wasn't able to determine the cause of death. The only thing he found was bruises on the biceps as if somebody had taken hold of her roughly. If there's going to be any charge at all, it will have to be manslaughter

317

and it will have to be based on circumstantial evidence."

"Unless we can persuade the murderer to confess," said Sergeant Kamp. "You do think it's murder, don't you?"

"Don't see what else it could be," replied Inspector Hummel. "The woman has a quarrel with her husband and goes off in her car at around midnight. Nineteen days later, we find the car with evidence that someone wearing gloves has driven it. A week later, the body is recovered from a lake fifty miles away. An explanation other than homicide requires more fantasy than is acceptable to the commissioner."

"Well, the motive wasn't money because her jewelry wasn't taken," said Sergeant Kamp, "and, if it was something personal, there doesn't seem any possibility other than the husband. I'm positive that she was not mixed up with some other man."

"The trouble with that is that Wietfeld would have to be stupid," said Hummel, "and he's a doctor so he shouldn't be."

"Stupid to murder his wife when he could simply divorce her?" asked Kamp.

"Stupid to leave her jewelry on her," replied Hummel. "If the jewelry had been missing, we would have assumed robbery and we'd be looking for a hitchhiker. As it is . . ."

"We still would have suspected him," said Kamp. "All the woman was wearing was a pink nightdress. She wouldn't have run off in that on a chilly March evening."

"A good point, Walter," said the inspector. "Go see Wietfeld and ask him what his wife was wearing when she left."

Before going to see Dr. Wietfeld, Sergeant Kamp read through the original missing person report and noted with surprise that the doctor had described his wife's jewelry in some detail, but had made no mention of what she was wearing.

The omission was strange enough that Kamp looked up the duty sergeant who had taken the report and asked him about it.

The duty sergeant replied that Dr. Wietfeld had said he did not know what his wife was wearing when she left. She had gone upstairs, had apparently packed and the first indication he had that she was going was when he saw her car pulling out of the driveway.

"So I didn't go to see Wietfeld," said Sergeant Kamp, reporting the circumstances to Inspector Hummel. "He'll only say that she presumably packed her nightdress in with her other things."

"Good thing you didn't," said the inspector. "I don't think I want Wietfeld to know that we suspect him. If he is guilty, it will only cause him to be more careful about covering his tracks."

"What tracks could he cover now?" asked Sergeant Kamp. "It's over a month since the murder. Any covering he could do, he's already done."

"No," said Inspector Hummel. "He thinks he's in the clear now so he won't be cautious about associating with the motive."

"You mean a woman," said the sergeant.

"What else?" asked the inspector. "If he did murder her, it wasn't for money. It would have to be a woman."

"Something like that shouldn't be hard to find out in Bad Salzuflen," said Sergeant Kamp.

Nor was it. A little discreet investigation at the orthopedic hospital quickly produced an astonishing number of statements to the effect that Dr. Wietfeld was not only having an affair with his secretary, but engaging in sexual relations with her in odd corners of the hospital, including the top of his own desk.

The secretary, Ilona Peters was, however, only 20 years old and had been working at the hospital for less than a year. The reports of the doctor's sexual activity went back six or seven years when Ilona had been only 13.

"Different secretary, of course," said Sergeant Kamp. "He apparently always has it on with his secretary. It's part of her job. Presumably hires on the basis of physical rather than professional qualifications. Miss Peters is too much. Makes me wish I'd studied medicine."

"I sometimes wish you had too, Walter," said Hummel thoughtfully. "All right. Let's have an in-depth background on the doctor and on his late wife. We'll be looking for evidence, not gossip, of marital infidelity, promises to divorce and marry and, in the case of the wife, threats of divorce and what unpleasant financial or social effects a divorce would have on the doctor. In short, motive."

The investigation was proceeding better than anyone had expected. Although it would probably not be possible to show that Dr. Wietfeld had murdered his wife, it might be possible to show that no one else had any reason to murder her. Then, if the doctor could be caught in a few contradictions, it might be possible to worm a partial confession out of him. The inspector could not hope for much more.

Much would depend upon how much the doctor knew of forensic medicine. He was, undoubtedly, highly qualified in orthopedics, but could he be sure that the medical expert in Muenster had not been able to determine the cause of death?

He had asked the inspector how she had died at the time the identification of the body was made by Monika's dentist, but Inspector Hummel had evaded the question.

"I haven't had the full report on the autopsy yet," he had said.

Wietfeld had nodded in understanding and he had not asked again.

Perhaps the question of his wife's death had slipped his mind. The doctor was a very busy man. In addition to his duties at the hospital, he had his secretary to cope with and, as the sergeant soon learned, not only his secretary. The doctor was, it seemed, almost pathologically attracted to sex and so avid for novelty that he had no less than three other affairs going on concur-

320

rently with the one with the secretary.

"Who," reported Sergeant Kamp, "appears to have the inside track, however. She attended the funeral with him and practically carried him back to his car."

"Why?" asked the inspector. "Was he sick?"

"Bowed down with sorrow," replied the sergeant. "The secretary was a great comfort in his time of need. Also, there's some evidence that she moved into the villa in Langenberg Strasse on the same night Mrs. Wietfeld is supposed to have disappeared."

"Good God!" exclaimed Inspector Hummel. "How can the man be a doctor and so stupid? Something like that is almost enough to get him indicted."

"But not convicted," said Sergeant Kamp. "The fact that a man is cheating on his wife doesn't automatically mean that he's murdered her and he could easily say, 'Why now?' because he's been cheating on her for years and he did on his first wife too and he didn't murder her."

"This was his second wife?" asked the inspector.

The sergeant nodded. "The first one lives in Hannover now," Kamp said. "I'm going over this afternoon and talk to her."

The interview produced nothing significant other than further information of the doctor's near-frenzied sex life.

The former Marianne Wietfeld had been married for seven years to the doctor and had two daughters, 20-year-old Caroline and 18-year-old Ingeborg, to show for it.

She had divorced Wietfeld, she explained, because he was the world's greatest tomcat. She had suffered patiently through seven years of his endless affairs in the belief that he would eventually exhaust himself, but as he entered his 30s going as strong as ever, Marianne had given up and filed for divorce.

"He's forty-six now and still going strong," said Sergeant Kamp. "Did he oppose the divorce?"

"He hardly noticed it," replied Marianne. "He had his

321

mind on other things, most of them around the age of eighteen."

The divorce had taken place in 1974 and that same year the doctor had met the second Mrs. Wietfeld, a medical technician, in Zurich where he was attending a conference. They had married in Kiel in 1976.

Wietfeld had been paying support money for the girls, but since the youngest had now passed 18, that had automatically ceased.

"Exactly the wrong sort of testimony," commented Kamp. "Wietfeld didn't give a damn whether his first wife divorced him or not, so why the second one?"

Inspector Hummel looked worried.

"Maybe we're looking at the wrong man," he muttered, "but who else . . . ? The whole thing is so phony . . . Wietfeld's obviously lying . . . Have you gone into what effect a divorce would have had on him?"

"Yes," answered Kamp. "None at all. Neither financially nor socially. Mrs. Wietfeld was threatening divorce. She'd seen a lawyer. But she wasn't pressing for settlement or a division of property. In fact, according to the lawyer, she didn't even want a divorce. She only wanted to scare her husband into stopping all his tomcating."

"She might have told him something different from what she told the lawyer," observed Hummel. "She could have threatened to ruin him financially."

"Well, maybe," said Kamp, "but, to tell the truth, the impression I get of Wietfeld is that he's not terribly concerned with money. He's got a safe, high income as a doctor and as long as the supply of girls holds out, he's happy."

"Damn!" exclaimed Hummel. "That's the impression I get too."

However, despite the negative aspects of the case, the investigation plodded on and, on May 13th, Dr. Klaus Wietfeld was taken into custody. He was not immediately charged and was so confident that he would be returning home that day that he told Andree and Nadine that he would see them at dinner.

In fact, he would not see them at all for a considerable time. He quickly made so many contradictory and confusing statements that a formal charge of concealing information in connection with the investigation of a felony was brought against him.

By this time, Wietfeld had admitted to having been present at his wife's death, but not to killing her.

There had been, he explained, an argument over washing the dishes following the party and Monika had suddenly collapsed. When he had examined her, he found that she was dead of a heart attack.

Inspector Hummel pointed out that Monika had undergone a number of physical examinations, one less than a month before her death, and that there had been no mention of a heart condition.

Dr. Wietfeld said that he could not understand it himself. Perhaps, it had been something else. He suggested that the inspector consult the autopsy report.

"Very well," said the inspector, who did not want to admit that the autopsy had failed to establish the cause of death. "How did your wife's car get over by Exeter, if she died right in the house?"

"I drove it there," replied Dr. Wietfeld. "I was afraid of being accused of murdering her and I panicked. After I had left the car there, I ran all the way home."

"All five miles?" asked the inspector incredulous. "What purpose did that serve?"

"I thought it would confuse the investigation," murmured the doctor.

If that had been his purpose, he had succeeded for the act seemed utterly senseless to Inspector Hummel.

"And the body?" the inspector demanded. "How did that get in Lake Aa, fifty miles from here?"

"I took it there," answered Wietfeld. "I had to do something with it because I was afraid it would start to smell."

"You had it in the house with your children?" exclaimed the inspector, shocked in spite of himself.

"Of course not," replied Wietfeld indignantly. "I couldn't take a chance on their seeing it so, that same night, I took it down and put it in the trunk of my car."

"And drove it over to Lake Aa," Inspector Hummel added.

"Well, not right away," said Wietfeld. "I had things I had to do at the hospital and I was driving around with it all day Wednesday. It was only on Thursday that I found the time to go to the lake."

"Your secretary spent Tuesday night at your house," said Hummel. "Did she know your wife's body was in the trunk of your car outside?"

"Of course not," answered Wietfeld. "She knows nothing about this at all."

Klaus Wietfeld's car, an Audi sports coupe, was impounded and the trunk was examined by specialists from the police laboratory in Hannover. They reported that there was evidence that a human body had been transported in the trunk, but there were no traces of blood or other indications of violence.

Wietfeld's secretary, Ilona Peters, was arrested and questioned, but denied all knowledge of the manner in which Monika Wietfeld had died. She and the doctor, she said, were just good friends.

Since there was no evidence that she had any connection with whatever had taken place, she was released.

Dr. Klaus Wietfeld was not, however. Although the police could not show enough evidence of homicide to obtain an indictment, the doctor was, by his own admission, guilty of the legal disposal of a corpse and the circumstances were too suspicious to permit his release.

In the end, a compromise was reached. Dr. Wietfeld agreed to an indictment on charges of unintentional homicide and concealment of a crime and the police terminated their investigation of him. It was, in any case, the maximum with which he could be charged on the basis of the evidence.

EDITOR'S NOTE:
Herta Obermeyer, Ilona Peters, Boris Hummel, Walter Kamp and Adelbert Hortig are not the real names of the persons so named in the foregoing story. Fictitious names have been used in order to comply with German police regulations.

"THE CRIME AT HILLDROP CRESCENT"

by L.L. Alberts

No one meeting him on the street or seeing him at his place of business would ever have suspected Dr. Hawley Harvey Crippen of being a Lothario. He was a rather undersized fellow of middle age, balding a bit, who affected a sandy mustache and goatee, and whose eyes seemed to blink in bewilderment behind a pair of thick-lensed spectacles. Decidedly not a romantic figure.

Nevertheless, this same Dr. Crippen was destined to go down in history as a great lover, as well as one of the most cunning poisoners ever to plunge Scotland Yard into a fantastic guessing game. He is still remembered today as the monster of London's Hilldrop Crescent.

Although his crime took place in England, Crippen was an American, a native of Michigan.

Something of a rolling stone, he studied medicine in Cleveland, London and New York, and served internships in three or four different hospitals in the States. When he was 30, after practicing for only a few years, he met a flashing-eyed brunette named Cora Turner, who was only 17. He promptly married her and took her off to St. Louis to live. Later, they moved to Philadelphia where he also practiced for a while.

It was evident from the outset that Cora Crippen's primary interest did not lie in homemaking or raising a family.

"Everybody says I have a good voice, and there certainly is nothing wrong with my figure," she told her spouse. "I deserve to be on the stage, and I aim to get there."

Crippen objected, but Cora had the proverbial "whim of iron" and his arguments were in vain. She embarked on what was to be a long and expensive series of lessons in singing and dancing. She even picked out a stage name for herself: "Belle Elmore."

In 1900, some 11 years after their marriage, Crippen unexpectedly received an offer to go to work for a London patent medicine company called Munyon's. The job tempted him—and he was fed up with private practice, and he'd become fond of London while there as a student—but before accepting it he consulted his wife.

"By all means, let us go," was her reaction. "The stupid theatre managers in this country don't appreciate my talents, but I'm sure I'll go over big in England. You'll be seeing the name Belle Elmore right up at the top of the playbills!"

Crippen, who had his own opinion of Cora's histrionic ability, uttered a noncommittal grunt and began making preparations for the move.

In London, they settled down in a rented, semi-detached house at No. 39 Hilldrop Crescent, a quiet, tree-lined street in a middle-class residential neighborhood. Crippen went about his business with Munyon's, which netted him an adequate if modest salary, and Cora resumed her strivings toward the stage.

Unfortunately, the managers of the London music halls were as unappreciative of her talents as their American counterparts had been. Cora—or Belle, as she still liked to call herself—never even got to carry a spear or appear in the back line of a chorus. She did, however, succeed in striking up friendships with a number of the-

327

atrical people, among them being Mr. and Mrs. Peter Baylor, Ruth Walker, Dorothy Crane and James Forbes. She also managed to wangle herself a job as treasurer of the Music Hall Ladies' Guild.

Though she had put on considerable weight, Cora retained some of her youthful beauty and was able to attract male admirers from time to time. These she met outside the house and, quite naturally, without Crippen's knowledge. Some of them showered her with costly jewelry. When the doctor expressed curiosity about the gems, Cora passed them off as "mere baubles — nothing but costume pieces."

As the years passed and her hopes of appearing behind the footlights receded further and further, Cora became increasingly flamboyant in dress and manner. She decked herself out in the gaudiest of garments — her favorite color was pink — and applied makeup to match. And she delighted in throwing parties for her friends, which imposed a serious strain on the family budget.

Three of four nights a week, weary from his labor at Munyon's, Crippen would come home to 39 Hilldrop Crescent to find the house filled with people who were utterly alien to him. Their loud jokes and singing and dancing gave him a splitting headache. Yet when he protested, Cora said in effect, "You go your way and I'll go mine." She also intimated she had plenty of chances to run off with men who were more compatible than the doctor. Their endless quarrels became more and more bitter.

The pattern for murder took more definite form in the summer of 1909 when a girl named Lisa Montclair came to work at Munyon's as a secretary.

Crippen was smitten at once. In the midst of dictating his first letter to her, he said, "My dear, you're lovely. Tell me all about yourself."

Just why Lisa should return the interest of a man so much older than herself is difficult to understand, but return it she did. She had yet to pass her 21st birthday, she told him, she was all alone in the world, and this job was her very first venture into the business field. Crippen added some observations of his own; Miss Montclair had blonde curly hair and deep blue eyes, and her figure was slim and bewitching.

Before long the doctor was taking Lisa out to lunch, then to dinner. He began seeing her several times a week outside the office. If other workers at Munyon's found their goings-on suspicious, they prudently kept their mouths shut.

The situation ran along into the first of 1910 with growing tension for Crippen. Lisa began talking rather insistently about marriage—something that the doctor himself desired—and at the same time he found life with Cora becoming more irksome every day.

The music hall couple, Mr. and Mrs. Baylor, dined at Hilldrop Crescent about once a week. In recent months Crippen had dodged these occasions, but on the night of January 31st he made it a point to come home from the office early.

Crippen was much more attentive to his wife than usual during the dinner and the hours that followed, and the whole evening went off pleasantly except for a slight indisposition on the part of Baylor.

The following day the doctor called at the home of the couple to inquire after Baylor's health. Mrs. Baylor said he seemed better but was upstairs asleep. "And how is Belle?" she asked.

"Oh, she's fine," Crippen replied.

On the next afternoon, February 1st, Lisa Montclair delivered a note to Miss Walker, another theatrical friend of Cora's, who also was an officer of the Music Hall Ladies' Guild. It read: "Dear Miss Walker: Illness of a near relative has called me to America on only a few hours' notice, so I must ask you to bring my resignation as Treasurer before the next meeting of the Guild so that a new Treasurer can be elected at once. You will appreciate my haste when I tell you that I have not been to bed—packing all night and getting ready to go. I shall hope to see you in a few months, but cannot spare a moment to call on you before I go."

The note was signed "Belle Elmore, per H.C.C."

Considering it strange that the woman had dictated the note to Crippen, Miss Walker showed it to the Baylors. They, too, considered it suspicious, particularly in view of what the doctor had said when he called at their house. A day or two later Baylor dropped around to Crippen's office to seek an explanation. Crippen was strangely vague. It was true, he said, that Cora, or Belle, had been called to America—he simply hadn't seen fit to mention it when he talked to Mrs. Baylor the day before the note was delivered.

In some respects Dr. Crippen was clever; in others, he was exceedingly stupid. On the 7th, for instance, he pawned a ring and brooch that belonged to his wife for 115 pounds. A few nights later he attended a ball given by the Music Hall Benevolent Fund, accompanied by lovely Lisa Montclair. And friends noted that the girl was wearing pieces of Cora Crippen's jewelry!

Finally, even though he must have sensed the suspicion that was building up against him, Crippen persuaded Lisa to quit her job and move in with him at Hilldrop Crescent.

Trying frantically to build up a fabrication that would protect him, the doctor wrote to the Baylors around the 20th of March saying he'd received word that his wife was "desperately ill" with double pneumonia.

Two days later he followed up this letter with a telegram sent from Victoria Station: BELLE DIED YESTERDAY AT SIX O'CLOCK. PLEASE PHONE HER FRIENDS. WILL BE AWAY A WEEK."

As if that were not enough, Crippen inserted a brief obituary notice in one of the London newspapers. Then he and Miss Montclair embarked for the French resort town of Dieppe to pass a one-week Easter holiday. While he was away he wrote to two of Cora's friends, James Forbes and Dorothy Crane, telling them of her passing. But he set her death as having occurred two days after the date of his telegram to the Baylors.

Forbes, Miss Crane and the Baylors got together and compared notes, but despite all the suspicious circumstances they refrained from going to the authorities. Crippen's mixup in dates, they reasoned, could be the natural mistake of a grief-stricken man. It was terribly bad taste for Crippen to let Lisa Montclair wear Cora's jewels—but, then, it didn't prove him guilty of any wrongdoing.

"We'd better go easy on this," Baylor said, with the reluctance of the average citizen to become involved with the police.

Upon Crippen's return, Baylor went to see him again. What steamship had his wife taken to the States? Crippen didn't know. Where were the relatives she visited? He couldn't recall. The doctor stubbornly refused to answer several similar questions.

Next, Baylor talked to Forbes. "Do you think we ought to do anything?" he asked.

Forbes shook his head. "Let's play a waiting game. I'll question him from time to time, and so will Miss Crane. If Belle met with foul play it's too late now to help her. A few weeks' delay in going to the authorities won't make any difference."

In subsequent conversations with Cora's friends, Crippen grimly stuck to the main thesis of his story concerning her disappearance, although every account he gave was marked by minor discrepancies. At last he came up with the statement that, actually, his wife had died in San Francisco; she had been cremated and the ashes had been sent to him for interment.

Forbes happened to know that his friend had had a

strong feeling against cremation on religious grounds. "Why didn't you notify us so that we could attend the last rites?" he demanded.

"Oh, I thought best that the services be very, very private," the doctor replied.

Forbes decided the time finally had come to take action. Late in June he went to the office of Chief Inspector Walter Dew and told him the entire story.

Dew, like Cora's friends, was inclined to be circumspect, particularly when investigation disclosed that Crippen had previously been untouched by scandal and bore an excellent reputation among his business associates. It wasn't until July 8th that he and Sergeant John Mitchell paid a call at No. 39 Hilldrop Crescent. They found Miss Montclair there, and she directed them to Crippen's office.

As soon as the officers announced their identity, Crippen showed signs of being extremely upset.

"I had better tell you the absolute truth, gentlemen," he stammered. "I made up that story about Cora's death and cremation to save myself from possible humiliation—I'm afraid she may have taken up with another man. For all I know, she can still be alive. She—she just dropped out of sight on February 1st, and because of things she said in the past I suspect she went to America. That's all I can tell you."

Dew and Mitchell went with the doctor to his home. A search turned up clothing, furs and jewelry that belonged to the missing woman.

"Why do you suppose she didn't take these things with her?" the chief inspector demanded.

"I haven't the slightest idea," Crippen said, "except that she apparently left in an awful hurry. That's what made me think it was an elopement of some kind."

Dew glanced quizzically at Crippen and then at Lisa Montclair, whose presence in the house the doctor had made no effort to explain. "Well," he said, "we simply have got to find your wife. Matter of routine, you understand. I'll have circulars on her printed and sent all over Britain and the Continent. Also, I'll see that advertisements requesting information about her are placed in several newspapers in the United States."

"Can't you wait a few weeks before you do that?" Crippen pleaded.

"No, we had better act right away," the chief inspector said grimly.

When the doctor showed up at his office the following morning, he appeared so agitated that one of his assistants, Walter Ford, asked him if he weren't feeling well.

"Oh, it's nothing, nothing, Walter," Crippen replied. "Just a case of some people doing too much silly talking. By the way, do you mind going down to Oxford Street on an errand for me?"

Ford assented, and the doctor handed him some banknotes and a slip of paper. "I want you to buy the articles of boy's clothing on this list," he said. "You can tell the clerk the lad is 16 and not too large for his age. I want a brown tweed suit, a felt hat size six and one-half, some shirts and collars, shoes. Well, it's all on the list. Be quick about it, will you?"

Ford made the purchases and returned to the office. Crippen grabbed up the parcels and headed for the door. "I'm leaving for the day," he said over his shoulder. "In fact, I may be gone for several days. An important business trip."

Hawley Harvey Crippen was off on a trip, all right, but it certainly had nothing to do with business. He scurried back to Hilldrop Crescent, handed the boy's clothing to Lisa Montclair, and ordered her to don the disguise.

It was obvious that Miss Montclair apparently had subordinated her will completely to that of her lover. She always did his exact bidding without asking questions. Furthermore, she was completely in the dark as to the manner of Mrs. Crippen's disappearance.

To alter his own appearance, Crippen shaved off his mustache and goatee, discarded his glasses, and put on a suit he'd never worn before.

The transformations completed, the doctor and his youthful mistress took a boat to Antwerp. Failing there to book immediate passage for America, they proceeded to Brussels but soon were back in Antwerp again. Crippen now found accommodations available on the *Montrose,* one of the slower steamships, which was bound for Quebec. For the purser's list he signed himself "Mr. Robinson" and his companion as "Robinson, Junior."

Back in London, on the 12th, Chief Inspector Dew decided to have another talk with Crippen and went to his office, only to learn that the doctor had gone away on a "business trip." Accompanied by Sergeant Mitchell, he continued on to the house on Hilldrop Crescent. As the officers had half anticipated, Miss Montclair was not there and the doors were tightly locked. They located the landlord and ordered him to let them into the building.

On their previous visit Dew and his aide had confined their attention to the ground floor and the two upper floors, on none of which were there any indications of foul play. Now they concentrated on the basement. The results were set forth with typical British restraint in the chief inspector's official report: "Finally we came to the coal cellar, which had a brick floor. There was a very small quantity of coal there, and also a little rubbish. Mitchell and I got down on our knees and probed about with a small poker which I had got out of the kitchen.

"I found that the poker went in somewhat easily between the crevices of the bricks, and I managed to get one or two up, and then several others came up pretty easily. I then got a spade from the garden and dug the clay that was immediately underneath the bricks. After digging down to about a depth of four spadefuls I came across what appeared to be human remains."

Dew now summoned Dr. Alexander Marshall, a police

334

surgeon, Sir Melville MacNaughten, chief of the Criminal Investigation Department, and other officers to the scene. Continued digging exposed the complete skeletal framework of a human being. Portions of scalp and long hairs still adhered to the skull. Besides the bones, a few hair curlers and some feminine clothing were found.

Without doubt, the bones and rotting flesh were all that remained of Cora Turner Crippen, otherwise known as Belle Elmore.

The grisly cellar find was removed to a mortuary, where the Scotland Yard experts went to work on it. They definitely established that the victim had been female, and that her measurement corresponded to those of Mrs. Crippen. Moreover, they discovered strong indications that death had been caused by poison.

"An entirely logical means of murder for a medical man like Crippen," Dew told Mitchell. "Let's have an immediate survey of all chemists' shops with which the doctor, in behalf of Munyon's, had any dealings."

It was quickly established that there were several such shops. In all but one Crippen's purchases had been of non-poisonous materials. On the records of Lewis and Burrows, however, there was a significant entry dated the 18th of January. The sheet read: "Name and quantity of poison: five grains hyoscin hydrobromide. Purpose for which required: homeopathic preparation. Signature of purchaser: H.H. Crippen."

Dr. W.H. Wilcox, highly skilled scientific analyst employed by Scotland Yard, assisted Dew and Mitchell in going over the ledgers of the various pharmaceutical firms. "There's little doubt in my mind but what this is the poison used to kill Mrs. Crippen," he declared. "It is extremely rare, and so far as I know never has been employed in a murder case before—proof of Dr. Crippen's cunning."

Immediately after the bones were found an alarm had gone out through the British Isles and the Continent giving descriptions of the missing Dr. Crippen and Lisa Montclair and asking for their apprehension. Now something happened that caused Chief Inspector Dew to alter his "wanted" appeal.

Walter Ford came forward to tell how Crippen had sent him out to make the purchases of boy's clothing. "I'm familiar with Miss Montclair, sir," he told Dew, "and if you ask me, those things I bought would be a pretty good fit for her."

As a result of this information, Dew informed British and Continental authorities that Crippen's companion probably was masquerading as a boy.

"You know," Sergeant Mitchell pointed out, "Dr. Crippen came originally from America, and he may be heading back there. Don't you think police on the other side should be alerted?"

"That is being done, both for the States and Canada," the chief inspector said. "I've spent a small fortune in cable tolls. Come to think of it, at this very moment Crippen and Miss Montclair may be on shipboard, and in that case—"

Dew drafted a detailed description of the crime and the missing suspects, and Scotland Yard men took the message around to all the shipping companies for transmission via the wireless to their ships at sea.

Among the vessels whose aerials picked up the bulletin was, of course, the *Montrose,* just a few days out of Antwerp and plodding across the Atlantic toward Quebec. As soon as Captain Fred Kendall read the message handed to him by the wireless operator he snapped his fingers and exclaimed, "The Robinsons! I thought there was something funny about that pair the minute they came aboard!"

The *Montrose* skipper was a man of brimming curiosity who fancied himself as something of an amateur detective. One of the first things he noticed about the Robinsons—Senior and Junior—was that they were continually holding hands. More than once, on a dark part of the deck, he came upon them embracing—rather an unusual behavior for father and son.

Then there was the matter of Junior's figure. The brown tweed suit failed to conceal curves and contours which were undeniably feminine. Junior's voice and handling of knife and fork at the table were decidedly ladylike.

Captain Kendall answered Dew's bulletin with an immediate message. "Keeping couple under observation," he said. "Doing nothing to alarm them."

A promontory called Father Point was the first port of call for the *Montrose* on the American mainland, and it was at this point that the ship picked up a pilot. Checking with marine officials, Chief Inspector Dew found that he could beat the *Montrose* to Father Point if he embarked at once on a faster boat.

It was the 31st of July when a pilot vessel came alongside the *Montrose* off Father Point and Dew climbed the ladder. Kendall escorted him to the Robinson cabin and threw open the door.

"Inspector Dew!" gasped Hawley Harvey Crippen. "This is impossible!"

"Some people still think the wireless is an impossible invention," the Scotland Yard man observed. "Dr. Crippen, you are under arrest for the murder of your wife. And I must hold you, Miss Montclair, as an accessory."

Kendall and the chief inspector made a search of Crippen's effects. He carried no weapons, but there was a scrap of paper in his coat pocket which gave partial indication of his guilt.

"I cannot stand this horror I go through every night any longer," the message read, "and as I see nothing bright ahead, and my money has come to an end, I have made up my mind to jump overboard."

Thanks to Marconi's wireless and the quick action of Chief Inspector Dew, Crippen never had a chance to carry out this threat. He and Lisa Montclair were promptly returned to England to face justice.

The middle-aged doctor went on trial first, in Old Bailey, on October 18th. After three days of testimony it took a jury only 20 minutes to find him guilty as charged, and he was sentenced to be hanged.

Lisa Montclair's trial on charges of being an accessory to the murder resulted in a "not guilty" verdict.

The last act in the drama of Hilldrop Crescent took place at gloomy Pentonville Prison on November 22nd, 1910, when Hawley Harvey Crippen mounted the steps to the gallows and the trap was sprung.

EDITOR'S NOTE:
The name, Lisa Montclair, is fictitious.

"DEADLY Rx SNUFFED THREE LIVES!"

by Krist Boardman

No one suspected that Sunday, November 1, 1987, would be Dawn Marie Garvin's last day alive. The attractive 20-year-old woman had been seen very recently by loved ones and had too much going for her simply to drop out of the realm of the living.

But, as impossible as that seemed, it was her last day.

An outstanding business administration student at Harford Community College in northeast Maryland, Dawn had only recently married. She and her beau had tied the knot a few months earlier and established a residence at an apartment in nearby Baltimore County, not far from her family's Joppatowne home and her college in Harford County. While her husband worked for the U.S. Navy, Dawn attended classes and also worked part time.

But, unfortunately, November 1, 1987 is forever engraved on the minds of those who loved her. It was a Sunday. Her husband was at home on the last day of his leave from the Norfolk, Virginia Navy base. He had to be back in Norfolk later that night. As it was about a four- or five-hour trip, he left at 7:30 p.m. He was to call Dawn to let her know that he had arrived safely.

But when he did call home from Norfolk, no one answered the phone. This was odd because Dawn never left the apartment late at night and furthermore, she had said she would be home expecting his call.

After Dawn's husband left, another relative stayed with Dawn for about two or three hours, then left for home. Thus, it was only a short time since the relative left the apartment to the time that her husband should have reached her on the phone. Yet inexplicably, Dawn never answered.

The husband's worries weren't known to Dawn's other relatives until he called them from Norfolk and told them of his concerns. Another relative of Dawn's decided to go directly to the couple's apartment to see what had happened. When he arrived, it was already 1:30 a.m. on Monday.

Dawn Marie Garvin was found nude and dead in her bed. She had been shot several times in the head. The relative promptly called the Baltimore County Police, who quickly responded and secured the crime scene.

Detectives were at a loss for a clue or even a motive. In the apartment there was no sign of a struggle. There were no overturned chairs. Except for Dawn's body, nothing was out of order.

Nor was there any sign of forced entry into the apartment, leading investigators to believe initially that Dawn knew her assailant and voluntarily let him in.

By the time the autopsy was completed, detectives knew they had a sex crime as well as a murder. Although initially police reports spoke of just some kind of sexual assault, later statements made public spoke of rape and also possible mutilation.

Detectives Robert Capel and Milton Duckworth headed up the probe for the county police. They looked into Dawn's background and found no extramarital or illicit love affairs, shady connections, or any behavior on the victim's part that was less than exemplary. Without such activity, it was very unlikely that there may have been an unknown lover with an ax to grind.

"We really don't have a whole lot to go on," remarked Baltimore County Police Sergeant Brian Uppercue.

Without any leads from Dawn's background, police assumed that there weren't any and focused on canvassing the apartment complex for additional information. Eventually they did locate three neighbors who reported seeing a suspicious man who tried to gain entry into several nearby dwellings the day before Dawn was killed. The accounts of the neighbors were being assembled to assist a police artist in putting together a composite sketch.

"We had a few people who reported that there was a man who went through the building the day before who didn't belong there," said E. Jay Miller, information officer for the county police. "He knocked on doors and tried to get in by saying he needed to use the phone or asking for directions; nobody let him in.

"After the fact (the murder), we found that this had occurred," Miller elaborated. "It didn't seem that important until this happened. Right now, we're still hoping to come up with a composite."

Baltimore County police never did come up with a composite, however. The painstaking work of completing a composite was overtaken by other events.

The lack of any solid leads led to the creation of a reward fund by friends of Dawn's family and husband. The shock and outrage generated by the rape-murder made it easy for the reward fund coordinator to collect money.

"We've gotten a very good response, and the response from the community has been overwhelming," said a reward fund coordinator. A relative of Dawn's "has asked

341

that we let the public know that the friendship and assistance are appreciated."

Hardly was the reward fund established then the case took an unexpectedly dramatic turn.

On the morning of Monday, November 16th, scarcely a mile from Dawn Garvin's apartment, highway workers traveling along White Marsh Boulevard as it approaches the interchanges with I-95 spotted a nude female body at the bottom of a ravine alongside the road. They notified Baltimore County police. The body was completely unclothed and little could be done to identify the woman, who had apparently died form a gunshot wound to the head. However, there was no evidence of rape or sexual abuse. The victim appeared to be in her late 30s or early 40s.

At about the same time, relatives of 43-year-old Patricia Antoinette Hirt were worried about what might have happened to her the previous day. Patricia, a divorcee who worked as a secretary and who had raised two daughters to college age, had left that Sunday afternoon to deliver a camera to her brother-in-law's house.

Steven Oken and his wife were planning on traveling to the Virgin Islands the following month, and Patricia had visited Steven to deliver the camera. At the time, Oken's wife was on a business trip to California and was not at the house when Patricia arrived.

When Patricia failed to return home after the delivery or to contact them to explain where she was, relatives called Oken's house. The 25-year-old pharmacy employee answered and explained that Hirt had never arrived.

The following morning, when Patricia still didn't show up, relatives left for the Oken house and went in. Steven had already left. When they entered they found blood in the kitchen and on the living room floor. In addition, they saw signs of a struggle in the house and blood on the door.

A member of Hirt's family called the police.

It didn't take long for the police to link the dumping of the nude woman's body near I-95 with the disappearance of Patricia Hirt. They were one and the same case.

Suddenly, the need to find Steven Oken became urgent.

Described by friends and relatives as a nice guy who liked collecting guns and target practice, Oken had suddenly disappeared. His pickup truck was parked close to his townhouse. What was missing was Patricia Hirt's 1979 white Ford Mustang. Authorities began to wonder if he had taken that car and fled.

A tight-lipped E. Jay Miller said of the rapidly breaking crime spree, "We know she [Hirt] was there, because we have evidence she was in the house."

Miller said a search was made of the entire house and the shed on Oken's property, but he did add that someone saw Oken leaving his backyard shed at about 6:00 p.m. on Sunday.

"We can place him where the body was found and we know she was in the house," he said.

But was Oken also an active suspect in Dawn Garvin's murder, which took place only a few blocks away and only two weeks earlier?

Miller wasn't closing the door to that possibility. He said there were definite similarities between the deaths of Garvin and Hirt—for example, both were shot in the head—and that Oken could not be dismissed as a suspect in the Garvin slaying.

However, Miller qualified his statement by adding, "There are also dissimilarities."

At this time, more information surfaced about Oken's activities leading up to the time of his alleged spree.

One story that gained currency was that Oken was having family problems and was "acting out" prior to these events.

Some of Oken's acquaintances saw him drunk late at night—not anything of great note, but indicative that he might have been disturbed about something.

Police also noted that only three weeks earlier, Oken had been arrested for punching a female desk clerk at a motel in East Baltimore. He had pleaded guilty to battery and been placed on probation.

An investigation into that incident revealed that the woman clerk was afraid Oken was going to rape her, and she protected herself by kneeing him in the groin.

It remained unclear whether Oken was still in the area or had left for parts unknown. But local residents weren't taking anything for granted, given the occurrence of two homicides in their community.

"I've got a gun now," confided a resident of the apartment building where Dawn Garvin was slain. "I did it because of this. I have two daughters and I keep my eye on them at all times. We have got to be careful."

"We put another dead bolt [lock] on our door," said another apartment resident. "We are petrified to live here. My wife and I have only lived here for six weeks. We're really unhappy and would move except that we have a nine-month lease. It seemed like a safe place to live."

A resident of Oken's street, just a few blocks away, said, "I'm naturally suspicious. When someone comes to the door, I stand at the top of the stairs and sometimes I call down."

Another resident of the same street said, "I guarantee it's not going to help real estate any. Before this, people weren't really concerned. Now, it's close to home."

Baltimore County police swore out arrest warrants for

Oken, but didn't know where to serve them. Because of the possibility he had fled the area, teletypes were sent to police agencies all over the country.

"We have issued a national and international lookout for Oken," said Jay Miller, "because he may try to leave the country and head to the Virgin Islands."

He also said that Oken's proclivity for camping may have led him to camp in remote areas to elude police. Because of Oken's fondness for firearms, Miller said he should be considered extremely dangerous.

Just how dangerous he would be was revealed only a couple of days later. On Monday, November 16th, at approximately 6:00 p.m. at a motel on U.S. 1 in Kittery, Maine, motel employees found the body of 25-year-old Lori Ward, the victim of a sexual assault and shooting.

Reconstructing the events of that night, motel employees told police that Lori Ward had called Oken at his room in the motel to inform him that he had left a credit card at the desk. That was at 5:00 p.m. An hour later, she was dead.

When Kittery police arrived to investigate, they searched the motel's guest rooms. The room reserved for Steven Oken was empty, even though he had planned to spend the night. When Maine authorities discovered that Oken was also wanted in connection with two homicides in Maryland, they issued their own all-points bulletins statewide. The elusive Oken could be anywhere.

In the meantime, a Baltimore County police ballistics examiner was comparing projectiles fired from a pistol seized from Oken's house with those recovered from the Dawn Garvin slaying. According to police information released at the time, there was a match between the gun and the Garvin bullets, establishing a definite link.

The fears of Oken's relatives for his safety during the

345

massive police manhunt in Maine prompted one of them to make this unusual televised plea from Maryland:

"Steven, we love you. We want to help you. Please call us. Please, please, please get in touch with us. We will work this thing out together."

Soon after, authorities working with Oken's wife made arrangements for her to make an unusual televised plea over Maine television via satellite from Maryland, for the purpose of asking him to surrender.

At the same time, police began to develop plans to inform law enforcement agencies in New Hampshire and Canada, as well as Interpol, of Oken's fugitive status.

But before these plans could be implemented, another event got in the way.

Sixty-five miles northeast of Kittery is Freeport, a town best known as the home of the internationally renowned mail-order firm of L.L. Bean. An alert motel manager noticed that one of his recent guests was driving the Mustang that police had noted Oken was driving. He called local police and informed them of the unusual coincidence.

Surrounding the motel between 3:30 and 4:00 p.m. on November 17th, police sealed off any possible escape routes. A hostage negotiator called Oken's room and asked him to surrender. At 5:09 p.m., he did.

Oken came out of his room unarmed, with his hands behind his head, and then dropped to his knees. According to police reports, he was believed to have been carrying an AR-15 semiautomatic military rifle, a .380-caliber automatic pistol, a 9-millimeter handgun, high-powered, armor-piercing Teflon-coated bullets, and a bulletproof vest. These items were recovered from his room, according to reports.

Oken was taken to the Portland County Jail. He was

arraigned the following morning on the Kittery murder charge and held for trial.

In 1988, Steven Oken pleaded guilty to the shooting death of Kittery motel clerk Lori Ward. Under the terms of his plea agreement, Oken was sentenced to life without possibility of parole.

This guilty plea should have cleared the way for Oken's extradition to Maryland on the two additional murder charges, but Maine attorney Richard S. Emerson Jr. of Portland found grounds for appeal. Because of announced intentions that the death penalty would possibly be sought for Oken in Maryland, Emerson tried to prevent his extradition.

In an appeal before the Supreme Court of Maine, Emerson argued that Oken's conviction should be vacated because police searched his motel room in Kittery without a warrant. In that search, police found a bloodstained shirt.

But the Maine justices disagreed. They denied Oken's appeal, ruling that Oken had abandoned his motel room by the time police searched it, so he had no constitutional right to privacy. Oken's room was listed as unoccupied, although he had not formally checked out.

The denial of the appeal clears one of the few remaining obstacles preventing Oken's extradition to stand trial in the slayings of Patricia Hirt and Dawn Garvin. Until and unless Steven Oken does stand trial on those charges, he is entitled to the presumption of innocence under the law that all untried suspects must be accorded.

"ALMOST PERFECT CRIME!"
by Bill Kelly

The last time anyone laid eyes on 32-year-old Ellis Henry Greene while he was still alive, he was steering a rather unsteady course on his way out of a Burbank Boulevard bar in North Hollywood at about eleven o'clock on Friday night, April 15, 1988. The next time anyone saw him, Greene was a corpse. The only hitch was, no one knew the corpse was Greene.

Later, in the early-morning hours of Saturday, April 16th, a couple of patrolmen stood in the Glendale office of Dr. Richard Pryde Boggs, who had made the emergency call, and they silently stared down at a limp body. Dr. Boggs identified the dead man as his patient, Melvin Eugene Hanson, and said that he had come to the physician's office after having called and complained of chest pains.

The doctor told the officers that he'd left the outer office for only a moment when he suddenly heard a thud. He rushed back in to find Hanson stretched out on the floor. After dialing 911 and finding the line busy, he proceeded to administer CPR (cardiopulmonary resuscitation). He finally got through to the emergency operator, and a team of medics arrived shortly afterward. But they could do nothing for him, said the doctor. Hanson was already beyond human help.

The body was removed to the medical examiner's office, where toxicological tests determined that Hanson's bloodstream contained a very high level of alcohol, but nothing else of consequence. The coroner, taking into account Dr. Boggs' information that Hanson had a heart ailment, attributed the cause of death to inflammation of the heart. No signs of foul play were present, but the coroner did photograph the body and take a set of fingerprints. The dead man had already been identified through the papers and credit cards found in his pockets.

Since both Dr. Boggs and the coroner possessed the most impeccable of credentials, the Glendale police were satisfied with the autopsy findings. The file on the death of Melvin Hanson, a 48-year-old businessman from Columbus, Ohio, was marked closed. No one had an inkling yet that something was amiss.

Melvin Hanson had a business partner, a 26-year-old former bartender named John Barrett Hawkins, who was also his sole heir. Muscular and handsome, with long, curly dark hair, Hawkins had a reputation as a womanizer and a male hustler. While Hanson had been more engrossed in their business dealings, Hawkins had lived it up.

The day after Hanson's death, Hawkins flew from Ohio to Southern California. He claimed Hanson's body and had it cremated.

In 1985, the two partners had opened a stylish sportswear store in Columbus, Ohio, called Just Sweats Inc. The business soon branched out into 22 stores. No sooner had they achieved success and respectability, however, than they converted most of Just Sweats' currency. That was in 1986, the same year when Hanson began applying for several life insurance policies, three of which listed Hawkins as the sole beneficiary.

Now Hawkins began pressuring the life insurance company in Mercer Island, Washington, to pay off the benefits on Hanson's death. Finally, the firm mailed him a couple of checks for $1 million. As a follow-up, a claims representative requested a thumbprint of the deceased man to close out the file. Hawkins complied. The print arrived at the Glendale Police Department four days after the request.

In September 1988, the Department of Insurance discovered that the dead man was listed in the U.S. Department of Justice computer file of missing persons. The thumbprint had been matched to the name Ellis Greene, not Melvin Hanson. A relative of Greene's who'd filed the missing-person report positively identified him by his police photograph taken before the quick cremation.

Their curiosity aroused, investigators began checking into Ellis Greene's background.

The mild-mannered Greene was born and raised in San Diego, but he'd lived in Ohio, and more recently, with a relative in North Hollywood. He worked as a bookkeeper for a Burbank accountant.

The question arose: If Ellis was the dead man who'd been cremated under the name Hanson, then where was the real Hanson? An investigation quickly got under way.

In late January 1989, police picked up Melvin Hanson, alive and well, at Dallas-Fort Worth International Airport. Traveling under the name Wolfgang von Snowden, he had tried to veil his true identity through cosmetic surgery.

In his luggage, customs officials found identification papers under several pseudonyms. One name in particular stood out—Ellis Greene. There was also a book titled, *How To Create A New Identity*. And tucked in the lining of his gear was $14,000 in cash.

This turn of events prompted the investigators to dig hard and deep into Melvin Hanson's background They learned that he'd embarked in his new identity as Wolfgang von Snowden—which he often misspelled—two months before his "death." The sleuths also discovered that he had signed a rental agreement for a Miami condominium using the nom-de-plume Wolfgang Eugene Vonsnowden. For character references, he had put down John B. Hawkins and Dr. Richard Boggs.

The investigators quickly checked out the telephone records of Hanson, Hawkins, and Boggs. They established that numerous calls had been made between the three men during the months leading up to Hanson's connived death. The probers also established that Hanson had flown from Miami to Los Angeles on April 15, 1988, and checked in at the Holiday Inn in Glendale under the name of Wolfgang Vonsnowden. He'd taken a flight back to Miami on the following afternoon.

On May 31, 1988, Boggs received a check for $6,500 from Hawkins. Phone calls between the three continued throughout the summer. Painstakingly carrying on the probe, homicide sleuths under the direction of Glendale Police Sergeant Jon Perkins discovered that Hanson had opened a sizable bank account in Key West, Florida, under the name Ellis Henry Greene.

By now, a private investigator hired by the insurance company was dogging Hanson's trail. An arrest warrant was issued for Hawkins and Hanson in Ohio.

Meanwhile, Hawkins had seemingly vanished into thin air, but Hanson was picked up and sent to Columbus. There, he faced embezzlement and insurance fraud charges. He was lodged at the Franklin County Jail and he appealed his extradition.

During the investigation into the mysterious death of

the man found on the floor of Dr. Boggs' office, something else had aroused police suspicions. On the body, all too obviously, a copy of Hanson's birth certificate had turned up, along with two major credit cards in the name of Hanson. Who, Sergeant Perkins wondered, carries around his birth certificate?

The sleuths also took a long, hard look at Dr. Boggs. They began to wonder whether Ellis Greene's death had indeed been natural—or homicidal. Careful investigation into Boggs' activities revealed that the onetime child of the Depression, and later "perfect citizen," never failed to make a great impression on everyone whose path he crossed.

Richard Boggs was born in Hot Springs, South Dakota, and raised for the most part, in Casper, Wyoming. His family moved to Los Angeles County in 1939 and settled in Glendale. Boggs graduated with honors from Glendale High School in 1951. In 1956 he graduated from UCLA at the top of his class with a degree in zoology.

A Wyoming friend, who admired Richard's drive and determination to become a physician, loaned him the money to attend medical school, since Richard's own family couldn't afford it. Boggs repaid the medical school loan, but he neglected to repay $31,000 the friend gave him to start a business. "I don't care," she told the investigators. "He's a brilliant doctor, and I think the world of him."

Richard Boggs joined the College of Medical Evangelists, today called the Loma Linda Medical School, and he adopted the San Bernadino-based Adventists' creed of abstinence from alcohol, tobacco, and meat. His brilliance and charm won him many friends and admirers.

In 1961 he married a woman who worked as a mathematics teacher to help support him during his medical training. Eager to begin a family, they adopted two boys.

At the Los Angeles County General Hospital, Boggs impressed several doctors who eventually helped him get into Boston City Hospital. In 1967, he returned to finish his neurology training in Los Angeles.

Boggs, his wife, and their two sons appeared to be happy. They became known as good neighbors who lived quietly in a Tudor mansion on a beautiful plot, now called La Canada Flintridge. Over the fireplace hung a life-size portrait of the doctor. Weekends featured barbecues and backyard parties, always with fellow doctors and their families. At 35, Boggs was already head of the neurology department at the Rancho Los Amigos Hospital in Downey.

Furthermore, while practicing medicine at a feverish, headlong pace, he conceived of a way to provide medical care for as many as 100,000 people. He gathered a group of investors, and, in 1970, he incorporated an operation called Satellite Health Systems. With 22 contract doctors working from a medical building in Hollywood, 25,000 patients were registered with Satellite and receiving medical attention.

Then the walls came tumbling down. By 1974, the large overhead and small membership sent the company into debt. Boggs declared bankruptcy.

Two years later, his bills multiplied into the millions. He owed the government back taxes. He owed banks and leasing agencies and countless friends. His American Medical Association membership lapsed for nonpayment of dues, along with his membership in the American Neurological Association.

Legal and financial woes mounted. Boggs began borrowing from Peter to pay Paul. Once he borrowed

$14,000 from a fellow physician to satisfy the IRS. His friend had to take Boggs to court to get his money back.

In 1978, his marriage of 17 years ended. His wife told friends that she simply couldn't cope with the irrational route Boggs' life had taken.

At one point Boggs began carrying a pistol. He allegedly bragged to one of his attorneys that he had important mob connections.

As time went by, people around Los Angeles County began hearing about a new diagnostician phenomenon. Among the legions of patients who saw Boggs as some magnanimous godlike healer was a Beverly Hills woman with a neurological condition that had left her almost completely paralyzed. Dozens of doctors had failed to help the long-suffering woman, but, she said, Boggs immediately diagnosed the problem. With the joint cooperation of an orthopedist, she claimed, she was completely cured.

"Dr. Boggs was the most brilliant neurologist around," she told the investigators. "He saved my life."

Not everyone was so mesmerized by Boggs' charms and abilities. In 1976, an official of a San Diego hospital who said he'd been trying to recruit gifted physicians, found that Boggs concentrated more on moonlighting and less on the needs of the hospital.

"He showed us that he really wasn't interested in our plans," the man said. "To me, that was a terrible keen disappointment. We thought he was very bright, but he was always looking for the easy way out. He started not minding the store too much. I was glad when he finally up and quit one day. We didn't have to fire him."

In 1976, the investigators discovered, both Glendale Memorial Hospital and Verdugo Hills Hospital released

354

Boggs from their staff for disciplinary purposes.

The detectives also learned that Boggs practiced medicine at an almost breakneck pace, very often starting his day at 5:00 a.m., and making rounds, or assisting a neurosurgeon in surgery, then running back to his office, or from one hospital to another, sometimes not returning home until 11 or 12 o'clock that night.

In 1981, Boggs' wife sued him to collect $33,000 in unpaid child support, contending that a court filing showed that his income for that year was $155,000. At that hearing she told the court that her husband owned a gun and had threatened to shoot her on several occasions. She said that he'd once told her, "I could hire someone to snuff you."

In a mad tangle of litigation Boggs had racked up over $1 million in uncollectible debts through 60 liens and judgments. Collectors dogged his footsteps. They garnished his office receipts and repossessed his furniture and office equipment. County marshals sought him in an effort to repossess his Rolls-Royce Silver Wraith II. The IRS slapped a padlock on his office for default on back taxes.

So, Boggs opened another office across the street.

When detectives questioned Boggs' receptionist of 15 years, she said she frequently received calls from pharmacies questioning the quantity of his prescriptions. The detectives who searched his office found paraphernalia for manufacturing metheamphetamines.

And now, Ellis Greene's death had emerged as the main element in an alleged million-dollar insurance rip-off. Investigators across the country began a seven-month quest to solve the mystery of the drunken man's last nine hours. It took them three months to confirm Greene's identity, and four more months to build a case against Dr. Boggs.

Boggs' careworn medical practice skidded to an abrupt halt on February 3, 1989. Having just been evicted from his North Central Avenue office suite for nonpayment of rent, he was in the midst of clearing out his possessions when the Glendale police arrested him. He was taken to the district attorney's office and charged with nine counts of murder, conspiracy and insurance fraud, and assault with a stun-gun. Along with Melvin Hanson, Dr. Richard Boggs was held in the Los Angeles County Jail without bail.

At his arraignment on Monday, February 6, 1989, the 6-foot-2-inch, 56-year-old neurologist pleaded not guilty to the charges. Deputy District Attorney Al MacKenzie alleged that Boggs had murdered Greene, and that John Hawkins had flown in from Ohio to claim Greene's body as Hanson's, and have it cremated.

The D.A. said that the crime would have never been detected had it not been for the insurance company claims worker.

"He just happened to ask whether the police had checked the thumbprint of the corpse against that of the policy holder. They had not. The suspicious claims agent phoned the cops and the scheme began to unravel."

As the trial date approached, Deputy D.A. MacKenzie was hoping to try Hanson and Boggs together. Hanson had appealed his extradition, however, and remained in the Franklin County Jail in Columbus. Thus, the chance of getting one to testify against the other for a lesser sentence seemed slight.

With two of the three suspects in custody, detectives continued the search for John Hawkins. In mid-July, they found his Mercedes-Benz convertible at the airport with its top down. Columbus Detective James Lanfear reported that Hawkins had swindled $1.8 million from the company he and Hanson had operated—Just Sweats Inc.—which had since declared bankruptcy, and he had flown the coop.

With Hawkins still on the lam, the lawyers began preparing for what promised to be a trial with an almost Byzantine complexity. Deputy D.A. MacKenzie focused on the circumstantial evidence linking the three suspects as equal accomplices in a conspiracy to commit murder in order to collect the insurance money.

Thus far, the evidence MacKenzie had been correlating and indexing for the coming trial seemed to be forming into a tight-fitting noose for the three men: records of dozens of phone calls the three made to one another shortly before the murder; insurance policies paid for by Hanson; Hanson's change of identity; Hawkins' disappearance shortly after the insurance company paid off; the testimony of Hawkins' roommate in whom Hawkins had confided that the body found in Boggs' Glendale office was not Hanson's.

Moreover, when the investigators searched Boggs' fashionable mansion, the Department of Insurance found paraphernalia for manufacturing illegal drugs, as well as a stun-gun—a weapon that can disable a person with an electrical charge. Deputy D.A. MacKenzie said that the stun-gun was being viewed as a possible murder weapon.

He himself was victimized—that was how Dr. Richard Boggs tried to explain his role in these events. He asserted that he'd been completely taken in by Hawkins and the real Hanson, and that for seven years, he'd known the man who dropped dead in his office as Melvin Hanson, not Ellis Greene.

Although Boggs' attorney refused to explain their defense tactics in detail, one of the defendant's earlier attorneys had admitted to a newspaper reporter, "There

357

certainly is a circumstantial case for the insurance fraud, but there's a very difficult case to prove as to the homicide."

Before his lawyers were able to put a lid on Boggs' yakking away, he told the *Wall Street Journal:* "If I did it, I'd be in Rio," and, "I keep thinking I'll wake up from a bad dream."

When Boggs' trial got under way before Superior Court Commissioner Florence-Marie Cooper, the prosecutor's opening statement alleged that Dr. Boggs was the mastermind behind the nearly perfect scam. He asserted that Boggs had lured Ellis Greene, who bore a striking resemblance to Melvin Hanson, into his office and used his medical knowledge to murder Greene without leaving a perceptible trace in order to carry out an insurance swindle.

A former patient of Boggs' who described himself as a security expert, told the six-man, six-woman jury that after having witnessed a "kook" in an Army uniform shouting threats at Boggs in his office, he bought the doctor several stun-guns. The witness said that Boggs carried the stun devices as protection against threatening patients.

Another doctor testified that, later on, Boggs began carrying a pistol for protection.

Defense Attorneys Dale Rubin and Charles Lindner described Boggs as a victim of circumstances, a brilliant doctor still adored by patients who refused to give up on him, and commended by former President Richard M. Nixon for his work in starting one of the first health maintenance clinics.

They presented witnesses who described Dr. Boggs as a witty conversationalist and a man who cherished art, music, and people, often overgenerous when picking up the tab when dining with friends. One doctor said he

358

was trusting to the point of naivete.

In contrast, the prosecutor presented witnesses who testified that Boggs had a terrible temper. He would suddenly fly off the handle for little reason, they said. One colleague testified that the good doctor could be a practical joker one minute, and the next, a stuffed-shirt perfectionist.

The prosecutor said that once, Dr. Boggs forced a medical student who had put on rubber gloves backwards, to do it over ten times. Another time he allegedly stood up in a wedding in mock protest when the minister asked if there was anyone present who had any reason why the couple should not be married.

On Wednesday, July 11, 1990, Boggs' attorneys made an eleventh-hour admission that he was "unquestionably guilty" of conspiring to swindle life insurance benefits by falsely substituting Ellis Greene's identity for that of Melvin Hanson. But Defense Attorney Rubin insisted, in the final arguments, that the object of the swindle was money, not murder. He declared that the prosecuting attorneys had failed to prove that there had even been a murder.

In conceding the insurance scam, the defense attorneys maintained that the body of a recently deceased person had been taken from the morgue to carry out the planned scam.

"What the plan needed was not a murder, but a recently deceased body somehow obtained from the county morgue," the defense attorney told the jury.

The defense had brought in a county pathologist who testified that she had ruled Greene's death to be the result of a natural heart attack, but she'd changed it to homicide only after she had learned of the identity switch. She said she actually had no idea what the actual cause of death was.

Throughout the final arguments, Dr. Boggs sat slumped over the defense table, doodling away and infrequently looking up while the prosecutors portrayed him as a selfish con artist who'd picked up 32-year-old Ellis Greene in a bar, lured him to his office in Glendale, subdued him with a stun-gun, and then suffocated the man.

"Then the doctor summoned paramedics and identified Greene as his patient, one Melvin Hanson, the apparent victim of a heart attack," the prosecutor declared.

The prosecutors had entered into evidence a photocopy of Hanson's birth certificate and two credit cards found on Greene's corpse.

The 48-year-old Melvin Hanson appeared at the trial to prove to jurors that he was still alive, but he steadfastly refused to testify against his friend, Dr. Boggs. At this report was written, he was awaiting trial on charges that he faked his own death and conspired to commit murder. In accordance with his constitutional rights, Hanson must be considered innocent of the charges against him until and unless proven otherwise in a court of law.

While describing the case as "an almost perfect crime," Deputy D.A. MacKenzie said that Ellis Greene had died of suffocation hours before Boggs dialed 911 for help. The prosecutor brought in a pathologist who testified that Greene had died from the combined effects of alcohol and "poppers," a nitrite stimulant.

It took the jury only two hours to find 57-year-old Dr. Richard Boggs guilty of first-degree murder and eight other counts connected with a scheme to fraudulently obtain money from Hanson's life insurance policies. The eight other counts included criminal conspiracy, grand theft, and assault with a stun-gun.

Afterward, the district attorney said that he had hoped to get one or the other to testify against his co-conspirator, but he added, "It doesn't really matter anymore."

The district attorney's office praised Glendale Police Sergeant Jon Perkins, the detective who had tenaciously conducted the investigation into the puzzling crime.

Asked to comment on the outcome of the trial, Sergeant Perkins said with a big grin, "It's sweet."

At the time this report was filed, Melvin Hawkins remained at large. He must be considered innocent of any charges pending against him until and unless proved otherwise in court under due process of law.

"CLEVER WITH A KNIFE"

by Edward S. Sullivan

The erratic Los Angeles River, bone-dry most of the year but flashing into an occasional torrent, is the subject of jokes today since its bed and banks from the San Fernando Valley to the sea have been concreted to end the flood menace. Its brief trickle or deluge now flows decorously down the long straight concrete channel, which most of the time doesn't even look like a river bed and is the dry, sun-baked scene of hot-rod races and similar events.

But a few years ago the river was no joke. Storms in the mountains were likely to send it raging overnight, inundating hundreds of acres of farms and lowland homes southeast of the city, to diminish again just as quickly. Receding flood waters, after heavy rains had ushered in a boisterous April, left a litter of debris for miles along the soggy banks and bottoms. Pieces of broken furniture, lumber, old tires, all sorts of things washed down from the upland communities lay forlornly in the reeds, potential treasure-trove for the industrious little bands of lowland dwellers who made a regular thing of river salvage, for meager profits.

By noon on the crisp spring morning of April 4th, the air clear and electric and the mountains etched

362

against a vivid blue sky after the storm, the river level was falling rapidly. Juan Mandriquez and his son, 14-year-old Ramon, set out from their home on Wright Road in Lynwood, near Long Beach, to comb the west bank for items of possible salvage value.

It was young Ramon who spotted a large square box floating downstream. *"Mira, Padre*—that looks like a brand new box, with the lid nailed on! Must be something in it!"

Father and son waded into the shallows and tried to reach the box with their long poles, but it was too far out and was being carried along too swiftly.

Regretfully, they watched the intriguing mystery box float farther from their reach and become a bobbing speck disappearing in the direction of the ocean. Then, as they turned back, they glimpsed a strange object about a hundred yards behind the box and equally inaccessible without a boat. It was something grayish white and long, and it danced like a cork in the turbulent muddy flood water.

"Wonder what that is?" Ramon shaded his eyes with his hand and squinted at the peculiar piece of flotsam.

"Lots of funny things floating down the river today, *nino,*" Juan Mandriquez shrugged. "Could be almost anything. We can't bother with it. Come on, let's get busy."

Father and son spent the afternoon without much luck in their plodding search for salvage, working downstream as the river waters rapidly ebbed, and at dusk they were turning homeward when sharp-eyed Ramon pointed to a grayish something lying snagged in a clump of marsh reeds, half in, half out of water.

"Look, Dad! There's that thing we saw floating behind that box—remember?"

They worked their way through the sticky mud to investigate, and a moment later they dropped their burdens and stood sinking to their ankles in the ooze, hastily crossing themselves as they stared with bulging eyes at the frightful thing in the rushes.

It was the headless, armless and legless torso of a woman completely nude—a grisly hulk cast up by the waters.

Forgetting their salvage hoard, father and son splashed and scrambled back over the flats and up the bank to the road where they hailed a passing motorist, who heard their terrified story and drove them to the office of Constable Roselle in nearby Compton.

The suburban constable flashed the electrifying word to the headquarters of Sheriff William I. Traeger in downtown Los Angeles, and shortly after the river salvagers had guided him back in the gathering darkness to the lonely spot in the marshes, they were joined by a party of deputies from the sheriff's Homicide Detail and the coroner's office, followed by a carload of newspapermen.

It was an eerie scene in the desolate mud-flats as they examined the butchered torso under the glow of flashlights. There wasn't much they could determine. The gruesome find lay like a broken marble statue, dark gashes where arms, legs and head had been.

"I'd say it was a young girl about 20," one of the coroner's men pronounced, "and she hasn't been in the water very long. Maybe a day or so."

Juan Mandriquez and his son told them about the mysterious looking nailed-up box that had preceded the torso down the river, and the officers agreed that it very likely contained the head and the missing members. A party of men went downstream to search for it, without much hope in the darkness, while the severed trunk was loaded into the coroner's black van and removed to the county morgue.

There Dr. A. F. Wagner, chief autopsy surgeon, began his examination at once, while Captain William J. Bright, sheriff's Homicide Chief, looked on. Dr. Wagner confirmed that the well-preserved torso appeared to be that of a girl or young woman, between the approximate ages of 17 and 25 years, of slight build, and weighing 118 pounds. Her complexion was light, clear and milky. Hair in the armpits was dark brown, giving an index to that of the missing head. Unless body and face were badly mismatched, the girl must have been very beautiful.

Other than the obvious and horrid dismemberment, there were no marks of external violence on the body itself and the cause of the death was not apparent. The doctor judged the victim had been dead some 36 to 48 hours, and in the water just about that length of time. The flesh was unblemished; there were no operation scars, moles nor other identifying marks.

"This was an expert job of dissection," the veteran surgeon commented as he studied the mute evidence of murder under the glaring lights of the autopsy room. "See here—the neck is severed cleanly between the fifth and sixth vertebrae, and in cutting into the flesh of the neck, the killer came within an eighth of an inch of his mark. He knew his anatomy, all right. There was no fumbling or hacking."

"What sort of tool would you say was used?" Captain Bright wondered.

"Hard to tell, but it looks almost like a professional job, with a scalpel and surgical saw, or their equivalents."

365

Bright assigned deputies to check the files on missing girls. In cooperation with the Los Angeles Police Department, throughout the night they contacted a score of families that had filed reports, and a dozen anguished relatives viewed the grisly remains but shook their heads mutely.

By morning, as the headline news spread, there was no need for further seeking out of relatives. The sheriff's office was deluged with reports and inquiries from parents, husbands, friends and neighbors of missing girls and young women. Several wandering girls even called in to identify themselves and relieve their parents of anxiety.

Scores of civilian volunteers joined a posse of 50 deputies and made a thorough search of the lower reaches of the river, using boats as well as patrolling both banks, probing every clump of reeds in search of the missing box. After a day-long futile hunt they decided it must have floated out to sea. The Coast Guard was alerted and beach patrolmen kept their eyes open.

Sheriff Traeger meanwhile assigned additional men to Captain Bright's detail, as they ran down scores of reports including hysterical stories of mystery men seen carrying ominous bundles or boxes through the streets at night.

One suburbanite turned in by a suspicious neighbor had a bad time till he proved that he had been lugging a dress-form home for his wife.

Telephone calls and letters poured in day by day from all over the western states, and the morgue continued to be besieged by people with legitimate inquiries as well as the curious, for the peculiar horror of a dismemberment murder always creates a great public

366

stir. Newspaper stories brought results.

Deputy Sheriff Frank Gompert, the crime lab technician, had his hands full with checking out possible identifications. Careful calculations of the slain girl's probable height and weight enabled him to eliminate many possibilities on the basis of description and photographs. Dr. Wagner's estimate of the age also narrowed it down. The autopsy surgeon completed his examination, still unable to determine the cause of death. Principal further information in his final report was that the dead girl, while she might have been married, had never borne any children. Neither was she the victim of an abortionist, as had been theorized.

Then there was the matter of the torso's lack of scars or blemishes, which served further as an index for elimination. In several cases, physicians who had attended young women now missing were called in to examine the remains. Most possibilities were checked out, but several remained open and the Homicide detectives patiently followed them up.

An important guide for the technician was the hair from the armpits, strands of which he extracted and put under a microscope. Gompert announced that specimens of hair for comparison, while not positive, might provide a clue to identification. He was immediately flooded with samples of hair of all hues and varieties, belonging to missing girls—baby curls taken from trunks, long braids preserved when hair was bobbed, treasured ringlets in keepsakes and lockets.

Many he discarded at once on the basis of color, for the slain girl's hair was definitely dark brown. Other specimens he tested with microscope and chemicals. Again, a few possibilities remained for active investigation.

Captain Bright's men and the city police, following up every lead, located more than a dozen missing young women as by-products of the murder investigation. A man whose bride had disappeared was picked up and held for questioning when neighbors informed the Homicide detectives that he had threatened to "blow her up." Her description fitted that of the river victim; the young husband was jittery and evasive, and Bright began to think he really had something—till the missing wife showed up indignantly at the Hall of Justice to demand her husband's release.

As one possibility after another petered out, a squad of deputies was assigned to examine every shack and shed along the river in its upper reaches, in search of bloodstains or other clues to the place where the body had been cut up. River habitues and transients were questioned.

But days went by without any further development, the inquiries dwindled to a trickle, and it began to look as though the Lynwood Torso Mystery was to go down in the books as one of Southern California's unsolved murder riddles. The Jane Doe torso, treated with preservatives, was kept in a special refrigerated viewing compartment at the morgue, but not many people came to look at it.

The torso case had long since vanished from the news columns and the Homicide men were routinely checking out belated inquiries from other parts of the country, when six weeks later, on the sunny afternoon of May 18th, it was revived in grotesque and dramatic fashion.

An excited and almost incoherent housewife telephoned Police Chief Harry R. Smith of the small town of Bell, a few miles up the river from Lynwood.

368

"Some boys—they're parading down Florence Avenue with a human head—on a stick!"

This was a new one on the veteran chief, who had all but forgotten the torso sensation under the press of other police work, and it sounded like a hysterical false alarm of some sort. Probably the boys had a dummy head or a mask. Who ever heard of a human head on a stick, on the main street of quiet suburban Bell in broad daylight? Nevertheless, Chief Smith had to do his duty, so with a sigh he put on his cap and climbed into his patrol car.

But it proved no false alarm. Smith caught up with the boys at the busy intersection of Florence and Atlantic Boulevard—a little band of half a dozen serious-faced youngsters in a tight defensive knot, surrounded by a growing crowd of excited elders. The boys' leader, a sturdy 10-year-old, held the gruesome trophy—a human skull with bits of mummified flesh adhering—aloft on a three-foot stick.

"Where did you get that, sonny?" the chief asked the boy mildly.

"We found it, down by the river where we were hunting frogs!"

Smith persuaded the lads to take a ride in his police car. They let him take the skull off the stick, which had been thrust through the jaw. He held the macabre brown thing gingerly at arm's length and inspected it. It had apparently been lying in the open for some time, but a few tufts of hair clung to the scraps of leather scalp, and the incongruously white teeth seemed to be almost intact. No telling whether it was the head of a man or a woman.

Smith put the severed skull in a sack he obtained from a storekeeper, and notified the sheriff's office,

369

for the river was in county territory. Then he had the willing boys guide him out along the road to the river bottoms, where they pointed out the exact spot where they had found their grisly prize, on a small muddy island left by the receding waters.

When the latest grim yield of the river was brought to Dr. Wagner's office at the morgue late that afternoon, the autopsy surgeon, after brief scrutiny, pronounced it to be the skull of a woman between 40 and 50 years old.

"I judge it to be a small-boned woman, rather than a man, by the small cranial cavity, the narrow lower jaw, and the small proportion of the face in relation to the cranium," Dr. Wagner explained to Captain Bright.

"As for the age, we can estimate that from the degree of ossification—hardening, that is—of the bones. Then there are certain characteristics of the lower jawbone that change with the different periods of life. And the sutures on top of the skull—they close up between 25 and 50, and here they're almost completely closed."

"Then this skull doesn't belong to the Lynwood torso?" Bright queried, frowning as he eyed the dark brown tufts of hair. "We've got two unidentified victims, then?"

"That's right. The torso is that of a young girl, and this head belongs to a mature woman. But it shouldn't go unidentified very long, with all this dental work to go on. That's another indication of her age, by the way; a young girl would hardly have all these gold fillings and those crowns."

"Can you tell how long the victim has been dead? Any indication of the cause?"

The autopsy surgeon shrugged. "Hard to tell how long. Anywhere from a few weeks to a few months. I'd say a month anyway. The cause is right here — this fracture above the right temple. She was hit with some sort of heavy instrument, probably a hammer."

Late the next day Captain Bright and Chief Criminal Deputy Harry Wright decided to explore a new angle that had occurred to them: to make a quiet check of the medical and embalming schools, on the outside chance that the dismembered remains had been thrown in the river by students as a macabre prank. This possibility had been discussed and rejected in the case of the torso, since it seemed too freshly dead to have come from a dissection room. But the browned skull, traditional student prop for practical jokes, was another matter.

Deputies were starting their canvass of the medical schools for missing cadavers, when Dr. Wagner telephoned and asked Bright to step over to his office down the hall right away.

He led the puzzled detective to a white-topped table where the Lynwood torso lay — with the Bell skull neatly fitted into place on the severed neck!

"Then — ?"

"Yes. That's where it belongs. There's only one Jane Doe after all. You see, the bones of the skull are a much more positive index of age than those of the body, which vary considerably with the individual. And in this case, the torso was so well preserved and the texture of the skin so fine and youthful that I just hadn't examined the bones too closely.

"Even at that, she must have been a remarkable woman, to keep herself in such shape. In life, she probably looked 15 years younger than she was. But

371

the skull tells the story: our victim was in her middle 40s, Bill. She wasn't a young girl at all."

This startling news meant that the investigation had to go back to its beginning again. Bright's men dug out of the files a score or more of still-open March and April missing persons reports and inquiries that had previously been passed over when they were interested only in young women from 17 to 25.

Technician Gompert confirmed that the hairs of the skull were of the same color and general characteristics as those from the torso's armpits; and now he enlisted the aid of University of Southern California dental experts in preparing a detailed chart of the slain woman's teeth, which was given wide prominence in the newspapers, with an appeal to dentists to search their records.

Three days after the latest find, scores of reports had been checked out, the dismembered body still lay unidentified, and Chief Wright had ordered several thousand circulars printed for distribution to dentists throughout the nation, when a man came to Captain Bright's office with still another report on a missing woman.

He was afraid the river victim might be his sister, Laura Belle Sutton, well-to-do 45-year-old divorcee missing since the end of March from her home at 2012 West 30th Street on the southwest side of Los Angeles.

"The description fits her. Laura was a beautiful woman who looked a lot younger than her age. And that dental work—I'm no expert, but it sounds like some of the work she had done in the last few years. Her dentist was Dr. Edwin C. Hyde. He has an office downtown here."

The busy Homicide captain had listened to many such stories in the past six weeks, but this one had an impressive ring of truth, and somehow the name Laura Belle Sutton seemed familiar.

When their visitor had gone, the deputies checked through the files and found where the name Laura Belle Sutton had cropped up previously. On May 17th, just a day before the skull was found, her disappearance had been reported to the Los Angeles police by one Frank P. Westlake, who described himself as a close friend of the missing divorcee and spokesman for several other anxious friends who had been trying vainly to locate her. The slain woman's brother had mentioned Westlake as one of the friends to whom he had spoken.

At the time of the police report, of course, the 45-year-old woman was not linked with the Lynwood torso; there was no suspicion of murder, and Westlake had expressed the opinion that she had run away for personal reasons. He, too, had mentioned her brooding over her mother's death, and thought perhaps she had simply wanted to get away from things for a while. "But she left everything behind her, and there are some business affairs that have to be taken care of. I thought it best to make an official report."

The police had sent a copy of this report to the sheriff's office, where it had not attracted much attention and was shortly forgotten in the excitement over finding of the head.

Gray and Allen called on Dr. Hyde and showed him the dental chart. He produced Mrs. Sutton's record card from his file cabinet and frowned as he compared them. "This certainly looks like some of my work, gentlemen," he finally pronounced. "You understand,

Mrs. Sutton hasn't visited me for more than a year, and she may have had some other work done since then, by someone else. But that porcelain-faced Richmond crown on the upper right incisor, in combination with those gold fillings — "

The dentist accompanied the two deputies to the morgue and examined the skull at first-hand. Several molars were missing, but the remaining teeth checked exactly with Dr. Hyde's chart, plus a couple of unrecorded fillings. Hyde was almost sure that the Richmond crown was his work; and Frank Gompert agreed that the number of check-points made it virtually certain that the severed head belonged to Laura Belle Sutton.

"To be positive," the technician said, "I'd like to have some samples of Mrs. Sutton's hair for comparison. We should be able to find some around her house. A vacuum cleaner would do the trick."

Before taking up this suggestion, Gray and Allen, joined by Lieutenant W. C. Allen of the Missing Persons Bureau, drove out to interview relatives and friends of the vanished divorcee, whose names her brother and Frank Westlake had supplied. In a short time they had accumulated considerable thought provoking information on Laura Belle's rather complicated life history.

She was described as a fragilely beautiful woman who looked not more than 30, with large innocent blue eyes and not a single streak of gray in her lustrous dark brown hair. Women envied her creamy complexion and trim, petite figure, and she took extreme care of herself, with frequent visits to the beauty parlor.

By nature vivacious, gay and gregarious, the childless Laura Belle had led an active social life since her divorce in 1927 from a prosperous young Beverly Hills man, from whom she had been separated for some time before the divorce.

She continued to occupy the large bungalow on West 30th Street, in the polite neighborhood where they had lived for six years, and got along comfortably on the alimony as well as the income from some investments of her own.

An old friend, Louis Neal, a mechanic who worked at night, occupied the garage apartment behind the house and Mrs. Sutton cooked his meals for him. At first she told people she just wanted to have a man around the place for protection, but in the past year she had confided that she and Neal planned to be married.

Frank Westlake, who lived not far away, was an older man she had met a year or so before. He visited her often and they went out together on occasion. It was understood that the reputedly wealthy retired businessman, who dabbled in contracting and made a hobby of carpentry, was more or less a fatherly adviser to the lively divorcee. But again the detectives heard rumors of romantic attachment; she had told several friends recently that she might marry Westlake, who was a recent widower.

There was also talk of renewed acquaintance with an old boy friend from World War I days, to whom she had been engaged before she married the handsome Sutton. Apparently Laura Belle had led a full life, and took some innocent pleasure in giving out piecemeal and contradictory reports on her romances, to keep her women friends and relatives guessing.

The investigators talked to Sutton, who said he

375

hadn't seen his ex-wife for about six months, but that she had called him on the telephone several times when he was late with his alimony payments. He had last spoken with her late in March, he said. Sutton emphasized that they were on good terms and their talks had been friendly. He had no idea what had become of her.

Gray and Allen also interviewed the missing woman's sister, who said she had last seen Laura at their mother's funeral in February. They had talked on the telephone several times since then, and Laura had been extremely depressed over the death of their mother; but she had said nothing about going away. Sutton and the sister had had several visits and phone calls from both Neal and Westlake, inquiring about the missing brunette divorcee.

Laura Belle's attorney, Willedd Andrews, had apparently been the last to see her. She had called at his office at Fourth and Spring Streets on the afternoon of March 29th, he said, and asked his advice about going to see the judge who had granted her the divorce in Ventura, 75 miles north of Los Angeles, to ask for increased alimony. Andrews advised her that it would be all right to visit the judge by herself, and she said she planned to do so the next day.

"She appeared to be upset about something," Andrews recalled. "It wasn't the alimony matter, and she wouldn't tell me what it was. I walked downstairs with her and helped her onto a Spring Street car, southbound. She said she was going to visit her sister."

But Laura Belle had not arrived at her sister's house that afternoon. Her sister had no idea what she might have wanted to see her about. Neither had Laura ever shown up in Ventura—Andrews had checked with the judge.

The lawyer said Laura had $450 in her purse when she visited his office. She had happened to mention the amount. "Laura always used to keep about $500 at home or in her handbag. She said she liked to have ready cash on hand. She was a bit careless that way — a year or so ago she was robbed of about $1000 worth of Liberty Bonds she kept in an envelope at home."

The Homicide men drove out to the silent bungalow on West 30th Street. Lou Neal had moved out a couple of weeks before, and the nextdoor neighbor had the key. The woman explained that Lou had taken Laura's personal belongings, including her canary birds, over to Westlake's house for safekeeping until she should return.

They went through the decorously furnished house, which was stripped of clothing, documents and all personal articles, but found nothing that might provide a clue to the divorcee's vanishment. However, recalling Frank Gompert's comment about the hair, Gray emptied the bag of the vacuum cleaner that stood in a closet and found the required sample all ready for them: a twisted and knotted strand of long brown hair taken up by the cleaner along with the household dust. The neighbor confirmed that Laura had employed no cleaning woman and the hair must be hers.

It was evening now, and since the deputies already had Frank Westlake's story in his report, they looked up Lou Neal, first of the two apparently friendly love rivals. They located him through his company and found him eating lunch, reading the latest newspaper account of the torso mystery.

"I've been expecting you fellows since Frank made that report," he told them. "I'm glad you're finally getting busy and looking for Laura. But you're on the wrong track if you think she's this murder victim. Laura's alive and around here somewhere. Why, she's been putting flowers on her mother's grave every few days!"

The mechanic told the officers he had last seen Mrs. Sutton at 3 A.M. on March 29th, when he came home from work and went to the kitchen to eat the sandwich she customarily left out for him. Laura called to him from her darkened bedroom and asked him to bring her a glass of water. He did so, said goodnight to her and went to his own apartment. When he got up that afternoon there was no sign of her about the house.

He didn't see her the next day, and two nights later he found a note from Frank Westlake on the kitchen table, asking him to call as soon as possible, at the older man's house at 1810½ West 11th Street.

When Neal drove over the following morning, Westlake wanted to know if he had seen or heard from Laura Belle. She had planned to go to Ventura on the afternoon of the 29th Westlake said, and had been due back by train the next night. Westlake had gone to the depot to meet her, but she wasn't on the train. He was seriously worried, because Laura had been carrying $450 she had drawn out of the bank that morning. He had been visiting her home several times daily—he had a key—and feeding the canaries.

After a week went by with still no word, the two men, forgetting their love rivalry in their mutual anxiety, began to make inquiries among the divorcee's other friends and relatives. No one had had any word from her. Westlake drove up to Ventura, thinking she might have decided to stay over, but found no trace of

378

her at the hotels.

By this time the papers were headlining the torso case, but Neal and Westlake never connected it with Laura Belle, since the victim was described as not more than 25 years old.

Recalling the divorcee's inconsolable grief over her dead mother and how she had visited the grave every few days, they went out to San Gabriel Cemetery. To their great relief they found a bunch of fresh red carnations, Laura's favorite flower, in a vase at the mother's grave. This proved to them that the elusive woman was alive and somewhere near.

"I took a week off work and hung around the cemetery every day," Neal told the deputies. "I put a big bunch of roses on the grave, with a note to Laura in the middle of them, asking her to get in touch with me. When I came back from lunch one day, my note was gone and there was a fresh bouquet of carnations! That was about April 15th—so you see, that body in the morgue can't belong to Laura."

But the note didn't elicit any response, and when another week had gone by, the two men took it on themselves to move Laura's things to Westlake's house. Neal knew Laura had entrusted Frank with many business affairs—in fact they had a joint bank account for investment purposes—and he was sure she wouldn't mind. Neal himself stayed with Westlake for a while, but had recently moved to a furnished room. Westlake took care of Laura's utility bills and saw that the lawn and garden of the deserted bungalow were kept up.

The voluble mechanic readily told the history of his association with the grass widow. He had met her four years before, he said, when he was selling cakes and cookies from door to door in the neighborhood. The unhappy housewife told him her troubles, and he became a frequent visitor. When the Suttons separated, Neal moved into the garage apartment at Laura's invitation—she didn't want to be alone. He insisted their friendship had remained on a platonic basis until after her divorce. He was in the habit of turning over his $20 weekly paycheck to her for his room and board, and kept only his tips for pocket money.

They had talked of marriage after the divorce, but complications arose when in 1928 Laura met Frank Westlake. The elderly part-time building contractor dropped around to play cards at night or to do little carpentry jobs at the house in the daytime, and he seemed to hold some sort of magical fascination for the beautiful divorcee.

"I asked her right out if she was in love with Frank," Neal related, "and she said no, she still wanted to marry me. But she kept putting it off, and Frank hung around more and more. I didn't like it, and we had a few arguments, but there wasn't much I could do. Laura was a free woman, after all!"

Next morning, while Gompert was running his microscopic and chemical tests of the hair sample, comparing it with hair from the mummified head, the Homicide deputies and the Missing Persons detective interviewed Frank P. Westlake at his home.

The short, wiry, 57-year-old gray-haired man expressed horrified incredulity when they told him they believed Laura Belle Sutton was the torso victim. Like the mechanic he had taken the fresh flowers on her mother's grave as absolute proof that she was simply staying undercover somewhere around Los Angeles, although he knew of no reason why she should behave so erratically.

"I last saw her on the morning of the 29th, about 10:30," Westlake told the officers. "We met at the bank at Seventh and Spring, to draw some money from our joint savings account. I drew out $750 and gave her $450 in cash. She didn't say what she needed it for—only that she was going to Ventura and would be back the next night. I was to meet her at the train."

He was puzzled to learn that Laura had visited her attorney in Los Angeles that same afternoon and spoken of going to Ventura the next day. He was at a loss to explain this discrepancy.

Like the mechanic, Westlake freely discussed his relationship with the attractive divorcee. He had met her through mutual friends, and she had sought his experienced advice about investing some money she had inherited. With his guidance Laura had made some profitable stock market deals, and had bought a business lot in the fast-growing Westwood district. He more or less had come to manage all of Laura's business affairs, Westlake told the officers modestly. In addition to the joint bank account they had a joint safe deposit box.

Love? Yes, you could call it that. Westlake liked to do things for Laura. For two weeks he had sat up every night with her dying mother, and Laura vowed eternal gratitude. Yes, they had discussed marriage, but both wanted to be sure before making the jump.

Did Westlake know of any enemies Laura might have had? Assuming she was the murder victim, did he suspect anyone?

No, the little man frowned thoughtfully, he couldn't name anyone, but there was a thing the officers should know about. One night early in March he and

Laura had been walking down the street near her house when a tough-looking young man accosted them and without a word struck Westlake in the face, knocking him down and breaking his glasses. The fellow started to manhandle Laura but her screams put him to flight. They hadn't reported the incident to the police, disliking notoriety. They thought the attacker must have been a strong-arm robber, a common purse-snatcher. But he *hadn't* snatched Laura's well-filled purse.

Thanking Westlake for his information, the sleuths headed back to headquarters, where they found Captain Bright plunged into gloom by surprising and disconcerting news from the crime lab. "Gompert says the hair isn't Mrs. Sutton's," he told them. "Something about the structure of the shafts. A capillary canal down the center of the dead woman's hair. None in the Sutton samples. Different shade, too, under the microscope. Says there's no doubt about it. So now we're back where we started!"

The crestfallen Homicide deputies shelved their investigation of the missing Laura Belle, and went back to the tedious work of trying to identify the dismembered Jane Doe. However, Police Lieutenant Allen, in whose jurisdiction the Sutton disappearance case lay, followed it up actively. Struck by the fact that the missing woman hadn't come forward although the newspapers had blazoned her name in connection with the torso, he ordered circulars bearing her photograph and description circulated throughout the West. And he assigned men to interview a long list of her friends and relatives.

Deputies Allen and Gray meanwhile busied themselves with a promising new inquiry from the police of

382

Seattle, Washington. A woman of the northern city thought the torso murder victim might be her sister, who had vanished in 1927 after leaving Seattle for Los Angeles, on her way to Chicago. The description fitted, and the dental chart was very similar.

Captain Bright's men were endeavoring to trace the cold trail of this woman, when the next afternoon came an electrifying call from Lieutenant Allen. "Bill, I've been talking to Laura Sutton's hairdresser. It seems she wore a switch to disguise her thinning hair! There's a good chance that sample that threw you off came from the switch. I've just gone through her effects, over at Westlake's house, and I've found some of her own hair that she was saving. I'm bringing it right in!"

This time Gompert's test was affirmative. The new hair sample matched that of the slain woman in every particular. To be doubly sure, Bright called in Mrs. Sutton's husband and her physician, Dr. John Clayton, to view the remains. Both said the torso, with its square shoulders and narrow hips, resembled hers completely. And the mummified ears of the skull were pierced for earrings, as Laura's had been.

The sheriff's men were now thoroughly convinced that the murdered woman was Laura Belle Sutton, and the investigation went ahead in high gear. Deputies set out to make a thorough check on the backgrounds of both Frank Westlake and Lou Neal, as well as probing still further into the brunette beauty's past and talking to her old boy friend from World War I. Several friends confirmed the story of the mystery attack on the street.

Now that it was definitely a murder case, Westlake with apparent reluctance told the officers that he

383

strongly suspected his rival, Neal. The young mechanic was extremely jealous, he said, and on occasion had displayed a violent temper. Westlake had advised Laura to evict him. And he added the ominous sounding information that Neal had once worked as a butcher.

On the strength of this, Neal was invited to headquarters for questioning and willingly came along. "Why, the old goat!" he exploded when he gathered that Westlake had inspired this action. "What motive would I have for killing Laura? Frank is the one who profits by her death!"

The mechanic revealed that Westlake, in an expansive mood shortly after Laura disappeared, had shown him a deed conveying the Westwood property to him, some stock certificates the divorcee had signed over to him, and a bill of sale for her household furniture. There was also a $500 life insurance policy naming him beneficiary. "After all, we're going to be married soon, you know!" Westlake had explained with a grin.

Neal had thought it odd that Laura hadn't told him about these transfers—especially since the lot had been bought largely with his paychecks. And now he divulged an incident that he hadn't seen to mention previously, lest he cast unjust suspicion on Westlake.

On March 26th, talking to his employer's bookkeeper, he had learned, quite by accident that his last four paychecks had been endorsed and cashed by Frank Westlake. When he asked Laura about the checks in Westlake's presence, she answered evasively that she must have misplaced them. Neal then took the checks from his pocket and confronted her with his rival's signature.

"Certainly I signed those checks!" Westlake flared up. "There's nothing wrong with that, young man! I'm

Mrs. Sutton's business manager, and I deposited them in our joint account."

As they continued to argue, Laura Belle suddenly pulled a revolver from the sideboard drawer and put it to her head. "I can't stand this sordid wrangling! I'll shoot myself!" she cried. Neal wrested the gun away from her, unloaded it, and left without further words.

"And as for his telling you I used to be a butcher," the aroused mechanic added, "sure I was a butcher once, but that doesn't mean I go around cutting up people! That's more in Frank Westlake's line. Don't you know that he used to be a doctor—a *surgeon?*"

Investigation confirmed Neal's story of the checks. Further, inquiry at the bank showed that the $750 withdrawal, made on Westlake's signature on March 29th, had reduced the balance to a few dollars. And county records revealed that Westlake had recorded the deed to Laura's lot in his name only two weeks after the torso was found.

Now it was Frank Westlake's turn to be invited down to headquarters. He expressed surprise that there was any question about the checks, bill of sale, deed and certificates. "Naturally, I've been handling all Laura's affairs. We were going to be married!" As for the furniture, they had planned to sell it and move to a new house. He said he alone had signed for the $750 on the 29th, because Laura had her gloves on.

Grudgingly, he agreed to let the authorities examine the transferred documents, and he gave a specimen of his own handwriting. He also let them take Laura Belle's old revolver, which was among her effects. He modestly confirmed that he had formerly been a surgeon in Pike County, Illinois, and later in the army medical corps. Wearying of medical practice, he had retired some 15 years before and come to California. Only a few close friends knew of his former profession.

Westlake was sent home with an admonition to hold himself available for further questioning, and two deputies tailed him unobtrusively.

Frank Gompert examined the .38 revolver, but his findings were negative; it hadn't been fired for years. More encouraging was the report of J. Clark Sellers, eminent handwriting expert retained by the sheriff, who said Mrs. Sutton's signatures on all the documents were forgeries apparently written by Frank Westlake.

Brought in again and confronted with this evidence, the cold-eyed ex-doctor shrugged it off. "Yes, I signed her name. She gave me permission. She didn't want to be bothered by business details. She told me to sign her name to anything I wanted. We trusted each other completely, you understand."

"Yes, I can see that," Captain Bright remarked dryly. "After all, you were going to be married!"

Now that the hunt was in full cry, further incriminating facts piled up against the glib-tongued little man. A friend of his late wife came forward with a dress Westlake had given her early in April, saying it belonged to a woman friend who had died. The dress was identified as one of Laura Belle's.

More significant, deputies located an Alhambra florist who identified Westlake's photo as that of a man who had bought red carnations on several occasions in April and May—thus accounting for the fresh flowers on the grave which had fooled Lou Neal.

The case was building up, and Bright was discussing with his superiors the advisability of an arrest on the

386

circumstantial evidence in hand, when on May 24th Dr. Westlake came to the Homicide office and with a broad smile displayed a note he said he had just received from Laura Belle, mailed two days before in Arizona. Neatly typewritten, it read: "My Dear: What did you do with the furniture and the birdies? If stored, where? Is Mr. Neal still in town and what shift is he working? Please answer these questions in any of the personal columns. Will see you soon."

The note was signed with the penciled initials "L.B.S." The doctor didn't have the envelope; he said he had thrown it away in his excitement, but assured Captain Bright that it had been postmarked Holbrook, Arizona. He was convinced the note was genuine, and planned to insert the reply as directed.

Though Bright didn't take much stock in the note, he telegraphed the Holbrook police to look for a woman of Laura's description. Clark Sellers shortly reported that the initials were not in Laura's handwriting—but neither were they in Frank's, and the little ex-surgeon was not known to be proficient at typewriting.

That same night, Deputies Gray and Allen tailed Dr. Westlake when he drove to his son's home in Pasadena, and watched him go surreptitiously to the garage at the rear before entering the house. When he had gone they searched the garage. Up in the rafters they found a set of surgical instruments with the knives and scalpels missing. It was wrapped in a newspaper dated March 24th.

While significant enough, this find didn't constitute direct evidence; and there was still the matter of the "Arizona" note. However, this was shortly cleared up. A friend and distant relative of Westlake's came forward to disclose that the ex-physician had asked him to type and sign the note for him, "to play a joke on a friend." He produced the original copy, scrawled in pencil, which Westlake had given him and which he had prudently retained in his safe.

He added the sinister information that his grandparents, Mr. and Mrs. W. H. Brown, who had shared their home with Westlake and his wife, a relative of theirs, had both died suddenly within a short time in 1927, leaving their entire estate including the house to Lizzie Westlake. Within a few months Mrs. Westlake followed them in sudden death, and cold-eyed Frank came into sole possession. Death certificates of all three, who had been in good health, were signed by a doctor friend of Westlake's. Other relatives were highly suspicious at the time and had gone to the district attorney, but he advised them there was no evidence on which to act.

This story of the typed note was sufficient to tip the scales of evidence. The D. A. agreed with Sheriff Traeger that it was time to move in, and Gray and Allen at long last arrested the gray-haired ex-doctor and booked him on suspicion of murder.

Clamming up now, his steel-gray eyes flashing hostility, Westlake retained an attorney who sought his release on the ground that the corpus delicti had not been established—that there was no proof that Laura Belle was the torso victim.

The D. A. soon remedied this. Gompert, City Chemist Rex Welch and other experts had been working with Laura's dentist and physician, quietly building up their identification evidence. Now Coroner Frank Nance called a belated inquest and the medicos and technicians presented their testimony. The jurors returned a verdict that the remains were those of Laura Belle Sutton, and that she had been killed with a blunt instrument with homicidal intent. Westlake was formally charged with murder and pleaded not guilty.

Other loose ends were shortly tied up. With Westlake safely behind bars, Gompert and Welch, seeking the scene of the murder and dismemberment, made a thorough examination of the accused man's house. Disconnecting the plumbing fixtures, in the outlet gooseneck of the bathtub they found a quantity of congealed human blood. There was also blood on the wall behind the tub.

And probing Frank and Laura's financial records, Bright's men established that the divorcee had had the $450 in her purse at home several days before the 29th; this indicated that Westlake had withdrawn the whole $750 for himself, probably without her knowledge. They also found that Westlake had paid the premiums on Laura's life insurance policy. They suspected him of stealing her Liberty Bonds a year before, but couldn't prove it.

Lou Neal, completely exonerated of any suspicion, cooperated fully with the officers in the investigation.

Deputy District Attorney Wayne Jordan summed up the evidence at Westlake's preliminary hearing. Unimpressed by the defendant's contention that Laura Belle was still alive, Municipal Judge R. Morgan Galbreth on June 8th ordered him held for Superior Court trial.

While he awaited trial, information came from authorities of Pike County, Illinois, linking Westlake with still another decapitation murder almost 30 years before. In 1900 the skeleton of long-missing Joseph Van Zandt, a wealthy farmer and patient of Dr. Westlake's, had been found in a well, the head cut off with surgical instruments. The young doctor, who had benefited by the farmer's death, fell under suspicion and was questioned by the grand jury, but there was insufficient evidence for indictment.

Other ugly reports from his days of medical practice linked Westlake's name with the abortion business.

On August 27th, 1929, Westlake went to trial before Superior Judge Walton J. Wood. The gruesome head and torso, with arms and legs still missing, laying in plain view on a table throughout the sessions. Prosecutor Jordan asked the death penalty, contending that the ex-physician had killed Laura Belle for her money and property. He theorized that when the divorcee discovered Westlake had drawn the last $750 from their account, she went to his house to remonstrate, and he slugged her with a hammer and cut up her body in the bathtub. A score of witnesses told their damning stories.

Dr. Westlake's defense was that Laura Belle was still alive. His attorneys challenged identification of the torso, bringing up the original official statement that it was the body of a young woman. Westlake denied the note story as a frameup, and maintained the "L.B.S." note was genuine. He repeated his account of the mystery attack on the street.

But the parade of evidence was overwhelming, and on September 8th, after 31 hours deliberation, the jury of nine women and three men found Westlake guilty of murder in the first degree. Due to the circumstantial nature of the case, they recommended life imprisonment rather than the death penalty. Smiling coldly, the gray-haired little man on September 17th heard Judge Wood sentence him to life in San Quentin.

His appeals were denied and he was taken to prison,

still maintaining his innocence. He served 14 years of his life sentence, and was an old, sick and broken man when he was released on parole in 1944 at the age of 71. He died on January 30th, 1950 while still on parole.

EDITOR'S NOTE:
The name, Louis Neal, is fictitious.

"MURDER PARTED THE STAR-CROSSED LOVERS!"

by Joseph L. Koenig

Autumn in November brings frosty gusts of cold air; and with the cold come the hawks, thousands of them, darkening the crisp autumn skies, riding the thermals which funnel them south over the broad-leaf ridges of Eastern Pennsylvania. And with them come the hunters, huddled at the summit of Hawk Mountain for the sheer, brutal pleasure of blasting them to Earth. Or, rather, they did. For some 50 years ago, the craggy bottleneck on the raptors migration route was made into a bird sanctuary and bloodletting became a thing of the past at Hawk Mountain.

Or, it nearly did.

At 10:15 on the chilly Thursday morning of November 15, 1984, a rare traveler scavenging cans and bottles along a two-lane macadam road half a mile from the base of the Hawk Mountain Bird Sanctuary in West Brunswick Township made a chilling find, one which erased all thoughts of the pocketful of change he would receive for a few hours' work. Inside a sleeping bag which was swaddled in gray felt matting similar to the kind used as padding under a rug was the body of a stout, dark-haired woman in her mid-20s, her shattered skull a mass of gore. The scavenger looked long and hard at his grim find, then averted his gaze, and did not look back till he had reached a phone, which he used to summon help.

Responding to his call were Schuylkill County and Pennsylvania State Police, among them Trooper Eugene R. Taylor. When the matting was pulled away and the sleeping bag opened, Taylor saw that the dead woman was lying on her stomach, her white sweater blood-soaked, her tan culottes torn in back and her pantyhose and panties pulled down to the middle of her thighs. A search of the immediate vicinity produced little additional evidence and nothing which could be used to identify her. When forensic scientists had completed their work there, the remains were transported to the morgue where the autopsy and, hopefully, the identification would take place.

For two days, Keystone state police worked with no success to come up with a name for the Hawk Mountain corpse. Dr. Richard Bindie, who was a pathologist at Pottsville Hospital, confirmed that the woman had, without a doubt, been slain—the victim of massive injuries about the head inflicted with a dull, heavy instrument. But that brought them no closer to identifying her.

Then, on Saturday, November 17th, the Pennsylvania troopers received the break they had been hoping for. It came from 75 miles away, in Manalapan Township, New Jersey, where the police had put out a missing person report on Teresa C. Taylor, the 25-year-old mother of an infant son. The woman, who carried some 150 pounds on a five-foot, three-inch frame, had vanished from her modern, two-story brown-shingled house in the comfortable Knolls development on Monday. Her husband had reported her missing the day the body was found.

Because the description of the missing woman seemed

393

to fit so closely the Hawk Mountain victim a call was made to Manalapan Township, a comfortable, middle-class community close to the Atlantic shore. Not long after, two of the missing woman's relatives travelled to Pennsylvania where, at precisely 3:55 p.m., they made the formal identification.

In the Knolls, the neighborhood around the intersection of Valley and Woodward Roads where the Taylor home stood, news of Teresa Taylor's horrible death was met with stunned disbelief.

"It's sad, so very sad," one of the neighbors said. "The couple was married only last year and moved here less than a year ago, around Christmas. Their baby is only five months old. How could something like this have happened? It's incredible. Awful."

One neighbor recalled that the Taylors had him over for iced tea, the previous summer, while Teresa was still in the hospital with the baby.

"He seemed more outgoing than she," he said of Teresa's husband, Dr. Kenneth Taylor, a Staten Island, New York, dentist. "He said he only had one real conversation with Mrs. Taylor in which he said she was having a difficult pregnancy and could not walk upstairs to see the room that had been converted into a nursery for the expected child."

Commented another neighbor, "It seemed like she never came out of the house. I heard they had six cats.

"They had a lot of people come and visit them, though. They had barbecues."

"I remember saying to my husband after their baby was born," still another neighbor said, "that with a baby you have to go to the doctor and shop for food. But you never saw her."

Theresa C. Taylor, investigators learned, was a graduate of Moore Catholic High School on Staten Island

and had earned an associate degree in dental hygiene from City College of New York. Her 35-year-old husband, Dr. Kenneth Z. Taylor, a former Navy lieutenant, had attended Oakhill High School in Cincinnati, Ohio, and Ball State University in Muncie, Indiana, receiving his doctor of dental surgery degree in 1976 from the University of Indiana. The couple had met about two years before Teresa's death, while she was employed at a Brooklyn, New York, dental clinic. They married about a year later, in July, 1983, and lived on Staten Island before moving to Manalapan Township.

Dr. Taylor, the neighbors agreed, was an upcoming young man with a limitless future, the proprietor of a dental practice with two office addresses on Staten Island—one on Grandview Avenue, the other on Jersey Street. In the initial moments of the New Jersey investigation into his young wife's slaying, he consented to a search of his house and car. At the same time, he agreed to come to Manalapan Township police headquarters to talk at length about what he knew of his wife's final hours.

Taylor told his questioners that his wife was a woman of unpredictable behavior, the result of an addiction to codeine. Early on Sunday morning, November 11th, he said, he had awakened to find her "strung out again." The woman appeared to be nervous and upset and told him that she couldn't care for their baby any longer and needed to "clean up." Taylor suggested that she seek psychiatric help, but she refused and he went back to sleep.

Sometime between 8:00 and 8:30, his story continued, Teresa woke him to say that she had to get away from the house and that he should not tell anyone that she was going. Hours later, he drove her to Newark International Airport, leaving her at the terminal with some

$800-$1,000 in cash. Teresa indicated that she would be gone about two weeks.

Taylor went on to say that he drove home and packed some things in the car and then headed west for his parents' home in Indiana. Teresa had wanted his family to care for the baby in her absence. Taylor said he made it as far as Pennsylvania, where he spent the night in a motel. It was late the following night when he arrived in Indiana and dropped off the baby. Then he headed east again, visiting his former wife and daughter in Pittsburgh. The following night he returned to New Jersey and went to a bar on Staten Island.

When Teresa failed to contact him, he said, he reported her missing to the police and then did a little detective work on his own, hunting fruitlessly for clues to her whereabouts at the airport. Then he drove back to Pittsburgh, where his parents reached him with word that Teresa's body had been found.

The interrogation was proceeding smoothly when it was interrupted by detectives who had just completed their search of the Taylor home. In the garage of the big house on Valley Road they had found an earring showing traces of dried blood, an earring exactly like the one Teresa Taylor was wearing when her body turned up at the foot of Hawk Mountain.

Manalapan Township Police Lieutenant Peter Vanderwiel and Lieutenant William Lucia of the Monmouth County Prosecutor's Office told Kenneth Taylor that they did not believe he was being candid with them and advised him that he should be more truthful. Then a brief halt was called to the grilling. When questioning resumed, Taylor made another statement.

This time, the Staten Island dentist claimed that he had caught his wife sexually abusing their five-month-old son on the morning of November 11th. When she ran from him, he had followed her into another room where she swung a dumbbell at him. Taylor said that he ducked under the blow, twisted the heavy metal from her hand and swung it at her.

"I just couldn't take it any more," he allegedly said. "She was taking my prescriptions and stealing my money. I just couldn't take it any more."

At 3:00 on Sunday afternoon, November 18th, 35-year-old Kenneth Taylor was charged with the murder of his wife, Teresa.

"We believe the husband was solely responsible for her death," said First Assistant Monmouth County Prosecutor Paul Chaiet.

Arraigned, Monday, before Municipal Court Judge Leslie B. Tinkler, Kenneth Taylor pleaded innocent to the murder charge and was ordered held in lieu of $500,000 bond at the Monmouth County Jail in Freehold Township.

In a brief chat with newsmen, Taylor's attorney said the victim, who had been employed as a dental hygienist at her husband's Staten Island practice, took large quantities of codeine and cocaine and was in a drugged stupor when she allegedly molested her child.

"I believe the evidence will show his wife was a drug abuser and did harm to the child, and that precipitated the incident," he said.

Relatives of the victim, however, sought to portray Dr. Taylor as the drug abuser, a man who was in the habit of writing prescriptions in his wife's name and then taking the drugs himself.

The woman's former employer said that Teresa Taylor had returned from her 1983 Mexican honeymoon so badly beaten that she was hospitalized for several weeks at Staten Island Hospital before returning to work. Teresa had explained that she was beaten by "a bunch of Mexicans," and after her recuperation she had appeared "quite happy" until leaving her job to have her baby.

Two months after the slaying, in court papers filed in January, 1985 by Prosecutor Chaiet, it was revealed that six years earlier Dr. Taylor had been charged with the attempted murder of a former wife. The thrice-married dentist's second spouse had told police in 1979 that Taylor had attempted to kill her by covering her face with a chloroform-soaked sponge while she was asleep. Following the alleged assault, the document stated, Taylor was seen by a number of psychiatrists. Later, at his ex-wife's insistence, the attempted murder charges were dropped.

The document also stated that two partners in the Brooklyn dental clinic where Taylor was employed from July, 1980, to July 1983, said that the murder suspect had stolen some $4000-$5000 from them and had explained that he needed the funds to pay for his honeymoon. However, he had not gone back to work for them after returning from Mexico.

Chaiet also stated that his office was contacted by a clerk from "the Navy Credit Union in Virginia," who had said that Taylor owed about $26,000.

Chaiet went on to say that his office was attempting to look into the beating of Teresa Taylor during the couple's July, 1983, honeymoon in Acapulco. Although Taylor had said that the beating was the work of men who broke into the couple's room, his wife's family claimed the dentist had been taken into custody briefly by the Mexican police.

At Kenneth Taylor's murder trial, which got underway in Freehold in the last week of May, 1985, Prosecutor Chaiet said, "I will be calling for a murder conviction for this defendant because that's what he did when he broke Teresa's head into pieces on November 11, 1984.

Speaking of the defendant's claim that the victim had sexually assaulted the couple's five-month-old baby, he went on to say, "This perverted tale is just that, a perverted tale of a sinister and calculating mind."

Defense counsel insisted that his client had slain his wife in the course of defending himself after his wife sexually assaulted their child and then struck him with a dumbbell in a drug-clouded haze. The attack, he said, knocked Taylor to the floor, where he found another dumbbell and swung it at the woman. Then he blacked out and awoke to find Teresa dead.

Realizing what he had done, the lawyer said, Taylor "panicked. He was going to commit suicide" by poisoning himself with carbon monoxide. But he "could not go through with it."

Taylor, he went on, "is guilty of obstructing justice . . . and giving false information to the police, but he is not on trial on those charges.

"This is not a murder, this is a family tragedy. This was not a trouble-free marriage, but there was a loving and caring relationship between the two of them."

On Monday, June 3rd, Dr. Bindie, the pathologist who performed the autopsy, told the jury that a dumbbell which investigators found in the couple's home could have been used to inflict the deadly wounds on Teresa Taylor.

Investigator Glenn Meyer of the Monmouth Prosecutor's Office said that lab testing for blood on the dumbbell, on stains found in the couple's car and in their house—including a 55-foot "drag mark" leading from the weight room to the garage—had proved positive. Meyer went on to say that he had discovered a Pennsylvania road map opened to the general area of Schuylkill County during the search of the car.

On Tuesday, June 4th, a Willow Grove, Pennsylvania, toxicologist testified that although he saw traces of codeine and alcohol in Teresa Taylor's blood he did not believe the levels were high enough to have produced aggressive behavior in the woman. He attributed the alcohol found in her system to the natural fermentation of body sugar after her death. The level of codeine appeared consistent with that resulting from therapeutic usage. No cocaine was found.

Defense counsel suggested that the strange behavior ascribed to the victim might be explained by the presence of other drugs which the witness did not test for. He also cited pre-menstrual stress and post partum depression as influencing the woman's behavior.

Another prosecution witness, a relative of Teresa Taylor, said that the day before the woman's death she was discussing the problems of having sex while pregnant when her husband interrupted.

"Theresa wouldn't refuse him after the whipping he gave her the other night." The woman added that nothing further was said about the matter.

"I thought it was a joke," she told the court, noting that she did not notice any bruises on Teresa.

Wednesday, a friend of Teresa Taylor told the court that the victim "was always a loving mother."

She went on to say that along with her boyfriend she had taken cocaine with the Taylors one night in the summer of 1984. She recalled that they had a hard time getting "high" until they followed the cocaine with alcohol.

The woman added that Teresa Taylor took diet pills, codeine for her teeth and another prescription drug.

Testifying out of the hearing of the jury on Thursday, a Long Island woman related that she had met Kenneth and Teresa Taylor in Acapulco, Mexico, in

1983. Five or six days later, she had seen the defendant in the lobby of their hotel looking disheveled, unshaven and gaunt.

There were two policemen with him, she recalled, and he was waiting to get into the hotel safe for some money he said he needed to post bail. Taylor asked her if she would lend him some money if it turned out he didn't have all he needed to secure his release from custody and she had said no.

Taylor, the witness went on, explained that he had spent four days in jail following a fight with his bride.

" 'I knocked her teeth out,' " she quoted him as saying.

"He said, 'You know how it is. We had a few drinks and got into a fight.' "

A close relative of Teresa Taylor told the court that the American consul in Acapulco had informed him that Teresa was hospitalized and Kenneth was charged with beating her. When he flew to Mexico and saw the young woman in the hospital, the right side of her face was swathed in bandages and the left side severely swollen. Her front teeth were smashed.

"All I know is I went to bed in my hotel and I woke up in the hospital," Teresa had said to him.

The woman had added that her new husband could not have harmed her "because Ken loves me and he wouldn't do this to me."

On Monday, June 10th, the British consul in Acapulco told the court that Kenneth Taylor's story of having been mugged on his honeymoon was "possible, but highly improbable."

The assistant manager of the Taylors' hotel said that it was about 10:00 p.m. when he responded to a call of trouble at the Taylors' room from a man who moaned the words, "Beat, beat, heart attack."

401

When he arrived at the room, he remembered, he found the defendant in a daze on the floor near the bathroom. The shower was on and Taylor, wearing shorts and a shirt, was wet below the knees. His hands were bloody.

Scattered all about the room was broken glass from a lamp and a green bottle sent up from the bar. He saw drops of blood on the tablecloth, the bed and on one wall. Teresa Taylor, bleeding profusely, was sprawled on the floor about 15 feet from her husband.

"We saw the body and it was really in bad condition," the witness recalled. "Really bad, a lot of blood." The woman's throat had been cut.

The witness added that when the authorities brought her husband to see her at the hospital, Teresa embraced him and asked to be alone with him and said that the police should release him.

Taking the stand on Tuesday, June 11th, Kenneth Taylor, the last of 11 witnesses to testify about the incident, denied having beaten his wife in their Acapulco hotel room.

Following the incident, he said, he spent four days in a Mexican jail and was not released until he paid a bribe to his captors.

"I was told at the jail if I paid the man $500 I could leave so I could see my wife," he testified.

Taylor maintained that he and Teresa were asleep in bed when he heard a noise and got up to investigate. After checking the patio door—which, he said, had a broken lock—he was climbing back into bed when he was struck on the right side of the head with "something heavy." Then someone dragged him off the bed by his feet and kicked him in the back of the neck when he tried to stand up.

"I remember I saw stars," he said. He added that he

caught a glimpse of a second person on the other side of the bed as he was hitting the floor.

"The next thing I remember I was awake and I found my wife in her own blood."

Taylor explained that he crawled across broken glass to check Teresa's pulse, then phoned the front desk to get help. Later, he passed out on the bathroom floor.

At the close of Taylor's testimony, Superior Court Judge Michael D. Farren said that he did not believe the story and would allow testimony about the Acapulco incident.

"I don't find it to be credible," the jurist ruled. "The thing that sticks out is his conduct after this happened. She's absolutely devastated about the head, or should I say pulverized? What does he do? He takes her pulse, walks out to the balcony and claims he faints. Then he goes in and takes a shower while his wife is on the floor dying."

The jurist added that he found it hard to believe that the six-foot, one-inch 200-pound dentist could be subdued with "a negligible bump on the head."

Judge Farren said that he found the testimony of the woman who claimed that Taylor had told her he knocked out his wife's teeth after she bit him on the foot to be "very credible."

In his final argument to the jury, defense counsel referred to the incident as a "frame-up."

"I don't remember any Mexican police going up to that stand and saying one thing about Dr. Taylor ever saying he laid a finger on his wife."

The attorney described his client as "a 35-year-old man coming into his prime," while his wife was "a 25-year-old woman whose expectations were not always in line with reality."

He reminded the panelists that witnesses had described Taylor as devoted to his son, whose birth had seemed to draw the couple closer together.

"In fact, the two of them had only good things to say about each other. When Teresa wasn't using codeine, she was a good mother. She could cope."

The defense attorney told the panelists to use common sense in evaluating Taylor's claims that he had caught his wife attempting to perform sex on their son, "to see it through the eyes of a father who fears for his baby.

"Was that a tale that was made up with a view to a trial?" he asked. "Can you imagine the rage, the shock to a father to know that was going on? This was not a case of murder, it's a case of family tragedy. There are no winners here," he concluded. "These two were star-crossed lovers from the beginning. Fate was not on their side."

Prosecutor Chaiet countered by telling the jurors that Kenneth Taylor was a liar. "The answer to why Teresa died does not prove out like a mathematical word problem," he contended. "But there should be no mystery, no mystery at all, that this defendant is a murderer."

Chaiet asked the panelists to consider Taylor's actions in the moments after his wife had died. "He would have been devastated, he would have reached out for help. But what does he do? He wraps the body in a rug and dumps it in the woods. Does that sound like the family tragedy we've heard so much about?"

Chaiet reminded the panel that evidence indicated Teresa Taylor was not high on drugs the night she died. And even if the story her husband told were true, Chaiet said, he would still be guilty of murder.

"Do you believe his life was in imminent danger? And even if you believed that, when he took the bar (dumbbell) from her, how was she going to kill him?

404

When you consider what was done here, it was not reckless. It was purposeful and knowing."

On Tuesday, June 18th, after three and a half hours of debate over two days, the jury of ten men and two women found Kenneth Z. Taylor guilty of the murder of his wife. Judge Farren ordered him returned to the Monmouth County Jail to await sentencing on September 27th. Under New Jersey law, Taylor faces a mandatory term of life in prison without parole for 30 years.

" 'ANGEL' OF PAIN WHO USED A CHAINSAW ON RUTH"

by Julie Malear

Friday, March 4, 1988, dawned bright and clear in West Palm Beach, Florida. From the sandy Palm Beach surfside east of the Intracoastal Highway to the marshy Everglades on the western rim, people in the resort towns basked in the happy, subtropical warmth. Light breezes ruffled the myriad blooms on suburban mango trees, billowed the sails of boats on sea and intracoastal, and whipped the bright clothing of tourists who thronged the area for "the season." It was a typical South Florida day.

Unfortunately, the day would be anything but typical for retired schoolteacher Ruth Ann Nedermier, a regal, gray-haired widow with smiling hazel eyes who was much admired in the community by her former students and their parents. At 72, Ruth Nedermier was in excellent health except for the effects of a recent operation. A month before, doctors had inserted an artificial hip in her body and that day, like many days prior, she was relaxing a while in bed.

Although a young, nice-looking physical therapist came to the house regularly to teach Ruth to walk again and a nurse's aide stayed with her several hours each weekday, the elderly lady was still a semi-invalid. Ruth could get around her small, neat home with the help of a walker, but she had to rely on friends or the nurse's aide

406

to drive her wherever she needed to go, or more often, just let the aide run the errands herself.

Through the open door of her bedroom, Ruth Nedermier could see her employee now, moving around the house, getting ready to leave for the evening. The nurse's aide was a pretty woman of 23 with chocolate-colored skin and big dark eyes; she was well spoken and reasonably well educated, the mother of a little boy who stayed at nursery school while she worked. Ruth Nedermier liked this nurse far more than the previous aides. She'd employed several others before, each hired from the same nursing service.

As Ruth Nedermier, wearing a light-blue cotton housedress and blue-and-pink-print bedroom slippers, climbed down from her bed and shuffled across the room with her walker, the phone rang. She could hear the nurse's aide lift the receiver and answer. Moments later the young woman came into the bedroom and helped Ruth take the call. She then waved goodbye and walked out of the room. It was three o'clock.

The phone call was from an officer at the bank. After describing several transactions, the voice on the line asked Ruth Nedermier if she was alone in the house. When she replied that her nurse's aide was just leaving, the bank officer said she'd call back later when no one was around.

The words made a cold, disagreeable chill run up and down Ruth Nedermier's spine. What in the name of creation was the bank officer trying to tell her? she wondered. The caller had mentioned big checks drawn on her account. *She* hadn't signed those checks! Had one of her former employees been trying to get some extra cash? Ruth thought of all the people who'd been in and out of her house since her operation. Had one of them picked up her checkbook? No, of course not! They were all trusted friends and neighbors. Hanging up the phone at the caller's suggestion, Ruth made up her mind to get to the bottom of the problem right away.

A slight sound behind her caught Ruth's attention, but before she could turn around to see what it was, a sharp sudden pain tore into the back of Ruth's head with such force that she let out a cry. Darkness poured over Ruth like molasses from a pitcher. Dizziness spun her. The unexpected blow was robbing Ruth of the capacity to think or act. What was happening? "Help," she whimpered. No one could hear her. If only her nurse's aide had stayed with her a few minutes longer. . . .

Before Ruth could recover from the addling blow, a strong plastic bag plunged over her head, knocking off her glasses and making it difficult for Ruth to breathe. Although Ruth thrashed and struggled with all her might, in the end she fell unconscious from lack of oxygen.

Hopefully, Ruth did not awaken for the final atrocity—the screeching, terrifying, excruciating pain of cold steel chewing through bones. Once the chainsaw did its work, Ruth Ann Nedermier would never wake again.

At 3:30 p.m., the phone at the Nedermier house rang for a very long time. No one answered. Over four hours passed. At 7:45 p.m., Ruth Nedermier's physical therapist, a dedicated man whose brother was a West Palm Beach police officer, arrived at the house as scheduled. Finding the front door unlocked, he entered the house and turned on a light. It was likely, he surmised, that his patient had fallen. He pictured Ruth lying on the floor of her bedroom, hoping he'd come in and help her up. That sort of thing did happen. He ran to Ruth's bedroom. She wasn't there. As the therapist hurried from room to room, searching, he began to worry. Ruth Nedermier was definitely not home. She'd always been here

408

for his appointment before. He wondered: had she forgotten? Had someone come by to take Ruth shopping? Or—his worry made him think the worst—had some doped-up weirdo found her door unlocked?

Perhaps because his brother was a cop, the therapist was not content to simply go away. He began to conduct his own private investigation. He called on several of the neighbors. What he found displeased him. No way could his patient have "wandered off." Something was definitely wrong! The therapist went back in the house and called the police.

By the time West Palm Beach Detectives John Johnston and Mark Anderson received a "missing person" call around 10:20, officers and crime scene sleuths, Lieutenant Greg Parkinson, and Crime Scene Investigator (CSI) Jack McCall were already at the Churchill Road home. The responding officer, L.R. Foreman, quickly filled the investigators in on the known facts: A 72-year-old female was missing, and a robbery had taken place without forced entry into her home. The master bedroom showed signs of a disturbance. A full-size made-up bed had several items on top of it: a tan metal file box, a green file box, and a black jewelry box. These items had signs that someone had searched through each one and had dumped items onto the bed—items such as jewelry, checks, and various papers.

Crime scene detectives processed the room for latent prints, snapped photographs, and sealed the doors and windows with evidence tape.

By this time, several friends and neighbors of Ruth Nedermier's had gathered outside. They were talking to Officer Foreman, Sergeant Robertson, Lieutenant Wood, and Officer Harmer.

Detectives Johnston and Anderson had Officers Foreman and Harmer conduct a canvass of the neighborhood. The lawmen found it a friendly, primarily middle-aged group who looked out after each other to the best of their ability. They were all worried about the missing woman.

Two men who lived across the street said they had seen a white car around 1:30 with four black males — they couldn't see their faces — inside. The car might have been the nurse's boyfriend's car, the men told the sleuths. She'd often go out to the curb to talk to her boyfriend, and sometimes the two would sit in the car and eat a sandwich. But he never went in the house as far as the neighbors knew.

Detectives Anderson and Johnston found an address book in the house with the name and phone number of Mrs. Nedermier's best friend, Margaret Mays. At the detectives' call, Mrs. Mays immediately drove over. Sitting in the living room talking to the two sleuths, the friend told her interrogators an interesting story.

Mrs. Mays had been a close friend of Ruth Nedermier's for about 20 years, she said. That day, she'd called Ruth several times during the late afternoon with no response. Finally, just before six o'clock, Margaret drove by to check on her friend.

Persuading another worried neighbor to join her, Margaret knocked on the door. They got no answer. Margaret then used her key to enter with the other woman and look around. They noted the boxes on the bed but saw no signs of a struggle. The jewelry scattered there appeared to be all costume jewelry, nothing worth stealing.

Her friend Ruth did own several pieces of semi-expensive jewelry, Margaret told the detectives — two white-gold rings with multiple diamonds, two solid yellow-gold bangle bracelets, and a watch. The victim usually wore these items daily when not in bed or taking a nap. These items weren't found in the bedroom. Had a thief seen Ruth shopping and followed her home to rob her later?

Margaret Mays mentioned, too, that recently there was a problem with Ruth's checking account. Normally, Ruth maintained a checking balance of approximately $20,000 with CDs in other accounts. Still, when Margaret had taken Ruth to the doctor the week before and tried to write a check for what was owed him, there was not enough money in Ruth's account. Naturally, this upset Ruth, Margaret explained, since Ruth was usually meticulous about her records. As a result, Ruth gave Margaret the last few bank statements. Both women were aware of a large discrepancy in the account that showed the most recent balance to be only $3,000 to $4,000. Ruth decided to phone the nursing service, thinking it possible that one of her former nurse's aides, angry at being dismissed, was forging checks in her name.

Trying to balance Ruth's checking account, Margaret noted there were several missing and out-of-order check entries on the account. Margaret told Ruth that she'd check with a bank officer and get back to her quickly with the results.

Probing further into the witness's story, the detectives learned that Ruth Nedermier was attended now by a nurse's aide whom she liked. Previously, Ruth had let several women go. Her current nurse routinely took Ruth shopping, to various doctors, and to the bank, as well as on miscellaneous errands. Sometimes the aide even took her employer's clothes home to wash. Margaret Mays called the aide "well spoken and neat . . . in school to be a nurse."

In fact, the aide had called her that morning, Margaret Mays recalled, to ask if she could give her employer a bath. "No," Margaret had replied, "not until the physical therapist releases her." Margaret Mays had called at noon

411

and had asked the aide, "Let me speak to Ruth." The aide had replied, "She can't come to the phone. She's in the bathroom." To that Margaret had said, "Have her call me when she gets out of the bathroom."

Although the aide said "okay," Ruth never returned the call. Margaret, having business to attend to, left her house before 1:00 p.m. and visited the bank around 3:30. When she spoke with the bank officer, the woman told her she'd called Mrs. Nedermier at 3:00 p.m. The nurse's aide, she said, had answered the phone, then had put her employer on. The bank officer told Margaret Mays she'd spoken to Ruth Nedermier about four large-sum checks totaling over $4,000. "I never signed or wrote those checks!" the victim had replied. The bank officer had called back at 3:30 p.m., she told Margaret Mays, but there was no reply. The two women discussed the situation for an hour and then Margaret Mays left, she told Detectives Johnston and Anderson.

Later, the sleuths would hear the same story from the bank officer. But now, as they questioned her, the two sleuths could see that Margaret Mays was noticeably shaken and worried about her friend Ruth. Margaret promised to make all canceled checks and bank statements available to the investigators, adding that several checks were out of sequence.

When the detectives interviewed a neighbor across the street, the man told them he'd seen the aide's red Ford about 3:00 p.m. "pulled all the way up into the Nedermier carport." That was something she'd never done before, because Mrs. Nedermier always had her own car parked there and did not allow anyone, especially one of her employees, to pull up that far. Then, around 4:00 p.m., the neighbor believed, he noticed a carload of men parked in front of the house.

Another neighbor had been sitting at his desk when he

heard a car engine starting. Looking across the street toward the noise, he noticed the red, late-model compact Ford pulling away on Churchill Road, going east toward South Dixie. The time was about 3:30 p.m. as best he could recollect, but he couldn't see the car's occupants through the tinted windows.

Two other neighbors had gone to visit Ruth Nedermier just before 4:00 p.m. They found the front door locked. This surprised them because the ex-schoolteacher usually kept it unlocked so she could yell to any friends who might drop by to come inside. Thus, Ruth wouldn't have to go to the door herself.

Unable to enter in front, the two women then went to the back of the house thinking Ruth might be on the patio. When she wasn't, they tried that door, which was ordinarily kept locked. Surprisingly, it opened.

The two women went in and looked around. Nothing seemed to be out of order. Assuming Ruth had gone to the store, they wrote a note warning her to be more careful about her door and left it on the TV in the den. Then they locked the front and back entrances behind them.

Both witnesses told the sleuths that they'd known the missing woman for years and were also able to describe her jewelry. Each, interrogated separately, gave the same account.

After delving into the stories from all of the victim's friends and neighbors, Detectives Johnston and Anderson thought it very unlikely that Ruth Nedermier had merely wandered away.

After realizing that the nurse's aide was probably the last person to see Ruth Nedermier alive, the detectives tried at once to locate her. Margaret Mays had already given them the name of the nurses' home care service that Ruth had used. Although no one there answered the lawmen's calls, they raced down and used the emergency number, which they found posted on the door. The woman who managed the service came down at once and opened up. At the lawmen's request, she found the current aide's file. The nurse's aide's name was Inger LeMont. The address listed was on N.W. 3rd Avenue in Delray Beach, a small resort city less than 20 miles south.

The two sleuths sped there immediately, hoping the aide could shed some light on Ruth Nedermier's disappearance. Arriving at the house, they asked to speak to her. Relatives told them that the young woman did not live at the family home. She, her son, and her boyfriend had their own apartment on Gulfstream Road in Lake Worth, just south of West Palm Beach. The sleuths returned north and knocked on the door. It was now very late.

Inger LeMont came to the door in her nightgown. As they questioned the pleasant-sounding nurse's aide, both detectives were impressed with her sincerity. After taking her down to the West Palm Beach Police Station, the probers interrogated her further. She swore that Ruth Nedermier was alive when she left. "I answered the phone for Mrs. Nedermier and waved goodbye. Then my boyfriend came in about four p.m."

The two sleuths drove the woman back home. Her boyfriend, Leroy Harding, was waiting there for her. Like Inger, he seemed completely innocent.

By Monday, the detectives had nothing. They found an old photo of Ruth Nedermier at her house and released it to the newspapers, asking for help in finding the semi-invalid as she might have "wandered off." They told the press they were concerned she "had walked away and fallen."

Nurse's aide Inger LeMont began calling Detective Anderson that day, a practice she continued over a dozen times that week, usually at the beginning or end of his shift. She said on Monday that she was "worried about Mrs. Nedermier," and she made suggestions: "Did you call the hospital?" "Did you ask the neighbors?" "Did you go door to door?" "Is there anything I can do?" Le-Mont seemed concerned.

Also on Monday, the probers interviewed the bank officer who had informed Ruth Nedermier about the checks. Her story corroborated what Margaret Mays had said. The officer said she'd been watching Mrs. Neder-mier's account because there had recently been at least four checks made out to Inger LeMont that totaled in excess of $4,000. The checks had been "endorsed and cashed or split-deposited" in Inger LeMont's savings account at the same bank—checks for $884, $1,650, $1,320, and a last one for $1,150.

The bank officer repeated how she'd called the missing woman at 3:00 p.m. and the phone was answered by Inger LeMont. When Ruth Nedermier took the phone, the bank officer advised her of the suspect checks, saying she needed to talk to Ruth in depth after Inger LeMont left for the day. Upon hearing about the checks, Ruth Nedermier had stated emphatically, "I did not write those checks! I did not sign those checks!" As far as the bank officer could tell, Inger LeMont was within earshot because her voice could be heard in the background, although the gist of what she was saying was not understandable over the wire. The bank officer had asked Mrs. Nedermier to call her as soon as Inger Le-Mont left the house.

The sleuths informed their lieutenant, John Conklin, who in turn showed the checks to Sergeant Winifred Sadler, the department's check expert. The sergeant was able to determine from the signatures that the checks were indeed forgeries. Subsequently, after the checks were sent away for verification, Sergeant Sadler's statements were confirmed by forgery experts.

Now, of course, the sleuths were suspicious of the nurse's aide, but they didn't want to alert her until they had more evidence.

Soon after the missing woman's photo appeared in the media, the Delray Beach Police Department received an anonymous phone call that "a bag of things possibly related to Mrs. Nedermier's disappearance" had been found by a young boy. He'd found them in a dumpster behind the store in the Post Office Shopping Plaza in downtown Delray Beach.

The following day, Wednesday, March 9th, Detective Anderson drove to Delray Beach where he met with Delray Beach Police Detective-Sergeant Bob Brand and Jeff Galyon, who were searching the area behind a variety store in the plaza. The dumpsters were literally overflowing. Although their contents had been slated for pickup the previous day, luckily for the investigative team, the collector had not yet performed his duty. If he had, the detectives mused, they'd have missed it all.

Minutes after Detective Anderson's arrival, the huge garbage truck roared into the plaza alley beside the lawmen. Yesterday, the driver told them, he hadn't picked up the trash because he was sick. Now, the garbage claw scooped up the dumpsters and poured their contents into the truckbed.

It was a bright, sunny day. Quickly tossing off his coat, tie, and shirt, the tall, dark-haired detective dived into the trash pile along with Delray's Detective-Sergeant Brand. Knowing no other way to find what they were looking for, the lawmen pawed through the mess, coming out sticky with melted candy, rotting food, and various other gloppy throw-aways. Almost to the bottom, Detec-

416

tive Anderson found physical evidence—a bloodstained brick that appeared to match those on Ruth Nedermier's patio, and a blue and pink slipper like the one Margaret Mays had described as belonging to Ruth. He found her eyeglasses, too—broken, one lens bloody and shattered. There also were a number of prescription bottles and what could have been the contents of a ladies' purse.

Detective Anderson was excited. "Look at this bloody brick! But where is *she?* She's got to be dead," he told Brand.

A last handful brought out what seemed to be a cassette tape that had unwound. Actually, the slick, black tape was a typewriter-cartridge ribbon. The West Palm Beach sleuth started pulling the ribbon out and holding it up to the sun. Sticky and gooey as it was, there were literally several hundred words on its surface. Over and over again, one name appeared: "Inger LeMont, Inger LeMont, Inger LeMont . . ."

Elated, Detective Anderson read on. There was a letter dated the 26th of December to a girlfriend: "I just got an electric typewriter for Christmas. . . ." The things Inger had written made her sound like she was still a teenager. There were notes to herself and an order from a doctor with directions for a prescription: "One per day at lunch." There was also a pornographic love letter to her boyfriend.

For Detective Mark Anderson, seeing Inger LeMont's name over and over on the ribbon was enough to set his mind to work.

Detective Anderson suddenly recalled information that he'd learned when he delved into the nurse's background. Both Inger and a family member, Darlene, had previously worked at the store to which the dumpster belonged.

Even more incriminating, Anderson had learned Inger

417

was on probation for forgery—a similar case to the Nedermier one but without a disappearance.

When the lawmen returned to the Delray Beach Police Station, they were handed a call from the anonymous woman who'd phoned the day before about the dumpster. She now told them that her son went through the dumpsters every Saturday looking for what he could find, "like candy and stuff, and he'd found a bag." In the bag was a checkbook, which he had taken home, the woman told the sleuths. When the boy's mother saw the name on the checks—"Ruth Nedermier"—and knew she'd seen that name in the paper, she made the first call. Now, feeling bad that it had been anonymous, she gave the detectives her address.

Detectives Anderson, Brand, and Galyon drove over and interviewed the woman's teenaged son. They asked him when it was that he found the papers with Nedermier's name on them, the rag, and "the stone that's broken in two pieces."

"Saturday, March fifth," the youth replied, "about four o'clock." He described the container for the sleuths and told them he always searched the dumpster because "some things they throw away."

"Were they inside a bag or a box or anything?" they asked.

"Inside a black garbage bag . . . tied in a knot." He told the lawmen he had thrown everything back in "except the papers," which he'd taken home and shown to his mother.

It was nearly 8:00 p.m. when the detectives finished interviewing the youth. Detective Anderson, jubilant at the progress, headed north to the West Palm Beach station. En route, he stopped at the home of his partner, Detective Johnston, and made him come out to the car.

"Look what I found! This is practically yelling at us!"

418

Anderson said.

"Yes!" Johnston cheered, equally excited. But he knew the find was a mixed blessing, and he sobered his tone. "She must be dead, Mark. But where is she? The canal?"

Although by now it was half-past eight, Johnston accompanied Anderson to the crime lab. Everyone had already left for the day. When they phoned Lieutenant Parkinson at home, he quickly returned to the lab to confirm that the stain on the broken brick was, indeed, blood.

The next day, Inger LeMont kept calling. Not wanting to alert the suspect, Detective Anderson told her nothing about what they'd found. The nurse's aide wondered what the detectives had been doing. Why weren't they making more progress? she pressed. Thinking fast, Detective Anderson recalled how there was another officer involved in a shooting at that time. He asked Inger if she'd heard about it.

"Did you see the other story?" he asked, using that as an excuse not to have done more on the Nedermier case. "It's in all the papers." When Inger said that she had, Anderson added a partial truth: "Well, we've been working on that. Sorry I haven't been able to do more about your case."

"Oh, well," Inger replied, "when you get back to it, I'll help you any way I can." She sounded so sincere. Could it be, the detective wondered, that she was guilty only of the forgery and truthfully had no knowledge of her employer's whereabouts?

On Saturday, March 12th, Inger LeMont called several times. Detective Anderson just blew her off. He didn't want to warn her that she was a suspect. But shortly after 4:00 p.m., he and Detective Johnston drove over to Inger LeMont's apartment on Gulfstream Road in West Palm Beach, having called first to say they were coming.

419

In front of the duplex was the aide's red Ford EXP. The white Pontiac, which Inger's boyfriend supposedly drove, was not around.

Inger answered the lawmen's knock and invited them inside. They couldn't help but notice that she was an immaculate housekeeper. An array of books, papers, and a black compact portable typewriter on the den coffee table indicated where she'd been studying.

As Inger resumed her seat, the lawmen asked about her work. Inger explained she was a "certified nursing assistant" but was in the process of becoming a registered or licensed practical nurse. Inger still came across as very sincere, intelligent, and well spoken.

Detective Anderson feigned interest in her typewriter. "Boy, this is a neat typewriter. What kind is it? Are you doing your homework?"

"Yeah," Inger answered, then added, "but my typewriter isn't working right."

The sleuth lifted the lid of the machine as if to fix it. "Inger, no wonder! It's got no ribbon!"

"I used it. I threw it away," she told the investigators.

Right. Anderson congratulated himself silently, *and I've got it!*

The detectives asked Inger LeMont to describe what Mrs. Nedermier wore the last time she had seen her. She did so, mentioning the slippers were blue and pink cloth booties with pink rubber soles—exactly like the one found in the dumpster. Delving further, the sleuths listened as Inger described the "good jewelry" that her employer wore "even around the house." While giving the invalid a sponge bath that day, Inger remembered placing Ruth's rings and watch in a black and white ashtray on the nightstand, but the sleuths, recalling the crime scene search, knew the ashtray was empty when found.

The probing continued. As time when by, the nurse

became agitated and restless, spontaneously telling the detective duo she "was being truthful with the police." At the same time, she seemed to seek their approval.

Inge denied having parked her red Ford "under the carport," saying that neighbors who had described that scenario were lying. Besides, she told the detectives, she'd driven to pick up her son at nursery school as soon as she left the Nedermier home. She drove through a nearby fast-food restaurant before taking the boy to spend the night with her parents. When she left there for her Gulf-stream Road apartment around 7:00 p.m., a relative rode along. Because Inger was "busy," he left by cab soon after.

Growing more and more nervous and evasive as the interrogation continued, Inger LeMont finally went to the kitchen telephone and dialed a couple of numbers. An older relative of hers was sick in Delray, she informed them in a halting voice. She had to go tend to her soon. Fidgeting, Inger repeated that her boyfriend Leroy Harding had shown up of his own accord at the Nedermier house on Friday with three friends.

Inger denied harming, abducting, or stealing money from her employer, although she admitted that she had written checks recently and Mrs. Nedermier had signed them "to pay bills and all."

"Well, Inger, the bank suspects that *someone* has been committing forgeries on Mrs. Nedermier's account," Detective Johnston told her. Her only answer was that all the money she had received was "deserving" and that although she had written some checks to herself, she "deserved the extra money." She'd used the money to help her boyfriend, Leroy, who had a coke habit, Inger told them.

"If she didn't do it, she must know something about it," Detective Anderson said in a low voice to his partner.

"She's either lying or. . . ."

At that point, Inger asked the sleuths to leave. She then sped away from the house in her red Ford EXP.

That afternoon, about 5:00 p.m., the Delray Beach Police Department received a call reporting that an unspeakable stench was coming from a trunk in a closet in the home of Inger LeMont's relatives. The caller, a relative of the nurse's aide, feared the trunk held a dead body.

Officers T.J. Rubin and H. Noppe responded. Upon their arrival at the house, they were taken to view the trunk. Noting that there were layers of plastic bags covering some sort of decaying matter, the two officers called for Sergeant Robert Musco, Sergeant Tom Meister, Rich Ackerman, medical examiners, and crime scene detectives.

Once assembled, the lawmen cut into the bags and found a dismembered, decomposing body. First, they found the right foot and leg bone cut off below the knee. The body with its head attached was at the bottom wrapped in a shower curtain. A blindfold was on the eyes. Delray officers quarantined Inger's relative in his home while they investigated, then took him down to headquarters.

By that time, Detectives Anderson and Johnston, as well as Detective K.C. Myers, and Crime Scene Investigator McCall, and Lieutenant Parkinson, had been notified that the body might be their missing victim. They drove out to the LeMont home in Delray Beach about 7:45 p.m. where Detective-Sergeant Ken Herndon of that department, along with Detective-Sergeant Bob Brand and Detective Jeff Gaylon, filled them in on details. The chopped-up, partly flayed body had been found in plastic bags in a trunk in a closet, Herndon told them. Mothballs had been added to quell the stench.

Crime scene detectives took pictures and made charts. Forensic Investigator Sam Altschul and Medical Examiner Dr. John Marrachini soon sent the body to the county office in West Palm Beach for further examination. The other detectives, meanwhile, drove to the Delray Beach station and were further briefed before interviewing Inger's relative, Phillip, who had found the body.

After explaining that they merely wanted to record what he'd discovered, Detectives Anderson and Myers asked Inger's relative, "Why did you call the police?"

"I came from work," he began somewhat edgily. "I wanted to take a nap before I went to jai alai. So I smell this funny scent in the house so [I ask] my daughter over there, 'Darlene, what's in that suitcase in the house?' and she didn't know. So I turned the air conditioner on, so my wife said, 'Oh Lord, you going to turn that air on? . . .' She's sick. She can't take it. So I said, 'I got to get the scent out of here.' OK. I went and told my daughter, 'Let's open it [the trunk].' I said, 'I believe a body is in there.' She started to cry . . . and I said, 'We don't know what's in it . . . let's check it and see.' "

Phillip told the lawmen that he pried open the trunk with a screwdriver. "That scent would knock my head off. . . . A second time I open it again, raise the lid, and look and see different sections of garbage bags—you know, plastic bags—and I pass one layer plastic, and I go down to a sheet . . . a sheet or a blanket . . . I put my hand on it, and it was feeling very wet and very sandy. Lots of sand. And then that scent came up on me, and I said, 'Oooh!'—you know? So then I called my friend down the street, and she come up, and she said, 'Hurry up and call the police,' 'cause she knows it, 'cause she's a nurse."

As Detectives Myers and Anderson delved deeper into

the story, the man told them the trunk was in his two young daughters' clothes closet—Darlene's and Rhonda's—that it had been there since Thursday, according to his daughter Darlene.

"But you don't know how the trunk got in there?" the sleuths probed.

"No, I really don't know. I know when I came from work yesterday evening I smell this funny scent in the house and someone was in there spraying. I say, 'Why's the house smelled up? What's this spray?' "

"Was that Darlene spraying?"

"No, that was . . . that was . . . umm . . . oh God, I can't even find my own relative's name! Ain't that awful? . . . Inger!" The relative told how Inger was cleaning up and he was pleased, thinking she was doing something great. "But I guess all along she knew what she was doing."

He related that Darlene then admitted that Inger had put the trunk in her closet, and he answered, "So that's why the police came here that night?" When Phillip put two and two together, he said, "Uh-oh, I don't go for this!" He told them he "couldn't help but call the police."

"Do you remember," Detective Anderson queried, "when my other partner and I came down last week and we told you we were looking for that lady that Inger worked for?" When Phillip said yes, the sleuth asked, "Did you hear anything else about it until today?"

"No, I just saw it on television. Even when it came on the news, I asked Inger yesterday. I said, 'Did they ever find that lady?' She said, 'No, I haven't heard anything.' I said, 'Did you call your agency to find out anything? You not going to work—you waiting on that lady to come back?' She said she don't know. . . . Then she was in a hurry to go, and she leave. Dear God!"

Inger wasn't around that night, the relative said. He didn't know where she had gone. He was concerned about his wife and what the strain of the investigation might do to her if Inger were in the house."

"True," the detectives assured him as they terminated the interview. "We don't want her to cause problems with your wife."

After the body's discovery on Saturday, March 12th, the investigation became a joint affair between Delray Beach and West Palm Beach. Since West Palm Beach police suspected the corpse to be that of Ruth Nedermier, Delray Beach police more or less turned it over to them, assisting thereafter with whatever jurisdictional problems might arise.

Meanwhile, back at the station on the same evening, the detectives proceeded to interview other family members present. From one relative, sleuths learned that the very night before, Friday, March 11th, Inger LeMont had enlisted the aid of one of her relatives and two young male friends in moving the steamer trunk. They carried the heavy trunk out of the northeast bedroom closet, down the main hall of the residence, and then out the north side door, where some effort was made to "clean" the trunk's interior before putting it back into the closet. This information came from the detectives' questioning of Darlene, another relative of Inger's.

Inger, the girl told the sleuths, had washed the trunk out with a hose, claiming that the "meat" in the trunk, which she said she'd bought from a thief on the street and couldn't tell her boyfriend Leroy about, was spoiling. Neither Darlene, according to her testimony, nor the two young males saw what was actually in the bags in the trunk.

Sergeant Brand called on the Delray Beach Tactical Unit to locate the friend who had helped Inger move the

425

heavy piece. After checking various hangouts along Atlantic Avenue, the youth was found and escorted to headquarters. He told Detective K.C. Myers that Inger LeMont had knocked on his door sometime before 11:00 p.m. and had asked for his cousin, saying she needed him to help her "take something out" of her house. Since the cousin wasn't home, the youth enlisted a visiting friend to help. Both Darlene and Rhonda were in the house at the time, the youth told the detectives, and he and his friend noticed a "stink" in the house. They carried the trunk, which he described as measuring four feet by three feet with metal corners and leather handles on the end; he thought it was black in color. As they dragged it down the hall, he noticed red watery fluid on the floor spilling along their path. The youth said he suspected that it was blood but didn't press the issue. Instead, he negotiated with Inger to pay him for his trouble. She gave him seven dollars, which he and his friend used to buy liquor. Soon, police found the youth's friend and double-checked the story.

When that was done, the Delray sleuths returned to their stationhouse while Detectives Anderson, Johnston, and Myers drove to the medical examiner's office in West Palm Beach. They spent several hours completing the identification of the human remains, tagging them, and taking photographs. Heat and plastic had speeded decomposition. Still, whoever had chainsawed the woman—who may or may not have been alive as she was cut up—had hit the large steel pin that had been put into her hip. That particular pin had a serial number. When the detectives obtained the number from the pin and checked it with hospital records, they were able to positively identify the corpse as Ruth Ann Nedermier.

Before the three detectives went off duty in West Palm Beach in the early Sunday morning hours, they had

Communications broadcast a request for assistance in locating "black female Inger LeMont and her boyfriend, black male Leroy Harding, and their two vehicles."

The teletype brought fast results. At around 11:00 a.m. that morning, Lieutenant Conklin called Detective Myers to tell him that Officer C. Fragakis had stopped the white 1964 Pontiac noted in the message. The vehicle was occupied by Leroy Harding and a second male who was driving the car. The officer asked the occupants if they would voluntarily accompany him to headquarters so that detectives could speak with them further. Actually, had either man refused, they would have been legally free to leave. Instead, the pair accompanied Officer Fragakis.

At headquarters, Detective Myers interviewed the driver, who told him that he was merely an acquaintance of Leroy Harding's, having seen him on the streets. It was around 10:00, he recalled, when Harding cruised up and asked him, "Do me a favor. Go with me. I want to pick up this car." They drove to a motel, where Harding entered a small red car and drove off. The acquaintance described the car as an American-made hatchback with a "sheriff's badge sticker" on it, which he followed in his car until Harding backed the car under the carport of one of the buildings in a development. Harding then climbed back in the white car beside his acquaintance. As they drove away, Harding became very nervous, according to the acquaintance, and claimed that the police were behind them. The acquaintance asked Harding, "You got your license and registration?" to which Harding replied, "Yeah."

After the detectives completed the interview with Harding's acquaintance, they were aware that, based on the information developed during the investigation by this time, the red Ford Escort EXP usually driven by In-

427

ger LeMont had been used to deliver the trunk containing the remains of Ruth Nedermier to the residence on N.W. 3rd Avenue in Delray Beach. Now, with the lead given them by Harding's acquaintance, the lawmen completed a search warrant and sent it along with officers who located the red Ford and had it towed in to await processing by crime scene personnel.

Around 10:00 p.m., a neighbor of Inger LeMont's notified the investigators that two men and a woman had just loaded household furnishings from LeMont's apartment into a large truck. She gave the detectives the truck's tag number and description, which was subsequently broadcast countrywide. It wasn't long before Delray Beach police located the truck at the LeMont family home on 3rd Avenue. The vehicle belonged to Phillip Sr., Inger's relative. He, Darlene, and Phillip Jr. had transported Inger's belongings to their house. The combined Delray Beach-West Palm Beach detective team secured a search warrant and checked the truck.

The portable typewriter with its missing ribbon, towels similar to the bloody one recovered from the dumpster, and open boxes of trash bags were among the items seized for evidence.

Early Wednesday morning, March 16th, a former Palm Beach County deputy sheriff who was the brother of Leroy Harding stopped by West Palm Beach Police Headquarters and told Lieutenant Conklin he would bring in Inger LeMont in about 20 minutes. The lieutenant notified the detective trio of Myers, Johnston, and Anderson, who arrived soon after the suspect was brought in. The sleuths read Inger her rights and the interview was under way at about 10:30.

Inger said she'd called Leroy's brother, the deputy, and told him she wanted to be brought in. Speaking about her background, Inger told them she'd had a year of college in addition to technical school in which she'd studied nursing. The lawmen then asked Inger to tell them what she knew about Ruth Nedermier's disappearance.

"The only thing I know is that you guys came to my house Friday night . . . well . . . Saturday morning about four . . . and brought me down here . . . and I found out she was missing; and the only thing else that I know is that, on that following Thursday when I got up . . . I was getting ready to do some cleaning, and I looked at the shades in the back, and I saw that black trunk sitting there."

Inger continued by saying she thought about some "guys that came by sellin' meat and what they said. . . . They had meat that could last—I think they said a month or something—and you pay them so much money a month, and they have the freezer to go along with the meat." Thinking that's what was in the trunk which was on her patio, Inger said she went out there to open it. "It did have meat on top of it, and it had ice on top of it, too. . . . When I got to the bottom, I saw what it was, so I just shut it and sat there." The two men with the meat had come by the week before on a Tuesday night, Inger recalled. They came in a dark blue truck. The meat on top was like ribs, she said—"Meat you barbecue. Three pieces." Inger knew they'd been iced because they were cold. She did not see the trunk on Wednesday.

"So you look deeper into the trunk after the ribs?" the detectives probed.

"After I took those off, there was, ummm . . . there was like a . . . guess a sheet or whatever. And then I put my hand on it. . . ."

"You put your hand on the sheet that was underneath the ribs?"

"No. I put my hand on Mrs. Nedermier." As the sleuths interrogated her further, Inger told them she could tell it was her employer because of the dress she had on. She shut the trunk and did not open it again, she told the detectives. She didn't see if Mrs. Nedermier was all in one piece or not. At that point, Inger called a young male relative, Phillip Jr., and told him she wanted him to help her move a trunk. She drove to Delray Beach to get him.

When he saw the trunk at her house, Phillip Jr. questioned Inger. He wanted to open the trunk, but she said no, the meat's spoiled, and she "was taking it to Delray." "Why?" Phillip Jr. had asked. "Because I don't know what else to do," Inger told him.

But Phillip Jr. kept questioning her, Inger told the detectives. "He said he'd take it to his job, and they could cut it, you know, 'cause he thought it was all meat. He works at a . . . country club."

After dragging the trunk to the red Ford and putting it in Inger's hatchback, her relative drove them to the family home in Delray Beach. They then lifted the heavy object out of the car, dragged it into the house, and put it into Darlene and Rhonda's closet. Another family member, who was sick, didn't know. "I was the only one that knew what was in there. The first thing I wanted to do was talk to Leroy about it, but I can't even remember when I saw him."

She stayed at the house all day, Inger continued, finally driving to pick up her son at nursery school and go to the store for room deodorizer and other things before returning to N.W. 3rd Avenue. Soon the trunk began smelling, Inger told Detectives Anderson, Johnston, and Myers. When Darlene and Rhonda came home, she had to tell them something about the trunk. Inger said, as she had told Phillip Jr., that the trunk had meat in it. They asked why it was in the closet. "I told them the meats were stolen or something. I don't know . . . I can't

430

remember what I told them." The smell, with the door shut, became worse and the girls complained. Inger told them the meat was turning bad. " 'Why don't you just throw it out?' they kept saying, and I kept saying, 'Well, you just don't understand why I can't do that.' I left about nine Thursday night."

Back at her Gulfstream Road apartment, Inger Le-Mont saw Leroy but told him nothing. The next morning, he took her son to school. She returned to Delray Beach, telling him a family member wasn't well. She took the sick relative to an aunt's, she told the sleuths, then went to bring Darlene, who wasn't feeling well, home from school. The smell by then had become ferocious, even in the red Ford.

As the detective trio continued the interrogation, Inger said, "Nothing would kill the odor, and then by that time I was so panicked I didn't know what to do, and then I sat here and I dialed the Delray police, and then I hung the phone up right after . . . and I said, 'Well, what am I gonna tell them?' so I just hung the phone up."

The rest of the day was a blur to Inger, going through the motions of normal life — eating, taking a relative to church, picking up her son — but she mainly tried to combat the overwhelming smell that her family was noticing. Inger said she wanted to tell one family member, but she knew what a temper he had and was afraid to. She tried every type of air freshener and tried to shampoo the inside of her car. She also took it to the car wash, something she had done the night before with a girlfriend. But nothing helped get rid of the stench.

When Darlene complained terribly, Inger tried to push the trunk out and was going to pour bleach around it. Instead she sopped up the greasy liquid coming from the bottom of the trunk with towels and clothes, which she later threw in a garbage bag. "It was

. . . gosh, it was awful," Inger recalled.

After the entire family was home, someone said, "Gosh, what *is* that?" According to Inger, they thought it was the garbage. When Inger gave a relative a ride to a friend's that night, she tried to tell him about the body, but she couldn't.

"Even after I got home," Inger admitted, "I kept calling home to see if the smell had gotten worse . . . and then about three o'clock, when you guys got there, and then Darlene called and said to get there because [a relative] was, you know, being curious about the trunk. . . . And you notice I was impatient to get out of there, and you guys kept sitting there and asking me questions."

"Why didn't you just tell us what was going on?" the detectives asked.

". . . I was scared," Inger replied.

When an attorney, procured by Inger's family, advised her to interrupt the interview, she was charged with first-degree homicide and jailed.

A search warrant was executed for Inger LeMont's Gulfstream Road apartment. The county serologist, Richard Tanton, introduced luminol into the apartment. Although previously no blood could be seen with the naked eye, the luminol made the house—her little boy's room, especially—light up like a Christmas tree, each brilliant spot revealing where blood had been. This room, then, was where Ruth Nedermier had been chainsawed into pieces.

Oddly enough, Inger's small footprints could be seen in the midst of the blood-drenched floor—*only* her footprints. Observing this, the detectives knew that *she,* and not Leroy Harding or the other "three dudes" Inger mentioned, was responsible for the chainsaw massacre. When the mop on the back patio was sprayed, it too gave off a blinding glow.

After that, the detective trio discovered many lies in Inger's testimony. They found witnesses who knew she'd pawned her employer's jewelry, and fellow jailmates who said a relative of Inger's was seen wearing some of it. They also found the person who had sold her—and her alone—the steamer trunk.

On April 6th, the detectives again interviewed Inger LeMont at the state's attorney's office, at which time she waived her rights and issued a long, conflicting statement in an attempt to implicate Leroy Harding. It was obvious to all of those present that the nurse's aide was lying on many counts.

Inger admitted she'd purchased the trunk, but it was for innocent reasons, she said, before Ruth Nedermier disappeared. The luggage shop owner, who claimed it was the only such trunk sold by them in 1988, had a receipt marked March 7th. Inger did, however, confirm that the victim had been struck on the head with a brick and the victim's head was covered with a plastic bag to at least render her unconscious. The victim was then taken to Inger's apartment and dismembered with an electric chainsaw that Leroy had purchased, not the gas-powered chainsaw seized from a relative's home the night police discovered the body. Although Inger admitted the forgeries, she concocted a new character, "Eyes," whom she claimed helped Leroy kill Ruth Nedermier while she stole the jewelry. Inger LeMont changed her story repeatedly and was caught in too many lies to be believed.

In retrospect, the West Palm Beach detective team thought they knew what had really happened. Discussing the crime after the fact, Detective Anderson said, "I think after the call from the bank, Inger panicked. She ran outside and got a brick from the new construction, then hit Ruth Nedermier over the head— probably from behind. When she told Leroy, he took off

433

but still felt emotional ties to her."

Before she went to trial, Inger LeMont pleaded guilty and was sentenced to 75 years in prison. She is now serving her time.

EDITOR'S NOTE:

Leroy Harding, Phillip Sr. and Jr., Darlene, Rhonda, and Margaret Mays are not the real names of the persons so named in the foregoing story. Fictitious names have been used because there is no reason for public interest in the identities of these persons.

APPENDIX:

"The Doctor Prescribed Sex Orgies"
Master Detective, March, 1977
"12 Victims for the Angel of Death"
Inside Detective, February, 1985
"Were Killers Loose in Ann Arbor's V.A. Hospital?"
Master Detective, December, 1977
"12 Slugs Ended the Marriage on the Rocks!"
Front Page Detective, May, 1984
" 'Angel of Mercy' Was a Deadly Backstabber!"
Front Page Detective, February, 1988
"The Casanova Was a Chainsaw Killer!"
Inside Detective, April, 1985
"Chilling Confession of Cincinnati's Cyanide Killer"
Front Page Detective, August, 1989
"The Dentist Extracted Insurance Money from
   His Murder Victims!"
Inside Detective, August, 1981
"Floater in the Pink Nightie"
Front Page Detective, March, 1989
"The Crime at Hilldrop Crescent"
Master Detective, August, 1955
"Deadly Rx Snuffed Three Lives!"
Master Detective, October, 1990
"Almost Perfect Crime"
Inside Detective, October, 1991
"Clever with a Knife"
Master Detective, August, 1955
"Murder Parted the Star-Crossed Lovers!"
Front Page Detective, February, 1986
" 'Angel' of Pain Who Used a Chainsaw on Ruth"
Official Detective, August, 1991

COLD-BLOODED MURDER FROM PINNACLE BOOKS

NURSES WHO KILL   (449, $3.95)
Clifford L. Linedecker and William A. Burt
RICHARD ANGELO—convicted of killing four patients
by lethal injection in a New York hospital
GENENE JONES TURK—serving 99 years for maiming
and killing kinfants in a Texas pediatric clinic
DONALD HARVEY—convicted killer of terminally ill pa-
tients in Kentucky hospitals
INGER LEMONT—Florida homecare worker convicted of
hacking an shut-in woman to death in her home
ROBERT DIAZ—convicted killer of 12 elderly residents in
two California nursing homes

This is the grizzly true crime account of such hospital
killers—men and women who abused their scared role to
save lives in order to take them, hideously, coldly, without
remorse and often for pleasure.

SPREE KILLERS   (461, $4.95)
Edited by Art Crockett
 No one knows what triggers it. Maybe it's a look, maybe
a word. But the result is always the same: Innocent people
are wounded and killed.
 They are mass murderers, spree killers. If they escape the
scene of their bloody crime, they may never kill again. Unlike serial murderers like Ted Bundy, these killers claim
lives indescriminately, usually in one mad burst of violence. There's no way to hide from their insane acts once
the killing urge is triggered. (From the files of *TRUE DE-
TECTIVE* Magazine)

THE EXECUTIONER
by Don Pendleton